ÉLIPHAS LÉVI

THE HISTORY OF MAGIC
INCLUDING A CLEAR AND PRECISE EXPOSITION OF ITS PROCEDURE, ITS RITES AND ITS MYSTERIES

by
ÉLIPHAS LÉVI
(ALPHONSE LOUIS CONSTANT)

TRANSLATED, WITH A PREFACE AND NOTES, BY
ARTHUR EDWARD WAITE

ISBN:978-1-63923-234-5

All Rights reserved. No part of this book maybe reproduced without written permission from the publishers, except by a reviewer who may quote brief passages in a review to be printed in a newspaper or magazine.

Printed: June 2022

Cover Art By: Amit Paul

Published and Distributed By:
Lushena Books
607 Country Club Drive, Unit E
Bensenville, IL 60106
www.lushenabooksinc.com/books

ISBN: 978-1-63923-234-5

THE
HISTORY OF MAGIC

INCLUDING A CLEAR AND PRECISE EXPOSITION
OF ITS PROCEDURE, ITS RITES AND
ITS MYSTERIES

by
ÉLIPHAS LÉVI
(ALPHONSE LOUIS CONSTANT)

TRANSLATED, WITH A PREFACE AND NOTES, BY
ARTHUR EDWARD WAITE

RIDER AND COMPANY
1955

PREFACE TO THE ENGLISH TRANSLATION

IN several casual references scattered through periodical literature, in the biographical sketch which preceded my rendering of *Dogme et Rituel de la Haute Magie* and elsewhere, as occasion prompted, I have put on record an opinion that the *History of Magic*, by Alphonse Louis Constant, written —like the majority of his works—under the pseudonym of Éliphas Lévi, is the most arresting, entertaining and brilliant of all studies on the subject with which I am acquainted. So far back as 1896 I said that it was admirable as a philosophical survey, its historical inaccuracies notwithstanding, and that there is nothing in occult literature which can suffer comparison therewith. Moreover, there is nothing so comprehensive in the French language, while as regards ourselves it must be said that we have depended so far on a history by Joseph Ennemoser, translated from the German and explaining everything, within the domain included under the denomination of Magic, by the phenomena of Animal Magnetism. Other texts than this are available in that language, but they have not been put into English; while none of them has so great an appeal as that which is here rendered into our tongue. Having certified so far regarding its titles, it is perhaps desirable to add, from my own standpoint, that I have not translated the book because it is entertaining and brilliant, or because it will afford those who are concerned with Magic in history a serviceable general account. The task has been undertaken still less in the interests of any who may have other—that is to say, occult—reasons for acquaintance with "its procedure, its rites and its mysteries". I have no object in providing unwary and foolish seekers with material of this kind, and it so happens that the present History does not fulfil the promise of its subtitle in these respects, or at least to any extent that they would term practical in their folly. Through all my later literary life I have sought to make it plain, as the result of antecedent years spent in occult research, that the occult sciences—in all their general understanding—are paths of danger when they are not paths of simple make-believe and imposture. The importance of Éliphas Lévi's account at large of the claims, and of their story throughout the centuries, arises from the fact (*a*) that he is the authoritative exponent-in-chief of all the alleged sciences; (*b*) that it is he who, in a sense, restored and placed them under a new and more attractive vesture, before public notice at the middle period of the nineteenth century; (*c*) that he claimed, as we shall see, the very fullest knowledge concerning them, being that of an adept and master; but (*d*) that—subject to one qualification, the worth of which will be mentioned—it follows from his long examination that Magic, as understood not in the streets only but in the houses of research concerning it, has no ground in the truth of things, and is of the region of delusion only. It is for this reason that I have translated his History of

PREFACE TO THE ENGLISH TRANSLATION

Magic, as one who reckons a not too gracious task for something which leans toward righteousness, at least in the sense of charity. The world is full at this day of the false claims which arise out of that region, and I have better reasons than most even of my readers can imagine to undeceive those who, having been drawn in such directions, may be still saved from deception. It is well therefore that out of the mouth of the masters we can draw the fullest evidence required for this purpose.

In the present prefatory words I propose to shew, firstly, the nature of Éliphas Lévi's personal claims, so that there may be no misconception as to what they were actually, and as to the kind of voice which is speaking; secondly, his original statement of the claims, nature and value of Transcendental Magic; and, thirdly, his later evidences on its phenomenal or so-called practical side, as established by its own history. In this manner we shall obtain his canon of criticism, and I regard it as serviceable, because—with all his imperfections—he had better titles of knowledge at his own day than anyone, while it cannot be said that his place has been filled since, though many workers have risen up in the same field of inquiry and have specialised in the numerous departments which he covered generally and superficially.

Before entering upon these matters it may be thought that I should speak at some length of the author's life; but the outlines have been given already in an extended introduction prefixed to a digest of his writings which I published many years ago under the title of *Mysteries of Magic*, and again, but from another point of view, in the preface to the *Doctrine and Ritual of Transcendental Magic*, already mentioned. These things are still available in one edition or another, and very little has transpired subsequently, because—as a matter of fact—the salient biographical facts are not numerous.

In the present place it will be therefore sufficient to say that Alphonse Louis Constant was born at Paris in 1810, and was the son of a shoemaker, apparently in very poor circumstances. His precocity in childhood seemed to give some promise of future ability; he was brought to the notice of a priest belonging to his parish, and this in its turn led to his gratuitous education at Saint-Sulpice, obviously with a view to the priesthood. There his superiors must have recognised sufficient traces of vocation, according to the measures of the particular place and period, for he proceeded to minor orders and subsequently became a deacon. He seems, however, to have conceived strange views on doctrinal subjects, though no particulars are forthcoming, and, being deficient in gifts of silence, the displeasure of authority was marked by various checks, ending finally in his expulsion from the Seminary. Such is one story at least, but an alternative says more simply that he relinquished the sacerdotal career in consequence of doubts and scruples. Thereafter he must, I suppose, have supported himself by some kind of teaching, and by obscure efforts in literature. Of these the remains are numerous, though their value has been much exaggerated for bookselling purposes in France.

PREFACE TO THE ENGLISH TRANSLATION

His adventures with Alphonse Esquiros over the gospel of the prophet Ganneau are told in the pages that follow, and are an interesting biographical fragment which may be left to speak for itself. He was then approaching the age of thirty years. I have failed to ascertain at what period he married Mlle Noémy, a girl of sixteen, who became afterwards of some repute as a sculptor, but it was a runaway match and in the end she left him. It is even said that she succeeded in a nullity suit—not on the usual grounds, for she had borne him two children, who died in their early years if not during infancy, but on the plea that she was a minor, while he had taken irrevocable vows. Saint-Sulpice is, however, a seminary for secular priests who are not pledged to celibacy, though the rule of the Latin Church forbids them to enter the married state.

In the year 1851 Alphonse Louis Constant contributed a large volume to the encyclopædic series of Abbé Migne, under the title of *Dictionnaire de Littérature Chrétienne*. He is described therein as *ancien professeur au petit Séminaire de Paris*, and it is to be supposed that his past was unknown at the publishing bureau. The volume is more memorable on account of his later writings than important by its own merits. As a critical work, and indeed as a work of learning, it is naturally quite negligible, like most productions of the series, while as a dictionary it is disproportioned and piecemeal; yet it is exceedingly readable and not unsuggestive in its views. There is no need to add that, as the circumstances of the case required, it is written along rigid lines of orthodoxy and is consequently no less narrow, no less illiberal, than the endless volumes of its predecessors and successors in the same field of industry. The doubting heart of Saint-Sulpice had become again a convinced Catholic, or had assumed that mask for the purpose of a particular literary production. Four years later, however, the voice of the churchman, speaking the characteristic language of the Migne Encyclopædias, was succeeded by the voice of the magus. The *Doctrine of Transcendental Magic* appeared in 1855, the *Ritual* in 1856, and henceforth Alphonse Louis Constant, under the pseudonym of Éliphas Lévi, which has become almost of European celebrity, was known only as an exponent of occult science. It is these works which more especially embody his claims in respect of the alleged science and in respect of his own absolute authority thereon and therein. Certain later volumes, which followed from his pen in somewhat rapid succession, are very curious when compared with the *Doctrine and Ritual* for their apparent submission to church authority and their parade of sincere orthodoxy. I have dealt with this question at length in my introduction to the *Mysteries of Magic*, and I shall be dispensed therefore from covering the same ground in the present place. Such discrepancy notwithstanding, Éliphas Lévi became, in a private as well as in a public sense, a teacher of occult science and of Kabalism as its primary source: it was apparently his means of livelihood. He was in Paris during the siege which brought the Franco-German war to its disastrous close, and he died in 1875, fortified by the last rites of the Catholic Church. He left behind him a large sheaf of manuscripts, several of which have been published since, and some await an editor. The issue of his life and letters has been long promised in Paris, under the auspices of M. Lucien Mauchel, but the fact that over sixteen years have elapsed since the announcement was first made may signify that they are withheld permanently. Possibly the executors of Mme Constant, who is said to have married a second time in 1872, may have laid an interdict on the design.

Passing now to the subject-in-chief of this preface, it is affirmed as follows in the *Doctrine and Ritual of Transcendental Magic*: (1) There is a potent and real Magic, popular exaggerations of which are really below the truth. (2) There is a formidable secret which constitutes the fatal science of good and evil. (3) It confers on man powers apparently superhuman. (4) It is the traditional science of the secrets of Nature which has been transmitted to us from the Magi. (5) Initiation therein gives empire over souls to the sage and the adroitness for ruling wills. (6) Arising apparently from this science, there is one infallible, indefectible and truly catholic religion which has always existed in the world, but it is unadapted for the multitude. (7) For this reason there has come into being the exoteric religion of apologue, fable and nurse's stories, which is all that is possible for the profane: it has undergone various transformations, and it is represented at this day by Latin Christianity under the obedience of Rome. (8) Its veils are true in their symbolism, and it may be called true for the crowd, but the doctrine of initiates is not less than a negation of the absolute therein. (9) It is Magic alone which imparts true science.

Hereof is what may be termed the theoretical, philosophical or doctrinal part, the dogma of "absolute science". That which is practical follows, and it deals with the exercise of a natural power but one superior to the ordinary forces of Nature. It is to all intents and purposes comprised in a Grimoire of Magic, and is a work of ceremonial evocations—whether of elementary spirits, with the aid of pantacles, talismans and the other magical instruments and properties; whether of spirits belonging *ex hypothesi* to the planetary sphere; whether of the shades or souls of the dead in necromancy. These works are lawful, and their results apparently veridic, but beyond them is the domain of Black Magic, which is a realm of delusion and nightmare, though phenomenal enough in its results. By his dedications Éliphas Lévi happened to be a magus of light.

It will be observed that all this offers a clear issue, and—for the rest— the Grimoire of Transcendental Magic, according to Éliphas Lévi, does not differ generically from the *Key of Solomon* and its counterparts, except in so far as the author has excised here and enlarged there in obedience to his own lights. He had full authority for doing so on the basis of his personal claims, which may be summarised at this point. (1) He has discovered "the secret of human omnipotence and indefinite progress, the key of all symbolism, the first and final doctrine". (2) He is alchemist as well as magician, and he makes public the same secret as Raymund Lully, Nicholas Flamel and probably Heinrich Khunrath. They produced true

PREFACE TO THE ENGLISH TRANSLATION

gold, "nor did they take away their secret with them". (3) And finally: "at an epoch when the sanctuary has been devastated and has fallen into ruins, because its key has been thrown over the hedge to the profit of no one, I have deemed it my duty to pick up that key, and I offer it to him who can take it: in his turn he will be doctor of the nations and liberator of the world".

It must be said that these claims do not rest on a mere theory or practice of ceremonial evocations. There is no question that for Éliphas Lévi his secret doctrine of occult science is contained in a hypothesis concerning an universal medium denominated the Astral Light, which is neither more nor less than the odylic force of Baron Reichenbach, as the French writer himself admits substantially, but it is dilated in his speculation and issues therein greatly transformed as follows. (1) It is an universal plastic mediator, a common receptacle for vibrations of movement and images of form; it may be called the Imagination of Nature. (2) It is that which God created when He uttered the *Fiat Lux*. (3) It is the great medium of occult force, but as such it is a blind force, which can be used for good or evil, being especially obedient to the light of grace. (4) It is the element of electricity and lightning. (5) The "four imponderable fluids" are diverse manifestations of this one force, which is "inseparable from the First Matter" and sets the latter in motion. (6) It is now resplendent, now igneous, now electric, now magnetic. (7) It has apparently two modes, which tend to equilibrium, and the middle point of this equilibrium seems to be the attainment of the Great Work. (8) It is "ethereal in the infinite, astral in stars and planets, metallic, specific or mercurial in metals, vegetable in plants, vital in animals, magnetic or personal in men". (9) It is extracted from animals by absorption and from men by generation. (10) In Magic it is the glass of visions, the receptacle of all reflections. The seer has his visions therein, the diviner divines by its means and the magus evokes spirits. (11) When the Astral Light is fixed about a centre by condensation it becomes the Philosophical Stone of Alchemy, in which form it is an artificial phosphorus, containing the concentrated virtues of all generative heat. (12) When condensed by a triple fire it resolves into oil, and this oil is the Universal Medicine. It can then only be contained in glass, this being a non-conductor.

Again, here is a clear issue at its value, and I make this qualification because the Astral Light is, as I have said, a speculation, and personally I neither know nor care whether such a fluid exists, or, in such case, whether it is applicable to the uses indicated. It is enough that Éliphas Lévi has made his affirmations concerning it in unmistakable language.

Let us pass therefore to the *Histoire de la Magie*, though I have been borrowing from it already in respect of the putative universal fluid. Magic therein is still the science of the ancient Magi; it is still the exact and absolute science of Nature and her laws, because it is the science of equilibrium. Its secret, the secret of occult science, is that of God's

PREFACE TO THE ENGLISH TRANSLATION

omnipotence. It comprises all that is most certain in philosophy, all that is eternal and infallible in religion. It is the Sacerdotal Art and the Royal Art. Its doctrine is contained in Kabalism, and it derives apparently from primeval Zoroastrian doctrine, of which Abraham seems to have been a depositary. This doctrine attained its perfection in Egypt. Thereafter, on its religious side, the succession appears to have been: (a) from Egypt to Moses; (b) from Moses to Solomon, through certain custodians of the secret law in Jewry; (c) from the Temple at Jerusalem to St. Peter's at Rome, though the method of transition is obscure—as that which was previously affirmed is still maintained, namely that Rome has lost the Kabalistic Keys. It is naturally left to our conjecture as to when the church possessed them—from Éliphas Lévi's point of view, perhaps in the days of Dionysius, perhaps in those of Synesius, but not from my standpoint, and so the question remains.

Now, if these things do not differ specifically from the heads of the previous testimony, on the surface and in the letter thereof, it is no less certain that there is a marked distinction alike in general atmosphere and inward spirit. About this all can satisfy themselves who will compare the two texts, and I need not insist on it here. What, however, in the *Histoire de la Magie*, has befallen that practical side which, after all the dreamings, the high and decorative philosophy, the adornments—now golden, now meretricious—was the evidence, term and crown of the previous work? Those who are reading can again check me; but my answer is this: whether the subject of the moment is the art of evoking spirits, whether it is old cases of possession, whether it is witchcraft or necromancy, whether it is modern phenomena like direct-writing, table-rapping and the other properties of spiritism, as they were known to the writer and his period, they have one and all fallen under the ban of unreserved condemnation. It is not that they are imposture, for Éliphas Lévi does not dispute the facts and derides those who do, but they belong to the abyss of delusion and all who practise them are workers of madness and apostles of evil only. The advent of Christianity has put a decisive period to every working of Magic and anathema has been pronounced thereon. It is from this point of view that Lévi takes the disciple through each century of the subject, sometimes indeed explaining things from the standpoint of a complete sceptic, sometimes as Joseph Ennemoser might himself have explained them, but never—no, not once—like the authorised exponent of practical Magic who has tried the admirable and terrifying experiments, who returns to say that they are true and real, which is the testimony of the *Doctrine and Ritual*, if these volumes can be held to signify anything. Necromancy as a science of the abyss; spiritism as the abyss giving up every form of delusion; sorcery, witchcraft, as rich indeed in testimony but to human perversity alone, apart from intervention of diabolism belonging to the other world—I testify with my whole heart to the truth of these accusations, though I do not believe that the unseen world is so utterly cut off from the world of things manifest as Éliphas Lévi con-

PREFACE TO THE ENGLISH TRANSLATION

sidered in his own paradoxical moods. But once more—what has become of Magic? What has happened to the one science which is coeval with creation itself, to the key of all miracles and to almost omnipotent adeptship? They are reduced as follows: (*a*) to that which in its palmary respects is the "sympathetic and miraculous physics" of Mesmer, who is "grand as Prometheus" because of them; (*b*) to a general theory of hallucination, when hallucination has been carried by self-induced delusion or otherwise, to its *ne plus ultra* degree; and (*c*) but I mention this under very grave reserves, because—for the life of me—I do not understand how or why it should remain—to the physical operations of alchemy, which are still possible and actual under the conditions set forth in the speculation concerning the Astral Light. It is not as such, one would say, a thaumaturgic process, unless indeed the dream should rule—as it tends to do—that fulfilment depends on an electrifying power in the projected will of the adept. In any case, the ethical transliteration of alchemical symbolism is seemingly a more important aspect of this subject.

I need not register here that I disbelieve utterly in Lévi's construction of the art of metallic transmutation, or that I regard his allegorising thereon as a negligible product when it is compared with the real doctrine of Hermetic mysticism; but this is not the point at issue. The possessor of the Key of Magic, of the Kabalistic Keys, thrown aside or lost by the Church, comes forward to tell us that after the advent of Christ "magical orthodoxy was transfigured into the orthodoxy of religion"; that "those who dissented could be only *illuminati* and sorcerers"; that "the very name of Magic could be interpreted only according to its evil sense"; that we are forbidden by the Church to consult oracles, and that this is "in its great wisdom"; that the "fundamental dogma of transcendental science ... attained its plenary realisation in the constitution of the Christian world", being the equilibrium between Church and State. All that is done outside the lawful hierarchy stands under an act of condemnation; as to visions, all fools are visionaries; to communicate with the hierarchy of unseen intelligence we must seek the natural and mathematical revelations set forth in Tarot cards, but it cannot be done without danger and crime; while mediums, enchanters, fortune-tellers, and casters of spells "are generally diseased creatures in whom the void opens." Finally, as regards the philosophical side of Magic, its great doctrine is equilibrium; its great hypothesis is analogy; while in the moral sense equilibrium is the concurrence of science and faith.

What has happened to a writer who has thus gone back on his own most strenuous claims? One explanation is—and long ago I was inclined to it on my own part—that Éliphas Lévi had passed through certain grades of knowledge in a secret school of the Instituted Mysteries; that he was brought to a pause because of disclosures contained in his earlier books; and that he had been set to unsay what he had affirmed therein. I now know by what quality of school—working under what titles—this report was fabricated, and that it is the last with which I am acquainted

PREFACE TO THE ENGLISH TRANSLATION

to be accepted on its own statements, either respecting itself or any points of fact. An alternative is that Éliphas Lévi had spoken originally as a Magus might be supposed to speak when trafficking in his particular wares, which is something like a quack doctor describing his nostrums to a populace in the market-place, and that his later writings represent a process of retrenchment as to the most florid side of his claims. This notion is apart from all likelihood, because it offers no reason for the specific change in policy, while—if it be worth while to say so—I do not regard Lévi as comparable to a quack doctor. I think that he had been a student of occult literature and history for a considerable period, in a very particular sense; that he believed himself to have discovered a key to all the alleged phenomena; that he wrote the *Doctrine and Ritual* in a mood of enthusiasm consequent thereupon; that between the appearance of these volumes and that of the *Histoire de la Magie* he had reconsidered the question of the phenomena, and had come to the conclusion that so far from being veridic in their nature they were projected hallucinations variously differentiated and in successively aggravated grades; but that he still regarded his supposed universal fluid as a great explanatory hypothesis respecting thaumaturgic facts, and that he still held to his general philosophy of the subject, being the persistence of a secret tradition from remote times and surviving at the present day (1) in the tenets of Kabalism and (2) in the pictorial symbols of the Tarot.

It is no part of my province in the present connection to debate his views either on the fact of a secret tradition or in the alleged modes of its perpetuation: they are well known otherwise and have been expressed fully elsewhere. But in the explanation just given I feel that I have saved the sincerity of one who has many titles to consideration, who is still loved by many, and for whom my own discriminating sympathy has been expressed frequently in no uncertain way: I have saved it so far at least as can be expected; one does not anticipate that a Frenchman, an occultist and a magus is going to retract distinctly under the eye of his admirers, more especially when he has testified so much. I feel further that I have justified the fact of the present translation of a work which is memorable in several respects, but chiefly as the history of a magic which is not Magic, as a testimony which destroys indeed the whole imputed basis of its subject. It does not follow that Lévi's explanation of physical phenomena, especially of the modern kind, is always or generally correct; but much of it is workable in its way, and my purpose is more than served if those who are drawn toward the science of the mystics may be led hereby to take warning as to some of the dangers and false-seemings which fringe that science.

A few things remain to be said. Readers of his History must be prepared for manifold inaccuracies, which are to be expected in a writer like Éliphas Lévi. Those who know anything of Egypt—the antiquities of its religion and literature—will have a bad experience with the chapter on Hermetic Magic; those who know Eastern religion on its deeper side will regard the discourse on Magic in India as title-deeds of all incompetence; while in respect of later Jewish theosophy I have had occasion in certain annotations to indicate that Lévi had no extensive knowledge of those Kabalistic texts on the importance of which he dwells so much and about which he claims to speak with full understanding. He presents, however, some of its lesser aspects.

As regards the religion of his childhood, I feel certainly that it appealed to him strongly through all his life, and in the revulsion which seems to have followed the *Doctrine and Ritual* he was drawn back towards it, but rather as to a great hierarchic system and a great sequence of holy pageants of living symbolism. Respecting the literal truth of its teachings, probably he deceived himself better than he fooled his readers. In a multitude of statements and in the spirit of the text throughout, it is certain that the *Histoire de la Magie* offers "negation of dogma" on its absolute side. We obtain a continual insight into free sub-surface opinions, ill concealed under external conformity to the Church, and we get also useful sidelights on the vanity of the author's sham submissions. In this manner we know exactly what quality of sentiment led him to lay all his writings at the foot of the seat of Peter, for Peter to decide thereon. It is needless to add that his constructions of doctrine throughout are of the last kind that would be commended to the custodians of doctrine. At the same time there is very little doubt that he believed genuinely in the necessity of a hierarchic teaching, that, in his view, it reposed from a very early period in certain sanctuaries of initiation, that the existence of these is intimated in the records of the Mosaic dispensation, that they were depositaries of science rather than revelation, that Kabalistic literature is one of their witnesses, but that the sanctuaries were everywhere in the world, Egypt and Greece included. Of all these the Church of Christ is the heir, and though it may have lost the keys of knowledge, though it mistakes everywhere the sign for the thing signified, it is entitled to our respect as a witness and at least to qualified obedience.

I think that Éliphas Lévi has said true things and even great things on the distinctions and analogies between science and faith, but the latter he understood as aspiration, not as experience. A long essay on the mystics, which is perhaps his most important contribution to the *Dictionnaire de Littérature Chrétienne*, indicates that he was thinly acquainted with the mind of Suso, St. John of the Cross, St. Teresa and St. Francis of Sales. Accordingly he has a word here and there on the interior life and its secrets, but of that which remains for the elect in the heights of sanctity he had no consciousness whatever. For him the records of such experience are literature and mystic poetry; and as he is far from the term herein, so is he remote also when he discourses of false mystics, meaning Gnostic sects, Albigensian sects, *illuminati* so-called and members of secret heretical societies representing reformed doctrine. As the religion of the mystics is my whole concern in literature, let me add that true religion is not constituted by "universal suffrage" (see text, p. 370), but by the agreement of those who have attained in the Divine experience that which is understood by attainment.

In conclusion, after we have set aside, on the warrants of this History, the phenomenal side of Magic, that which may be held to remain in the mind of the author is Transcendental Magic—referred to when I spoke of a qualification earlier in these remarks; but by this is to be understood so much of the old philosophical systems as had passed within his consciousness and had been interpreted therein. It will be unacceptable to most readers at this day, but it has curious aspects of interest and may be left to stand at its value.

A. E. WAITE.

CONTENTS

PREFACE TO THE ENGLISH TRANSLATION . . . 5

INTRODUCTION

False definition of Magic—It is not to be defined at hazard—Explanation of the Blazing Star—Existence of the absolute—Absolute nature of magical science—Errors of Dupuis—Profanation of the science—Prediction of Count Joseph de Maistre—Extent and import of the science—The Divine Justice—Power of the adept—The devil and science—Existence of demons—False idea of the devil—Conception of the Manicheans—Crimes of sorcerers—The Astral Light—The so-called Imagination of Nature—Of what is to be understood hereby—The effects hereof—Definition of magnetism—Agreement between reason and faith—Jachin and Boaz—Principle of the hierarchy—Religion of Kabalists—Images of God—Theory of the light—Mysteries of sexual love—Antagonism of forces—The mythical Pope Joan—The Kabalah as an explanation and reconciliation of all—Why the Church condemns Magic—Dogmatic Magic an explanation of the philosophy of history—Culpable curiosity regarding Magic—Plan of the present work—The author's submission to the established order 29

BOOK I
THE DERIVATIONS OF MAGIC

CHAPTER I
FABULOUS SOURCES

The Book of Enoch concerning the Fall of the Angels—Meaning of the Legend—The Book of the Penitence of Adam—The Personality of Enoch—The Apocalypse of St. Methodius—Children of Seth and of Cain—Rationale of occultism—Error of Rousseau—Traditions of Jewry—The glory of Christianity—The *Sepher Yetzirah*, *Zohar* and *Apocalypse*—Opening of the Zohar 55

CHAPTER II
MAGIC OF THE MAGI

The true and false Zoroaster—Doctrines of the true Zoroaster—Transcendental fire-philosophy—Electrical secrets of Numa—A transcript from Zoroaster on demons and sacrifices—Important revelations on magnetism—Initiation in Assyria—Wonders performed by the

CONTENTS

Assyrians—Du Potet in accord with Zoroaster—Danger incurred by the unwary—Power of man over animals—Downfall of the priesthood in Assyria—Magical death of Sardanapalus . . . 65

CHAPTER III

MAGIC IN INDIA

The Indians as descendants of Cain—India the mother of idolatry—Doctrine of the Gymnosophists—Indian origin of Gnosticism—Some wise fables of India—Black Magic of the *Oupnek'hat*—Citation from J. M. Ragon—Indian Grand Secrets—The English and Indian insurrections 72

CHAPTER IV

HERMETIC MAGIC

The Emereld Table—Other writings of Hermes—Magical interpretation of the geography of Ancient Egypt—Ministry of Joseph—Sacred alphabet—The Isiac Tablet of Cardinal Bembo—The Tarot explained by the *Sepher Yetsirah*—The Tarot of Charles VII—Magical science of Moses 79

CHAPTER V

MAGIC IN GREECE

Fable of the Golden Fleece—Medea and Jason—The five magical epics—Aeschylus a profaner of the Mysteries—The Orpheus of legend—Orphic Mysteries—Göetia—The sorcerers of Thessaly—Medea and Circe 86

CHAPTER VI

MATHEMATICAL MAGIC OF PYTHAGORAS

Pythagoras an heir of the traditions of Numa—Identity of Pythagoras—His doctrine concerning God—A fine utterance against anarchy—Golden Verses—Symbols of Pythagoras—His chastity—His divination—His explanation of miracles—Secret of the interpretation of dreams—The belief of Pythagoras 92

CHAPTER VII

THE HOLY KABALAH

Origin of the Kabalah—The horror of idolatry in Kabalism—Kabalistic definition of God—Principles of the Kabalah—The Divine Names—Four forms of Tetragrammaton—The word which accomplishes all transmutations—The Keys of Solomon—The chain of spirits—

CONTENTS

Whether human spirits return—The world of spirits according to the Zohar—Of spirits which manifest—Fluidic larvæ—The Great Magical Agent—Obscure origin of larvæ 98

BOOK II
FORMATION AND DEVELOPMENT OF DOGMAS

CHAPTER I
PRIMITIVE SYMBOLISM OF HISTORY

Allegory of the Earthly Paradise—The Edenic Pantacle—The Cherub—Folly of a great mind—Mysteries of Genesis—Children of Cain—Magical secrets of the Tower of Babel—Belphegor—The mediæval Sabbath—Decadence of the hierarchy—Philosophy of chance—Doctrine of Plato—An oracle of Apollo—Rationalism of Aristotle—The Cubic Stone—Summary of Neoplatonism 107

CHAPTER II
MYSTICISM

Inviolability of magical science—Profane and mystic schools—The Bacchantes—Materialistic reformers and anarchic mystics—Imbecile visionaries—Their horror of sages—Tolerance of the true Church—False miracles—Rites of Black Magic—Barbarous words and unknown signs—Cause of visions—A theory of hallucinations . 115

CHAPTER III
INITIATIONS AND ORDEALS

The Great Work—The four aspects of the Sphinx and the Shield of Achilles—Allegories of Hercules and Œdipus—The Secret Doctrine of Plato—Of Plato as Kabalist—Difference between Plato and St. John—Platonic theosophy—Fatal experiences—Homœpathy practised by the Greeks—The cavern of Trophonius—Science of Egyptian priests—Lactantius and the antipodes—The Greek hell—Ministry of suffering—The Table of Cebes and the poem of Dante—Doctrines of the Phædron—The burial of the dead—Necromancy . 121

CHAPTER IV
THE MAGIC OF PUBLIC WORSHIP

Magnificence of the true Cultus—Orthodox traditions—Dissent of the profane—Their calumnies against initiates—An allegory concerning Bacchus—Tyresias and Calchas—The priesthood according to Homer—Oracles of sibyls—Origin of geomancy and cartomancy . 129

CONTENTS

CHAPTER V
MYSTERIES OF VIRGINITY

Of Hellenism at Rome—Institution of Vestals—Traditional virtue of virgin blood—Symbolism of Sacred Fire—Religious aspect of the history of Lucretia—Honour among Roman women—Mysteries of the *Bona Dea*—Numa as a hierophant—Ingenious notions of Voltaire on divination—Prophetic instinct of the masses—Erroneous opinions of Fontenelle and Kircher on oracles—Religious Calendar of Numa 134

CHAPTER VI
SUPERSTITIONS

Their origin and persistence—Beautiful thought of the Roman pontiff, St. Gregory—observation of numbers and of days—Abstinence of the magi—Opinions of Porphyry—Greek and Roman superstitions —Mythological data on the secret properties of animals—A passage from Euripides—Reasons of Pythagorean abstinence—Singular excerpt from Homer—Presages, dreams, enchantments and fascinations—Magical whirlpools—Modern phenomena—Olympus and Plotinus 138

CHAPTER VII
MAGICAL MONUMENTS

The Seven Wonders of the world and the seven magical planets—The Pyramids—Thebes and its seven gates—The pantacle of the sun— The pantacle of the moon—The pantacle of the conjugal Venus— The pantacles of Mercury, Jupiter and Mars—The Temple of Solomon—Philosophical summary of ancient wisdom . . . 144

BOOK III
DIVINE SYNTHESIS AND REALISATION OF MAGIA BY THE CHRISTIAN REVELATION

CHAPTER I
CHRIST ACCUSED OF MAGIC BY THE JEWS

The beginning of the Gospel according to St. John and its profound meaning—Ezekiel a Kabalist—Special character of Christianity— Accusations of the Jews against the Saviour—The *Sepher Toldos Jeshu*—A beautiful legend from the apocryphal gospels—The Johannites—Burning of magical books at Ephesus—Cessation of

CONTENTS

oracles—The great Pan is dead—Transfiguration of natural prodigy into miracle and of divination into prophecy 147

CHAPTER II

THE WITNESS OF MAGIC TO CHRISTIANITY

Absolute existence of religion—Essential distinction between science and faith—Puerile objections—Christianity proved by charity—Condemnation of Magic by the Christian priesthood—Simon the Magician—His history—His doctrine—His conference with SS. Peter and Paul—His downfall—His sect continued by Menander . 150

CHAPTER III

THE DEVIL

The question considered in the light of faith and science—Satan and Lucifer—Wisdom of the Church—The devil according to the initiates of occult science—Of possessions in the gospel—Opinions of Torreblanca—Astral perversities—The Sabbatic goat—The false Lucifer 158

CHAPTER IV

THE LAST PAGANS

The eternal miracle of God—Civilising influence of Christianity—Apollonius of Tyana—His allegorical legend—Julian the apostate—His evocations—Jamblichus and Maximus of Tyre—Birth of Secret Societies for the forbidden practices of Magic . . . 162

CHAPTER V

LEGENDS

The legend of St. Cyprian and St. Justin—Magical prayer of St. Cyprian—The Golden Legend—Apuleius and the Golden Ass—The fable of Psyche—Curious subtlety of St. Augustine—Philosophy of the Fathers of the Church 166

CHAPTER VI

SOME KABALISTIC PAINTINGS AND SACRED EMBLEMS

Gnosticism and the primitive Church—Emblems of the catacombs—True and false Gnostics—Profanation of the Gnosis—Impure and sacrilegious Rites—Eucharistic sacrilege—The Arch-heretic Marcos—Women and the priesthood—Montanus and his female prophets—Tertullian—The dualism of Manes—Danger of evocations—Divagations of Kabalism—Loss of the Kabalistic Keys . . . 171

CONTENTS

CHAPTER VII
PHILOSOPHERS OF THE ALEXANDRIAN SCHOOL

Ammonius Saccas—Plotinus—Porphyry—Hypatia—Incautious admissions of Synesius—Writings of this initiate—More especially his tract on Dreams—The commentary of Jerome Cardan thereon—Attribution of the works of St. Dionysius to Synesius—Their orthodoxy and their value 176

BOOK IV
MAGIC AND CIVILISATION

CHAPTER I
MAGIC AMONG BARBARIANS

Rome conquered by the Cross—History of Philinnium and Machates—The Bride of Corinth—Philosophical considerations thereon—Germanic and Druidic theology—College of the Druids at Autun—Druidic transmigration of souls—Some Druidic practices . . 180

CHAPTER II
INFLUENCE OF WOMEN

Female influence in early France—Velleda slandered by Chateaubriand—*Berthe au grand pied*—The fairy Mélusine—Saint Clotilda—The sorceress Frédégonde—The story of Klodswinthe—Frédégonde and Clovis—Further concerning her history 186

CHAPTER III
THE SALIC LAWS AGAINST SORCERERS

Laws attributed to Pharamond—Explanation of a Talmudic passage by Rabbi Jechiel—Belief in the immortality of the soul among the Jews—An ecclesiastical council on sorcery—The rise of Mohammed—The religious history of Charles Martel—The Reign of Pépin the Short—The Kabalist Zedekias—His fables concerning elementary spirits—An epidemic of visions 190

CHAPTER IV
LEGENDS OF THE REIGN OF CHARLEMAGNE

Charlemagne a prince of faerie—Charlemagne and Roland—The enchanted sword and magic horn—The *Enchiridion* of Leo III—The

CONTENTS

tradition therein—The pantacles—The Sabbath—The Free Judges—Their foundation and purpose—Power of this Tribunal—The fate of Frederick of Brunswick—Code of the Free Judges—Laws of Charlemagne—Knighterrantry—The cultus of the Blessed Virgin . 195

CHAPTER V

MAGICIANS

The pope and empire—The penalty of excommunication—Further concerning Rabbi Jechiel—The automaton of Albertus Magnus—Albertus and St. Thomas Aquinas—The legend of the automaton interpreted—Scholasticism and Aristotelian philosophy—The philosophical stone and the quintessence 202

CHAPTER VI

SOME FAMOUS PROSECUTIONS

The great religious orders and their power—The Knights Templar—Their origin—Their secret design—The Christian sect of Johannites—Their profanation of the history of Christ—Pontiffs of the Johannite sect—The Johannites and the Templars—Further concerning Templar secret doctrine—Development of the chivalry—Their projects discovered—Their suppression—The case of Joan of Arc—The history of Gilles de Laval 207

CHAPTER VII

SUPERSTITIONS RELATING TO THE DEVIL

Apparitions of Satan—Possessions—A philosophy of superstitions—The crime of Black Magic—Pathological states—The soul of the world—Modern phenomena—Fourier and M. de Mirville—Baron de Guldenstubbé 219

BOOK V

THE ADEPTS AND THE PRIESTHOOD

CHAPTER I

PRIESTS AND POPES ACCUSED OF MAGIC

Inviolable sanctity of the priesthood—Accusations of false adepts—Groundless charges against Pope Sylvester II—Scandalous story of Polonus reproduced by Platina—The legend of Pope Joan—Its derivation from ancient Tarot cards representing Isis crowned with a tiara—Further concerning Sylvester II—Opinion of Gabriel

CONTENTS

Naudé—The Grimoire attributed to Pope Honorius III—The antipope Honorius II as its possible author—An excursus on the content and character of the work 223

CHAPTER II
APPEARANCE OF THE BOHEMIAN NOMADS

Their entrance into Europe early in the fifteenth century—Their name of Bohemians or Egyptians—An account of their encampment near Paris, drawn from an ancient chronicle—A citation from George Borrow—Researches of M. Vaillant—The Gipsies and the Tarot—A conclusion on this subject—Communistic Experiment in 1840 . 234

CHAPTER III
LEGEND AND HISTORY OF RAYMUND LULLY

Story of the *Doctor Illuminatus* on its mythical side—Raymund Lully and the Lady Ambrosia—His immortality and liberation therefrom—The historical personage—Lully as an alchemist—The Rose Nobles—His philosophical testament—Colleges for the study of languages founded by his efforts—The Great Art—He appears at the Council of Vienna—Lully a disciple of the Kabalists—But the tradition in his hands had become Christian 242

CHAPTER IV
ON CERTAIN ALCHEMISTS

Nicholas Flamel and the book of Abraham the Jew—Mysterious figures of the work—A tradition concerning Flamel—Bernard Trevisan—Basil Valentine—John Trithemius—Cornelius Agrippa—The pantacle of Trithemius—William Postel—Illustrations of his teaching—The story of Mother Jeanne—The renewal of Postel—An opinion of Father Desbillons—Paracelsus—His doctrines of occult medicine—Mysteries of blood—Narrative of Tavernier—The *Philosophia sagax* of Paracelsus 250

CHAPTER V
SOME FAMOUS SORCERERS AND MAGICIANS

The Divine Comedy of Dante and its Kabalistic analysis—*The Romance of the Rose*—Luther and anarchical theology—His disputes with the devil—His sacrilegious marriage—Sorcerers during the reign of Henry III—Visions of Jacques Clément—Mystic symbolism of the rose—Union of the rose and the cross—The Rosicrucians—Henry Khunrath—His *Amphitheatrum Sapientiæ Æternæ*—Its pantacles—Oswaldus Crollius—Alchemists of the early seventeenth century—A Rosicrucian manifesto 260

CONTENTS

CHAPTER VI
SOME MAGICAL PROSECUTIONS

Introductory remarks—Real crime of sorcerers—Some deplorable condemnations—The case of Louis Gaufridi—The case of Urbain Grandier—The nuns of Louvier and some other processes—Interpretation of certain phenomena—Story of an apparition . . 269

CHAPTER VII
THE MAGICAL ORIGIN OF FREEMASONRY

Its appearance in Europe—Its allegorical and real end—The Legend of Hiram—Its meaning—Mission of the Rites of Masonry—Its profanations 283

BOOK VI
MAGIC AND THE REVOLUTION

CHAPTER I
REMARKABLE AUTHORS OF THE EIGHTEENTH CENTURY

Important discoveries in China—The *Y-Kim* of Fo-hi—Legend of its origin—Connection with the Zohar—An example of absolute philosophy—Opinion of Leibnitz—Emmanuel Swedenborg—His system and its Kabalistic derivation—The discovery of Mesmer—Its theory and its great importance—A comparison between Voltaire and Mesmer 288

CHAPTER II
THAUMATURGIC PERSONALITIES OF THE EIGHTEENTH CENTURY

The Comte de Saint-Germain—Unpublished particulars of his life—The report of Madame de Genlis—The Order of Saint Jakin—A pretended initiation—Further concerning the Rosicrucians—An appreciation of Saint-Germain—His alleged identity with the mysterious Althotas—The alchemist Lascaris—Count Cagliostro—An agent of the Templars—A successor of Mesmer—Explanation of his seal

CONTENTS

and Kabalistic name—His secret of physical regeneration—His trial by the Inquisition—He is said to be still alive . . . 295

CHAPTER III

PROPHECIES OF CAZOTTE

The school of Martinists—The supper of Cazotte—The romance of *Le Diable Amoureux*—Its interpretation according to the Kabalah—Lilith and Nehamah—Initiation of Cazotte—The Mystic Mountain —Cazotte and the Revolutionary Tribunal 305

CHAPTER IV

THE FRENCH REVOLUTION

The reveries of Rousseau and their fatal consequences—The tomb of Jacques de Molay—The Lodge in Rue Platriere—The doom of Louis XVI—A genius of massacre—Mademoiselle de Sombreuil—Madame Elizabeth—The Church of the Jacobins—Vengeance of the Templars—Further concerning the Apocalypse of St. Methodius—The prophecies of Abbé Joachim 309

CHAPTER V

PHENOMENA OF MEDIOMANIA

An obscure sect of Johannite mystics—Visions of Loiseaut—Dom Gerle and Catherine Théot—A visit from Robespierre—The prophecy of Catherine—Her fate and that of Dom Gerle—The Saviours of Louis XVII—Martin de Gallardon—Eugène Vintras—Naündorff . 312

CHAPTER VI

THE GERMAN ILLUMINATI

The adept Steinert—An account of Eckartshausen—Schroepter and Lavater—The spirit Gablidone—His prophecies—Stabs and Napoleon—Carl Sand and Kotzebue—The Mopses and their mysteries—The magical drama of Faust 317

CHAPTER VII

EMPIRE AND RESTORATION

Predictions relative to Napoleon—Mademoiselle Lenormand—Etteilla and cartomancy—Madame Bouche and the Czar Alexander—Madame de Krudener—Further concerning the Saviours of Louis XVII—Visions of Martin de Gallardon 322

CONTENTS

BOOK VII

MAGIC IN THE NINETEENTH CENTURY

CHAPTER I
MAGNETIC MYSTICS AND MATERIALISTS

Infectious follies of Fourier—The dogma of hell—An evocation in the Church of Notre Dame—Lesser prophets and divinities—Ganneau, Auguste Comte and Wronski—Sale of the Absolute . . . 327

CHAPTER II
HALLUCINATIONS

Yet again concerning the Saviours of Louis XVII—Singular hallucination of Eugène Vintras—His prophecies and pretended miracles—The sect of Vintras—Its condemnation by Gregory XVI—Pontificate of Vintras—His dreams and visions 332

CHAPTER III
MESMERISTS AND SOMNAMBULISTS

The Church and the abuse of somnambulism—Baron Du Potet—His secret work on Magic—Table-turning—A table burnt for heresy—Experiences of Victor Hennequin—A magical melodrama . . 339

CHAPTER IV
THE FANTASTIC SIDE OF MAGICAL LITERATURE

Alphonse Esquiros invents a romanesque Magic—Henri Delaage continues the work—His gifts of enchantment—His orthodoxy—Le Comte d'Ourches—Baron de Guldenstubbé—His miraculous writings—Their explanation—Exhumation of a fakir—History of a vampire—The cartomancist Edmond. 343

CHAPTER V
SOME PRIVATE RECOLLECTIONS OF THE WRITER

The author is presented by the magician Alphonse Esquiros to the divinity Ganneau—Eccentric doctrines of the *Mapah*—Another Louis XVII—A fatal result of this visit—Secret cause of the Revolution of 1848—The wife of Ganneau 355

CONTENTS

CHAPTER VI

THE OCCULT SCIENCES

A synthesis in summary—Recapitulation of principles—The search after the absolute 358

CHAPTER VII

SUMMARY AND CONCLUSION

The enigma of the sphinx and its solution—Paradoxical questions and their answers—Knowledge and faith—The communion of faith—The temporal power of the pope—The science of moral equilibrium—Consequences of its recognition—A citation from the Blessed Vincent de Lerins—Another from Comte Joseph de Maistre—An axiom of St. Thomas Aquinas—The liberation of Magic—Purpose of this work 361

APPENDIX 375

INDEX 377

LIST OF ILLUSTRATIONS

PLATE
I. Portrait of Éliphas Lévi in the Robe of a Magus — *Frontispiece*

		PAGE
II.	The Pentagram of the Absolute	31
III.	The Great Symbol of Solomon, reconstructed according to the Zohar	43
IV.	The Magical Head of the Zohar	51
V.	The Great Kabalistic Symbol of the Zohar	63
VI.	The Mystery of Universal Equilibrium, according to Indian and Japanese Mythology, together with the Pantomorphic Lynx, or Twenty-First Primitive Egyptian Tarot Key	73
VII.	The Bembine Tablet	83
VIII.	Pantacle of Kabalistic Letters, being the Key of the Tarot, Sepher Yetzirah and the Zohar	101
IX.	The Seal of Cagliostro, Seal of the Samian Juno, Apocalyptic Seal, Twelve Seals of the Cubic Stone in Masonry, with the Twenty-First Tarot Key in the centre of all	111
X.	Egyptian Symbols of Typhon, illustrating Goëtia and Necromancy. Typhon is depicted performing the renewal of the empire of darkness. From the Temple of Hermoutis. The smaller figures are from the Zodiac of Esne and the top is a *bas relief* in the same temple	117
XI.	The Seven Wonders of the World	145
XII.	A Public Disputation between St. Peter and St. Paul on the one side and Simon the Magician on the other. Ascent and fall of Simon. From an engraving of the fifteenth century	157
XIII.	Hermetic Magic. Reproduced from an ancient Manuscript	179
XIV.	The Philosophical Cross, or plan of the Third Temple, as prophesied by Ezekiel and planned in the building scheme of the Knights Templar	209
XV.	Two occult Seals are shewn in the left compartment; the first represents the Great Work; the second is that of Black Magic. Both are from the *Grimoire of Honorius*. The right hand compartment contains primitive Egyptian Tarots—the 2 of Cups at the top and beneath this, specimens of the Ace of Cups	227
XVI.	The Seven Planets and their Genii, according to the Magic of Paracelsus	257
XVII.	The Great Hermetic Arcanum, according to Basil Valentine	291
XVIII.	A general plan of Kabalistic Doctrine	325
XIX.	Apocalyptic Key: the Seven Seals of St. John	359

INTRODUCTION

MAGIC has been confounded too long with the jugglery of mountebanks, the hallucinations of disordered minds and the crimes of certain unusual malefactors. There are otherwise many who would promptly explain Magic as the art of producing effects in the absence of causes; and on the strength of such a definition it will be said by ordinary people—with the good sense which characterises the ordinary, in the midst of much injustice—that Magic is an absurdity. But it can have no analogy in fact with the descriptions of those who know nothing of the subject; furthermore, it is not to be represented as this or that by any person whomsoever: it is that which it is, drawing from itself only, even as mathematics do, for it is the exact and absolute science of Nature and her laws.

Magic is the science of the ancient magi; and the Christian religion, which silenced the counterfeit oracles and put a stop to the illusions of false gods, does, this notwithstanding, revere those mystic kings who came from the East, led by a star, to adore the Saviour of the world in His cradle. They are elevated by tradition to the rank of kings, because magical initiation constitutes a true royalty; because also the great art of the magi is characterised by all adepts as the Royal Art, as the Holy Kingdom—*Sanctum Regnum*. The star which conducted the pilgrims is the same Burning Star which is met with in all initiations. For alchemists it is the sign of the quintessence, for magicians it is the Great Arcanum, for Kabalists the sacred pentagram. Our design is to prove that the study of this pentagram did itself lead the magi to a knowledge of that New Name which was to be exalted above all names and to bend the knees of all beings who were capable of adoration. Magic, therefore, combines in a single science that which is most certain in philosophy, which is eternal and infallible in religion. It reconciles perfectly and incontestably those two terms, so opposed on the first view—faith and reason, science and belief, authority and liberty. It furnishes the human mind with an instrument of philosophical and religious certitude as exact as mathematics, and even accounting for the infallibility of mathematics themselves.

An Absolute exists therefore in the realms of understanding and faith. The lights of human intelligence have not been left by the Supreme Reason to waver at hazard. There is an incontestable truth; there is an infallible method of knowing that truth; while those who attain this knowledge, and adopt it as a rule of life, can endow their will with a sovereign power which can make them masters of all inferior things, all wandering spirits, or, in other words, arbiters and kings of the world.

If such be the case, how comes it that so exalted a science is still unrecognised? How is it possible to assume that so bright a sun is hidden in a sky so dark? The transcendental science has been known always, but

INTRODUCTION

only to the flowers of intelligence, who have understood the necessity of silence and patience. Should a skilful surgeon open at midnight the eyes of a man born blind, it would still be impossible to make him realise the nature or existence of daylight till morning came. Science has its nights and its mornings, because the life which it communicates to the world of mind is characterised by regular modes of motion and progressive phases. It is the same with truths as it is with radiations of light. Nothing which is hidden is lost, but at the same time nothing that is found is absolutely new. The seal of eternity is affixed by God to that science which is the reflection of His glory.

The transcendental science, the absolute science, is assuredly Magic, though the affirmation may seem utterly paradoxical to those who have never questioned the infallibility of Voltaire—that marvellous smatterer who thought that he knew so much because he never missed an opportunity for laughter instead of learning. Magic was the science of Abraham and Orpheus, of Confucius and Zoroaster, and it was magical doctrines which were graven on tables of stone by Enoch and by Trismegistus. Moses purified and re-veiled them—this being the sense of the word reveal. The new disguise which he gave them was that of the Holy Kabalah—that exclusive heritage of Israel and inviolable secret of its priests.[1] The mysteries of Eleusis and of Thebes preserved among the Gentile some of its symbols, but in a debased form, and the mystic key was lost amidst the apparatus of an ever-increasing superstition. Jerusalem, murderer of its prophets and prostituted over and over again to false Assyrian and Babylonian gods, ended by losing in its turn the Sacred Word, when a Saviour, declared to the magi by the holy star of initiation, came to rend the threadbare veil of the old temple, to endow the Church with a new network of legends and symbols—ever concealing from the profane and always preserving for the elect that truth which is the same for ever.

It is this that the erudite and ill-starred Dupuis should have found on Indian planispheres and in tables of Denderah; he would not have ended by rejecting the truly catholic or universal and eternal religion in the presence of the unanimous affirmation of all Nature, as well as all monuments of science throughout the ages.[2] It was the memory of this scientific

[1] The word signifies reception, and in Rabbinical Hebrew it denotes doctrine so communicated—that is to say, by a tradition handed down or received from the past. John Reuchlin specifies it as symbolical reception, signifying that the doctrine is not comprised simply in its surface meaning. He says further that it is of Divine Revelation, and that it belongs primarily to the life giving contemplation of God. This is in the universal sense, but it is concerned also with secret teaching respecting particular things, meaning things manifest—*contemplatio formarum separatarum*.
[2] The reference is to *L'Origine de tous les Cultes, ou Religion Universelle*, 12 vols. in 8vo, together with an atlas in 4to. Paris, 1794. The work endeavoured to shew the unity of dogma under the multiplicity of symbols and allegories. In other words, it explained religion by astronomy, the cultus in the light of the calendar, mysteries of grace by means of natural phenomena. An abridgment in a small volume appeared about 1821. The Table of Denderah or Dendra was a great zodiac sculptured on the ceiling of the portico belonging to the Temple at that place, which was the ancient Tentyrio.

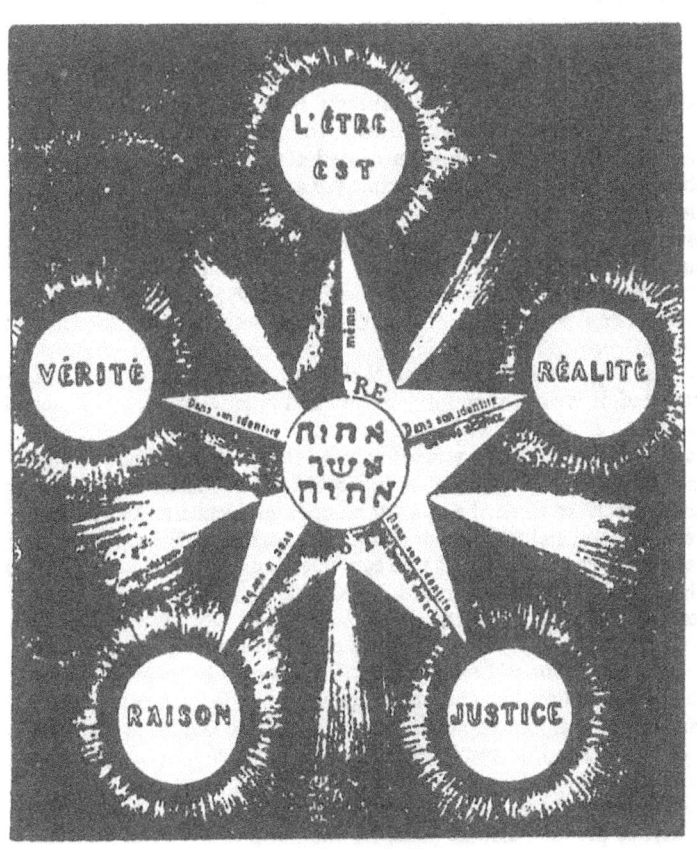

The Pentagram of the Absolute

INTRODUCTION

and religious absolute, of this doctrine summarised in a word, of this word alternately lost and recovered, which was transmitted to the elect of all antique initiations. Whether preserved or profaned in the celebrated Order of the Temple, it was this same memory handed on to secret associations of Rosicrucians, Illuminati and Freemasons which gave a meaning to their strange rites, to their less or more conventional signs, and a justification above all to their devotion in common, as well as a clue to their power.

That profanation has befallen the doctrines and mysteries of Magic we have no intention to deny; repeated from age to age, the misuse itself has been a great and terrible lesson for those who made secret things unwisely known. The Gnostics caused the Gnosis to be prohibited by Christians, and the official sanctuary was closed to high initiation. The hierarchy of knowledge was thus compromised by the intervention of usurping ignorance, while the disorders within the sanctuary were reproduced in the state, for, willingly or otherwise, the king always depends from the priest, and it is towards the eternal *adytum* of divine instruction that earthly powers will ever look for consecration and for energy to insure their permanence.

The key of science has been thrown to children; as might have been expected, it is now, therefore, mislaid and practically lost. This notwithstanding, a man of high intuitions and great moral courage, Count Joseph de Maistre, who was also a resolute catholic, acknowledging that the world was void of religion and could not so remain, turned his eyes instinctively towards the last sanctuaries of occultism and called, with heartfelt prayers, for that day when the natural affinity which subsists between science and faith should combine them in the mind of a single man of genius. "This will be grand," said he; "it will finish that eighteenth century which is still with us. . . . We shall talk then of our present stupidity as we now dilate on the barbarism of the Middle Ages."

The prediction of Count Joseph de Maistre is in course of realisation; the alliance of science and faith, accomplished long since, is here in fine made manifest, though not by a man of genius. Genius is not needed to see the sun, and, moreover, it has never demonstrated anything but its rare greatness and its lights inaccessible to the crowd. The grand truth demands only to be found, when the simplest will be able to comprehend it and to prove it also at need. At the same time that truth will never become vulgar, because it is hierarchic and because anarchy alone humours the bias of the crowd. The masses are not in need of absolute truths; were it otherwise, progress would be arrested and life would cease in humanity; the ebb and flow of contrary ideas, the clash of opinions, the passions of the time, ever impelled by its dreams, are necessary to the intellectual growth of peoples. The masses know it full well, and hence they desert so readily the chair of doctors to collect about the rostrum of mountebanks. Some even who are assumed to be concerned in philosophy, and that perhaps especially, too often resemble the children playing at

INTRODUCTION

charades, who hasten to turn out those who know the answer already, lest the game should be spoiled by depriving the puzzle of the questions of all its interest.

"Blessed are the pure in heart, for they shall see God" has been said by Eternal Wisdom. Purity of heart therefore purifies intelligence, and rectitude of will makes for precision in understanding. Whosoever prefers truth and justice before all things shall have justice and truth for his reward, because supreme Providence has endowed us with freedom in order that we may attain life; and very truth, all its exactitude notwithstanding, intervenes only with mildness, never does outrage to tardiness or violence to the errors of our will when it is beguiled by the allurements of falsehood.

It remains, however, according to Bossuet, that, antecedent to anything which may please or repel our senses, there is a truth, and it is by this that our conduct should be governed, not by our appetites. The Kingdom of Heaven is not the empire of caprice, either in respect of man or God. "A thing is not just because it is willed by God," said St. Thomas, "but God wills it because it is just." The Divine Balance rules and necessitates eternal mathematics. "God has made all things with number, weight and measure"—here it is the Bible speaking.[1] Measure an angle of creation, make a proportionally progressive multiplication, and all infinity shall multiply its circles, peopled by universes, passing in proportional segments between the extending symbolical arms of your compass. Suppose now that, from whatever point of the infinite above you, a hand holds another compass or square, then the lines of the celestial triangle will meet of necessity those of the compass of science and will form therewith the mysterious star of Solomon.[2]

"With what measure you mete, it shall be measured to you again," says the Gospel. God does not strive with man that He may crush man by His grandeur, and He never places unequal weights in His balance. When He would test the strength of Jacob, He assumes the form of man; the patriarch withstands the onset through an entire night; at the end there is a blessing for the conquered and, in addition to the glory of having sustained such a struggle, he is given the national title of Israel, being a name which signifies—Strong against God.[3]

We have heard Christians more zealous than instructed hazarding a strange explanation of the dogma concerning eternal punishment by suggesting that God may avenge infinitely an offence which itself is finite,

---

[1] *Sed omnia in mensura, ei numero, et pondere disposuisti*: "But Thou hast ordered all things in measure and number and weight."—Wisdom xi, 21.

[2] The conventional Hexagram presents in pictorial symbolism the root doctrine of the Hermetic Emerald Tablet: "That which is above is equal to that which is below." It is the sign of the interpenetration of worlds.

[3] According to the *Zohar*, Part I, fol. 21a, 21b, it was with the guardian angel of Esau that Jacob wrestled at the place which he named Peniel. The angel could not prevail against Jacob because the latter derived his strength from the Supreme Light, *Kether*, and from *Chokmah*, which is the second hypostasis. He therefore smote Jacob on the right thigh, which signifies the seventh *Sephira*, or *Netsach*

INTRODUCTION

because if the offender is limited the grandeur of the offended being is not. An emperor of the world might, on the strength of a similar pretext, sentence to death some unreasoning child who had soiled accidentally the hem of his purple. Far otherwise are the prerogatives of greatness, and St. Augustine understood them better when he said that "God is patient because He is eternal." In God all is justice, seeing that all is goodness; He never forgives after the manner of men, for He is never angered like them; but evil being, by its nature, incompatible with good, as night is with day, as discord is with harmony, and the liberty of man being furthermore inviolable, all error is expiated and all evil punished by suffering proportioned thereto. It is vain to invoke the help of Jupiter when our cart is stuck in the mud; unless we take pick and shovel, like the waggoner in the fable, Heaven will not draw us out of the rut. Help yourself and God will help you. In such a reasonable and wholly philosophical way is explained the possible and necessary eternity of punishment, with still a narrow way open for man to escape therefrom—being that of toil and repentance.[1]

It is by conformity with the rules of eternal power that man may unite himself to the creative energy and become creator and preserver in his turn. God has not limited narrowly the number of rounds on Jacob's ladder of light. Whatsoever Nature has constituted inferior to man is thereby to him made subject: it is for man to extend his domain in virtue of continual ascent. Length and even perpetuity of life, the field of air and its storms, the earth and its metallic veins, light and its wondrous illusions, darkness and the dreams thereof, death and its ghosts—all these do therefore obey the royal sceptre of the magi, the shepherd's staff of Jacob and the terrible wand of Moses. The adept becomes king of the elements, transmuter of metals, interpreter of visions, controller of oracles, master of life in fine, according to the mathematical order of Nature and conformably to the will of the Supreme Intelligence. This is Magic in all its glory. But is there anyone who in these days will dare to give credence to such words? The answer is—those who will study loyally and attain knowledge frankly. We make no attempt to conceal truth under the veil of parables or hieroglyphical signs; the time has come when everything should be told, and we propose to tell everything. It is our intention, in short, to unveil that ever secret science which, as we have indicated, is hidden behind the shadows of ancient mysteries, which the Gnostics betrayed clumsily, or rather disfigured unworthily, which is recognised dimly under the darkness shrouding the pretended crimes of Templars, which is met with once again beneath the now impenetrable enigmas of High-Grade Masonic Rites. We purpose further to bring into open day the fantastic King of the Sabbath, to expose the very roots of Black Magic

[1] The more usual argument of high orthodox theology in the Latin school is that a sin against the Infinite Being is one of infinite culpability. If it were suggested in rejoinder that it must be one of infinite inconsequence, so far as that Being is concerned, it might not be more reasonable than the argument, but it would do less outrage to logic.

and its frightful realities, long since surrendered to the derision of the grandchildren of Voltaire.

For a great number of readers Magic is the science of the devil—even as the science of light is identified with that of darkness. We confess boldly at the outset that we are not in terror of the devil. "My fear is for those who fear him," said St. Teresa. But we testify also that he does not prompt our laughter and that the ridicule of which he is often the object seems to us exceedingly misplaced. However this may be, it is our intention to bring him before the light of science. But the devil and science—the apposition of two names so strangely incongruous—must seem to have disclosed the whole intent in view. If the mystic personification of darkness be thus dragged into light, is it not to annihilate the phantom of falsehood in the presence of truth? Is it not to dispel in the day all formless monsters of the night? Superficial persons will think so and will condemn without hearing. Ill-instructed Christians will conclude that we are sapping the fundamental dogma of their ethics by decrying hell; and others will question the utility of combating error in which, as they imagine, no one believes longer. It is, therefore, important to enunciate our object clearly and establish our principles solidly.

We say, therefore, to Christians that the author of this book is a Christian like yourselves. His faith is that of a catholic strongly and deeply convinced; for this reason he does not come forward to deny dogmas, but to combat impiety under its most pernicious forms, which are those of false belief and superstition. He comes to drag from the darkness the black successor of Ahriman, in order to expose in broad day his colossal impotence and redoubtable misery. He comes to make subject the age-long problem of evil to the solutions of science, to uncrown the king of hell and to bow down his head at the foot of the cross. Is not virginal and maternal science—that science of which Mary is the sweet and luminous image—destined like her to crush the head of the old serpent?

The author, on the other hand, would say to pretended philosophy: Why seek to deny that which you cannot understand? Is not the unbelief which affirms in the face of the unknown more precipitate and less consoling than faith? Does the dreadful form of personified evil only prompt you to smile? Hear you not the ceaseless sobbing of humanity which writhes and weeps in the crushing folds of the monster? Have you never heard the atrocious laugh of the evil-doer who is persecuting the just man? Have you never experienced in yourselves the opening of those infernal deeps which the genius of perversity furrows in every soul? Moral evil exists—such is the unhappy truth; it reigns in certain spirits; it incarnates in certain men; it is therefore personified, and thus demons exist; but the most wicked of these demons is Satan. More than this I do not ask you to admit, and it will be difficult for you to grant me less.

Let it be otherwise and clearly understood that science and faith render mutual support to one another only in so far as their respective

INTRODUCTION

realms remain inviolably distinct. What is it that we believe? That which we do not know absolutely, though we may yearn for it with all our strength. The object of faith is not more than an indispensable hypothesis for science; the things which are in the domain of knowledge must never be judged by the processes of faith, nor, conversely, the things of faith according to the measures of science. The end of faith is not scientifically debatable. "I believe because it is absurd," said Tertullian; and this utterance—paradoxical on the surface as it is—belongs to the highest reason. As a fact, beyond all that we can suppose rationally there is an infinite towards which we aspire with unquenchable thirst, and it eludes even our dreams. But is not the infinite itself an absurdity for our finite appreciation? We feel all the same that it is; the infinite invades us, overflows us, renders us dizzy at its abysses and crushes us by its awful height.

Scientifically probable hypotheses are one and all the last half-lights or shadows of science; faith begins where reason falls exhausted. Beyond human reason there is that Reason which is Divine—for my weakness a supreme absurdity, but an infinite absurdity which confounds me, and in which I believe.

The good alone is infinite; evil is not; and hence if God be the eternal object of faith, then the devil belongs to science. In which of the catholic creeds is there any question concerning him? Would it not be blasphemy to say that we believe in him? In Holy Scripture he is named but not defined. Genesis makes no allusion to a reputed revolt of angels; it ascribes the fall of Adam to the serpent, as to the most subtle and dangerous of living beings. We are acquainted with Christian tradition on this subject; but if that tradition is explicable by one of the greatest and most diffused allegories of science, what can such solution signify to the faith which aspires only to God, which despises the pomps and works of Lucifer?

Lucifer—Light-bearer—how strange a name, attributed to the spirit of darkness! Is it he who carries the light and yet blinds feeble souls? The answer is yes, unquestionably; for traditions are full of divine disclosures and inspirations. "Satan himself is transformed into an angel of light," says St. Paul. And Christ Himself said: "I beheld Satan as lightning fall from heaven." So also the prophet Isaiah: "How art thou fallen from heaven, O Lucifer, son of the morning." Lucifer is then a fallen star—a meteor which is on fire always, which burns when it enlightens no longer. But is this Lucifer a person or a force, an angel or a strayed thunderbolt? Tradition supposes that it is an angel, but the Psalmist says: "Who maketh his angels spirits; his ministers a flaming fire." The word "angel" is applied in the Bible to all messengers of God—emissaries or new creations, revealers or scourges, radiant spirits or brilliant objects. The shafts of fire which the Most High darts through the clouds are angels of His wrath, and such figurative language is familiar to all readers of Eastern poetry.

Having been the world's terror through the period of the middle ages,

INTRODUCTION

the devil has become its mockery.[1] Heir to the monstrous forms of all false gods cast down successively from their thrones, the grotesque scarecrow has turned into a mere bugbear through very deformity and hideousness. Yet observe as to this that those only dare to laugh at the devil who know not the fear of God. Can it be that for many diseased imaginations he is God's own shadow, or is he not often the idol of degenerate souls who only understand supernatural power as the exercise of cruelty with impunity?

But it is important to ascertain whether the notion of this evil power can be reconciled with that of God—in a word, whether the devil exists, and in such case what he is. There is no longer any question of superstition or of ridiculous invention; it is a question of religion alone and hence of the whole future, with all the interests, of humanity.

Strange reasoners indeed are we: we call ourselves strong-minded when we are indifferent to everything except material advantages, as, for example, money; and we leave to their own devices the ideas which are mothers of opinions and may, or at least can, by their sudden veering, upset all fortunes. A conquest of science is much more important than the discovery of a gold mine. Given science, gold is utilised in the service of life; given ignorance, wealth furnishes only destroying weapons.

For the rest, it is to be understood absolutely that our scientific revelations pause in the presence of faith, that—as Christian and Catholic —our work is submitted entirely to the supreme judgment of the Church. This said, to those who question the existence of a devil, we would point out that whatsoever has a name exists; speech may be uttered in vain, but in itself it cannot be vain, and it has a meaning invariably. The Word is never void, and if it be written that it is in God, as also that it is God, this is because it is the expression and the proof of being and of truth. The devil is named and personified in the Gospel, which is the Word of truth; he exists therefore and can be considered as a person. But here it is the Christian who defers: let science or reason speak; these two are one.[2]

Evil exists; it is impossible to doubt it; we can work good or evil. There are beings who work evil knowingly and willingly. The spirit which animates these beings and prompts them to do ill is betrayed, turned aside from the right road, and thrown across the path of good as an obstacle; this is the precise meaning of the Greek word *diabolos*, which we render as devil. The spirits who love and perform evil are accidentally bad. There is therefore a devil who is the spirit of error, wilful ignorance, vertigo;

[1] It is to be noted, however, that there was mockery of its kind in the middle ages, that Satan and his emissaries in folk-lore appear under ridiculous lights. There is the prototypical story of the devil who gave a course of lectures on Black Magic at the University of Salamanca and demanded, as a consideration, the soul of one of his hearers; but he was cheated with the student's shadow.

[2] In his earlier work, *The Doctrine and Ritual of Transcendental Magic*, Éliphas Lévi affirms (a) on the authority of a writer whom he does not name, that the devil is God, as understood by the wicked; (b) on another authority, that the devil is composed of God's ruins; (c) that the devil is the Great Magical Agent employed for evil purposes by a perverse will; (d) that he is death masquerading in the cast-off garments of life; (e) that Satan, Beelzebub, Adramelek, etc., do not designate spiritual unities, but legions of impure spirits.

INTRODUCTION

there are beings under his obedience who are his envoys, emissaries, angels; and it is for this reason that the Gospel speaks of an eternal fire which is prepared, and in a sense predestined, for the devil and his angels. These words are themselves a revelation, so let us search their meaning, giving, in the first place, a concise definition of evil. Evil is the absence of rectitude in being. Moral evil is falsehood in action, as the lie is a crime in speech. Injustice is of the essence of lying, and every lie is an injustice. When that which we utter is just, there is no falsity. When that which we do is equitable and true in mode, there is no sin. Injustice is the death of moral being, as lying is the poison of intelligence. The false spirit is therefore a spirit of death. Those who hearken to him become his dupes and are by him poisoned. But if we had to take his absolute personification seriously, he would be himself absolutely dead, and absolutely deceived, which means that the affirmation of his existence must imply a patent contradiction. Jesus said that the devil is a liar like his father. Who then is the father of the devil? Whosoever gives him a personal existence by living in accordance with his inspirations; the man who diabolises himself is the father of the incarnate spirit of evil. But there is a rash, impious and monstrous conception, traditional like the pride of the Pharisees, and in fine there is a hybrid creation which armed the paltry philosophy of the eighteenth century with an apparent defence. It is the false Lucifer of the heterodox legend—that angel proud enough to think that he was God, brave enough to buy independence at the price of eternal torment, beautiful enough to worship himself in the plenary Divine Light; strong enough to reign still in darkness and in dole and to make a throne of his inextinguishable fire. It is the Satan of the heretical and republican Milton, the pretended hero of black eternities, calumniated by deformity, bedecked with horns and talons which would better become his implacable tormentor. It is the devil who is king of evil, as if evil were a kingdom, who is more intelligent than the men of genius that fear his wiles. It is (*a*) that black light, that darkness with eyes, that power which God has not willed but which no fallen creature could create; (*b*) that prince of anarchy served by a hierarchy of pure spirits;[1] (*c*) that exile of God who on earth seems, like Him, everywhere, but is more tangible, is more for the majority in evidence, and is served better than God himself; (*d*) that conquered one, to whom the victor gives his children that he may devour them; (*e*) that artificer of sins of the flesh, to whom flesh is nothing, and who therefore can be nothing to flesh, unless indeed he be its creator and master, like God; (*f*) that immense, realised, personified and eternal lie;

[1] In speaking of evil and a possible Prince of Darkness, it is necessary to proceed carefully, if we are confined, like Éliphas Lévi, within the measures of a theory of opposites. The definition of evil as the absence of rectitude is entirely insufficient to cover the facts of experience; it is that indeed, but it is also as much more as may be necessary to account for its positive and active side. The truth is that positive and negative are on both sides of the eternal balance of things postulated by the theory. So far as it goes, evil is the absence of rectitude, and, so far as it goes also, rectitude is the absence of evil; but the vital aspects of good and bad have slipped between the fingers of definition in both cases.

INTRODUCTION

(g) that death which cannot die; (h) that blasphemy which the Word of God will never silence; (i) that poisoner of souls whom God tolerates by a contradiction of His omnipotence or preserves as the Roman emperors guarded Locusta among the trophies of their reign; (k) that executed criminal, living still to curse his Judge and still have a cause against him, since he will never repent; (l) that monster accepted as executioner by the Sovereign Power, and who, according to the forcible expression of an old catholic writer, may term God the God of the devil by describing himself as a devil of God.

Such is the irreligious phantom which blasphemes religion. Away with this idol which hides our Saviour. Down with the tyrant of falsehood, the black god of Manicheans, the Ahriman of old idolaters. Live God and His Word incarnate, who saw Satan fall from heaven. And live Mary, the Divine Mother, who crushed the head of the infernal serpent.

So cry with one voice the traditions of saints, and so cry faithful hearts. The attribution of any greatness whatsoever to a fallen spirit is a slander on Divinity; the ascription of any royalty whatsoever to the rebel spirit is to encourage revolt and be guilty, at least in thought, of that crime which the horror of the middle ages termed sorcery. For all the offences visited with death on the old sorcerers were real crimes and were indeed the greatest of all. They stole fire from heaven, like Prometheus; they rode winged dragons and the flying serpent, like Medea; they poisoned the breathable air, like the shadow of the manchineel tree; they profaned sacred things and even used the body of the Lord in works of destruction and malevolence.

How is all this possible? Because there is a composite agent, a natural and divine agent, at once corporeal and spiritual, an universal plastic mediator, a common receptacle for vibrations of movement and images of form, a fluid and a force which may be called, in a sense at least, the imagination of Nature. By the mediation of this force every nervous apparatus is in secret communication together; hence come sympathy and antipathy, hence dreams, hence the phenomena of second sight and extra-natural vision. This universal agent of Nature's works is the *Od* of the Jews and of Reichenbach, the Astral Light of the Martinists,[1] which denomination we prefer as the more explicit.

---

[1] Saint-Martin recognises the existence of an astral region, which is apparently that of sidereal rule. There is, in his view, a certain science of this region, and of this the active branch is theurgic, while the passive engenders somnambulism. These divisions constitute the elementary science of the astral, but above these there is one which is more fatal and dangerous, of which he refuses to speak. There is no Martinistic doctrine concerning the Astral Light, understood as an universal medium. Éliphas Lévi seems to have used the term Martinism in a general sense, as if it included the school of Martines de Pasqually. Pasqually, however, has no doctrine concerning the Astral Light. Modern French Martinism has read it into Saint-Martin's rather ridiculous "epico-magical poem" or allegory, called *Le Crocodile*, much as another school of experiment might find therein a veiled account of the Akasic records and the mode of their study. I refer to the story of Atlantis, which begins at *Chant* 64 and occupies a large part of the book. The account of the Chair of Silence is very curious in this connection.

INTRODUCTION

The existence and possible employment of this force constitute the great secret of Practical Magic; it is the Wand of Thaumaturgy and the Key of Black Magic. It is the Edenic serpent who transmitted to Eve the seductions of a fallen angel. The Astral Light warms, illuminates, magnetises, attracts, repels, vivifies, destroys, coagulates, separates, breaks and conjoins everything, under the impetus of powerful wills. God created it on the first day when He said "Let there be light." This force of itself is blind but is directed by *Egregores*—that is, by chiefs of souls, or, in other words, by energetic and active spirits.[1]

Herein is the complete explanatory theory of prodigies and miracles. How, as a fact, could good and bad alike compel Nature to reveal her hidden forces, how could there be divine and diabolical miracles, how could the reprobate and bewrayed spirit have more power in certain ways and cases than the just spirit, which is in truth so powerful in simplicity and wisdom, unless we postulate an instrument which all can use, upon certain conditions, but some for the great good and others for the great evil?

Pharaoh's magicians accomplished at first the same miracles as Moses. The instrument which they used was therefore the same; the inspiration alone differed; when they confessed themselves conquered, they proclaimed that, for them, human powers had reached their limit, and that there must be something superhuman in Moses.[2] This took place in Egypt, that mother of magical initiations, that land where it was all occult science, hierarchic and sacred instruction. Was it, however, more difficult to make flies appear than frogs? No, assuredly; but the magicians knew that the fluidic projection by which the eyes are biologised cannot proceed beyond certain bounds, and these had been passed already by Moses.[3]

A particular phenomenon occurs when the brain is congested or overcharged by Astral Light; sight is turned inward, instead of outward; night falls on the external and real world, while fantastic brilliance shines on the world of dreams; even the physical eyes experience a slight quivering and turn up inside the lids. The soul then perceives by means of images the reflection of its impressions and thoughts. This is to say that the analogy subsisting between idea and form attracts in the Astral Light a reflection representing that form, configuration being the essence of the vital light; it is the universal imagination, of which each of us appropriates a lesser or greater part according to our grade of sensibility and memory. Therein is the source of all apparitions, all extraordinary visions and all the intuitive phenomena peculiar to madness or ecstasy.

The appropriation or assimilation of the light by clairvoyant sensibility is one of the greatest phenomena which can be studied by science. It may

[1] If the word is of Greek origin it seems to connect with the idea of watchers rather than leaders. Cf. ὁ ἐγρήγορος = Vigil, in the Septuagint.
[2] The Kabalistic explanation is (a) that Egyptian Magic was real Magic; (b) that its wisdom was of the lowermost degree only; (c) that it was overcome by the superior degrees, by which the serpent above, or Metatron, dominates the serpent below, namely, Samael. See *Zohar*, Part II, fol. 28a.
[3] Elsewhere Éliphas Lévi suggests that Pharaoh's magicians refused rather than failed and that the production of flies was beneath the dignity of their Magic.

INTRODUCTION

be understood in a day to come that seeing is actually speaking and that the consciousness of light is a twilight of eternal life in being. The word of God Himself, Who creates light, and is uttered by all intelligence that conceives of forms and seeks to visualise them. "Let there be light." Light in the mode of brightness exists only for eyes which look thereon, and the soul enamoured with the pageant of universal beauty, and fixing its attention on that luminous script of the endless book which is called things manifest, seems to cry on its own part, as God at the dawn of the first day, the sublime and creative words: *Fiat lux*.

We do not all see with the same eyes, and creation is not for all the same in colour and form. Our brain is a book printed within and without, and with the smallest degree of excitement, the writing becomes blurred, as occurs continually in cases of intoxication and madness. Dream then triumphs over real life and plunges reason in a sleep which knows no waking. This condition of hallucination has its degrees; all passions are intoxications; all enthusiasms are comparative and graduated manias. The lover sees only infinite perfections encompassing that object by which he is fascinated. But, unhappy infatuation of voluptuaries, tomorrow this odour of wine which allures him will become a repugnant reminiscence, causing a thousand loathings and a thousand disgusts.

To understand the use of this force, but never to be obsessed and never overcome thereby, is to trample on the serpent's head, and it is this which we learn from the Magic of Light; in such secrets are contained all mysteries of magnetism, which name can indeed be applied to the whole practical part of antique Transcendental Magic. Magnetism is the wand of miracles, but it is this for initiates only; for rash and uninstructed people, who would sport with it or make it subserve their passions, it is as dangerous as that consuming glory which, according to the allegorical fable, destroyed the too ambitious Semele in the embraces of Jupiter.

One of the great benefits of magnetism is that it demonstrates by incontestable facts the spirituality, unity and immortality of the soul; and these things once made certain, God is manifested to all intelligences and all hearts. Thereafter, from the belief in God and from the harmonies of creation, we are led to that great religious harmony which does not exist outside the miraculous and lawful hierarchy of the Catholic Church, for this alone has preserved all traditions of science and faith.

The primal tradition of the one and only revelation has been preserved under the name of Kabalah by the priesthood of Israel. Kabalistic doctrine, which is that of Transcendental Magic, is contained in the *Sepher Yetzirah*, the *Zohar* and the *Talmud*.[1] According to this doctrine,

---

[1] It should be mentioned that this enumeration is in the reverse order of chronology, and it is not, as it happens, even in accordance with what may be called traditional chronology. Legend says—and Éliphas Lévi himself mentions subsequently—that the *Sepher Yetzirah* was the work of Abraham and that the *Zohar* is in its root-matter a literal record of discourses delivered by R. Simeon Ben Jochai, after the fall of Jerusalem, A.D. 70. The Jerusalem and Babylon Talmuds are admittedly growths of some centuries.

INTRODUCTION

the absolute is Being, and therein is the Word, which expresses the reason of Being and of life. The principle therefore is that Being is being, אהיה אשר אהיה. In the beginning the Word was, which means that it is, has been and shall be; and this is reason which speaks. In the beginning was the Word. The Word is the reason of belief, and therein also is the expression of that faith which gives life to science. The Word, or Logos, is the wellspring of logic. Jesus is the Incarnate Word. The concord of reason with faith, of science with belief, of authority with liberty, has become in these modern days the real enigma of the sphinx. Coincidentally with this great problem there has come forward that which concerns the respective rights of man and woman. This was inevitable, for between the several terms of a great and supreme question there is a constant analogy, and the difficulties, like the correspondences, are invariably the same. The loosening of this Gordian knot of philosophy and modern politics is rendered apparently paradoxical, because in order to effect an agreement between the terms of the required equation there is always a tendency to confuse the one with the other. If there is anything that deserves to be called supreme absurdity it is to inquire how faith becomes a reason, reason a belief and liberty an authority; or, reciprocally, how the woman becomes a man and the man a woman. The definitions themselves intervene against such confusion, and it is by maintaining a perfect distinction between the terms, and so only, that we can bring them into agreement. The perfect and eternal distinction between the two primal terms of the creative syllogism, for the demonstration of their harmony in virtue of the analogy of opposites, is the second great principle of that occult philosophy veiled under the name of Kabalah and indicated by all sacred hieroglyphics of the old sanctuaries, as by the rites, even now understood so little, of ancient and modern Masonry.

We read in Scripture that Solomon erected two brazen columns before the door of his Temple, one of them being called *Jachin* and the other *Boaz*, meaning the strong and the weak.[1] These two pillars represented man and woman, reason and faith, power and liberty, Cain and Abel, right and duty. They were pillars of the intellectual and moral world, the monumental hieroglyphic of the antinomy inevitable to the grand law of creation. The meaning is that every force postulates a resistance on which it can work, every light a shadow as its foil, every convex a concave, every influx a receptacle, every reign a kingdom, every sovereign a people, every workman a first matter, every conqueror something to overcome.

---

[1] The meanings ascribed to the names and inscriptions on the two Pillars of the Temple will be of curious interest to members of the Masonic Fraternity, who will be reminded of variants with which they are themselves familiar. It must be said, however, that the explanation of Lévi corresponds neither to Masonic nor Kabalistic symbolism. According to the latter *Boaz* is the left-hand Pillar, being that of Severity in the scheme of the Sephirotic Tree; it answers to *Hod*, and the meaning attached to its name is Strength and Vigour. *Jachin* is on the right hand, answering to *Netzach* on the Tree; it signifies the state of becoming established. That which is made firm between *Hod* and *Netzach* is *Malkuth*, or the kingdom below. This is the late Kabalism of the tract entitled *Garden of Pomegranates*.

The Great Symbol of Solomon

INTRODUCTION

Affirmation rests on negation; the strong can only triumph because of weakness; the aristocracy cannot be manifested except by rising above the people. For the weak to become strong, for the people to acquire an aristocratic position, is a question of transformation and of progress, but it is without prejudice to the first principles; the weak will be ever the weak and it matters nothing if they are not always the same persons. The people in like manner will ever remain the people, the mass which is ruled and is not capable of ruling. In the vast army of inferiors, every personal emancipation is an automatic desertion, which, happily, is imperceptible because it is replaced, also automatically; a king-nation or a people of kings would presuppose the slavery of the world and anarchy in a single city, outside all discipline, as at Rome in the days of its greatest glory. A nation of sovereigns would be inevitably as anarchic as a class of experts or of scholars who deemed that they were masters; there would be none to listen; all would dogmatise and all give orders at once.

The radical emancipation of womanhood falls within the same category. If, integrally and radically, the woman leaves the passive and enters the active condition, she abdicates her sex and becomes man, or rather, as such a transformation is impossible physically, she attains affirmation by a double negation, placing herself outside both sexes, like a sterile and monstrous androgyne. These are strict consequences of the great Kabalistic dogma respecting that distinction of contraries which reaches harmony by the analogy of their proportions. This dogma once recognised, and the application of its results being made universally by the law of analogies, will mean a discovery of the greatest secrets concerning maternal sympathy and antipathy; it will mean also a discovery of the science of government in things political, in marriage, in all branches of occult medicine, whether magnetism, homœopathy, or moral influence. Moreover, and as it is intended to explain, the law of equilibrium in analogy leads to the discovery of an universal agent which was the Grand Secret of alchemists and magicians in the middle ages. It has been said that this agent is a light of life by which animated beings are rendered magnetic, electricity being only its accident and transient perturbation, so to speak. The practice of that marvellous Kabalah to which we shall turn shortly, for the satisfaction of those who look, in the secret sciences, after emotions rather than wise teachings, reposes entirely in the knowledge and use of this agent.

The religion of the Kabalists is at once hypothesis and certitude, for it proceeds from known to unknown by the help of analogy. They recognise religion as a need of humanity, as an evident and necessary fact, and it is this alone which for them is divine, permanent and universal revelation. They dispute about nothing which is, but they provide the reason for everything. So also their doctrine, by distinguishing clearly the line of demarcation which must exist for ever between science and faith, provides a basis for faith in the highest reason, guaranteeing its incontestable and

INTRODUCTION

permanent duration. After this come the popular forms of doctrine, which alone can vary and alone destroy one another; the Kabalist is not only undisturbed by trivialities of this kind, but can provide on the spot a reason for the most astonishing formulæ. It follows that his prayer can be joined to that of humanity at large, to direct it by illustrations from science and reason and draw it into orthodox channels. If Mary be mentioned, he will revere the realisation in her of all that is divine in the dreams of innocence, all that is adorable in the sacred enthusiasm of every maternal heart. It is not he who will refuse flowers to adorn the altars of the Mother of God, or white banners for her chapels, or even tears for her ingenuous legends. It is not he who will mock at the new-born God weeping in the manger or the wounded victim of Calvary. He repeats nevertheless, from the bottom of his heart, like the sages of Israel and the faithful believers of Islam: There is no God but God. For the initiates of true science this signifies: There is but one Being, and this is Being. But all that is expedient and touching in beliefs, but the splendour of rituals, the pageant of divine creations, the grace of prayers, the magic of heavenly hopes—are not these the radiance of moral life in all its youth and beauty? Could anything alienate the true initiate from public prayers and temples, could anything raise his disgust or indignation against religious forms of all kinds, it would be the manifest unbelief of priests or people, want of dignity in the ceremonies of the cultus—in a word, the profanation of holy things. God is truly present when He is worshipped by recollected souls and feeling hearts; He is absent, sensibly and terribly, when discussed without light or zeal—that is to say, without understanding or love.

The adequate conception of God according to instructed Kabalism is that which was revealed by St. Paul when he said that to attain God we must believe that He is and that He recompenses those who seek Him out. So is there nothing outside the idea of being, in combination with the idea of goodness and justice: these alone are absolute. To say that there is no God, or to define what He is, constitutes equal blasphemy. Every definition of God hazarded by human intelligence is a recipe of religious empiricism, out of which superstition will subsequently extract a devil.

In Kabalistic symbolism the representation of God is always by a duplicated image—one erect, the other reversed; one white, and the other black.[1] In such manner did the sages seek to express the intelligent and vulgar conceptions of the same idea—that of the God of light and the God of shadow. To the miscomprehension of this symbol must be referred the Persian Ahriman—that black but divine ancestor

---

[1] This is the particular construction which is placed by Lévi on the texts with which he is assuming to deal, and it is not really justified by these. The *Zohar* has, however, a doctrine of the Unknown Darkness. The Infinite is neither light nor splendour, though all lights emanate therefrom. It is a Supreme Will, exceeding human comprehension, and more mysterious than all mysteries. See *Zohar*, Part I, fol. 239a.

of all demons. The dream of the infernal king is but a false notion of God.

Light in the absence of shadow would be invisible for our eyes, since it would produce an overpowering brilliance equal to the greatest darkness. In the analogies of this physical truth, understood and considered adequately, a solution will be found for one of the most terrible of problems, the origin of evil. But to grasp it fully, together with all its consequences, is not meant for the multitude, who must not penetrate so readily into the secrets of universal harmony. It was only after the initiate of the Eleusinian mysteries had passed victoriously through all the tests, had seen and touched the holy things, that, if he were judged strong enough to withstand the last and most dreadful secret, a veiled priest passed him at flying pace and uttered in his ear the enigmatic words: Osiris is a black god. So was Osiris—of whom Typhon is the oracle—and so was the divine religious sun of Egypt, eclipsed suddenly, becoming the shadow of that grand, indefinable Isis who is all that has been and shall be, and whose eternal veil no one has lifted.

Light is the active principle for Kabalists, while darkness is analogous to the passive principle, for which reason they regarded the sun and moon as emblems of the two divine sexes and the two creative forces. So also they attributed to woman the first temptations and sin, and subsequently the first labour—the maternal labour of redemption: it is from the bosom of the dark itself that light is reborn. The void attracts the *plenum*, and thus the abyss of poverty and wretchedness, pretended evil, seeming nothingness and the ephemeral rebellion of creatures, attracts eternally an ocean of being, wealth, mercy and love. This interprets the symbol of the Christ descending into hell after pouring out upon the cross all immensities of the most marvellous forgiveness.

By the same law of harmony in the analogy of opposites the Kabalists explain also all mysteries of sexual love. Why is this passion more permanent between two unequal natures and two contrary characters? Why is there in love one always who immolates and one who is victim? Why are the most obstinate passions those the satisfaction of which would seem impossible? By this law also they would have decided once and for ever the question of precedence between the sexes, as brought forward in all seriousness by the Saint-Simonism of our own day. The natural strength of woman being that of inertia or resistance, they would have ruled that modesty is the most imprescriptible of her rights, and hence that she must neither perform nor desire anything demanding a species of masculine boldness. Nature has otherwise provided to this end by giving her a soft voice, not to be heard in large assemblies, unless raised to a ridiculously discordant pitch. She who would aspire to the functions of the opposite sex must forfeit thereby the prerogatives of her own. We know not to what point she may arrive in the ruling of men, but it is certain at least that in reaching it she will lose the love of men and, that which will be more cruel for her, the love of children.

INTRODUCTION

The conjugal law of the Kabalists[1] furnishes further, by analogy, a solution of the most interesting and difficult problem of modern philosophy, being the agreement between reason and faith, authority and liberty of conscience, science and belief. If science be the sun, belief is the moon—a reflection of day amidst night. Faith is the supplement of reason in the darkness left by science before and behind it. It emanates from reason but can neither be confounded therewith nor bring it to confusion. The trespasses of reason upon faith or of faith upon reason are eclipses of sun or moon. When they come about, both source and reflector of light are rendered useless.

Science perishes on account of systems which are no other than beliefs and faith succumbs to reason. In order to sustain the edifice, the two pillars of the temple must be parallel and separate. When they are brought by force together, as Samson brought them, they are thrown down, and the whole building collapses on the blind zealot or revolutionary, whose personal or national resentment has destined him beforehand to death. The struggles between the spiritual and temporal powers at all periods of humanity have been quarrels over domestic management. The papacy has been a jealous mother, seeking to supplant a husband in the temporal power, and she has lost the confidence of her children, while the temporal power in its usurpation of the priesthood is not less ridiculous than a man who should pretend to know better than a mother how to manage the home and nursery. The English, for example, from the moral and religious point of view, are like children swaddled by men, as we may appreciate by their spleen and dullness.

If religious doctrine is comparable to a nurse's story, on the understanding that it is ingenious and beneficial morally, it is perfectly true for the child, and the father would be very foolish to contradict it. Give therefore to mothers a monopoly in tales of faërie, in songs and household solicitudes. Maternity is a type of the priesthoods, and it is because the Church must be a mother only that the catholic priest renounces the right of man and transfers in advance to herself his claim on fatherhood. It must never be forgotten that the papacy is either nothing or that it is the universal mother. It may be even that Pope Joan, out of which protestants have constructed a tale of scandal, is only an ingenious allegory, and when sovereign pontiffs have ill-used Emperors and Kings it has been Pope Joan trying to beat her husband, to the great scandal of the Christian world. So also schisms and heresies have been other conjugal quarrels;

---

[1] Éliphas Lévi does not seem always to have made the most of his opportunities as regards the texts of Kabalism and the literature thereto belonging which were available at his period in Latin and certain modern languages, including his own. He had otherwise little opportunity of learning the real message of the Zoharic cycle. Taking all the circumstances into consideration, his guesses were sometimes very shrewd, and here and there carry with them the suggestion of intuitions. The teaching of the *Zohar* on the subject of sex postulates, like so much of its doctrine, a secret tradition to which it never gives expression in fulness, though it is incessantly lifting now one and now another corner of the veil. It is, however, impossible to speak of it within the limit of a note.

INTRODUCTION

the Church and Protestantism speak evil one of another, lament one another, make a show of avoiding and being weary one of another like spouses living apart.

It is by the Kabalah, and this alone, that all is explained and reconciled. All other doctrines are vivified and made fruitful thereby; it destroys nothing but, on the contrary, gives reason to all that is. So all the forces of the world are at the service of this one and supreme science, while the true Kabalist can make use at his pleasure, without hypocrisy and without falsehood, of the science possessed by the wise and the zeal of believers. He is more catholic than M. de Maistre, more protestant than Luther, more Jewish than the chief rabbi, and a prophet more than Mahomet. Is he not above systems and the passions which darken truth? Can he not at will bring together their scattered rays, so variously reflected in all the fragments of that broken mirror which is universal faith—fragments which are taken by men for so many opposite beliefs? There is one being, one law and one faith, as there is only one race of man—אהיה אשר אהיה.

On such intellectual and moral heights it will be understood that the human mind and heart enter into the deep peace. "Peace profound, my brethren"—such was the master-word of High-Grade Masonry, being the association of Kabalistic initiates.[1]

The war which the Church has been forced to make against Magic was necessitated by the profanations of false Gnostics, but the true science of the Magi is catholic essentially, basing all its realisation on the hierarchic principle. Now, the only serious and absolute hierarchy is found in the Catholic Church, and hence true adepts have always shewn for it the deepest respect and obedience. Henry Khunrath alone was a resolute protestant, but in this he was a German of his period rather than a mystic citizen of the eternal Kingdom.[2]

The essence of anti-Christianity is exclusion and heresy; it is the partition of the body of Christ, according to the beautiful expression of St. John: *Omnis spiritus qui solvit Christum hic Antichristus est*. The reason is that religion is charity and that there is no charity in anarchy. Magic had also its anarchists, its makers and adherents of sects, its thaumaturgists and sorcerers. Our design is to vindicate the legality of the science from the usurpations of ignorance, fraud and folly; it is in this respect more especially that our work will stand to be useful, as it will be also entirely new. So far the History of Magic has been presented as

---

[1] It was not a master-word but a mode of greeting; it was neither Masonic nor Kabalistic; it was a Rosicrucian formula. It may be added that "Peace profound, my brethren" was answered by "Emanuel; God is with us." It is a perfect and highly mystical mode of salutation.

[2] Perhaps the true explanation in respect of Henry Khunrath is that, seemingly, he was of the Lutheran persuasion as one of the accidents of his birth, but in the higher consciousness he was, as he could be only, catholic. As regards the resolute protestantism, Éliphas Lévi says in his *Ritual of Transcendental Magic* that Khunrath "affects Christianity in expressions and in signs, but it is easy to see that his Christ is the Abraxas, the luminous pentagram radiating on the astronomical cross, the incarnation in humanity of the sovereign sun celebrated by the Emperor Julian". See my translation of the *Doctrine and Ritual of Transcendental Magic*, p. 257.

INTRODUCTION

annals of a thing prejudged, or as chronicles—less or more exact—of a sequence in phenomena, seeing that no one believed that Magic belonged to science. A serious account of this science in its rediscovery, so to speak, must set forth its developments or progress. We are walking in open sanctuary instead of among ruins, and we find that the Holy Places, so long buried under the débris of four civilisations, have been preserved more wonderfully than the mummified cities which excavation has unearthed, in all their dead beauty and desolate majesty, beneath the lava of Vesuvius.

Bossuet in his magnificent work has shewn us religion bound up everywhere with history; but what would he have said had he known that a science which, in a sense, was born with the world, provides an explanation of primeval dogmas, belonging to the one and universal religion, in virtue of their combination with the most incontestable theorems of mathematics and reason? Dogmatic Magic is the key of all secrets as yet unfathomed by the philosophy of history, while Practical Magic alone opens the Secret Temple of Nature to that power of human will which is ever limited, yet ever progressive.

We are far from any impious pretence of explaining the mysteries of religion by means of Magic, but our intention is to indicate after what manner science is compelled to accept and revere those mysteries.[1] It shall be said no longer that reason must humble itself in the presence of faith; on the contrary, it must do honour to itself by believing, since it is faith which saves reason from the horrors of the void on the brink of the abyss, and it is its bond of union with the infinite. Orthodoxy in religion is respect for the hierarchy as the sole guardian of unity. Let us therefore not fear to repeat that Magic is essentially the Science of the Hierarchy, remembering clearly that, before all things else, it condemns anarchic doctrines, while it demonstrates, by the very laws of Nature, that harmony is inseparable both from power and authority.

The chief attraction of Magic for the great number of curious persons is that they see therein an exceptional means for the satisfaction of their passions. The unbeliever's horizon is of the same order. The avaricious would deny that there is any secret of Hermes corresponding to the transmutation of metals, for otherwise they would buy it and so enjoy wealth. But they are fools who believe that such a secret is sold. Of what use would be money to those who could make gold? That is true, says the sceptic, but if you, Éliphas Lévi, possessed it, would you not be richer than we are? Who has told you that I am poor? Have I asked for anything at your hands? Where is the sovereign in the world who can boast that he has acquired from me any secret of science? Where is the millionaire whom I have given reason to believe that I would set my fortune against his? When we look at earthly wealth from beneath it, we

---

[1] Éliphas Lévi has said previously (a) that the Church ignores Magic—for she must either ignore it or perish; (b) that Magic, as understood by him, is absolute religion as well as absolute science; (c) that it should regenerate all forms of worship.

INTRODUCTION

may yearn for it as the sovereign felicity, but it is despised when we consider it from above and when one realises how little temptation there can be to recover that which has been dropped as if it were hot iron.

But apart from this, a young man will exclaim that if magical secrets were true, he would attain them that he might be loved by all women. Nothing of the sort; a day will come, poor child, when it will be too much to be loved by one of them, for sensual desire is a dual orgy, the intoxication of which causes disgust to supervene quickly, after which anger and separation follow. There was once an old idiot who would have liked to have become a magician in order to upset the world. But if you were a magician, my hero, you would not be an imbecile, and before the tribunal of your conscience you would find no extenuating circumstances did you become a criminal.

The Epicurean, on his part, demands the recipes of Magic, that he may enjoy for ever and suffer nothing at all. In this case the science itself intervenes and says, as religion also says: Blessed are those who suffer. But that is the reason why the Epicurean has lost faith in religion. "Blessed are those who mourn"—but the Epicurean scoffs at the promise. Hear now what is said by experience and by reason. Sufferings test and awaken generous sentiments; pleasures promote and fortify base instincts. Sufferings arm against pleasure; enjoyment begets weakness in suffering. Pleasure squanders; pain ingarners. Pleasure is man's rock of peril; the pain of motherhood is woman's triumph. Pleasure fertilises and conceives, but pain brings forth.[1] Woe to him who cannot and will not suffer; he shall be overwhelmed by pain. Nature drives unmercifully those who will not walk; we are cast into life as into an open sea: we must swim or drown. Such are the laws of Nature, as taught by Transcendent Magic. And now reconsider whether one can become a magician in order to enjoy everything and suffer nothing. Yet the world will ask: In such case what profits Magic? What would the prophet Balaam have replied to his she-ass had the patient brute asked him what profits intelligence? What would Hercules have answered to a pigmy if he had inquired what profits strength? We do not compare worldly people to pigmies and still less to Balaam's ass: it would be wanting in politeness and good taste. We say therefore, with all possible graciousness, to such brilliant and amiable people, that for them Magic is absolutely useless, it being understood further that they will never take it seriously. Our work is addressed to souls that toil and think. They will find an explanation therein of whatsoever has remained obscure in our *Doctrine and Ritual*. On the pattern of the Great Masters, we have followed the rational order of sacred numbers in the plan and division of our works, for which reason this History of Magic is arranged in seven books, having seven chapters in

---

[1] If it be worth while to say so the translation of this passage does not follow the text, which suggests that the act of conception—on the female side—involves suffering. The text reads: *C'est le plaisir qui féconde, mais c'est la douleur qui conçoit et enfante.*

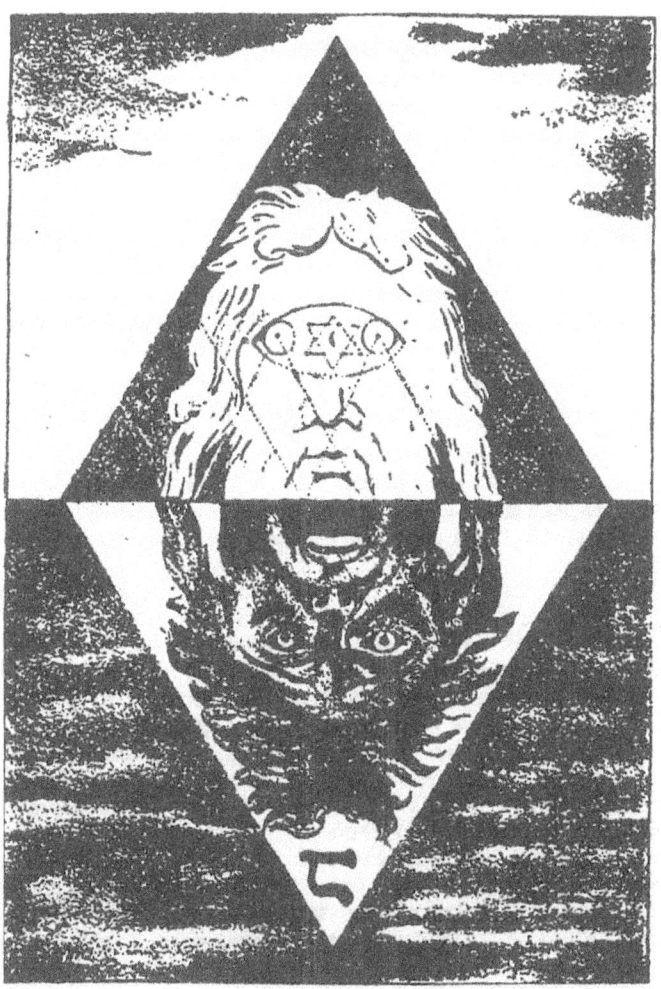

The Magical Head of the Zohar

INTRODUCTION

each. The first book is dedicated to the Sources of Magic; it is the genesis of that science, and we have provided it with a key in the letter *Aleph*, expressing Kabalistically the original and primal unity. The second book contains historical and social formulæ of the magical word in antiquity; its seal is the letter *Beth*, symbolising the duad as an expression of the word which realises, the special character of the Gnosis and occultism. The third book is concerned with the realisations of antique science in Christian society. It shews after what manner, even for science itself, the word takes flesh. The number three is that of generation, of realisation, and the key of this book is the letter *Gimel*, a hieroglyph of birth. We are introduced in the fourth book to the civilising power of Magic among barbarous races, to the natural productions of this science amidst peoples still in their childhood, to the mysteries of Druids and their miracles, to the legends of bards, and it is shewn after what manner these things concurred in the formation of modern societies, thus preparing a brilliant and permanent victory for Christianity. The number four expresses Nature and force, while the letter *Daleth*, which stands for it in the Hebrew alphabet, is represented in that of the Kabalists by an emperor on his throne. The fifth book is consecrated to the sacerdotal era of the middle ages, and we are present at the dissensions and struggles of science, the formation of secret societies, their unknown achievements, the secret rites of grimoires, the mysteries of the *Divine Comedy*, the divisions within the sanctuary which must lead later on to a glorious unity. The number five is that of the quintessence, religion and the priesthood; its character is the letter *He*, represented in the magical alphabet by the symbol of a high priest. The sixth book exhibits the intervention of Magic in the work of the Revolution. The number six is that of antagonism and strife in preparation for universal synthesis, and the corresponding letter is *Vau*, symbol of the creative *lingam* and the reaper's sickle. The seventh book is synthetic, containing an exposition of modern workings and discoveries, new theories on light and magnetism, the revelation of the great Rosicrucian secret, the explanation of mysterious alphabets, the science of the word and its magical works; in fine, the summary of the science itself, including an appreciation of what has been accomplished by contemporaneous mystics. This book is the complement and the crown of the work, as the septenary is the crown of numbers, uniting the triangle of idea to the square of form. Its corresponding letter is *Zain*, and the Kabalistic hieroglyphic is a victor mounted on a chariot, drawn by two sphinxes.[1]

Far from us be the ridiculous vanity of posing as a Kabalistic victor; it is the science alone which should triumph; and that which we expose before the intelligent world, mounted on the cubic chariot and drawn by

---

[1] According to the *Zohar*, the letter *Aleph* is a sacrament of the unity which is in God, and it is thereby and therein that man obtains unity. *Beth* is the basis of the work of creation and in a sense also its instrument. *Gimel* represents the charity and beneficence which are the help of poverty, designated by the letter *Daleth*. The letters *He* and *Vau* are part of the mystery which is contained in the Divine Name—יהוה. The letter *Zain* is likened to a sharp sword or dagger.

INTRODUCTION

sphinxes, is the Word of Light, the Divine Fulfiller of the Mosaic Kabalah, the human Sun of the Gospel, that man-God who has come once as Saviour and will manifest soon as Messiah—that is, as definitive and absolute king of temporal institutions. It is this thought which animates our courage and sustains our hope. But now it remains to submit all our conceptions, all our discoveries and all our labours to the infallible judgment of the hierarchy. To the authorised men of science be that which belongs to science, but the things which connect with religion are set apart to the Church alone and to that one hierarchic Church, the preserver of unity, which has been catholic, apostolic and Roman from the days of Christ Jesus to our own. To scholars our discoveries, to bishops our aspirations and beliefs. Woe to the child who believes himself wiser than his parents, to the man who acknowledges no masters, to that dreamer who thinks and prays by himself. Life is an universal communion and in such communion do we find immortality. He who isolates himself is given over to death thereby, and an eternity of isolation would be eternal death.

ÉLIPHAS LÉVI.

BOOK I

THE DERIVATIONS OF MAGIC

א—ALEPH

CHAPTER I

FABULOUS SOURCES

THE apocryphal *Book of Enoch* says that there were angels who consented to fall from heaven that they might have intercourse with the daughters of earth.[1] "For in those days the sons of men having multiplied, there were born to them daughters of great beauty. And when the angels, or sons of heaven, beheld them, they were filled with desire; wherefore they said to one another: 'Come, let us choose wives from among the race of man, and let us beget children.' Their leader, Samyasa, answered thereupon and said: 'Perchance you will be wanting in the courage needed to fulfil this resolution, and then I alone shall be answerable for your fall.' But they swore that they would in no wise repent and that they would achieve their whole design. Now there were 200 who descended on Mount Armon, and it was from this time that the mountain received its designation, which signifies Mount of the Oath. Hereinafter follow the names of those angelic leaders who descended with this object: Samyasa, chief among all, Urakabarameel, Azibeel, Tamiel, Ramuel, Danel, Azkeel, Sarakuyal, Asael, Armers, Batraal, Anane, Zavebe, Samsaveel, Ertrael, Turel, Jomiael, Arazial. They took wives, with whom they had intercourse, to whom also they taught Magic, the art of enchantment and the diverse properties of roots and trees. Amazarac gave instruction in all secrets of sorcerers; Barkaial was the master of those who study the stars; Akibeel manifested signs; and Azaradel taught the motions of the moon".

This legend of the Kabalistic Book of Enoch is a variant account of the same profanation of Mysteries which we meet with under another form of symbolism in the history of the sin of Adam. Those angels, the sons of God, of whom Enoch speaks, were initiates of Magic, and it was this that

[1] The account which follows may be compared with that which is found, *s.v. Apocryphes* in Éliphas Lévi's *Dictionnaire de Littérature Chrétienne*, mentioned in my preface to the present translation. It describes the legend concerning the fall of certain angels as *une assez singulière histoire*. He refers also to the various extant versions of the book, and to those in particular which differ from the "primitive" codex, being (a) that which he uses, and (b) "that which St. Jude cites in his catholic epistle as an authentic" work, actually composed by the prophet Enoch, to whom it is attributed.

55

they communicated to profane men, using incautious women as their instruments. They split upon the rock of sense-attraction, becoming enamoured of the female sex, and the secrets of royalty and priesthood were extracted from them unawares. Primitive civilisation collapsed as a consequence, and the giants, who typified brute force and unbridled appetite, fought together for the world, which escaped only by immersion in the waters of the deluge, wherein all traces of the past were effaced. This deluge symbolised that universal confusion into which humanity is brought of necessity when it ignores and does outrage to the harmonies of Nature.[1] There is kinship between the fall of Samyasa and that of Adam; the lure of sense seduced both; both profaned the Tree of Knowledge; and both were driven far away from the Tree of Life. It is needless here to discuss the views, or rather the simplicity, of those who take everything literally and believe that knowledge and life were once manifested under the form of trees; let us confess rather and only to the deep meaning of sacred symbols. The Tree of Knowledge does actually inflict death when its fruit is eaten; that fruit is the adornment of this world; those golden apples are the glitter of earth.

In the Arsenal Library there is a very curious manuscript entitled *The Book of the Penitence of Adam*, and herein Kabalistic tradition is presented under the guise of legend to the following effect: "Adam had two sons—Cain, who signifies brute force, and Abel, the type of intelligence and mildness. Agreement was impossible between them; they perished at each other's hands; and their inheritance passed to a third son, named Seth." Here is the conflict of two opposing forces diverted to the advantage of a synthetic and united force. "Now Seth, who was just, was permitted to approach as far as the entrance of the Earthly Paradise, without being threatened by the Kerub and his flaming sword." In other words, Seth represented primeval initiation. "It came to pass in this manner that Seth beheld the Tree of Knowledge and the Tree of Life, incorporated together after such a manner that they formed but a single tree"— signifying the harmony of science and religion in the transcendental Kabalah. "And the angel gave him three seeds containing the vital power of the said tree." The reference is here to the Kabalistic triad. "When Adam died, Seth, in obedience to the directions of the angel, placed the three seeds in the mouth of his father, as a token of eternal life. The

[1] The *Zohar* says that the Ark of Noah was a symbol of the Ark of the Covenant, that his entrance therein saved the world, and that this mystery is in analogy with the Supreme Mystery. At this point there is a sex-implicit throughout the Kabalistic commentary, and the nature of the "unbridled appetite" which brought about the deluge is identified with that sin which caused the destruction of Judah's second son, as told in Genesis c. xxxviii. See *Zohar*, Part I, section *Toldoth Noah*. It is intimated also that the souls of those who perished in the deluge were to be blotted out, like the remembrance of Amalek. Part I, fol. 25a. They will not even be included in the resurrection which shall go before the Last Judgment. Fol. 68b. At the same time the chastisement would have been suspended had Noah prayed to God like Moses, but the tradition supposes him to have asked only concerning himself. *Zohar*, Part III, fol. 14b. The Holy Land was not covered by the waters of the deluge. Part II, fol. 197a.

THE DERIVATIONS OF MAGIC

saplings which sprang up from these, became the Burning Bush, in the midst of which God communicated to Moses his Eternal Name—

—אהיה אשר אהיה

signifying He Who is and is to come. Moses plucked a triple branch of the sacred bush and used it as his miraculous wand. Although separated from its root, the branch continued to live and blossom, and it was subsequently preserved in the Ark.[1] King David planted the branch on Mount Zion, and Solomon took wood from each section of the triple trunk to make the two pillars, *Jachin* and *Boaz*, which were placed at the entrance of the Temple. They were covered with bronze, and the third section was inserted at the threshold of the chief gate. It was a talisman which hindered things unclean from entering within. But certain nefarious Levites removed during the night this obstacle to their unholy freedom and cast it, loaded with stones, to the bottom of the Temple reservoir. From this time forward an angel of God troubled the waters of the pool, imparting to them a miraculous value, so that men might be distracted from seeking the tree of Solomon in its depths. In the days of Jesus Christ the pool was cleansed and the Jews, finding the beam of wood, which in their eyes seemed useless, carried the latter outside the town and threw it across the brook Cedron. It was over this bridge that our Saviour passed after his arrest at night in the Garden of Olives. His executioners cast him from it into the water; and then in their haste to prepare the instrument-in-chief of His passion, they took the beam with them, which was made of three kinds of wood, and formed the cross therewith."[2]

This allegory embodies all the great traditions of the Kabalah and the secret Christian doctrine of St. John, which is now utterly unknown. It follows that Seth, Moses, David, Solomon and Christ obtained from the same Kabalistic Tree their royal sceptres and pontifical crooks. We can understand in this manner why the Christ was adored in His manger by the Magi. Let us recur, however, to the *Book of Enoch*, as greater authority attaches to it than can be attributed to an unknown manuscript; the former is cited in the New Testament by the Apostle St. Jude. Tradition refers the invention of letters to Enoch, and it is to him that we must therefore trace back the teachings embodied in the *Sepher Yetzirah*, which

---

[1] It was the Rod of Aaron, not that of Moses, which, according to Heb. ix, 4, was placed in the Ark of the Covenant, together with the Tables of the Law and the Pot of Manna. It is said, however, most clearly in 1 Kings viii, 9, that "there was nothing in the ark save the two tables of stone, which Moses put there at Horeb".

[2] Whatever the date to which the *Book of the Penitence of Adam* may be referable, it represents one form of a legend which was spread widely in the middle ages. *The Gospel of Nicodemus* seems to have instituted the first analogy between the Tree of Knowledge and the Tree of the Cross. "All ye who have died through the wood which this man"—Adam—"hath touched: all of you I will make alive again by the wood of the cross." The legend of the triple branch, under a strange transformation, reappears in that chronicle of the Holy Graal which has been ascribed to the authorship of Walter Map. There is no end to the stories which represent Christ dying upon a tree which was a cutting from the Tree of Knowledge. This is how the Tree of Knowledge becomes the Tree of Life in Christian legend.

is the elementary work of the Kabalah, its compiler—according to the Rabbins—being the patriarch Abraham, as the heir of the secrets of Enoch and as the father of initiation in Israel. Enoch would seem in this manner to be identical with the Egyptian Hermes Trismegistus, while the famous *Book of Thoth*, written throughout in hieroglyphics and in numbers, would be that occult Bible, anterior to the book of Moses and full of mysteries, to which the initiated William Postel alludes so frequently throughout his works, under the title of the *Genesis of Enoch*.[1]

The Bible says that Enoch did not die, but that God translated him from one life to another. He is to return and confound Anti-Christ at the end of time, when he will be one of the last martyrs, or witnesses of truth, mentioned in the Apocalypse of St. John. That which is said of Enoch in this respect has been said also of all the great initiators recorded in Kabalism. St. John himself, according to the primitive Christians, was saved from death, and it was long thought that he could be seen breathing in his tomb.[2] The explanation is that the absolute science of life preserves against death, as the instinct of the people has always led them to divine. However this may be, the extant memorials of Enoch are contained in two books, one of which is hieroglyphic and the other of the nature of allegory. The first comprises the hieratic keys of initiation, while the second is the history of a great profanation which caused the destruction of the world and the reign of chaos after that of the giants.

St. Methodius, a bishop in the early days of Christianity, whose writings are found in the collection of the Fathers of the Church, has left a prophetic Apocalypse which unfolds the world's history in a series of visions. It is not included among the saint's acknowledged writings, but it was preserved by the Gnostics and has been printed in the *Liber Mirabilis* under the assumed name of Bermechobus, which illiterate compositors have substituted in place of Bea-Methodius, an abbreviation of *Beatus Methodius*.[3] This book corresponds in several respects with the allegorical treatise entitled *The Penitence of Adam*. It tells how Seth migrated eastward with his family and so reached a mountain in the vicinity of the Earthly Paradise. This was the country of initiates, whilst the posterity of Cain invented a spurious or debased Magic in India, the land of fratricide, and put witchcraft into the hands of the reckless.

St. Methodius predicts in a later place the struggles and successive

---

[1] The *Clavis Absconditorum à Constitutione Mundi*, which is the chief work of Postel, outside his translation of the *Sepher Yetzirah*, affirms that Enoch was born at the time when Christ the Mediator would have been manifested in the flesh as the incarnation of perfect Virtue, supposing that man had remained in his first estate. There is no reference to a *Genesis of Enoch*.

[2] *Hic intrat vivus foveam*—he, being still alive, enters the tomb, says Adam of St. Victor in his third Sequence for Dec. 27.

[3] There were two canonised bishops bearing the name of Methodius at widely different periods, and as both were writers it is an open question to which of them the reference is intended. It is probably to Methodius of Olympus, who was martyred about 311. Methodius, the Patriarch of Constantinople, died in 846. There is not the least reason to suppose that the Apocalypse under the name of Bermechobus was the work of either.

THE DERIVATIONS OF MAGIC

predominance of the Ishmaelites, being the name given in his apocalypse to those who conquered the Romans; of the Franks, who overcame the Ishmaelites; and then of a great race from the North whose invasion will precede the personal reign of Anti-Christ. An universal kingdom will be founded thereafter and will fall into the hands of a French prince, after which there will be the reign of justice for a long period of years. We are not concerned with prophecy in the present place, but it is desirable to note the distinction between good and evil Magic, between the Sanctuary of the Sons of Seth and the profanation of science by the descendants of Cain.[1] Transcendental knowledge, as a fact, is reserved for those who are masters of their passions, and virgin Nature does not deliver the keys of her nuptial chamber to adulterers.

There are two classes—freemen and slaves; man is born in the bondage of his passions, but he can reach emancipation through intelligence. Between those who are free already and those who as yet are not there is no equality possible. The part of reason is to rule and of instinct to obey. On the other hand, if you impose on the blind the office of leading the blind, both will end in the abyss. We should never forget that liberty does not consist in the licence of passion emancipated from law, which licence would prove the most hideous of tyrannies; liberation consists in willing obedience to law; it is the right to do one's duty, and only just men can be called free. Now, those who are in liberation should govern those who are in bondage, and slaves are called to be released, not from the government of the free but from the yoke of brutal passions, as a consequence of which they cannot exist without masters.

Confess with us now for a moment to the truth of the transcendental sciences. Suppose that there does actually exist a force which can be mastered and by which the miracles of Nature are made subservient to the will of man. Tell us, in such case, whether the secrets of wealth and the bonds of sympathy can be entrusted to brutal greed; the art of fascination to libertines; the supremacy over other wills to those who cannot attain the government of their proper selves. It is terrifying to reflect upon the disorders which would follow from such a profanation; some cataclysm is needed to efface the crimes of earth when all are steeped in slime and blood. Now, it is this state of things that is indicated by the allegorical history of the fall of the angels, according to *The Book of Enoch*; it is this which was the sin of Adam, and hereof are its fatal consequences. Of such also was the Deluge and its wreckage; of such at a later period the malediction of Canaan. The revelation of occult secrets is typified by the insolence of that son who exposes his father's nakedness. The intoxication of Noah is a lesson for the priesthood of all ages. Woe to

---

[1] Compare Lopukhin's *Quelques Traits de l'Église Intérieure*, where the sanctuary which was inaugurated by Adam is connected more especially with Abel, and was presumably maintained afterwards by Seth. In opposition thereto was the Church of Cain, which was anti-Christian from its beginning. See my introduction to Mr. Nicholson's translation, pp. 6, 7, and the text, p. 59—*Some Characteristics of the Interior Church*, 1912.

those who lay bare the secret of divine generation to the impure gaze of the crowd. Keep the sanctuary shut, all ye who would spare your sleeping father the mockery of the imitators of Ham.[1]

Such is the tradition of the children of Seth respecting the laws of the human hierarchy; but the latter were not acknowledged by the family of Cain. The Cainites of India invented a genesis to consecrate the oppression of the strong and to perpetuate the ignorance of the weak. Initiation became an exclusive privilege of the high castes, and entire races of humanity were doomed to unending servitude on the pretence of inferior birth: they issued, as it was said, from the feet or knees of Brahma. Now, Nature engenders neither slaves nor kings, but all men indifferently are born to labour. He who pretends that man is perfect at birth but is degraded and perverted by society is the wildest of anarchists, though he may be the most poetic of maniacs. But in vain was Jean Jacques a sentimentalist and dreamer; his deep implicit of misanthropy when explicated by the logic of fanatical partisans, bore fruits in hate and destruction. The consistent architects of the Utopia imagined by the susceptible philosopher of Geneva were Robespierre and Marat.

Society is no abstract personality that can be rendered responsible separately for the stubbornness of man; society is the association of men; it is defective by reason of their vices and sublime in respect of their virtues; but in itself it is holy, like the religion which is bound up inseparably therewith. Is not religion, as a fact, an association of the highest aspirations and the most generous endeavours? After this manner does the blasphemy of anti-social equality and of right in the teeth of duty give answer to the lie about castes privileged by Nature; Christianity alone has solved the problem by assigning supremacy to self-sacrifice and by proclaiming him as the greatest who offers up his pride for society and his appetites for the sake of the law.

Though they were the depositaries of the tradition of Seth, the Jews did not preserve it in all its purity, and were infected by the unjust ambitions of the posterity of Cain. Believing that they were a chosen people, they deemed that God had allotted them truth as a patrimony rather than as a security held in trust for humanity at large.[2] Side by side with the sublime traditions of the *Sepher Yetzirah* we meet with very curious revelations among the Talmudists. For example, they do not shrink from ascribing the idolatry of the Gentiles to the patriarch Abraham himself; they say that to the Israelites he bequeathed his inheritance, namely the knowledge of the true Divine Names; in a word, the Kabalah was the lawful and hereditary property of Isaac; but the patriarch gave,

---

[1] According to the *Zohar*, the intoxication of Noah contains a mystery of wisdom. He was really sounding the depths of that sin which was the downfall of the first man, and his object was to find a remedy. In this he failed, and "was drunken", seeking to lay bare the divine essence, without the intellectual power to explore it. *Section Toldoth Noah.*

[2] The *Sepher Ha Zohar* affirms in several places that the Law was offered to the Gentiles, and was by them refused.

THE DERIVATIONS OF MAGIC

as they tell us, certain presents to the children of his concubines; and by such presents they understand veiled dogmas and cryptic names, which became materialised speedily, and were transformed into idols.[1] False religions and their absurd mysteries, oriental superstitions, with all their horrible sacrifices—what a gift from a father to his disowned family! Was it not sufficient to drive Hagar with her son into the desert? To their one loaf and their pitcher of water must he add the burden of falsehood, as a torment and poison in their exile?

The glory of Christianity is that it called all men to truth, without distinction of races and castes, though not without distinction in respect of intelligence and of virtue. "Cast not your pearls before swine," said the Divine Founder of Christianity, "lest treading them under foot, they turn and rend you." The Apocalypse or Revelation of St. John, which comprises all the Kabalistic secrets concerning the doctrine of Christ Jesus, is a book no less obscure than the *Zohar*. It is written hieroglyphically in the language of numbers and images, and the Apostle appeals frequently to the knowledge of initiates. "Let him understand who has knowledge—let him who understands compute"—he says frequently, after reciting an allegory or giving a mystic number. St. John, the beloved disciple and depositary of all the secrets of the Saviour, did not therefore write to be understood by the multitude.

The *Sepher Yetzirah*, the *Zohar* and the *Apocalypse* are the masterpieces of occultism; they contain more meanings than words; their method of expression is figurative, like poetry, and exact, like numerical formulæ. The Apocalypse summarises, completes and surpasses all the science of Abraham and Solomon, as we will prove by explaining the Keys of the transcendent Kabalah.

It is not less astonishing to observe at the beginning of the *Zohar*[2] the profundity of its notions and the sublime simplicity of its images. It is said as follows: "The science of equilibrium is the key of occult science. Unbalanced forces perish in the void. So passed the kings of the elder world, the princes of the giants. They have fallen like trees without roots, and their place is found no more. Through the conflict of unbalanced forces the devastated earth was void and formless, until the Spirit of

---

[1] The authority for this statement is wanting. The *Zohar* dwells on Genesis xxi, 9: "And Sarah saw the son of Hagar," etc., implying that she did not acknowledge him as the son of Abraham, but of the Egyptian only. The Patriarch, however, regarded him as his own son. Sarah's desire to expel them is justified on the ground that she had seen Ishmael worshipping the stars of heaven. See *Zohar*, Part I, fol. 118. There is no allusion to the alleged gifts of the father, the scripture making it evident abundantly that the bread and bottle of water are for once to be understood literally.

[2] Even at the period of Éliphas Lévi it did not require a rabbinical scholar or a knowledge of Aramaic to prevent any fairly informed person from suggesting that the *Book of Concealed Mystery*, being the text here referred to, is the beginning of the *Zohar* It follows the *Commentary on Exodus*, about midway in the whole collection, which covers the entire Pentateuch. It so happens that the little tract in question is the first of three sections rendered into Latin by Rosenroth, and this must have deceived Lévi, as a consequence of utterly careless reading. There was plenty of opportunity for correction in the *Kabbala Denudata*, and so also in *La Kabbale*—an interesting but very imperfect study by AdolpheFranck, which appeared in 1843.

God made for itself a place in heaven and reduced the mass of waters. All the aspirations of Nature were directed then towards unity of form, towards the living synthesis of equilibrated forces; the face of God, crowned with light, rose over the vast sea and was reflected in the waters thereof. His two eyes were manifested, radiating with splendour, darting two beams of light which crossed with those of the reflection. The brow of God and His eyes formed a triangle in heaven, and its reflection formed a second triangle in the waters. So was revealed the number six, being that of universal creation."

The text, which would be unintelligible in a literal version, is translated here by way of interpretation. The author makes it plain that the human form which he ascribes to Deity is only an image of his meaning and that God is beyond expression by human thought or representation by any figure. Pascal said that God is a circle, of which the centre is everywhere and the circumference nowhere. But how is one to imagine a circle apart from its circumference? The *Zohar* adopts the antithesis of this paradoxical image and in respect of the circle of Pascal would say rather that the circumference is everywhere, while that which is nowhere is the centre. It is, however, to a balance and not to a circle that it compares the universal equilibrium of things.[1] It affirms that equilibrium is everywhere and so also is that central point where the balance hangs in suspension. We find that the Zohar is thus more forcible and more profound than Pascal.

Its author continues as follows his sublime dream. That synthesis of the word, formulated by the human figure, ascended slowly and emerged from the water, like the sun in its rising. When the eyes appeared, light was made; when the mouth was manifested, there was the creation of spirits and the word passed into expression. The entire head was revealed, and this completed the first day of creation. The shoulders, the arms, the breast arose, and thereupon work began. With one hand the Divine Image put back the sea, while with the other it raised up continents and mountains. The Image grew and grew; the generative organs appeared, and all beings began to increase and multiply. The form stood at length erect, having one foot upon the earth and one upon the waters. Beholding itself at full length in the ocean of creation, it breathed on its own reflection and called its likeness into life. It said: Let us make man—and thus man was made. There is nothing so beautiful in the masterpiece of

[1] There is no real analogy between the image attributed to Pascal and that of the Zoharic *Book of Concealment*. I have not verified the reference to Pascal, as the opportunity is not given by Lévi, but I have explained elsewhere that the idea was probably drawn from S. Bonaventura, who speaks of that *sphæra intelligibilis, cujus centrum est ubique et circumferentia nusquam*. See *Itinerarium Mentis ad Deum*. I have inferred that S. Bonaventura himself derived from a Hermetic book. As regards the symbolism of the Balance, the *Book of Concealed Mystery* says (a) that, in creating the world, God weighed in the Balance what had not been weighed previously, (b) that the Balance was suspended in a region where before there was no Balance, (c) that it served for bodies as well as souls, for beings then in existence and for those who would exist subsequently. These are the only references to this subject found in the tract.

The Great Kabalistic Symbol of the Zohar

any poet as this vision of creation accomplished by the prototype of humanity. Hereby is man but the shadow of a shadow, and yet he is the image of divine power. He also can stretch forth his hands from East to West; to him is the earth given as a dominion. Such is Adam Kadmon, the primordial Adam of the Kabalists. Such is the sense in which he is depicted as a giant; and this is why Swedenborg, haunted in his dreams by reminiscences of the Kabalah, says that entire creation is only a titanic man and that we are made in the image of the universe.

The *Zohar* is a genesis of light; the *Sepher Yetzirah* is a ladder of truth. Therein are expounded the two-and-thirty absolute symbols of speech —being numbers and letters. Each letter produces a number, an idea and a form, so that mathematics are applicable to forms and ideas, even as to numbers, in virtue of an exact proportion and a perfect correspondence. By the science of the *Sepher Yetzirah* the human mind is rooted in truth and in reason; it accounts for all progress possible to intelligence by means of the evolution of numbers. Thus does the *Zohar* represent absolute truth, while the *Sepher Yetzirah* furnishes the method of its acquisition, its discernment and application.

CHAPTER II

MAGIC OF THE MAGI

IT is within probability that Zoroaster is a symbolical name, like that of Thoth or Hermes. According to Eudoxus and Aristotle, he flourished 6000 years before the birth of Plato, but others say that he antedated the siege of Troy by about 500 years. He is sometimes represented as a king of the Bactrians, but the existence of two or three distinct Zoroasters is also one of the speculations.[1] Eudoxus and Aristotle alone would seem to have realised that his personality was magical, and this is why they have placed the Kabalistic epoch of an entire world between the birth of his doctrine and the theurgic reign of Platonic philosophy. As a fact, there are two Zoroasters, that is to say, two expounders of mysteries, one being the son of Ormuzd and the founder of an enlightened instruction, the other being the son of Ahriman and the author of a profanatory unveiling of truth. Zoroaster is the incarnate word of the Chaldeans, the Medes and the Persians; his legend reads like a prophecy concerning that of Christ, and hence it must be assumed that he had also his Anti-Christ, in accordance with the magical law of universal equilibrium.

To the false Zoroaster must be referred the cultus of material fire and that impious doctrine of divine dualism which produced at a later period the monstrous Gnosis of Manes and the false principles of spurious Masonry. The Zoroaster in question was the father of that materialized Magic which led to the massacre of the Magi and brought their true doctrine at first into proscription and then oblivion. Ever inspired by the spirit of truth, the Church was compelled to condemn—under the names of Magic, Manicheanism, Illuminism and Masonry—all that was in kinship, remote or approximate, with the primitive profanation of the mysteries. One signal example is the history of the Knights Templar, which has been misunderstood to this day.

The doctrines of the true Zoroaster are identical with those of pure Kabalism, and his conceptions of divinity differ in no wise from those of the fathers of the Church. It is the names only that vary; for example, the triad of Zoroaster is the Trinity of Christian teaching, and when he postulates that Triad as subsisting without diminution or division in each of its units, he is expressing in another manner that which is understood by our theologians as the circumincession of the Divine Persons. In his multiplication of the Triad by itself, Zoroaster arrives at the absolute reason of the number 9 and the universal key of all numbers and forms.

[1] As such it is old, and a monograph on the subject is included by Jacob Bryant in his *Analysis of Antient Mythology*, vol. ii, p. 38 *et seq*. Following the authorities of his period, and especially Huetius, he says that "they have supposed a Zoroaster, wherever there was a Zorastrian: that is, wherever the religion of the Magi was adopted, or revived". The two Zorasters of Lévi represent two principles of religious philosophy.

But those whom we term the three Divine Persons are called the three depths by Zoroaster. The first, or that of the Father, is the source of faith; the second, being that of the Word, is the well of truth; while the third, or creative action, is the font of love. To check what is here advanced, the reader may consult the commentary of Psellus on the doctrine of the ancient Assyrians: it may be found in the work of Franciscus Patricius on *Philosophical Magic*, p. 24 of the Hamburg edition, which appeared in 1593.

Zoroaster established the celestial hierarchy and all the harmonies of Nature on his scale of nine degrees. He explains by means of the triad whatsoever emanates from the idea and by the tetrad all that belongs to form, thus arriving at the number 7 as the type of creation. Here ends the first initiation and the scholastic hypotheses begin; numbers are personified and ideas pass into emblems, which at a later period became idols. The Synoches, the Teletarchæ and the Fathers, ministers of the triple Hecate; the three Amilictes and the threefold visage of Hypezocos—all these intervene; the angels follow in their order, the demons and lastly human souls. The stars are images and reflections of intellectual splendours; the material sun is an emblem of the sun of truth, which itself is a shadow of that first source whence all glory springs. This is why the disciples of Zoroaster saluted the rising day and so passed as sun-worshippers among barbarians.

Such were the doctrines of the Magi, but they were the possessors in addition of secrets which gave them mastery over the occult powers of Nature. The sum of these secrets might be termed transcendental pyrotechny, for it was intimately related to the deep knowledge of fire and its ruling. It is certain that the Magi were not only familiar with electricity but were able to generate and direct it in ways that are now unknown. Numa, who studied their rites and was initiated into their mysteries, possessed, according to Lucius Pison, the art of producing and controlling the lightning. This sacerdotal secret, which the Roman initiator would have reserved to the kings of Rome, was lost by Tullus Hostilius, who mismanaged the electrical discharge and was destroyed. Pliny relates these facts on the authority of an ancient Etruscan tradition and mentions that Numa directed his battery with success against a monster named Volta, which was ravaging the district about Rome. In reading this story, one is almost tempted to think that Volta, the discoverer, is himself a myth and that the name of Voltaic piles goes back to the days of Numa.

All Assyrian symbols connect with this science of fire, which was the great secret of the Magi; on every side we meet with the enchanter who slays the lion and controls the serpents. That lion is the celestial fire, while the serpents are the electric and magnetic currents of the earth. To this same great secret of the Magi are referable all marvels of Hermetic Magic, the extant traditions of which still bear witness that the mystery of the Great Work consists in the ruling of fire.

The learned Patricius published in his *Philosophical Magic* the Oracles

THE DERIVATIONS OF MAGIC

of Zoroaster, collected from the works of Platonic writers—from Proclus on Theurgy, from the commentaries on the *Parmenides*, commentaries of Hermias on the *Phædrus* and from the notes of Olympiodorus on the *Philebos* and *Phaidon*.[1] These Oracles are firstly a clear and precise formulation of the doctrine here stated and secondly the prescriptions of magical ritual expressed in such terms as follow.

DEMONS AND SACRIFICES

We are taught by induction from Nature that there are incorporeal dæmons and that the germs of evil which exist in matter turn to the common good and utility. But these are mysteries which must be buried in the recesses of thought. For ever agitated and ever leaping in the atmosphere, the fire can assume a configuration like that of bodies. Let us go further and affirm the existence of a fire which abounds in images and reflections. Term it, if you will, a superabundant light which radiates, which speaks, which goes back into itself. It is the flaming courser of light, or rather it is the stalwart child who overcomes and breaks in that heavenly steed. Picture him as vested in flame and emblazoned with gold, or think of him naked as love and bearing the arrows of Eros. But if thy meditation prolongeth itself, thou wilt combine all these emblems under the form of the lion. Thereafter, when things are no longer visible, when the Vault of Heaven and the expanse of the universe have dissolved, when the stars have ceased to shine and the lamp of the moon is veiled, when the earth trembles and the lightning plays around it, invoke not the visible phantom of Nature's soul, for thou must in no wise behold it until thy body has been purified by the Holy ordeals. Enervators of souls, which they distract from sacred occupations, the dog-faced demons issue from the confines of matter and expose to mortal eyes the semblances of illusory bodies. Labour round the circles described by the rhombus of Hecate. Change thou nothing in the barbarous names of evocation, for they are pantheistic titles of God; they are magnetised by the devotion of multitudes and their power is ineffable. When after all the phantoms thou shalt behold the shining of that incorporeal fire, that sacred fire the darts of which penetrate in every direction through the depths of the world—hearken to the words of the fire.[2]

[1] An English translation of the Chaldæan Oracles by Thomas Taylor, the Platonist, claims to have added fifty oracles and fragments not included in the collection of Fabricius. Mr. Mead says that the subject was never treated scientifically till the appearance of J. Kroll's *De Oraculis Chaldaicis* at Breslau, in 1894.

[2] It must be understood that this summary or digest is an exceedingly free rendering, and it seems scarcely in accordance with the text on which Éliphas Lévi worked. Following the text of Kroll, Mr. Mead translates the first lines as follows: "Nature persuades us that the Daimones are pure, and things that grow from evil matter useful and good." The last lines are rendered: "But when thou dost behold the very sacred Fire with dancing radiance flashing formless through the depths of the whole world, then hearken to the Voice of Fire."

THE HISTORY OF MAGIC

These astonishing sentences, which are taken from the Latin of Patricius, embody the secrets of magnetism and of things far deeper, which it has not entered into the heart of people like Du Potet and Mesmer to conceive. We find (*a*) the Astral Light described perfectly, together with its power of producing fluidic forms, of reflecting language and echoing the voice; (*b*) the will of the adept signified by the stalwart child mounted on a white horse—a symbol met with in an ancient Tarot card preserved in the *Bibliothèque Nationale*;[1] (*c*) the dangers of hallucination arising from misdirected magical works; (*d*) the *raison d'être* of enchantments accomplished by the use of barbarous names and words; (*e*) the magnetic instrument termed *rhombos*,[2] which is comparable to a child's humming top; (*f*) the term of magical practice, which is the stilling of imagination and of the senses into a state of complete somnambulism and perfect lucidity.[3]

It follows from this revelation of the ancient world that clairvoyant extasis is a voluntary and immediate application of the soul to the universal fire, or rather to that light—abounding in images—which radiates, which speaks and circulates about all objects and every sphere of the universe. This application is operated by the persistence of will liberated from the senses and fortified by a succession of tests. Herein consisted the beginning of magical initiation. Having attained the power of direct reading in the light, the adept became a seer or prophet; then, having established communication between this light and his own will, he learned to direct the former, even as the head of an arrow is set in a certain direction. He communicated at his pleasure either strife or peace to the souls of others; he established intercourse at a distance which those fellow-adepts who were his peers; and, in fine, he availed himself of that force which is represented by the celestial lion. Herein lies the meaning of those great Assyrian figures which hold vanquished lions in their arms. The Astral Light is otherwise represented by gigantic sphinxes having the bodies of lions and the heads of Magi. Considered as an instrument made subject to magical power, the Astral Light is that golden sword of Mithra used in his immolation of the sacred bull. And it is the arrow of Phœbus which pierced the serpent Python.

Let us now reconstruct in thought the great metropolitan cities of

[1] See my *Key to the Tarot*, 1910, p. 32, and the cards which accompany this handbook. See also my *Pictorial Key to the Tarot*, 1911, pp. 144-7.
[2] One of the Chaldæan Oracles has the following counsel: "Labour thou around the *Strophalos* of Hecate," which Mr. G. R. S. Mead translates: "Be active (or operative) round the Hecatic spinning thing." He adds by way of commentary that *Strophalos* may sometimes mean a top. "In the Mysteries tops were included among the playthings of the young Bacchus, or Iacchus. They represented . . . the fixed stars (humming tops) and planets (whipping tops)."—*The Chaldæan Oracles*, vol. ii, pp. 17, 18.
[3] Accepting this definition of the term of occult research, we can discern after what manner it differs from the mystic term. The one, by this hypothesis, is lucidity obtained in artificial sleep which stills the senses, and the other is Divine Realisation in the spirit after the images of material things and of the mind-world have been cast out, so that the sanctified man is alone with God in the stillness.

Assyria, Babylon and Nineveh; let us restore to their proper place the granite colossi; let us formulate the massive temples, held up by elephants and sphinxes; let us raise once more those obelisks from which dragons look down with shining eyes and wings outspread. Temples and palaces tower above these wondrous piles. For ever concealed, but manifested also for ever by the fact of their miracles, the priesthood and the royalty, like visible divinities of earth, abide therein. The temple is surrounded with clouds or glows with supernatural brilliance at the will of the priests; now it is dark in the daylight and again the night is enlightened; the lamps of the temple spring of themselves into flame; the gods are radiant; the thunders roll; and woe to that impious person who may have invoked on his own head the malediction of initiates. The temples protect the palaces and the king's retainers do battle for the religion of the Magi. The monarch himself is sacred; he is a god on earth; the people lie prone as he passes; and the maniac who would attempt to cross the threshold of his palace falls dead immediately, by the intervention of an invisible hand, and without stroke of mace or sword. He is slain as if by the bolt, blasted by fire from heaven. What religion and what power! How mighty are the shadows of Nimrod, of Belus, of Semiramis! What can surpass these almost fabulous cities, where such mighty royalties were enthroned—these capitals of giants, capitals of magicians, of personalities identified by tradition with angels and still termed sons of God or princes of heaven! What mysteries have been put to sleep in these sepulchres of past nations; and are we better than children when we exalt our enlightenment and our progress, without recalling these startling memorials?

In his work on Magic,[1] M. Du Potet affirms, with a certain timidity, that it is possible to overwhelm a living being by a current of magnetic fluid. Magical power extends beyond this limit, but it is not confined within the measures of the putative magnetic fluid. The Astral Light as a whole, that element of electricity and of lightning, can be placed at the disposition of human will. What must be done, however, to acquire this formidable power? Zoroaster has just told us; we must know those mysterious laws of equilibrium which subjugate the very powers of evil to the empire of good. We must have purified our bodies by sacred trials, must have conquered the phantoms of hallucination and taken hold bodily of the light, imitating Jacob in his struggle with the angel. We must have vanquished those fantastic dogs which howl in the world of dreams. In a word, and to use the forcible expression of the Oracle, we must have heard the light speak. We are then its masters and can direct it, as Numa did, against the enemies of the Holy Mysteries. But if in the absence of perfect purity, and if under the government of some animal passion, by which we are still subjected to the fatalities of tempestuous life, we proceed to

---

[1] This was *La Magie Dévoilée*, which was circulated in great secrecy. Later on, and probably after the decease of the author, it appeared in the ordinary way, and in 1886 an English translation was announced under the editorship of Mr. J. S. Farmer, but I believe that it was never published.

this kind of work, the fire which we kindle will consume ourselves; we shall fall victims to the serpent which we unloose and shall perish like Tullus Hostilius.

It is not in conformity with the laws of Nature for man to be devoured by wild beasts. God has armed him with the power of resistance; his eyes can fascinate them, his voice restrain, his sign bring them to a pause. We know indeed, as a literal fact, that the most savage animals quail before a steady human glance and seem to tremble at the human voice. The explanation is that they are paralysed and awe-stricken by projections of the Astral Light. When Daniel was accused of imposture and false Magic, both he and his accusers were subjected by the king of Babylon to an ordeal of lions. Such beasts attack those only who fear them or of whom they are themselves afraid. It is utterly certain that the tiger will recede before the magnetic glance of a brave man, although the latter may be disarmed.

The Magi utilised this power and the kings of Assyria kept tigers, leopards and lions in their gardens, in a state of docility. Others were reserved in vaults beneath the temples for use in the ordeals of initiation. The symbolic bas-reliefs are the proof; they depict trials of strength between men and animals, and the adept, clothed in his priestly garb, controls the brutes by a glance of his eye and stays them with his hand. When such animals are depicted in one of the forms ascribed to the sphinx, they are doubtless symbolical, but in other representations the brute is of the natural order, and then the struggle seems to illustrate a theory of actual enchantment.

Magic is a science; to abuse is to lose it, and it is also to destroy oneself. The kings and priests of the Assyrian world were too great to be free from this danger, if ever they fell; as a fact, pride did come upon them and they did therefore fall. The great magical epoch of Chaldea is anterior to the reigns of Semiramis and Ninus. At this time religion had begun already to materialise and idolatry to prevail. The cultus of Astarte succeeded that of the heavenly Venus and royalty arrogated to itself divine attributes under the names of Baal and of Bel, or Belus. Semiramis made religion subservient to politics and conquests, replacing the old mysterious temples by ostentatious and ill-advised monuments. This notwithstanding, the magical idea continued to prevail in art and science, sealing the constructions of that epoch with the characteristics of inim table power and grandeur. The palace of Semiramis was a building synthesis of entire Zoroastrian dogma, and we shall recur to it in explaining the symbolism of those seven masterpieces of antiquity which are called the wonders of the world.

The priesthood became secondary to the empire as the result of an attempt to materialise its own power. The fall of the one was bound to involve the other, and it came to pass under the effeminate Sardanapalus. This prince, abandoned to luxury and indolence, reduced the science of the Magi to the level of one of his courtesans. What purpose did marvels serve if they failed in ministration to pleasure? Compel, O enchanters, compel the winter to produce roses; double the savour of wine; apply your power over the light to make the beauty of women shine like that of divinities. The Magi obeyed and the king passed from intoxication to intoxication. But it came about that war was declared and that the enemy was already on the march. That enemy might signify little to the sybarite steeped in his pleasures. But it was ruin, it was infamy, it was death. Now Sardanapalus did not fear death, since for him it was an endless sleep, and he knew how to avoid the toils and humiliations of servitude. The last night came; the victor was already upon the threshold; the city could stand out no longer; the kingdom of Assyria must end on the morrow. The palace of Sardanapalus was illuminated and blazed with such splendour that it lightened all the consternated city. Amidst piles of precious stuffs, amidst jewels and golden vessels, the king held his final orgy. His women, his favourites, his accomplices, his degenerate priests surrounded him; the riot of drunkenness mingled with the music of a thousand instruments; the tame lions roared; and a smoke of perfumes, going up from the vaults of the palace, enveloped the whole edifice in a heavy cloud. But tongues of fire began to penetrate the cedar panelling; the frenzied songs were replaced by cries of terror and groans of agony. The magic which, in the hands of its degraded adepts, could not safeguard the empire of Ninus, did at least mingle its marvels to emblazon the terrible memories of this titanic suicide. A vast and sinister splendour, such as the night of Babylon had never seen, seemed suddenly to set back and enlarge the vault of heaven; a noise, like all the thunders of the world pealing together, shook the earth, and the walls of the city collapsed. Thereafter a deeper night descended; the palace of Sardanapalus melted, and when the morrow came his conqueror found no trace of its riches, no trace even of the king's body and all his luxuries.

So ended the first empire of Assyria, and the civilisation founded of old by the true Zoroaster. Thus also ended Magic, properly so called, and the reign of the Kabalah began. Abraham on coming out from Chaldea carried its mysteries with him. The people of God increased in silence, and we shall meet before long with Daniel confounding the miserable enchanters of Nebuchadnezzar and Belshazzar.[1]

---

[1] Éliphas Lévi adds in a note that, according to Suidas, Cedrenus and the *Chronicle of Alexandria*, it was Zoroaster himself who, seated in his palace, disappeared suddenly and by his own will, with all his secrets and all his riches, in a great peal of thunder. He explains that every king who exercised divine power passed for an incarnation of Zoroaster, and that Sardanapalus converted his pyre into an apotheosis.

CHAPTER III

MAGIC IN INDIA

WE are told by Kabalistic tradition that India was peopled by the descendants of Cain, and thither at a later period migrated the descendants of Abraham and Keturah; in any case it is, above all others, the country of Göetia and illusionary wonders. Black Magic has been perpetuated therein, as well as the original traditions of fratricide imposed by the powerful on the weak, continued by the dominant castes and expiated by the pariahs. It may be said of India that she is the wise mother of all idolatries. The dogmas of her gymnosophists would be keys of highest wisdom if they did not open more easily the gates leading to degradation and death. The astounding wealth of Indian symbolism seems to suggest that it is anterior to all others, and this is supported by the primeval freshness of its poetic conceptions. But the root of its tree seems to have been devoured by the infernal serpent. That deification of the devil against which we have already entered an energetic protest is displayed in all its grossness. The terrible Trimurti of the Brahmans comprises a Creator, a Destroyer and a Preserver. Their Adhi-nari, who represents the Divine Mother, or Celestial Nature, is called also Bohani, to whom the thugs or stranglers make votive offerings of their murders. Vishnu, the preserver, incarnates only to destroy an inferior devil, who is always brought back to life by the intervention of Siva, or Rudra, the god of death. One is conscious that Siva is the apotheosis of Cain, but there is nothing in all this mythology which recalls the mildness of Abel. The mysteries of India are notwithstanding grandiose in their poetry and singularly profound in their allegories; but they are the Kabalah in profanation, and hence so far from sustaining the soul and leading it to supreme wisdom, Brahminism, with its learned theories, plunges it into gulfs of madness.

It was from the false Kabalism of India that the Gnostics borrowed their reveries—by turns horrible and obscene; it is also Indian Magic, manifesting on the threshold of the occult sciences with a thousand deformities, which terrifies reasonable minds and provokes the anathemas of all the understanding churches. It is this false and dangerous knowledge, so often confounded by the ignorant and by smatterers with true science, which has involved all that bears the name of occultism in a general condemnation, to which the author of these pages himself subscribed sincerely before he had attained the key of the magical sanctuary. For theologians of the Vedas, God manifests as force only; all progress and all revelations are determined by conquest; Vishnu incarnates in monstrous leviathans of the sea and in enormous wild boars, which mould the primeval earth with their snouts.

Still, it is a marvellous pantheistic genesis, and the authors of its fables

The Indian and Japanese Mystery of Universal Equilibrium and the Egyptian Pantomorphic Iyinx

are lucid at least in their somnambulism. The ten Avatars of Vishnu correspond numerically to the *Sephiroth* of the Kabalah. The god in question assumed successively three animal or elementary forms of life, after which he became a sphinx and then a human being. He appeared next as Brahma and in a guise of assumed humility possessed the whole earth. He was a child on another occasion, and as such the consoling angel of the patriarchs. After this he assumed the mask of a warrior and gave battle to the oppressors of the world. Again he was embodied as diplomacy, opposing it to violence, and seems at this point to have abandoned the human form to assume the agility of the monkey. Diplomacy and violence consumed each other, and the world awaited some intellectual and moral redeemer. Vishnu thereupon incarnated as Krishna. He was proscribed even in his cradle, beside which there watched the symbolical ass. He was carried far away to save him from the power of his enemies; he attained manhood and preached the doctrine of mercy and good works. He descended into hell, bound the infernal serpent and returned gloriously to heaven. His annual festival is in August, under the sign of the Virgin. Here is astonishing intuition concerning Christian mysteries and so much the more impressive when we remember that the sacred books of India passed into writing many centuries before the Christian era. To the revelation of Krishna succeeded that of Buddha, who married the purest religion to philosophy of the highest kind. The happiness of the world was thus held to be secured and there was nothing further to expect, pending the tenth and final incarnation, when Vishnu will return in his proper form, leading the horse of the last judgment—that dread steed whose forefoot is raised always and when it is set down the world will be strewn in atoms.

We may note herein the presence of the sacred numbers and prophetic calculations of the Magi. Gymnosophists and Zoroastrian initiates drew from the same sources, but it was the false and black Zoroaster who remained master of theology in India. The final secrets of this degenerate doctrine are pantheism and its legitimate consequence, being absolute materialism masquerading as the absolute negation of matter. But what, it may be asked, does it signify whether spirit is materialised or matter spiritualised so long as the equality and identity of the two terms are postulated? But the consequence of such pantheism is, however, mortal to ethics: there are neither crimes nor virtues in a world where all is God. We may expect after such teachings a progressive degradation of the Brahmans into a fanatical quietism; but as yet the end was not reached. It remained for their great magical ritual, the Indian book of occultism, otherwise the *Oupnek'hat*, to furnish the physical and moral means of consummating the work of their stupefaction and arriving by a graduated method at that raving madness termed by their sorcerers the Divine State. The work in question is the progenitor of all grimoires and the most curious among the antiquities of Göetia. It is divided into fifty sections and is a darkness spangled with stars. Sublime maxims are blended with false oracles.[1] At times it reads like the Gospel of St. John, as, for example, in the following extracts from the eleventh and forty-eighth sections.

"The angel of creative fire is the word of God, which word produced the earth and the vegetation that issues therefrom, together with the heat which ripens it. The word of the Creator is itself the Creator and is also His only Son." Now, on the other hand, the reveries are worthy only of the most extravagant arch-heretics: "Matter being only a deceptive appearance, the sun, the stars and the very elements are genii, while animals are demons and man is a pure spirit deceived by the illusions of forms." We are perhaps sufficiently edified by these extracts in respect of doctrinal matters and may proceed to the Magical Ritual of the Indian enchanters.

"In order to become God, the breath must be retained—that is to say, it must be inhaled as long as possible, till the chest is well distended—and in the second place, the divine OM must be repeated inwardly forty times while in this state. Expiration, in the third place, follows very slowly, the breath being mentally directed through the heavens to make

---

[1] The analysis of Eliphas Lévi requires to be checked at all points. He followed the Latin version of Anquetil Duperron, made from a Persian text, and this is so rare as to be almost unobtainable. I shall therefore deserve well of my readers by furnishing the following extract from Deussen's *Religion and Philosophy of India*, regarding the *Oupnek'hat*:

"A position apart from the 52 and the 108 Upanishads is occupied by that collection of 50 Upanishads which, under the name of *Oupnek'hat*, was translated from the Sanskrit into the Persian in the year 1656 at the instance of the Sultan Mohammed Dara Shakoh, and from the Persian into the Latin in 1801-2 by Anquetil Duperron. The *Oupnek'hat* professes to be a general collection of Upanishads. It contains under twelve divisions the Upanishads of the three older Vedas, and with them 26 Atharva Upanishads that are known from other sources. It further comprises eight treatises peculiar to itself, five of which have not up to the present time been proved to exist elsewhere, and of which therefore a rendering from the Persian-Latin of Anquetil is alone possible. Finally the *Oupnek'hat* contains four treatises from the Vaj. Samh. 16, 31, 32, 34, of which the first is met with in a shorter form in other collections also, as in the Nilarudra Upanishad, while the three last have nowhere else found admission. The reception of these treatises from the Samhita into the body of the Upanishads, as though there were danger of their falling otherwise into oblivion, makes us infer a comparatively later date for the *Oupnek'hat* collection itself, although as early as 1656 the Persian translators made no claim to be the original compilers, but took the collection over already complete. Owing to the excessive literality with which Anquetil Duperron rendered these Upanishads word by word from the Persian into Latin, while preserving the syntax of the former language—a literality that stands in striking contrast to the freedom with which the Persian translators treated the Sanskrit text—the *Oupnek'hat* is a very difficult book to read; and an insight as keen as that of Schopenhauer was required in order to discover within this repellent husk a kernel of invaluable philosophical significance, and to turn it to account for his own system. An examination of the material placed at our disposal in the *Oupnek'hat* was first undertaken by A. Weber, Ind. Stud. 1, 11, ix, on the basis of the Sanskrit text. Meanwhile the original texts were published in the *Bibliotheca Indica* in part with elaborate commentaries, and again in the Anandas'rama series. The two longest and some of the shorter treatises have appeared in a literal German rendering by O. Bohtlingk. Max Müller translated the twelve oldest Upanishads in *Sacred Books of the East*, vol. i, 15. And my own translation of the 60 Upanishads contains complete texts of this character which, upon the strength of their regular occurrence in the Indian collections and lists of the Upanishads, may lay claim to a certain canonicity. The prefixed introductions and the notes treat exhaustively of the matter and composition of the several treatises."

contact with the universal ether. Those who would succeed in this exercise must be blind, deaf and motionless as a log of wood. The posture is on knees and elbows, with the face turned to the North. One nostril is stopped with a finger, the air is inhaled by the other, which is then also closed, the action being accompanied by dwelling in thought on the idea that God is the Creator, that He is in all animals, in the ant even as in the elephant. The mind must be absorbed in these thoughts. OM is at first recited twelve times and afterwards twenty-four times during each inspiration, and then as rapidly as possible. This regimen must be continued for three months—without fear, without remission, eating and sleeping little. In the fourth month the Devas will manifest; in the fifth you will have acquired all qualities of the Devatas; in the sixth you will be saved and will have become God."

What seems certain is that in the sixth month the fanatic who is sufficiently imbecile to persevere in such a practice will be dead or insane. If, however, he should really survive this exercise in mystic breathing the *Oupnek'hat* does not leave him in the happy position mentioned but makes him pass to other experiences.

"With the end of one finger close the anus, and then draw the breath from below upwards on the right side; make it circulate three times round the second centre of the body; thence bring it to the navel, which is the third centre; then to the fourth, which is the middle of the heart; subsequently to the throat, which is the fifth; and finally to the sixth, which is the root of the nose. There retain the breath: it has become that of the universal soul."

This seems simply an auto-hypnotic method of inducing a certain cèrebral congestion. But the author of the treatise continues:

"Think therefore of the great OM, which is the name of the Creator and is that universal, pure and indivisible voice which fills all things. This voice is the Creator Himself, Who becomes audible to the contemplative after ten manners. The first sound is like that of a little sparrow; the second is twice the first in volume; the third is like the sound of a cymbal; the fourth is as the murmur of a great shell; the fifth is comparable to the song of the India lyre; the sixth is like the sound of the instrument called *tal*; the seventh resembles the sound of a *bacabou* flute, held close to the ear; the eighth is like that of the instrument called *Pakaoudj*, which is struck with the hand; the ninth is like the sound of a little trumpet and the tenth like that of a thunder cloud. At each of these sounds the contemplative passes through different states, and at the tenth he becomes God. At the first sound the hairs of his whole body rise erect; at the second his limbs become torpid; at the third he feels through all his frame the kind of exhaustion which follows the intercourse of love; at the fourth his head swims and he is as one intoxicated; at the fifth the life-force flows back into his brain; at the sixth this force descends into him and he is nourished thereon; at the seventh he becomes the master of vision, can see into the hearts of others, and hears the most distant voices; at the ninth he becomes so ethereal that he can pass wheresoever he will and can see without being seen, like the angels; at the tenth he becomes the universal and indivisible voice. He is the great creator, the eternal being, exempt from all and, having become the perfect peace, he dispenses peace to the world."

What is noticeable in these most curious extracts is their exhaustive description of phenomena which characterise lucid somnambulism combined with a complete practice of auto-hypnosis; it is the art of inducing ecstasy by tension of the will and fatigue of the nervous system. We recommend therefore to mesmerists a careful study of the mysteries of the *Oupnek'hat*. The graduated use of narcotics and of a scale of coloured discs will produce effects analogous to those described by the Indian sorcerer. M. Ragon has provided the recipe in his work on *La Maçonnerie Occulte*.[1] The *Oupnek'hat* gives a simpler method of losing consciousness and arriving at ecstasy; it is to look with both eyes at the end of the nose and to maintain this act, or rather this grimace, until paralysis of the optic nerve supervenes. All such practices are equally painful, dangerous and ridiculous; we are far from recommending them to anyone; but we do not question that in a shorter or longer time, according to the sensibility of the subjects, they will induce ecstasy, catalepsy and even a dead swoon. In order to obtain vision and the phenomena of second sight, a state must be reached which is akin to that of sleep, death and madness. It is in this that the Indians excel, and it is perhaps to their secrets that we must refer the strange power of certain American mediums.

Black Magic may be defined as the art of inducing artificial mania in ourselves and in others; but it is also and above all the science of poisoning. What is, however, generally unknown, and the discovery in our days is due to M. Du Potet, is that it is possible to destroy life by the sudden congestion or withdrawal of the Astral Light. This may take place when, through a series of almost impossible exercises, similar to those described by the Indian sorcerer, our nervous sytem, having been habituated to all tensions and fatigues, has become a kind of living galvanic pile, capable of condensing and projecting powerfully that light which intoxicates or destroys.

We are not, however, at the end of the *Oupnek'hat* and its magical wonders; there is a final arcanum which the darksome hierophant entrusts to his initiates as the supreme secret of all; it is actually the shadow and reverse side of the great mystery of Transcendent Magic. Now, the latter is the absolute in morality and consequently in the direction of activity and in freedom. On the other hand, that of the *Oupnek'hat* is the absolute in immorality, in fatality and in deadly quietism: it is expressed as follows

---

[1] This forms the second book of the collection entitled *Orthodoxie Maçonnique*, which was published in 1853. The account of magical discs and the planets corresponding to them will be found on pp. 498–501. Ragon pretended that there was a system of Occult Masonry in three Degrees.

by the author of the Indian work: "It is lawful to lie in order to facilitate marriages, to exalt the virtues of a Brahman or the good qualities of a cow. God is truth, and in Him shadow and light are one. Whosoever is acquainted with this truth never lies, for his very falsehood turns true. Whatever sin he commits, whatever evil he performs, he is never guilty; if he committed a double parricide; if he killed a Brahman initiated into the mysteries of the Vedas; in a word, whatever he did, his light would not be impaired, for God says: I am the Universal Soul; in Me are good and evil, which are moderated one by the other; he who knows this cannot sin, for he is universal even as Myself."

Such doctrines are incompatible with civilisation, and furthermore, by stereotyping its social hierarchy, India has imbedded anarchy in the castes whereas social life is a question of exchange. Now, exchange is impossible when everything belongs to a few and nothing to others. What do social gradations signify in a putative civil state wherein no one can fall or rise? Herein is the long-delayed punishment of the fratricide; it is one which involves his entire race and condemns it to death. Should some alien, proud and egotistic nation intervene, it will sacrifice India—even as oriental legends tell us that Cain was killed by Lamech. Woe, notwithstanding to the murderer of Cain—so say the sacred oracles of the Bible.

CHAPTER IV

HERMETIC MAGIC

It is in Egypt that Magic attains the grade of completion as a universal science and is formulated as a perfect doctrine. As a summary of all the dogmas which obtained in the ancient world, nothing surpasses and indeed nothing equals those few paragraphs graven on precious stone by Hermes and denominated the Emerald Tablet. Unity of being and unity in the harmony of things, according to the ascending and descending scales; progressive and proportional evolution of the Word; immutable law of equilibrium and graduated progress of universal analogies; correspondence between the idea and its expression providing a measure of likeness between Creator and created; essential mathematics of the infinite, proved by the dimensions of a single angle in the finite: all this is expressed by the one proposition: "that which is above is like that which is below, and that which is below is like that which is above, for the fulfilment of the wonders of the one thing". Hereunto are added the revelation and illuminating description of the creative agent, the pantomorphic fire, the great medium of occult force—in a word, the Astral Light.

"The sun is its father and the moon its mother; the wind has borne it in the belly thereof." It follows that this light has emanated from the sun and has received form and rhythmical movement from the influences of the moon, while the atmosphere is its receptacle and prison. "The earth is its nurse"—that is to say, it is equilibrated and set in motion by the central heat of the earth. "It is the universal principle, the TELESMA of the world."

Hermes goes on to set forth in what manner this light, which is also a force, can be applied as a lever, as a universal dissolvent and as a formative and coagulative agent; how also this light must be extracted from the bodies in which it lies latent in order to imitate all the artifices of Nature by the aid of its diverse manifestations as fire, motion, splendour, radiant gas, scalding water or finally igneous earth. The Emerald Tablet contains all Magic in a single page.[1] The other works attributed to Hermes,[2]

---

[1] The legend concerning the Emerald Tablet is that it was found by Alexander the Great in the tomb of Hermes, which was hidden by the priests of Egypt in the depths of the Great Pyramid of Gizeh. It was supposed to have been written by Hermes on a large plate of emerald by means of a pointed diamond. I believe that there is no Greek version extant, and it is referred by Louis Figuier to the seventh century of the Christian era, or thereabouts. See *L'Alchimie et les Alchimistes*, p. 42.

[2] In his *Lexicon Alchemiæ* Rulandus reminds us that "the old astronomers dedicated the Emerald to Mercury", and Berthelot says that this was in conformity with Egyptian ideas, which classed the Emerald and Sapphire in their list of metals. See *Collection des Anciens Alchimistes Grecs, première livraison*, p. 269. The planet Mercury was the planet Hermes and it may be that some mystical connection was supposed between quicksilver and the precious stone. This would have been in Græco-Alexandrian times, if ever, as ancient Egypt does not seem to have been acquainted with quicksilver.

such as the *Divine Pymander, Asclepius, Minerva of the World*, &c. are generally regarded by critics as productions of the School of Alexandria; but they contain notwithstanding the Hermetic traditions which were preserved in theurgic sanctuaries. For those who possess the keys of symbolism the doctrines of Hermes can never be lost; amidst all their ruin, the monuments of Egypt are as so many scattered leaves which can be collected and the book of those doctrines thus reconstructed entirely. In that vast book the capital letters are temples and the sentences are cities punctuated with obelisks and by the sphinx.

The physical division of Egypt was itself a magical synthesis, and the names of its provinces corresponded to the ciphers of sacred numbers. The realm of Sesostris was divided into three parts; of these Upper Egypt, or the Thebaid, was a type of the celestial world and the land of ecstasy; Lower Egypt was the symbol of earth; while Middle or Central Egypt was the land of science and of high initiation. Each of these parts was subdivided into ten provinces, called Nomes, and was placed under the particular protection of a god. There were therefore thirty gods and they were grouped by threes, giving symbolical expression in this manner to all possible conceptions of the triad within the decad, or otherwise to the threefold material, philosophical and religious significance of absolute ideas attached primitively to numbers. We have thus the triple unity, or the first triad; the triple binary[1] formed by the first triad and its reflection, being the Star of Solomon; the triple triad, or the complete idea under each of its three forms; the triple quaternary, being the cyclic number of astral revolutions, and so onward. The geography of Egypt under Sesostris is therefore a pantacle or symbolical summary of the entire magical dogma originating with Zoroaster and rediscovered or formulated more precisely by Hermes.

In this manner did the land of Egypt become as a great volume and the instructions contained therein were multiplied by translation into pictures, sculptures, architecture through the length and breadth of the towns and in all temples. The very desert had its eternal teachings, and its word of stone was set squarely on the foundations of the pyramids. The pyramids themselves stood like boundaries of the human intelligence, in the presence of which the colossal sphinx meditated age after age, sinking by insensible degrees into the desert sand. Even at this day its head, defaced by the work of time, still emerges from its sepulchre, as if waiting expectantly the signal for its complete entombment at the coming of a human voice revealing to a new world the problem of the pyramids.

Egypt from our standpoint is the cradle of science and of wisdom, for it clothed with images the antique dogma of the first Zoroaster more exactly and more purely, if not more richly, than those of India. The

---

[1] The text says: *le triple binaire ou le mirage du triangle*, but it is obvious that the reflected triad cannot be termed binary. The expression is confused, but the meaning is that the first triangle equals unity, or the number 1; the second triad corresponds to the duad, or number 2; the third triad to the number 3, and so onward.

THE DERIVATIONS OF MAGIC

Sacerdotal Art and the Royal Art made adepts by initiation in Egypt, and such initiation was not restricted within the egotistic limits of caste. We know that a Jewish bondsman himself attained not only initiation but the rank of minister-in-chief, perhaps even of Grand Hierophant, for he espoused the daughter of an Egyptian priest, and there is evidence that the priesthood in that country tolerated no misalliance. Joseph realised in Egypt the dream of communion; he established the priesthood and the state as sole proprietors and thus sole arbiters of labour and wealth. In this way he abolished distress and turned the whole of Egypt into a patriarchal family. It is a matter of common knowledge that his elevation was due to skill in the interpretation of dreams, a science which even devout Christians now refuse to credit, though they recognise that the Bible, which narrates the wonderful divinations of Joseph, is the word of the Holy Spirit. The science of Joseph was none other than a comprehension of the natural analogies which subsist between ideas and images, or between the Word and its symbols. He knew that the soul, when immersed by sleep in the Astral Light, perceives the reflections of its most secret thoughts and even of its presentiments; he knew further that the art of translating the hieroglyphics of sleep is the key of universal lucidity, seeing that all intelligent beings have revelations in dreams.

The basis of absolute hieroglyphical science was an alphabet in which deities were represented by letters, letters represented ideas, ideas were convertible into numbers, and numbers were perfect signs. This hieroglyphical alphabet was the great secret which Moses enshrined in his Kabalah; its Egyptian origin is commemorated in the *Sepher Yetzirah*, in which it is referred to Abraham. Now this alphabet is the famous Book of Thoth, and it was divined by Count de Gebelin that it has been preserved to our own day in the form of Tarot cards. It passed later on into the hands of Etteilla, who interpreted it in the wrong sense, for even a study extending over thirty years could not atone for his want of common sense or supply deficiencies in his education. The record exists still among the drift and waste of Egyptian monuments; and its most curious, most complete key is found in the great work on Egypt by Athanasius Kircher. It is the copy of an Isiac tablet which belonged to the celebrated Cardinal Bembo. The tablet in question is of copper with figures in enamel, and it has been unfortunately lost. The copy supplied by Kircher is, however, exact.[1] The learned Jesuit divined that it contained the hieroglyphic key of sacred alphabets, though he was unable to develop the explanation. It is divided into three equal compartments; above

[1] The reference is to Athanasius Kircher's *Œdipus Ægyptiacus*, 3 vols. in folio, bound usually in four, published at Rome, 1652–1654. The *Mensa Isiaca*, being the Bembine Tablet, so called because its discovery is connected with the name of Cardinal Bembo, is in the third volume—a folding plate beautifully produced. The original is exceedingly late and is roughly termed a forgery. In 1669 the Tablet was reproduced on a larger scale by means of a number of folding plates in the *Mensa Isiaca* of Laurentius Pignorius. Both works are exceedingly rare. I suppose that these are the only records of the Tablet now extant, with the exception of a large copy in my possession made from the above sources.

are the twelve houses of heaven and below are the corresponding distributions of labour throughout the year, while in the middle place are twenty-one sacred signs answering to the letters of the alphabet. In the midst of all is a seated figure of the pantomorphic IYNX, emblem of universal being[1] and corresponding as such to the Hebrew *Yod*, or to that unique letter from which all other letters were formed. The IYNX is encircled by the Ophite triad, answering to the Three Mother Letters of the Egyptian and Hebrew alphabets.[2] On the right are the ibimorphic and serapian triads; on the left are those of Nepthys and Hecate, representing active and passive, fixed and volatile, fructifying fire and generating water. Each pair of triads in conjunction with the centre produces a septenary, and a septenary is contained in the centre. The three septenaries furnish the absolute number of the three worlds, as well as the complete number of primitive letters, to which a complementary sign is added, like zero to the nine numerals. The ten numbers and the twenty-two letters are termed in Kabalism the Thirty-two Paths of Wisdom, and their philosophical description is the subject of that venerated primæval book known as the *Sepher Yetzirah*, the text of which will be found in the collection of Pistorius and elsewhere.[3] The alphabet of Thoth is the original of our Tarot only in an indirect manner, seeing that the latter is of Jewish origin in the extant copies and that its pictures are not older than the reign of Charles VII. The cards of Jacquemin Gringonneur are the first Tarots of which we have any knowledge, but they reproduce symbols belonging to the highest antiquity. The game in its modern form was an experiment on the part of astrologers to restore the king, who has been mentioned, to reason.[4] The oracles of the Tarot give answers as exact as

[1] Mr. G. R. S. Mead tells us that *Iynx* in its root-meaning, according to Proclus, signifies the "power of transmission" which is said in the Chaldæan Oracles "to sustain the fountains". Mr. Mead thinks that the *Iyinges* were reproduced (a) as Living Spheres and (b) as Winged Globes. He thinks, also, that (a) the Mind on the plane of reality put forth (b) the one *Iyinx*, (c) after this three *Iyinges*, called paternal and ineffable, and finally (d) there may have been hosts of subordinate *Iyinges*. They were "free intelligences". It seems to follow that the *Iynx* was not "an emblem of universal being", but a product of the Eternal Mind.

[2] It may be mentioned that the Hebrew alphabet was divided into (a) Three Mother Letters, namely, *Aleph*, *Mem* and *Shin*; (b) Seven Double Letters, being *Beth, Gimel, Daleth, Kaph, Pe, Resh, Tau*; and (c) Twelve Simple Letters, or *He, Vau, Zain, Heth, Teth, Yod, Lamed, Nun, Samech, Ayin, Tsade, Quoph*.

[3] The *Sepher Yetzirah* was first made known to Latin-reading Europe by William Postel. Publication took place at Bâle in 1547. It is said to have been reissued at Amsterdam in 1646. The collection of Pistorius, entitled *Artis Cabalisticæ Scriptores*, belongs to 1587. Later and modern editions of the *Book of Formation* are fairly numerous. It was translated into French, together with the Arabic commentary of R. Saadya Gaon, by Mayor Lambert, in 1891. An English version by Dr. W. Wynn Westcott will serve the purpose of the general reader.

[4] The Tarots of this period belong to the year 1393, and it has been suggested recently in France that the artist Charles Gringonneur was really their inventor. It is useful to note this opinion, but I do not think that any importance attaches to it. The extant Gringonneur examples in the *Bibliothèque Nationale* have also been said to be of Italian origin and not therefore his work. The Venetian Tarots have been sometimes regarded as the oldest known form. The historical question is obscure beyond all extrication at present.

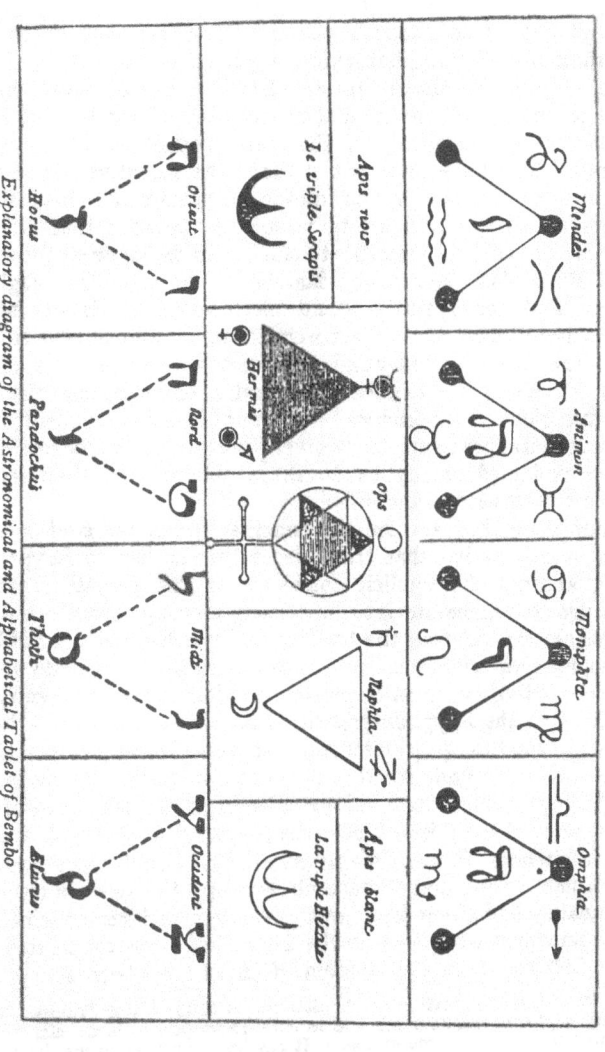

Explanatory diagram of the Astronomical and Alphabetical Tablet of Bembo

mathematics and measured as the harmonies of Nature. Such answers result from the varied combination of the different signs. But it requires a considerable exercise of reason to make use of an instrument belonging to reason and to science; the poor king, in his childish condition, saw only the playthings of an infant in the artist's pictures and he turned the mysterious Kabalistic alphabet[1] into a game of cards.

We are told by Moses that the Israelites carried away the sacred vessels of the Egyptians when they came out of the land of bondage. The account is allegorical, for the great prophet would scarcely have encouraged his people in an act of theft; the sacred vessels in question were the mysteries of Egyptian knowledge, acquired by Moses himself at the court of Pharaoh. We are by no means suggesting that the miracles of this man of God are referable to Magic; but we know on the authority of the Bible that Jannes and Mambres, who were the magicians of Pharaoh and consequently grand hierophants of Egypt, began by performing in virtue of their art wonders which were similar to those of Moses. They transformed wands into serpents and serpents again into wands, which might be explicable by prestige or fascination; they change water into blood; they produced a swarm of frogs in a moment; but they could not cause flies to appear or other parasitic insects, for reasons which we have explained already, as also the manner in which they were forced to confess themselves vanquished.

Moses triumphed and led the Israelites out of the land of bondage. It was at this period that true science became lost to Egypt, for the priests, abusing the implicit confidence of the people, allowed that knowledge to degenerate into brutalising idolatry. Such is the rock of peril for esoteric science; the truth must be veiled, yet not hidden from the people; symbolism must not be disgraced by a lapse into absurdity; the sacred veil of Isis must be preserved in its beauty and dignity. It was over this that the Egyptian priesthood failed; the vulgar and the foolish understood the hieroglyphic forms of Isis and Hermanubis as real things, so that Osiris was understood to be an ox, while the wise Hermes was a dog. The transformed Osiris masqueraded in the fantastic guise of the bull of Apis, nor did the priests hinder the people from adoring flesh intended for their kitchens. It was time to save the holy traditions; Moses established a new nation and forbade all worship of images; but the people unfortunately had dwelt long among idolaters, and memories of the bull of Apis remained with them in the desert. We know the history of that Golden Calf to which the children of Israel have been always a little

[1] In face of existing evidence, the description of the Tarot Trumps Major as a Kabalistic alphabet has as much and as little to support it as the claim that they constitute an Egyptian *Book of Thoth*. It has been reported to me, however, that there is an unknown Jewish Tarot, and it may interest students of the subject to know that before long. I hope to be able to give some account at first hand concerning it. There is little reason to suppose that it will prove (a) ancient or (b) Kabalistic; but as one never knows what is at one's threshold, I put the fact on record for whatever it may be worth in the future. Meanwhile, it is quite idle to say that our popular fortune-telling Tarots are of Jewish origin.

addicted. Moses, however, did not wish the sacred hieroglyphics to pass out of memory, and he sanctified them by their consecration to the purified worship of the true God. We shall see how all objects which entered into the cultus of Jehovah were symbolic in character and recalled the venerable signs of primæval revelation. But we must first finish with the Gentiles and follow through pagan civilisation the story of materialised hieroglyphics and of ancient rites degenerated.

CHAPTER V

MAGIC IN GREECE

WE pass now to the period when the exact sciences of Magic assumed their natural external form, being that of beauty. We have seen in the *Zohar* how the human prototype rose in heaven and was reflected below in the waters of being. This ideal man, this shadow of the pantomorphic god, this virile phantom of perfect form, was not destined to dwell alone in the world of symbolism. There was given to him a companion under the beneficent sky of Hellas. The celestial Venus, the chaste and fruitful Venus, the triple mother of the three Graces, rose in her turn, no longer from the sleeping deeps of chaos, but from the living and flowing waves of that echoing archipelago of poetry, where islands embroidered with green trees and flowers seem as the vessels of gods.

The magical septenary of Chaldea passes into music on the seven strings of the Orphic lyre. It is harmony which transforms the woods and wildernesses of Greece. To the melody of the songs of Orpheus the rocks are smoothed, the oaks sway in measures and the wild beasts become subject to man. By such magic did Amphion raise up the walls of Thebes—that wisdom-city of Cadmus, the city of initiation, itself a pantacle like the seven wonders of the world. As Orpheus gave life to numbers, so Cadmus bound thought to the sigils of letters. The one established a nation dedicated to all things beautiful, and for that nation the other provided a native land, corresponding to its genius and its love.

In the ancient Greek traditions Orpheus is numbered among the heroes of the Golden Fleece, who were the primeval conquerors of the Great Work. The Golden Fleece is the vesture of the sun itself; it is light in application to the needs of man; it is the grand secret of magical works; it is, in fine, initiation as this should be understood essentially; and it was the quest of these or this which carried the allegorical heroes into a mystic Asia. On the other hand, Cadmus was a voluntary exile from the glorious Thebes of Egypt; he brought into Greece the knowledge of letters and that harmony of which they are images. The new Thebes, the typical city of wisdom, was built to the measures of that harmony, for science consists in the rhythmic correspondence between hieroglyphical, phonetic and numeral characters, the inherent motion of which follows the eternal laws of mathematics. Thebes is circular and its citadel is square; like the sky of Magic, it has seven gates, and its legend was destined to become the epic of occultism and the foreshadowed history of human genius.

All these mysterious allegories, all these inspired traditions, are the soul of Greek civilisation; but we must be dissuaded from seeking the real history of their poetic heroes otherwise than in the transformations of oriental history carried into Greece by unknown hierophants. It was only the history of ideas which was written by the great of those days, and they were at little pains to acquaint us with the human struggles belonging to the birth of empires. Homer followed in their path, marshalling the gods, who are the immortal types of thought; it was in this sense that a world's upheaval followed on the frown of Jupiter. If Greece carried fire and sword into Asia, it was to avenge the profanations of science and virtue in their sacrifice to lust; it was to restore the empire of the world to Minerva and Juno, in despite of that sensuous Venus who ruined her devoted lovers. Such is the sublime mission of poetry, which substitutes gods for men, or causes in places of effects and eternal concepts for the sorry incarnations of greatness on earth. Ideas raise up and they also cast down empires; a faith of some kind is at the root of all grandeur, and in order that faith may be poetry, or in other words creative, it must be founded on truth. The only history which is worthy to occupy the wise is that of the light which is victorious over darkness for ever. That which is called a civilisation is one great day of this sun.

The fable of the Golden Fleece connects Hermetic Magic with Greek initiations. The Golden Fleece of the solar ram, which must be obtained by those or by him who would possess universal sovereignty, is figurative of the Great Work. The Argonautic vessel, built of timber from the prophetic oaks of Dodona, the speaking vessel, is the ship of the mysteries of Isis, the ark of life-force and renewal, the coffer of Osiris, the egg of divine regeneration. The adventurer Jason is he who is prepared for initiation, but he is a hero in his valour only; he has all the inconstancy and all the weakness of humanity, but he takes with him the personifications of all power. Hercules, who signifies brute force, has no real part in the work, for he goes astray from the path in pursuit of his unworthy loves. The others arrive in the land of initiation, of Colchis, where the remnant of Zoroastrian secrets is still preserved. The question is how to obtain the key of these mysteries, and science is once again betrayed by a woman. Medea delivers to Jason the arcana of the Great Work, with the kingdom and the life of her father; for it is a fatal law of the occult sanctuary that the revelation of its secrets entails death upon him who has proved unable to preserve them. Medea informs Jason of the monsters with which he must do battle and of that which will ensure his victory. There is firstly the winged serpent of earth, the astral fluid which must be seized and fixed; its teeth must be drawn and sown in a waste place which has been previously ploughed by the bulls of Mars. The dragon's teeth are those acids[1] which dissolve the metallic earth after its preparation

---

[1] The interpretation of Lévi seems to hesitate between several fields of symbolism, and what follows at this point suggests that the Golden Fleece is an allegory of metallic transmutation by means of alchemy. It was so regarded by many of the later disciples of this art. According to Antoine Joseph Pernety, the Golden Fleece is the symbol of the matter of the Great Work; the labours of Jason are an allegory concerning the operations therein and of the signs of progress towards perfection. The attainment of this Fleece signifies that of the Powder of Projection and the Universal Medicine. See *Dictionnaire Mytho-Hermétique* and *Les Fables Egyptiennes et Grecques*, both by Pernety, and in particular vol. i of the latter work, pp. 437–94.

by a double fire and by the earth's magnetic forces. A fermentation follows, comparable to a great battle; the impure is devoured by the impure, and the splendid Fleece is the reward of the adept.

So ends the magical romance of Jason and that of Medea follows, for Greek antiquity sought to include in this history the complete epic of occult science. Hermetic Magic is succeeded by göetia, parricide, fratricide, infanticide, sacrificing all to its passions but never enjoying the harvest of its crimes. Medea betrays her father like Ham and assassinates her brother like Cain. She stabs her children, poisons her rival and reaps the hatred of him whose love she has coveted. It may be surprising on the surface that Jason does not gain in wisdom by the mastery of the Golden Fleece, but it must be remembered that he owes the discovery of its secrets to treason only. He is a ravisher after the manner of Prometheus and not an adept like Orpheus; he is in search of wealth and power rather than of knowledge. Hence he perishes miserably, for the inspiring and sovereign virtues of the Golden Fleece will be never understood except by the disciples of Orpheus.

Prometheus, the Golden Fleece, the Thebaid, the Iliad and the Odyssey—these five great epics, full of the mysteries of Nature and human destinies, constitute the bible of ancient Greece, a cyclopean monument, a Pelion piled upon an Ossa, masterpiece over masterpiece, form on form, beautiful as light itself and throned upon eternal thoughts, sublime in truth. It was, however, at their proper risk and peril that the hierophants of poetry committed to the Greek people these marvellous fictions in which truth was shrined. Aeschylus, who dared to depict the Titanic struggles, superhuman woes and divine hopes of Prometheus —Aeschylus, the awe-inspiring poet of the family of Œdipus—was accused of betraying and profaning the mysteries and escaped with difficulty a severe condemnation. We are unable at this day to realise his whole intent, which was a dramatic trilogy embracing the entire symbolic history of Prometheus. It follows that he exhibited to the assembled people how Prometheus was delivered by Alcides and how Jupiter was cast from his throne. The omnipotence of genius in its suffering and the decisive victory of patience over power are fine, no doubt, but the crowd might see therein the future triumph of impiety and anarchy. Prometheus overcoming Jupiter might be understood as the people destined to be liberated one day from their priests and kings; and guilty hopes might count for much in the prodigal applause accorded to him who unveiled this prospect imprudently. To the leanings of dogma towards poetry we owe the masterpieces in question, and we are not therefore to be counted among the austere initiates who would wish, like Plato, to crown and then exile the poets; for the true poets are ambassadors of God on earth and those who cast them forth deserve no blessing from heaven.

The great Greek initiator and he who civilised it first was also its first poet, for, even in allowing that Orpheus was a mystical or fabulous personality, we must believe in the existence of Musæus and attribute to him the verses which pass under the name of his master.[1] It matters little to us otherwise whether one of the Argonauts was called Orpheus or not, for the poetic creator has done more than live; he lives in immortality for ever. The Orphic fable is a complete dogma, a revelation of priestly destinies, a new ideal form of the worship of beauty. The regeneration and redemption of love are indicated already therein. Orpheus descends into hell, seeking Eurydice, and must bring her back without seeing her; so must the pure man create his companion, raise her to himself by devotion and not by desire of her. It is in renouncing the object of passion that we deserve to possess the object of true love. We are already in the atmosphere of the pure dreams of Christian chivalry. But the hierophant is still a man; he falters, questions and looks. *Ah miseror Eurydicem*. She is lost, the error is committed, the expiation must now begin. Orpheus is widowed and remains as such in purity; the marriage with Eurydice had not attained consummation, and as the widower of one who was a virgin he rested himself in virginity. The poet is not two-hearted, and children of the race of gods love once and once alone. Paternal inspirations, yearnings for an ideal which shall be found beyond the tomb, widowhood made holy in its consecration to the sacred muse. What a revelation in advance of inspirations yet to come! Orpheus, bearing in his heart a wound that nothing but death shall heal, becomes a doctor of souls and bodies; he dies at length, the victim of his chastity—the death which he suffers is that of initiators and prophets. He perishes proclaiming the unity of God and the unity also of love: this at a later period was the root of the Orphic Mysteries.

Having shewn himself raised so far above his own epoch, Orpheus earned in due course the reputation of a sorcerer and enchanter. To him, as to Solomon, was attributed the knowledge of simples and minerals, of celestial medicine and the philosophical stone. With these he was doubtless acquainted, since he personifies primitive initiation, fall and reparation in his legend—the three divisions of the great work of humanity.

Orphic initiation may, according to Ballanche, be summarised in the following manner: "Made subject in the first place to the influence of the elements, man's own influence must afterwards govern these. Creation is the act of a divine magism which is continuous and eternal. True being resides for man in self-knowledge. Responsibility is for him a conquest and the very penalty of sin is another occasion for victory. All life is founded on death, and palingenesis is the law of reparation. Marriage is the reproduction in humanity of the great cosmogonical mystery. It should be one, as God and Nature are one. It is the unity of the Tree of Life, while debauch is division and death. Astrology is a synthesis, because the Tree

[1] Among several bearers of this name, I suppose that the reference is to him who, by tradition, was either the disciple or son of Orpheus, commemorated by Virgil. None of his poems are extant, so that the argument seems to fail. The antiquity of the Orphic poems—*Argonautica*, Hymns, etc.—is another question, and the conclusions of criticism on the subject are well known.

of Life is a single tree and because its branches—spread through heaven and bearing flowers of stars—are in correspondence with its roots, which are hidden in earth. The knowledge of the medical and magical virtues resident in plants, metals and bodies endowed with varying degrees of life, is also a synthetic knowledge. The capacities for organisation in their various grades are revealed by a synthesis. The aggregations and affinities of metals, like the vegetative soul of plants and like all powers of assimilation, are also made known by a synthesis."

It has been said that the beautiful is the splendour of the true, and it is therefore to this great light of Orpheus that we must ascribe the perfection of form which was manifested for the first time in Greece. To him also—as to a source—is referable the school of divine Plato, that pagan father of all high Christian philosophy. From him did Pythagoras and the *illuminati* of Alexandria alike derive their mysteries. Initiation does not suffer vicissitude; it is one and the same, wheresoever we meet it through the ages. The last disciples of Martines de Pasqually are still the children of Orpheus; but they adore the Realiser of antique philosophy, Who is the incarnate Word of Christians.

We have said that the first part of the fable concerning the Golden Fleece embodies the secrets of Orphic Magic and that the second part is dedicated to judicious warnings against the abuses of Göetia or the Magic of darkness. False or Göetic Magic, known at the present day under the name of sorcery, can never rank as a science: it is the empiricism of fatality. All excessive passion produces a factitious force of which will cannot be the master, but that force is obedient to the tyranny of passion. This is why Albertus Magnus counsels us to curse no one in our wrath. It is the story of the malediction of Hippolytus by Theseus. Excessive passion is real madness, and the latter in its turn is an intoxication or congestion of Astral Light. This is why madness is contagious and why passions in general operate as a veritable witchcraft. Women are superior to men in sorcery because they are more easily transported by excess of passion. The word "sorcerer" clearly designates victims of chance and, so to speak, the poisonous mushrooms of fatality.

Greek sorcerers, but especially those of Thessaly, put horrible precepts to the proof and were given over to abominable rites. They were mostly women wasted by desires which they could no longer satisfy, antiquated courtesans, monsters of immorality and ugliness. Jealous of love and life, those wretched creatures found lovers only in the tombs, or rather they violated sepulchres to devour with foul caresses the icy bodies of young men. They stole children and stifled their cries by pressing them to their dangling breasts. They were known as *lamiæ, stryges, empusæ*; children were the objects of their envy and thus of their hatred, and they sacrificed them for this reason. Some, like that Canidia who is mentioned by Horace, buried them as far as the head and left them to die of hunger, surrounded with food which they could not reach; others cut off the heads, hands and feet, boiled their fat and grease, in copper basins, to the consistence of an ointment, which they afterwards mixed with the juice of henbane, belladonna and black poppies. With this unguent they anointed the organ which was irritated unceasingly by their detestable desires; they rubbed also their temples and arm-pits, and then fell into a lethargy full of unbridled and luxurious dreams. There is need to speak plainly—these are the origins and this is the traditional practice of Black Magic; these are the secrets which were handed down to the middle ages; and such in time are the pretended innocent vicims whom public execration, far more than the sentence of inquisitors, condemned to the flames. It was in Spain and in Italy above all that the race of *stryges*, *lamiæ* and *empusæ* abounded, even at a late period; those who doubt should consult the most experienced criminologists of these countries, digested by Franciscus Torreblanca,[1] Roual Advocate of the Chancelry of Granada, in his *Epitome Delictorum*.

Medea and Circe are the types of Malefic Magic among the Greeks. Circe is the vicious female who bewitches and debases her lovers; Medea is the brazen poisoner who dares everything and makes Nature itself the abettor of her crimes. There are actually creatures who enchant like Circe and whose proximity defiles. They can inspire nothing but brutal passions; they exhaust and then disdain you. They must be treated according to the policy of Ulysses, by compelling them to obedience through fear and by being able to leave them in the end without regret. They are beautiful, heartless monsters and their vanity is their whole life. They were depicted by antiquity in the form of syrens.

As to Medea, she is perversity incarnate, willing and working evil. She is capable of love and does not yield to fear, but her love is more terrible than her hate. She is a bad mother and the destroyer of children; she loves the night and under the rays of the moon she gathers noxious herbs for the brewing of poisons. She magnetises the air, brings dole to earth, infects water and makes even the fire venomous. Reptiles provide her with their skins; she mutters frightful words; the track of blood follows her; and mutilated limbs fall from her hands. Her counsels madden, her caresses beget horror.

Such is the woman who has sought to rise beyond the duties of her sex by familiarity with forbidden sciences. Men avoid her, children hide when she passes. She is devoid of reason, devoid of true love, and the stratagems of Nature in revolt against her are the ever-renewing torment of her pride.

---

[1] Almost any of the demonologists will serve at need. The Jesuit Martinus Delrio who wrote *Disquisitionum Magicarum Libri Sex* has plenty to say about *Lamiæ* and *Stryges*. There is also Joannes Wierus, the pupil of Cornelius Agrippa, whose famous work on the Illusions and Impostures of Sorcery—*Histoires, Disputes et Discours*—was rendered from Latin into French in 1885.

CHAPTER VI

MATHEMATICAL MAGIC OF PYTHAGORAS

HE who initiated Numa, and of whose proficiency in Magic something has been said already, was a personage known as Tarchon, himself the disciple of a Chaldean named Tages. Science had then its apostles who went to and fro in the world, making priests and kings therein. Not infrequently persecution itself was overruled to fulfil the designs of Providence, and so it came about towards the seventy-second Olympiad, or four generations after the reign of Numa, that Pythagoras of Samos sought a refuge in Italy from the tyranny of Polycrates. The great promoter of the philosophy of numbers had visited all the sanctuaries of the world and had even been in Judæa, where he suffered circumcision[1] as the price of his admission into the mysteries of the Kabalah, communicated to him, though not without a certain reserve, by the prophets Ezekiel and Daniel. Subsequently, but again not without difficulty, he obtained Egyptian initiation, being recommended by the King Amasis. The capacities of his own genius supplemented the imperfect revelations of the hierophants, so that he became himself a master and one who expounded the mysteries.

Pythagoras defined God as a living and absolute truth clothed in light; he defined the Word as number manifested by form; and he derived all things from the *Tetractys*—that is to say, the tetrad. He said also that God is supreme music, the nature of which is harmony. Religion was, according to him, the highest expression of justice; medicine was the most perfect practice of science; the beautiful was harmony; force, reason; felicity, perfection; while truth in application consisted in distrusting the weakness and perversity of men.

When he made his dwelling at Crotona, the magistrates of that city, seeing that he exercised so great an influence over minds and hearts, were at first in some anxiety concerning him; but ultimately they sought his advice. Pythagoras counselled them to cultivate the muses and maintain the most perfect accord among themselves, because feuds between masters fomented rebellion among servants. Thereafter he imparted to them his grand religious, political and social precept: There is no evil which is not to be preferred before anarchy—an axiom of universal application and

---

[1] I do not know how this fable originated and the question is not worth the pains which would be necessary to elucidate it. It is narrated by Éliphas Lévi as matter of historical fact; but there is no question that M. Edouard Schuré, who owes so much to the occultist who preceded him, would have been glad to include it in his romantic biography of Pythagoras, if it had not been too mythical even for his purpose. He is content as it is to suggest that the sage of Samos had studied Jewish monotheism during a stay of twelve years at Babylon.

almost infinite depth, though one which even our own age is not as yet sufficiently enlightened to understand.

Outside the traditions of his life, the remains of Pythagoras are his Golden Verses and his Symbols, of which the former have passed into commonplaces of popular morality, so great has been their success through the ages. They have been rendered as follows:[1]

"First worship the immortal gods as they are established and ordained by the Law. Reverence the oath and next the heroes, full of goodness and light. . . . Honour likewise thy parents, and those most nearly related to thee. Of all the rest of mankind, make him thy friend who distinguishes himself by his virtue. Always give ear to his mild exhortations, and take example from his virtuous and useful actions. Avoid as much as possible hating thy friend for a slight fault. Understand that power is a near neighbour to necessity. . . . Overcome and vanquish these passions—gluttony, sloth, sensuality, and anger. Do nothing evil, neither in the presence of others nor privately, and above all things respect thyself. In the next place, observe justice in thy actions and in thy words. . . . The goods of fortune are uncertain; as they may be acquired, so may they likewise be lost. Always make this reflection, that it is ordained by destiny that all men shall die. . . . Support with patience thy lot, be it what it may, and never repine at it; but endeavour what thou canst to remedy it. Consider that fate does not send the greatest portion of these misfortunes to good men. . . . Let no man by his words or by his deeds seduce thee, nor entice thee to say or to do what is not profitable for thyself. Consult and deliberate before thou act, that thou mayst not commit foolish actions. For it is the part of a miserable man to speak and to act without reflection. But do that which will not afflict thee afterwards, nor oblige thee to repentance. Never do anything which thou dost not understand; but learn all that thou oughtest to know, and by that means thou wilt lead a very pleasant life. In no wise neglect the health of thy body; but give it drink and meat in due measure, and also the exercise of which it has need. . . . Accustom thyself to a way of living that is neat and decent without luxury. . . . Do only the things which cannot hurt thee, and deliberate before thou dost them. Never suffer sleep to close thy eyelids, after thy going to bed, till thou hast examined by thy reason all thine actions of the day. Wherein have I done amiss? What have I done? What have I omitted that I ought to have done?"

Up to this point the Golden Verses seem to be only the instructions of a schoolmaster. They bear, however, a very different construction. They are the preliminary laws of magical initiation, which constitute the first

---

[1] The authorship of the *Golden Verses* is of course a debated point; and it is an old suggestion that their real writer was Lysis, the preceptor of Epaminondas and an exponent of Pythagorean philosophy about 388 B.C., his master being referred to the beginning of the sixth century B.C. I should add that Éliphas Lévi has presented the Verses in a metrical form of his own, which reflects the originals at a very far distance. I have not followed this rendering but have had recourse to that of Mr. G. R. S. Mead.

part of the Great Work, that is to say the creation of the perfect adept. This is proved by the following verses:

"I swear by him who has transmitted into our souls the Sacred Quaternion, the source of nature, whose cause is eternal. Never begin to set thy hand to any work till thou hast prayed the gods to accomplish what thou art going to begin. When thou hast made this habit familiar to thee thou wilt know the constitution of the Immortal Gods and of men. Even how far the different beings extend, and what contains and binds them together ... and nothing in this world shall be hid from thee. ... O Jupiter, our Father! if thou wouldst deliver men from all the evils that oppress them, shew them of what daimon they make use. But take courage; the race of men is divine. ... When, having divested thyself of thy mortal body, thou arrivest at the most pure Æther, thou shalt be a god, immortal, incorruptible, and death shall have no more dominion over thee."

Pythagoras said otherwise: "As there are three divine concepts and three intelligible realms, so is there a triple word, because hierarchic order is ever manifested by the triad. There are (a) simple speech, (b) hieroglyphical speech and (c) symbolical speech. In other terms, there is the word which expresses, there is the concealing and, finally, there is the word that signifies: all hieratic intelligence in in the perfect science of these three degrees." After this manner he enshrined doctrine in symbols, but eschewing personifications and images, which, in his opinion, begot idolatry sooner or later. He has been even charged with detestation of poets, but it was the makers of bad verses to whom he forbade the art: "Thou who hast no harp, seek not to sing in measures," he says in his symbols. A man so great as he could never disregard the exact correspondence between sublime thoughts and beautiful figurative expressions; indeed his own symbols are full of poetry: "Do not scatter the flowers of which crowns are made." In such terms he exhorts his disciples never to diminish glory and never to flout that which it seems good for the world to honour.

Pythagoras was chaste, but, far from commanding celibacy to his disciples, he married on his own part and had children. A beautiful saying of his wife has remained in memory: she had been asked whether purification was not requisite in a woman after intercourse with a man, and in such case after what lapse of time she might regard herself as sufficiently purified to approach holy things. She replied: "Immediately, if it be with her husband; but if it be with another, never."

The same severity of principles, the same purity of manners, qualified in the school of Pythagoras for initiation into the mysteries of Nature and so was attained that empire over self by which the elementary powers could be governed. Pythagoras possessed the faculty which by us is termed second sight and was known then as divination. Being with his disciples one day on the seashore, a vessel appeared on the horizon. "Master," said one of the companions, "would it mean wealth if they gave me the cargo carried by that ship?" "To you it would be more than useless." Pythagoras answered. "In such case I would keep it for my heirs." "Would you wish to bequeathe them two corpses?" The vessel came into port and proved to be bearing the body of a man who desired to be buried in his own country.

It is related furthermore that beasts were obedient to Pythagoras. Once in the middle of the Olympic Games he signalled to an eagle winging its way through heaven; the bird descended, wheeling circle-wise, and again took rapid flight at the master's token of dismissal. There was also a great bear, ravaging in Apulia; Pythagoras brought it to his feet and told it to leave the country. It disappeared accordingly, and when asked to what knowledge he owed such a marvellous power, he answered: "To the science of light." Animated beings are, in fact, incarnations of light. Out of the darkness of ugliness forms emerge and move progressively towards the splendours of beauty; instincts are in correspondence with forms; and man, who is the synthesis of that light whereof animals may be termed the analysis, is created to command them. It has come about, however, that in place of ruling as their master, he has become their persecutor and destroyer, so that they fear and have rebelled against him. In the presence of an exceptional will which is at once benevolent and directing they are completely magnetised, and a host of modern phenomena both can and should enable us to understand the possibility of miracles like those of Pythagoras.

Physiognomists have observed that the majority of men have a certain facial resemblance to one or another animal. It may be a matter of imagination only, produced by the impression to which various physiognomies give rise, and revealing some prominent personal characteristics. A morose man is thus reminiscent of a bear, a hypocrite has the look of a cat, and so of the rest. These kinds of judgments are magnified in the imagination and exaggerated still further in dreams, when people who have affected us disagreeably during the waking state transform into animals and cause us to experience all the agonies of nightmare. Now, animals—as much as ourselves and more even than we—are under the rule of imagination, while they are devoid of that judgment by which we can check its errors. Hence they are affected towards us according to the sympathies or antipathies which are excited by our own magnetism. They are, moreover, unconscious of that which underlies the human form and they regard us only as other animals by whom they are dominated, the dog taking his master for a dog more perfect than himself. The secret of dominion over animals lies in the management of this instinct. We have seen a famous tamer of wild beasts fascinate his lions by exhibiting a terrible countenance and acting himself as if he were a lion enraged. Here is a literal application of the popular proverb which tells us to howl with the wolves and bleat with the sheep. It must also be realized that every animal form manifests a particular instinct, aptitude or vice. If we suffer the character of the beast to predominate within us, we shall tend to assume its external guise in an ever-increasing degree and shall even come to impress its perfect image on the Astral Light; more even than this, when we fall into dreams or ecstasy, we shall see ourselves as ecstatics and somnambulists would see us and as we must appear undoubtedly in the eyes of animals. Let it happen in such cases that reason be extinguished, that persistent dreams change into madness, and we shall be turned into beasts like Nebuchadnezzar. This explains those stories of were-wolves, some of which have been legally established. The facts were beyond dispute, but the witnesses were not less hallucinated than the were-wolves themselves.[1]

Cases of coincidence and correspondence in the dream-state are neither rare nor extraordinary. Persons in the state of magnetic ecstasy can see and talk to one another from opposite ends of the earth. We ourselves may meet someone for the first time and he or she will seem to be an old acquaintance because we have encountered frequently in dream. Life is full of these curious occurrences, and as regards the transformation of human beings into animals the evidences are on every side. How many aged courtesans and gluttonous females, reduced almost to idiocy after threading all sewers of existence, are nothing but old she-cats egregiously enamoured of their tom?

Pythagoras believed above all things in the soul's immortality and in the perpetuity of life. The endless succession of summer and winter, day and night, sleeping and waking, illustrated amply for him the phenomenon of death. For him also the particular immortality of human souls consisted in persistence of memory. He is said to have been conscious of his previous incarnations, and if the report is true it was something suggested by his reminiscences, for such a man as he could have been neither impostor nor fool.[2] It is probable that he came upon former memories in his dreams, while simple speculation and hypothesis have been constructed

[1] Among the appendices to the second part of the *Zohar* there is a short section on physiognomy, and it embodies some very curious materials. We learn, for example, that if a man who has certain specified characteristics of colour and feature should turn to God, a white blemish will form on the pupil of his right eye. He who has three semi-circular wrinkles on his forehead and whose eyes are shining will behold the downfall of his enemies. A man who has committed an adultery and has not repented is recognisable by a growth beneath the navel, and thereon will be found two hairs. Should he do penance, the hairs will disappear but the swelling will remain. A man who has a beauty-spot on his ear will be a great master of the Law and will die young. Two long hairs between the shoulders indicate a person who is given to swearing incessantly in an objectless manner. It will be seen that these details belong to a neglected part of the science, and I am a little at a loss to know how Éliphas Lévi would have pressed them into his service, if he had been fully acquainted with the work which he quotes so often.

[2] It happens that the hypothesis of reincarnation was personally unwelcome to Éliphas Lévi, and he did not know enough of Zoharic Kabalism to realise that it is of some importance therein. The traditions concerning the teaching of Pythagoras must be taken at their proper value, but there is no question that, according to these, he was an important champion of what used to be called the doctrine of metempsychosis, understood as the soul's transmigration into successive bodies. He himself had been (*a*) Æthalides, a son of Mercury; (*b*) Euphorbus, son of Panthus, who perished at the hands of Menelaus in the Trojan war; (*c*) Hermotimus, a prophet of Clazomenæ, a city of Ionia; (*d*) a humble fisherman, and finally (*e*) the philosopher of Samos.

as positive affirmation on his part. However this may be, his thought was great, for the real life of our individuality consists in memory alone. Those waters of Lethe pictured by the ancients were the true philosophical type of death. The Bible appears to impart a divine sanction to this idea when it is said in the Book of Psalms that "the just shall be in everlasting remembrance".[1]

---

[1] *In memoria æterna erit iustus.*

CHAPTER VII

THE HOLY KABALAH

LET us now have recourse to the origin of true science by recurring to the Holy Kabalah, or tradition of the children of Seth, taken from Chaldea by Abraham, communicated by Joseph to the Egyptian priesthood, ingarnered by Moses, concealed by symbols in the Bible, revealed by the Saviour to St. John, and embodied in its fulness in hieratic images, analogous to those of all antiquity, in the Apocalypse of this Apostle.

Whatsoever was in kinship with idolatry was held in detestation by the Kabalists, which notwithstanding, God is represented by them under a human figure, but it is purely hieroglyphical. For them He is the intelligent, the loving, the living infinite. He is neither the totality of all beings, nor being in abstraction, nor a being who is philosophically definable. He is in all things, being more and greater than all. His very name is ineffable, and yet this name gives expression only to the human ideal of His divinity.[1] It is not possible for man to understand God in Himself. He is the absolute of faith, but the absolute of reason is Being. Being is self-existent and is because it is. The cause of Being is Being itself. It is matter of legitimate speculation why this or that exists, but it would be absurd to inquire why Being is, for it would be to postulate Being as antecedent to Being.

It is demonstrated by reason and science that the modes of existence in Being are equilibrated in accordance with harmonious and hierarchic laws. Now the hierarchy is graduated on an ascending scale, becoming more and more monarchic. At the same time reason cannot pause in the presence of one absolute chief without being overwhelmed by the heights which it discerns above this supreme king; it takes refuge therefore in silence and gives place to adoring faith. That which is certain, for science and for reason alike, is that the idea of God is the grandest, most holy and most serviceable of all aspirations in man; that mortality and its eternal sanction repose on this belief. In humanity it is therefore the most real phenomenon of being, and if it were false, therefore, Nature would formulate the absurd, the void would affirm life, and it might be said at one and the same time that there was God and there was no God. It is to this philosophical and incontestable reality, or otherwise the notion of Deity, that the Kabalists give a name, and all other names are contained

---

[1] Éliphas Lévi has forgotten that the word "ineffable" means something which cannot be expressed; he intended to say that, according to the Kabalists, the efficacious name was hidden.

THE DERIVATIONS OF MAGIC

therein.[1] The ciphers of this name produce all numbers and the hieroglyphical forms of its letters give expression to all laws of Nature, with all that is therein. We shall not recur in this place to that which has been dealt with already as regards the divine Tetragram in the *Doctrine of Transcendental Magic*; but it may be added that the Kabalists inscribe it in four chief ways: (1) as יהוה, JHVH, which is spelt but not pronounced. The consonants are YOD, HE, VAU, HE, and they are rendered as JEHOVAH by us in opposition to all analogy, for the Tetragrammaton so disfigured is composed of six letters.[2] (2) אדני, ADNI, meaning Lord and pronounced by us ADONAI.[3] (3) אהיה, AHIH, which signifies Being and is pronounced by us EIEIE![4] (4) אגלא, AGLA, pronounced as it is written and comprising hieroglyphically all mysteries of the Kabalah.[5]

The letter *Aleph*, א is the first of the Hebrew alphabet, and expressing as it does unity, it represents hieroglyphically the dogma of Hermes: that which is above is analogous to that which is below. In consonance with this the letter has two arms, one of which points to earth and the other to heaven with an identical gesture. The letter *Gimel*, ג, is third in the alphabet; it expresses the triad numerically, and hieroglyphically it signifies childbirth, fruitfulness. Lamed, ל, is the twelfth letter and is an expression of the perfect cycle. Considered as a hieroglyphical sign it represents the circulation of the perpetual movement and the relation of the radius to the circumference. The duplicated *Aleph* represents the synthesis. Therefore the name AGLA signifies: (1) unity, which accomplishes by the triad the cycle of numbers, leading back to unity. (2) The fruitful principle of Nature, which is one therewith. (3) The primal truth which fertilises science and restores it to unity. (4) Syllepsis, analysis, science and syn-

---

[1] All later Kabalists agree that *Tetragrammaton* is the root and foundation of the Divine Names. In the Sephirotic system one of the allocations makes *Chokmah*, or Supernal Wisdom, to correspond with the *Yod* of Tetragrammaton. *Kether*, which is the Crown, is said to have no letter attributed thereto, because the mystery of *Ain Soph*, the hidden abyss of the Godhead, is implied therein. However, the apex of *Yod* does in a sense intimate concerning *Kether*. *He* is the second letter in the Divine Tetrad, and it is ascribed to *Binah*, or Supernal Understanding, wherein is all life comprehended. This is the abode of the *Shekinah* in transcendence. The third letter is *Vau*, and it is said to contain the six *Sephiroth* from *Chesed* to *Yesod*. The second *He* is the fourth and last letter; it corresponds to *Malkuth*, or the Kingdom, wherein is the mystery of the unity of God. This is the abode of the *Shekinah* in manifestation. Thus, *Yod*, *He*, *Vau*, *He*, which we render Jehovah, contains all the ten *Sephiroth*. There are, however, other allocations.

[2] Éliphas Lévi must have meant to say seven letters, but the point does not signify. According to Rosenroth, the Tetragrammaton with vowel-points is the eighth Divine Name—יְהֹוָה. The points are those of *Elohim* and it is read as that Name. This signifies the concealment of the "Ineffable" Name, on account of the exile of Israel.

[3] This is the Divine Name which is most in proximity to created things. See the excursus thereon in *Kabbala Denudata*, vol. i, pp. 32–41.

[4] Cf. the *Zohar*, Part I, fol. 15a, on Exodus iii, 14: "And God said unto Moses: I am that I am"—אהיה אשר אהיה.

[5] According to the Rabbinical Lexicon of Buxtorf, *Agla* is formed from the initial letters of the sentence אתה גבור לעולם אדני = *Tu potens es in sæculum, Domine*. There seems to be no Kabalistic authority for its explanation by Lévi, and the word occurs very seldom in the *Zohar*.

thesis. (5) The Three Divine Persons Who are one God; the secret of the Great Work, which is the fixation of the Astral Light by a sovereign act of will and is represented by the adepts as a serpent pierced with an arrow, thus forming the letter *Aleph*. (6) The three operations of dissolution, sublimation and fixation, corresponding to the three essential substances, Salt, Sulphur and Mercury—the whole being expressed by the letter *Gimel*. (7) The twelve keys of Basil Valentine, represented by *Lamed*. (8) Finally, the Work accomplished in conformity with its principle and reproducing the said principle.

Herein is the origin of that Kabalistic tradition which comprises all Magic in a single word. To know how this word is read and how also it is pronounced, or literally to understand its mysteries and translate the knowledge into action, is to have the key of miracles. In pronouncing the word AGLA it is said that one must turn to the East, which means union of intention and knowledge with oriental tradition. It should be remembered further that, according to Kabalah, the perfect word is the word realised by acts, whence comes that expression which recurs freqently in the Bible: *facere verbum*, to make a word—that is, in the sense of performing an act. To pronounce the word AGLA Kabalistically is therefore to pass all tests of initiation and accomplish all its works.[1]

It has been said in the *Doctrine of Transcendental Magic* that the name Jehovah resolves into seventy-two explicatory names, called *Shemahamphorash*.[2] The art of employing these seventy-two names and discovering therein the keys of universal science is the art which is called by Kabalists the Keys of Solomon. As a fact, at the end of the collections of prayers and evocations which bear this title there are found usually seventy-two magical circles, making thirty-six talismans, or four times nine, being the absolute number multiplied by the tetrad. Each of these talismans bears two of the two-and-seventy names, the sign emblematical of their number and that of the four letters of Tetragrammaton to which they correspond. From this have originated the four emblematical Tarot suits: the Wand, representing the *Yod*; the Cup, answering to the *He*; the Sword, referable to the *Vau*; and the Pentacle, in correspondence with the final *He*. The complement of the denary has been added in the Tarot, thus repeating synthetically the character of unity.[3]

[1] According to Petrus Galatinus, in *De Arcanis Catholicæ Veritatis*, the word *Agla* expresses the infinite power of the Divine Trinity. Like Éliphas Lévi, he gives us the separate significance of each letter and, like Buxtorf, he makes them the initials of the sentence already quoted, his rendering being: *Tu potens in æternum Dominus*. He terms *Agla Nomen Dei*, for which there seems to be as much and as little authority as there is for the suggestion that the *Divina potentia* is that of the Trinity.

[2] A very full exposition of this Name will be found in the section entitled *De Cabala Hebræorum*, forming part of Kircher's *magnum opus*, the *Œdipus Ægyptiacus*. It is curious that a tract so important as this, within its own measures, and written with the uttermost simplicity, does not appear to have been translated, even into the French language.

[3] I must admit that this reference escapes me. The Tarot consists of four suits of 14 cards each and there are 22 Trumps Major, making 78 cards in all.

Pantacle of Kabalistic Letters

The popular traditions of Magic affirm that he who possesses the Keys of Solomon can communicate with spirits of all grades and can exact obedience on the part of all natural forces. These Keys, so often lost, and as often recovered, are no other than the talismans of the seventy-two names and the mysteries of the thirty-two hieroglyphical paths, reproduced by the Tarot. By the aid of these signs and by their infinite combinations, which are like those of numbers and letters, it is possible to arrive at the natural and mathematical revelation of all secrets of Nature, and it is in this sense that communication is established with the whole hierarchy of intelligence.

The Kabalists in their wisdom were on their guard against the dreams of imagination and hallucinations of the waking state. Therefore they avoided in particular all unhealthy evocations which disturb the nervous system and intoxicate reason. Makers of curious experiments in phenomena of extranatural vision are no better than the eaters of opium and hasheesh. They are children who injure themselves recklessly. It may happen that one is overtaken by intoxication; we may even so far forget ourselves voluntarily as to seek the experience of drunkenness, but for the man who respects himself a single instance suffices. Count Joseph de Maistre says that one of these days we shall deride our present stupidity, much as we deride the barbarity of the middle ages. What would he think, did he see our table-turners or listen to makers of hypotheses concerning the world of spirits? Poor creatures that we are, we escape from one absurdity by rushing over to its opposite. The eighteenth century thought that it protested against superstition by denying religion, and we in return testify to the impiety of that period by believing in old wives' fables. Is it impossible to be a better Christian than Voltaire and still not believe in ghosts? The dead can no more revisit this earth which they have quitted than a child can return into the womb of its mother.[1] That which we call death is birth into a new life. Nature does not repeat what it has once done in the order of necessary progression through the scale of existence, and she cannot bely her own fundamental laws. Limited by its organs and served by these, the human soul can enter into communication with things of the visible world only by the intermediation of these organs. The body is an envelope adjusted to the physical environments in which the soul abides here. By confining the action of the soul it makes her activity possible. In the absence of body the soul would be everywhere, and yet in so attenuated a sense that it could act nowhere, but, lost in the infinite, would be swallowed up and annihilated in God.[2] Imagine a drop of fresh water shut

---

[1] The axiom has rather a convincing air, but the analogy is wrong, and the word "return" is a blunder of popular speech. The possibility of communication with those who have left this life is a question of the interpenetration of worlds. To say that the human spirit departs or comes back is a symbolic expression, like the statement that heaven is above us.
[2] The analogy is again wrong and the creation of a materialistic mind. The return of the soul to God is not annihilation but life for evermore, and it is union with all life.

up in a globule and cast in the sea; as long as that sheath is preserved intact, the drop of water will subsist in its separate form, but let the globule be broken and where shall we look for the drop in the vast sea?

In creating spirits, God could endow them with self-conscious personality only by their restriction in an envelope, so as to centralise their action and by restriction save it from being lost. When the soul separates from the body it changes environment of necessity, since it changes the envelope.[1] It goes forth clothed only in the astral form, or vehicle of light, ascending in virtue of its nature above the atmosphere, as air rises from the water in escaping from a broken vessel. We say that the soul ascends because the vehicle ascends and because action and consciousness are both attached thereto.[2] The atmospheric air becomes solid for luciform bodies which are infinitely rarer than itself, and they could only come down by assuming a grosser vehicle. Where would they obtain this in the region above our atmosphere? They could only return to earth by means of another incarnation, and such return would be a lapse, for they would be renouncing the state of free spirit and renewing their novitiate. The possibility of such a return is not admitted, moreover, by the catholic religion.

The doctrine here set forth is formulated by the Kabalists in a single axiom: The spirit clothes itself to come down and unclothes itself to go up. The life of intelligence is ascensional. In the body of its mother the child has a vegetative life and draws nourishment through a cord to which it is attached, as the tree is attached to the earth by its root and is also nourished thereby. When the child passes from vegetative to instinctive and animal life, the cord breaks and henceforth he has free motion. When the child becomes man he escapes from the trammels of instinct and can act as a reasonable being. When the man dies he is liberated from the law of gravitation, by which he has been previously bound to earth. When the soul has expiated its offences it grows strong enough to emerge from the exterior darkness of the terrestrial atmosphere and mount towards the sun.[3] The unending ascent of the sacred ladder begins therein, for the eternity of the elect cannot be a state of idleness; they pass from virtue to virtue, from bliss to bliss, from victory to victory, from glory to glory. There is no break in the chain, and those of the superior degrees can still exercise an influence on those who are below, but it is in harmony with the hierarchic order and after the same way that a king who rules wisely does good to the humblest of his subjects. From stage to stage the prayers arise and the graces pour down, never mistaking the path. But spirits who have once gone up cannot again come down, for in proportion to their ascent the zones solidify below them. The great gulf is fixed, says Abraham, in the

---

[1] The soul sheds one envelope, in which it has prepared another.
[2] This expression may tend to confusion. The consciousness and activity of the soul are manifested by means of that vehicle in which it happens to reside. It is not they that belong to the vehicle, but it is the vehicle that is used by them.
[3] There is no Kabalistic authority for the sun as the abode of souls.

parable of the rich man, so that they which would pass from hence to you cannot.[1]

Ecstasy may so exalt the powers to the star-body that it can draw the material body after it, thus proving that the destiny of the soul is to ascend. The stories of aërial levitation are possible, but there is no instance of a man being able to live under the earth or in water. It would be not less impossible for a soul in separation from the body to subsist for a single moment in the density of our atmosphere. Therefore departed beings are not about us, as spiritists suppose. Those whom we love may see us and to us many still manifest, but only by mirage and reflection in the common mirror of the Astral Light. Furthermore, they can take interest no longer in mortal things; they hold to us only by that which is highest in our feelings and is in correspondence with their eternal mode.[2]

Such are the revelations of Kabalism as imbedded in the mysterious book of the Zohar; for science they are of course hypothetical, but they rest on a series of exact inductions and these inductions are drawn from facts uncontested by science.

We are brought at this point into touch with one of the most dangerous secrets in the domain of Magic, being the more than probable hypothesis concerning the existence of those fluidic *larvæ* known in ancient theurgy under the name of elementary spirits. Something has been said upon the subject in *The Doctrine and Ritual of Transcendental Magic*, and the ill-starred Abbé de Villars, who jested with these terrible revelations, paid for his imprudence with his life.[3] The reason that the secret is dangerous is because it verges on the great magical arcanum. The truth is that the evocation of elementary spirits implies power to coagulate fluids by a projection of the Astral Light, and this power, so directed, can produce only disorders and misfortunes, as will be shewn at a later stage. Meanwhile, the grounds of the hypothesis and the evidence of its probability follow: Spirit is everywhere, and is that which animates matter; it overcomes the force of gravity by perfecting the vehicle which is its form. We see every-

[1] Kabalism is silent on the question of communication with those who have left this life, though tacitly it must admit the possibility on the evidence of the case of Samuel. The axiom that the spirit clothes itself to come down and unclothes itself to go up is one of the so-called *conclusiones Kabbalisticæ* of Picus de Mirandula, but it is found substantially in the *Zohar*, and as regards the descent, this is just what occurs *ex hypothesi* in the phenomena of spiritistic materialisations. As regards the parable of the rich man, it has nothing to do with the question of so-called spirit-return; those who were in the bosom of Abraham had as much left this life as those who were in Sheol.

[2] It depends on those who have left us. What of the earthly and the evil? Why should the bond between them and us—supposing that there is a bond—be that of our highest feelings?

[3] The fact is that he was assassinated; the inference is that it was by or at the instance of those whose secrets he was supposed to have betrayed. The murderers, also by inference, were said to be Brethren of the Rosy Cross. It may be mentioned that the *Comte de Gabalis* contains the theory of communication with elementary spirits, being those of earth, air, fire and water; but the mode of treatment suggests that it is a *jeu d'esprit*. The *Nouveaux Entretiens sur les Sciences Secrètes, Les Genies-Assistants* and *Le Gnome Irréconcilable*, which are supposed sequels, are forgeries of later periods.

where around us how form develops with instincts, till intelligence and beauty are attained: these are efforts of the light attracted by the charm of the spirit; they are part of the mystery of progressive and universal generation.

The light is the efficient agent of forms and life, because it is both motion and heat. When fixed and polarised about a centre, it produces a living being and draws thereafter the plastic substance needed to perfect and preserve it. This plastic substance is, in the last analysis, formed of earth and water and, with good reason, is denominated slime of the earth in the Bible. But this light is in nowise spirit, as believed by the Indian hierophants and all schools of Göetia: it is only the spirit's instrument. Nor is it the body of the *protoplastes*, though so regarded by theurgists of the school of Alexandria. It is the first physical manifestation of the Divine Breath. God creates it eternally, and man, who is in the image of God, modifies and seems to multiply it.[1]

Prometheus, says the classical fable, having stolen fire from heaven, gave life thereby to images formed of earth and water, for which crime he was blasted and chained by Jupiter. Elementary spirits, say the Kabalists in their most secret books, are children of the solitude of Adam, born of his dreams when he yearned for the woman who as yet had not been given to him by God.[2] According to Paracelsus, the blood lost at certain regular periods by the female sex and the nocturnal emissions to which male celibates are subject in dream people the air with phantoms.[3] The hypothetical origin of *larvæ*, according to the masters, is here indicated with sufficient clearness and further explanation may be spared.

Such *larvæ* have an aërial body formed from vapour of blood, for which reason they are attracted towards spilt blood and in older days drew nourishment from the smoke of sacrifices. They are those monstrous offspring of nightmare which used to be called *incubi* and *succubi*. When sufficiently condensed to be visible, they are as a vapour tinged by the reflection of an image; they have no personal life, but they mimic that of the magus who evokes them, as the shadow images the body. They collect

---

[1] Elsewhere in his works Éliphas Lévi says that the Astral Light is (*a*) the *Od* of the Hebrews, (*b*) an electro-magnetic ether, (*c*) a vital and luminous caloric, (*d*) the instrument of life, (*e*) the instrument of the omnipotence of Adam, (*f*) the universal glass of visions. It follows the law of magnetic currents, is subject to fixation by a supreme projection of will-power, is the first envelope of the soul, and the mirror of imagination. He terms it also magnetised electricity. It would seem that his contemporary disciples in France have abandoned the theory of their master, or perhaps I should say rather its doctrinal part. On the other hand, it has perhaps reappeared, under theosophical auspices, as the reservoir of the akasic records.

[2] There are also references to Lilith, a demon-wife of Adam, in the *Zohar*; she is called the instigator of chastisements and was really the wife of Samael, the evil angel. It may be added that, according to Paracelsus, the elementaries *non sunt progeniti ex Adamo* See *Liber de Nymphis, Sulphis, Pygmæis et Salamandris, Tract. I, cap.* 1.

[3] In respect of male celibates, the physiological particulars referred to are the blind yearning of Nature after the nuptial state and, with a téntative reserve in respect of the life of sanctity, it is shame to those who neglect the warning or turn it to the account of sin.

above all about idiots and those immoral creatures whose isolation abandons them to irregular habits. The cohesion of parts being very slight in their fantastic bodies, they fear the open air, a great fire and above all the point of a sword. They become, in a manner, as vapourous appendages to the real bodies of their parents, since they live only by drawing on the life either of those who have created them or those who appropriate them by their evocation. It may come about in this manner that if these shadows of bodies be wounded, their parent may be maimed in real earnest, even as the unborn child may be hurt and disfigured by the imaginations of its mother. The world is full of such phenomena; they justify these strange revelations and can only be explained thereby.

Such *larvæ* draw the vital heat of persons in good health and they drain those who are weak rapidly. Hence come the histories of vampires, things of terrific reality which have been substantiated from time to time, as it is well known. This explains also why in the neighbourhood of mediums, who are persons obsessed by *larvæ*, one is conscious of a cooling in the atmosphere. Seeing that their existence is due to the illusions of imagination and divagation of the senses, such creatures never manifest in the presence of a person who can unveil the mystery of their monstrous birth.

BOOK II

FORMATION AND DEVELOPMENT OF DOGMAS

ב—BETH

CHAPTER I

PRIMITIVE SYMBOLISM OF HISTORY

To explain Holy Scripture from the religious and dogmatic standpoint forms no part of our warrant. Subject above all things to the hierarchic order, we surrender theology to the doctors of the Church and we render to human science whatsoever is included in the domain of experience and reason. Therefore on those occasions when we may appear to be risking a new application of some biblical passage, it is always with proper respect for ecclesiastical decisions. We do not dogmatise on our own part, and we submit our observations and researches to the lawful authorities.

On reading the earliest history of the human race in the sacred work of Moses, that which strikes one at once is the description of the Earthly Paradise, which is summarised in the figure of a perfect pantacle. It is circular or square, since it is watered equally by four rivers arranged in the form of a cross, while in the centre are found two trees representing knowledge and life, stable intelligence and progressive motion, wisdom and creation.[1] The serpent of Asclepios and Hermes is coiled about the Tree; beneath its shadow are the man and woman, active and passive, intelligence and love. The serpent, symbolising the primal attraction and the central fire of the earth, tempts her who is the weaker, and she causes the man to succumb; yet to the serpent she yields only in order that she may overcome it subsequently: one day she will crush the head of it by giving a Saviour to the world. All science is represented in this admirable scene.[2]

[1] This is one construction of the symbol and is a little tinctured by Éliphas Lévi's sincere admiration for the understanding which lay behind the *Romance of the Rose*. The text of Genesis says that a river rose to water the Garden "and from thence it was parted and became into four heads", or four sources of rivers. These rivers did not water the Garden but the world without, and their names are familiar in the geography of the ancient world. The mystic pantacle of Eden shews therefore an enclosure constituted by a ring or circle of water, an island like that of Avalon, which is another Garden of Apples, and the waters flow out therefrom towards the four points of heaven: they form therefore a cross, and in the centre of that cross is the Paradise. If the reader will bear in mind that, according to the secret tradition, Adam was set to grow roses in the Garden of Eden, he will understand at what place of the world the symbolism of the Rosy Cross takes its origin.

[2] This is true, but it is only the science of this world in the sense that the greater includes the lesser. It is really the supernal knowledge which is called *Daath* in Kabalism, arising from the union of *Chokmah* and *Binah*, or Wisdom and Understanding.

The man abdicates the realm of intelligence by yielding to the solicitations of the sensitive part; he profanes the fruit of knowledge, which should be the sustenance of the soul, by applying it to the uses of unjust and material satisfaction; he loses in consequence the sense of harmony and of truth. He is clothed thereafter with the skin of a beast, because the physical form takes shape sooner or later, and invariably, in correspondence to moral dispositions. He is cast out of the circle which is watered by the four rivers of life, and a cherub, armed with an ever-moving, burning sword, prevents his return into the domain of unity.

As we have observed in the *Doctrine of Magic*, Voltaire discovered that the Hebrew word for cherub signifies a bull, and was highly amused at the story. He might have been less entertained had he recognised in the angel with the head of a bull the image of an obscure symbolism and in the revolving sword of fire those flashes of ill-understood and illusory truth which provided, after the Fall, a pretext to the idolatry of nations. The burning sword typified also that light which man knew no longer how to direct, so that, instead of governing its force, he was made subject to its fatal influence. The great magical work, understood in an absolute sense, is the conquest and direction of the burning sword, and the cherub is the angel or soul of the earth, represented invariably under the figure of a bull in the Ancient Mysteries. Hence in Mithraic symbolism, the master of light is seen vanquishing the bull of earth and plunging into his flank that sword which sets free the life, represented by drops of blood.

The first consequence of Eve's sin is the death of Abel. By separating love from understanding she separated it also from power, and this, reduced to blindness and in the bondage of earthly desires, became jealous of love and slew it. The children of Cain perpetuated the crime of their father; the daughters whom they brought into the world were disastrously beautiful, but, being void of love, they were born for the damnation of angels[1] and for the scandal of the descendants of Seth.

After the deluge, and as a sequel to the prevarication of Ham, some part of the mystery of which has been already indicated, the children of men attempted to realise an insensate project, by constructing an universal pantacle and palace. It was a vast experiment in socialistic equality, and the phalansterium of Fourier is a sorry conception in comparison with the tower of Babel.[2] The latter was an active protestation against the

[1] The commentary of the *Zohar* on Genesis vi, 2—"the sons of God saw the daughters of men that they were fair"—affirms that the angels were cast out of heaven as soon as they had conceived the desire therein suggested. Aza and Azael were the chiefs of these fallen spirits. Subsequently they taught Magic to men.
[2] The design of the builders, according to the *Zohar*, Part I, fol. 75a, was to abandon the celestial domain for that of Satan. They desired to rebuild heaven, apparently in the likeness of their own evil desires. They were the same quality of souls as the "giants in the earth in those days" and "the mighty men which were of old, men of renown". See Genesis c. vi, v. 4 and *Zohar*, Part I, fol. 25b.

FORMATION AND DEVELOPMENT OF DOGMAS

hierarchy of knowledge, a citadel built against floods and tempests, a promontory from the elevation of which the deified people would soar above the atmosphere and its commotions. But one does not ascend to knowledge on ladders of stone; the hierarchic degrees of the spirit are not built with mortar like the stories of a tower. Against such a materialised hierarchy anarchy itself protested, and men ceased to understand one another—a fatal lesson and one misinterpreted utterly by those who in our own days have dreamed of another Babel. The negations of equality give answer to doctrines which are hierarchic only in the sense of brutality and materialism. Whenever the human race builds such a tower, the summit will be contested and the multitude will desert the base. To satisfy all ambitions, the summit must be broader than the base and the result an unstable edifice which will collapse at the smallest shock.

The scattering of men was the first result of the curse pronounced against the profane descendants of Ham, but the race of Canaan bore in a particular manner the burden of the malediction in question, which at a later period made all their posterity anathema.[1] That chastity which is the guardian of the family is also the distinctive character of hierarchic initiations; profanation and revolt are always unclean; they tend to promiscuity and infanticide. Desecration of the mysteries of birth and destruction of children were the basis of the religions of ancient Palestine, given over to the horrible rites of Black Magic; the black god of India, the monstrous priapic Rutrem, reigned therein under the name of Belphegor. The Talmudists and the Platonic Jew Philo recite things so shameful respecting the worship of this idol that they appeared incredible to the learned lawyer Seldenus. It is said to have been a bearded image, with gaping mouth and a tongue like a gigantic phallus; the worshippers exposed themselves without shame in the presence of such a visage and presented offerings of excrement. The idols of Moloch and Chamos were murderous machines which sometimes crushed unfortunate little children against their brazen breasts and sometimes consumed them in their red-hot arms. There was dancing to the sound of trumpets and tambourines, so that the cries of the victims were stifled, and these dances were led by the wretched mothers. Incest, sodomy and bestiality were the authorised practices among these infamous people, and even formed part of the sacred rites.

Such is the fatal consequence of doing violence to universal harmony; one does not sin against truth with impunity. In revolt against God, man is driven to the outrage of Nature, despite himself. Identical causes ever produce the same effects, and the Sabbath of the Sorcerers in the middle

[1] Zoharic Kabalism was dissatisfied with the visitation of the offence of Ham on his apparently innocent son, Canaan, and it accounted for the malediction pronounced upon the latter by the fact that he had removed the *testes* from the person of his grandfather Noah. On the surface this is a ridiculous enormity, but it is a concealed intimation that the whole Noetic myth is, like Paradise itself, a mystery of sex shadowed forth in symbolism.

ages was but a repetition of the festivals of Chamos and Belphegor. It is against such crimes that a decree of eternal death is pronounced by Nature itself. Worshippers of black gods, apostles of promiscuity, preachers of public wantonness, enemies of the family and hierarchy, anarchists in religion and politics are enemies of God and humanity; not to isolate them from the world is to consent that the world shall be poisoned, or such at least was the view of inquisitors; but we are far on our own part from desiring to re-establish the cruel executions of the middle ages. In proportion as society shall become more truly Christian it will realise more fully that we must heal those who are diseased and not destroy them; now, criminal instincts are surely the most appalling of mental maladies.

It must not be forgotten that transcendental Magic is called the Sacerdotal Art and the Royal Art; in Egypt, Greece and Rome it shared the grandeur and decadence of the kingdom and the priesthood. Every philosophy which is at issue with the cultus and its mysteries is baneful to the great political powers, for these, in the eyes of the multitude, lose in grandeur if they cease to be symbols of Divine power. Every crown is broken which comes into collision with the tiara. The eternal dream of Prometheus is to steal fire from heaven and cast down the gods therefrom. The popular Prometheus, unbound on Caucasus by Hercules, who typifies labour, will ever bear about with him his rivets and chains; he will carry his undying vulture, fastened on his gaping wound, till he shall learn obedience at the feet of Him, Who, being born the King of kings and God of gods, has elected in His turn to be nailed in hands and feet and pierced in the side for the conversion of all rebellious spirits.

By opening the career of power to intrigue, republican institutions endangered the principles of the hierarchy. The task of forming kings was confided no longer to the hierarchy and was either replaced by right of inheritance—which abandons the throne to the unequal chances of birth—or by popular election—which sets aside religious influence to establish the monarchy on a basis of republican principles. Those governments which presided successively over the triumphs and humiliations of Greek and Roman states were formed in this manner. The science reserved to the sanctuaries fell into neglect, and men of boldness or genius, who had not been accepted by those who dispense initiation, devised another science in opposition to that of the priests, substituting doubt or denial for the secrets of the temple. In the excess of their adventurous imagination such philosophers were landed quickly in absurdity and laid upon Nature the blame which belonged to their own systems. Heraclitus fell a-weeping, Democritus took refuge in laughter, and the one was a fool like the other. Pyrrhon ended by believing in nothing, which can scarcely exonerate him for the fact that he knew nothing. Into this philosophical chaos Socrates brought a certain light and good sense, by affirming the existence of pure and simple morality.

The Twenty-first Key of the Tarot, surrounded by Mystic and Masonic Seals

But what does morality profit in the absence of religion? The abstract Deism of Socrates was interpreted by the people as atheism. It came about, however, that Plato, the disciple of Socrates, attempted to supply that system of doctrine which was wanting in the latter and of which indeed he had never dreamed.

The doctrine of Plato was epoch-making in the history of human genius, but it was not his own invention, for, realising that there is no truth apart from religion, he went to consult the priests of Memphis and to obtain initiation into their Mysteries. He is even credited with a knowledge of the Jewish sacred books.[1] In Egypt, however, his initiation could have been imperfect only, for the priests by that time had forgotten themselves the import of their primeval hieroglyphics, as is indicated by the history of that priest who spent three days in deciphering a hieratic inscription found in the tomb of Alcmene and sent by Agesilaus, King of Sparta. Cornuphis, who was doubtless the most learned among the hierophants, consulted the old collections of signs and characters; in the end he found that the inscription was in the script of *proteus*, being the Grecian name of the *Book of Thoth*, consisting of movable hieroglyphics, capable of variations as numerous as there are possible combinations of characters, numbers and elementary figures. But the *Book of Thoth*, being the key of oracles and the elementary work on science, should not have involved such long research before its signs were identified, if Cornuphis had been really proficient in the Sacerdotal Art. Another proof that primeval truths were obscured at this period is the fact that the oracles which registered their protest on the subject were in a style that was understood no longer.

After his return from Egypt, Plato was journeying with Simmias on the confines of Caria when he was met by some men of Delos, who begged him to interpret an oracle of Apollo. It declared that to make an end of the woes in Greece the cubic stone must be doubled. The attempt had been made with a stone kept in the temple of Apollo; but the work of doubling it on every side resulted in a polyhedron having twenty-five surfaces; to restore the cubic form they had to increase it twenty-six times the original volume of the stone, by a process of successive doubling. Plato sent back the emissaries to the mathematician Eudoxus,[2] saying that the oracle had counselled the study of geometry. Whether he did not himself understand the deep sense of the symbol or disdained to unveil it to the ignorant are points which must be left to conjecture; but that which is certain is that the cubic stone and its multiplication explains all secrets of sacred numbers, including the mystery of perpetual motion, hidden by adepts and pursued by fools under the name of

---

[1] It should be needless to say that this is a mere presumption and is not even founded on any legend concerning the travels of Plato. He is said to have been in Egypt for a period which has been estimated at thirteen years.

[2] He was a disciple of Plato who is supposed not only to have been illustrious for his knowledge of geometry but to have paid the usual pilgrim's visit to Egypt and to have returned an adept in astronomy.

squaring the circle.[1] By this cubic agglomeration of twenty-six cubes about a single central cube, the oracle indicated to the Delians not only the elements of geometry but the key of creative harmonies, explained by the inter-relation of forms and numbers. The plan of all great allegorical temples throughout antiquity is found in the multiplication (*a*) of the cube by the cross, (*b*) about which a circle is described, and then (*c*) the cubic cross moving in a globe. These notions, which are rendered more intelligible by a diagram, have been handed on to our own days in Masonic initiations, and they are a perfect justification of the name attributed to the modern societies in question, for they are also the root-principles of architecture and the science of building.

The Delians thought to answer the geometrical question by reducing their multiplication by half, but they had already obtained eight times the volume of their cubic stone. For the rest, the number of their experiments may be extended at will, for the story itself is probably a problem set to his disciples by Plato. If the utterance of the oracle has to be taken as a fact, we can find a still deeper meaning in it: to double the cubic stone is to extract the duad from unity, form from idea, action from thought. It is to realise in the world the exactitude of eternal mathematics, to establish politics on the basis of exact sciences, to harmonise religious dogma with the philosophy of numbers.

Plato has more eloquence but less depth than Pythagoras: he aspires to reconcile the philosophy of logicians with the immutable dogmas of seers; he does not seek to vulgarise but would reconstruct science. So was his philosophy destined at a later date to provide dawning Christianity with theories prepared beforehand and with vivifying doctrines. Notwithstanding, however, that he based his theorems on mathematics, Plato was poet rather than geometrician; he was rich in harmonious forms and was prodigal of marvellous hypotheses. Aristotle, who was a calculating genius exclusively, referred everything to debate in the schools; he made everything subject to the demonstrations of numeral evolutions and the logic of calculations. Excluding the faith of Platonism, he sought to prove all and likewise to comprehend all in his categories; he turned the triad into syllogism and the binary into enthymeme. For him the chain of being became a *sorites*. He reduced everything to an abstraction and reasoned on everything, being itself passed into an abstraction in his process and was lost amidst the hypotheses of ontology. Plato was destined to inspire the Fathers of the Church; Aristotle to be the master of mediæval scholastics; God knows what clouds gathered about this

---

[1] We have, unhappily, to remember that Éliphas Lévi himself wrote a great deal, and assuredly to little purpose, on the subject of squaring the circle and on perpetual motion. Elsewhere he tells us that the revolution of a square about its centre describes a circle, and thus the circle is squared. He also invented, in imagination, a clock which wound itself up in the process of running itself down, and this was perpetual motion—presumably, unless the mechanism happened to stop working or to wear itself out. The reader may settle for himself whether in these phantasies he was in hiding like an adept or pursuing like a fool.

logic which had no faith in anything and yet set out to explain all. A second Babel was in plan and another confusion of tongues was at no far distance. Being is being and in being is the reason of being. In the beginning is the Word and the Word, or Logos, is logic formulated in speech, or spoken reason. The Word is in God and the Word is God Himself manifested to intelligence. But this is precisely a truth which exceeds all philosophies and is that, also precisely, which must be believed, under the penalty of knowing nothing and falling back into the irrational doubt of Pyrrho. As guardian of faith, the priesthood rests entirely on this ground of science, and we are compelled to salute in its reaching the Divine principle of the Eternal Word.

CHAPTER II

MYSTICISM

THE legitimacy of Divine Right is so rooted in the priesthood that true priesthood does not exist apart from it. Initiation and consecration are a veritable heritage. So is the sanctuary inviolable on the part of the profane and so also it cannot be seized by sectarians. For the same reason the glorious lights of divine revelation are diffused in accordance with supreme reason, because they come down in order and harmony. God does not enlighten the world by means of meteors and flashes, but He causes every planetary system to gravitate about its particular sun. It is this very harmony which vexes certain souls, who have grown impatient with duty, and it is thus that people come forward to pose as reformers of morals, having failed in coercing revelation to concur with their vices. Like Rousseau, they exclaim: "If God has spoken, why have I heard nothing?" And then presently they add: "He has spoken, but it is to me." Such is their dream, and they end by believing it themselves. So do the makers of sects begin, and these are fomenters of religious anarchy: we would by no means condemn them to the flames, but it is certainly desirable to intern them as sufferers from contagious folly. It is precisely in this manner that those mystic schools were founded which brought about the profanation of science. We have seen how the Indian fakirs attained their so-called uncreated light—that is to say, by the help of erethism and cerebral congestion. Egypt had also its sorcerers and enchanters, while Thessaly, in the days of Greece, swarmed with conjurations and witchcraft. To enter into direct communication with deities is to suppress the priesthood and subvert the basis of the throne—a fact which is realised keenly by the anarchic instinct of pretended illuminism. It was by the allurement of licence that such conspirators looked to recruit disciples, giving absolution beforehand to every scandal in manners, on the condition of strictness in revolt and energy in protestation against sacerdotal legitimacy.[1]

The Bacchantes, who dismembered Orpheus, believed themselves inspired by a god, and they sacrificed the great hierophant to their deified drunkenness. The orgies of Bacchus were mystical tumults; the apostles of mania have always had recourse to disordered movements, frenetic agitations and horrible convulsions. From the effeminate priesthood of Bacchus to the Gnostics, from whirling dervishes to epileptics at the tomb of Paris the deacon, the characteristics of superstition and fanatic exaltation have been always the same. It has been invariably under the

[1] The only remark which is requisite on this chapter is that it involves throughout an abuse of the word Mysticism, which has nothing to do with religious anarchy, sects or magic. See, however, my preface to the present translation.

pretext of purifying doctrine and in the name of an exaggerated spiritualism that the mystics of all times have materialised the symbols of the cultus. It has been the same precisely with those who have profaned the science of the Magi, for transcendental Magic, as it is needful to remember, is the primeval priestly art. It condemns all that is done outside the lawful hierarchy, and it justifies the condemnation—though not the torture—of sectarians and sorcerers. The two classes are here connected intentionally, because all heretics have been evokers of spirits and phantoms, whom they have foisted upon the world as gods; all have arrogated to themselves the power of working miracles in support of their falsehoods. On these evidences they were all practisers of Göetic—that is to say, of Black Magic.

Anarchy being the point of departure and the palmary characteristic of dissident mysticism, religious concord is impossible between sectarians, and yet they are in astonishing unanimity upon a single point, being the hatred of hierarchic and lawful authority. This in reality is the whole root of their religion, as it is the sole bond which links them one to another. Is is ever the crime of Ham, contempt of the family principle and outrage offered to the father, whose nakedness and shame they expose with sacrilegious mirth. All the anarchic mystics confuse the Intellectual with the Astral Light; they worship the serpent instead of doing honour to that dutiful and pure wisdom which crushes its head. So are they intoxicated by vertigo and so fall inevitably into the abyss of folly.

All fools are visionaries, and may no doubt believe sincerely that they work wonders; indeed hallucination is contagious and things inexplicable occur, or seem to occur, frequently enough in their vicinity. Moreover, the phenomena of the Astral Light in the excess of its attraction or projection are themselves of a kind to confuse those who are half-educated. It is centralised in bodies and, as the result of violent molecular distention, it imparts to them so high a degree of elasticity that bones may be twisted and muscles stretched out of all measure. It forms whirlpools and waterspouts, so to speak, which levitate the heaviest bodies and can sustain them in the air for a length of time proportionate to the force of the projection. The sufferers feel on the point of bursting and cry for compression or percussion to relieve them. The most violent blows and the utmost constriction, being counterpoised by the fluidic tension, cause neither bruises nor wounds and relieve instead of crushing the patient.

As fools hold physicians in horror, so the hallucinated mystics detest wise men; they flee them in the first place and afterwards persecute them blindly, as if against their own will. In so far as they are mild and indulgent, it is in respect of vices; towards reason in submission to authority they are implacable; the most tolerant of heretics in appearance will be seized with fury and hatred if conformity and the hierarchy are mentioned. Hence heresies have led to disturbances invariably. The false prophet must slay if he cannot pervert. He clamours for tolerance towards himself

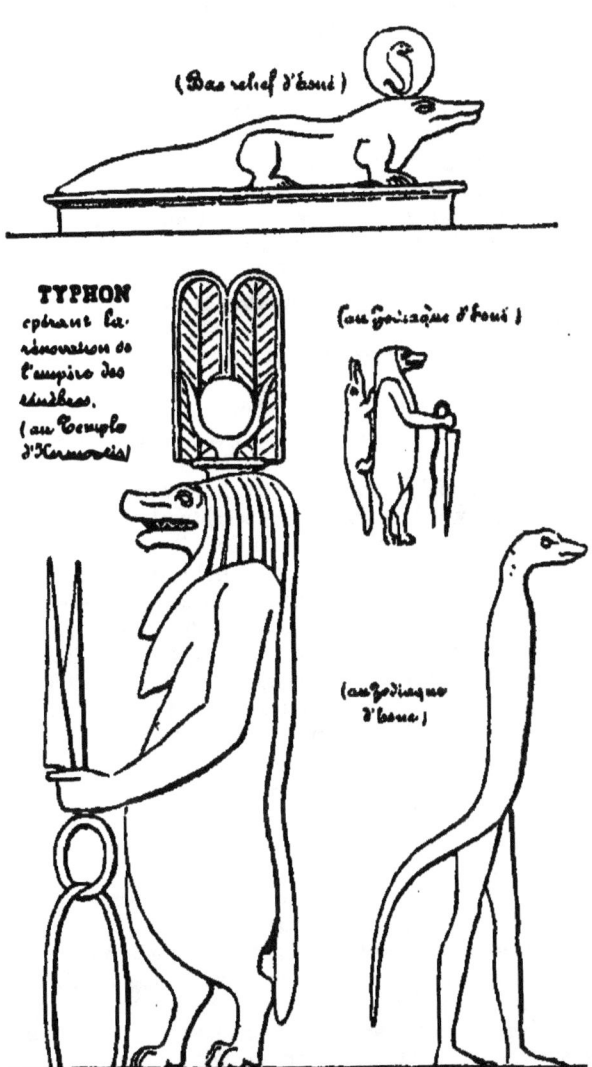

Egyptian Symbols of Typhon

but takes good care in what sense it shall be extended to others. Protestants were loud in their outcries against the faggots and pyres of Rome at the very time that John Calvin, on the warrant of his private judgment, condemned Servetus to be burnt. The crimes of the Donatists, Circumcisionists, and others too many for enumeration, drove Catholic rulers into excess and caused the Church to abandon those who were guilty to the secular arm. Would it not be thought that Vaudois, Albigensians and Hussites were lambs if one gave heed to the groans of irreligion? Where was the innocence of those darksome Puritans of Scotland and England who brandished the dagger in one hand and their Bible in the other, while preaching the extermination of Catholics? One only Church in the midst of so many reprisals and horrors has always postulated and in principle at least has maintained its hatred of blood: this is the hierarchic and legitimate Church.[1]

Now, in admitting the possibility and actuality of diabolical miracles, that Church recognises the existence of a natural force which can be applied for good or evil; and hence it has decided in its great wisdom that although sanctity of doctrine can legalise miracle, the latter of itself can never authorise novelties in religious teaching. To say that God, Whose laws are perfect and never falsify themselves, makes use of a natural instrument to produce effects which to us seem supernatural—this is to affirm the supreme reason and immutable power of God; it is to exalt our notion of His providence; and sincere Catholics should realise that such view by no means challenges His intervention in those marvels which operate in favour of truth. The false miracles caused by astral congestions have invariably an anarchic and immoral tendency, because disorder invokes disorder. So also the gods and familiars of heretics are athirst for blood and commonly extend their protection at the price of murder. The idolaters of Syria and Judea drew oracles from the heads of children torn from the bodies of the poor little victims. They dried these heads, and, having placed beneath the tongues a golden lamen bearing unknown characters, they fixed them in the hollows of walls, built up a kind of body beneath them composed of magical plants secured by bands, lighted a lamp at the foot of the frightful idols, burnt incense before them and proceeded to their religious consultation. They believed that the heads spoke, and the anguish of the last cries had doubtless distracted their imaginations; moreover, as said already, blood attracts *larvæ*. The ancients, in their infernal sacrifices, were accustomed to dig a pit, which they filled with warm and smoking blood; then from all the deep places of the night they beheld feeble and pallid shadows ascending, descending, creeping and swarming about the cavity. With a sword's point steeped in the same blood, they traced the circle of evocation and kindled fire

---

[1] The history of persecution may be left to speak for itself on the validity of this plea, and the postulated principle mentioned by Éliphas Lévi may even be thought to have concealed a stab from behind in the dark. In any case, the alleged horror of blood is best illustrated by the method of pyre and faggot.

of laurel, alder and cypress wood, on altars crowned with asphodel and vervain. The night seemed to grow colder and still more dark; the moon was hidden behind clouds; and they heard the feeble rustling of phantoms crowding about the circle, while dogs howled piteously over the countryside.

All must be dared in order to achieve all—such was the axiom of enchantments and their associated horrors. The false magicians were banded together by crime and believed that they could intimidate others when they had contrived to terrify themselves. The rites of Black Magic have remained revolting like the impious worships it produced; this was the case indifferently in the association of criminals who conspired against the old civilisations and among the barbaric races. There was always the same passion for darkness; there were the same profanations, the same sanguinary processes. Anarchic Magic is the cultus of death. The sorcerer devotes himself to fatality, abjures reason, renounces the hope of immortality, and then sacrifices children. He forswears marriage and is given over to barren debauch. On such conditions he enjoys the plenitude of his mania, is made drunk with iniquity till he believes that evil is omnipotent and, converting his hallucinations into reality, he thinks that his mastery has power to evoke at pleasure all death and Hades.

Barbarian words and signs unknown, or even utterly unmeaning, are the best in Black Magic.[1] Hallucination is insured more readily by ridiculous practices and imbecile evocations than by rites or *formulæ* which keep intelligence in a waking state. Du Potet says that he has tested the power of certain signs on ecstatics, and those which are published in his occult book, with precaution and mystery, are in analogy, if not absolutely identical, with pretended diabolical signatures found in old editions of the Grand Grimoire.[2] The same causes always produce the same effects, and there is nothing that is new beneath the moon of sorcerers, any more than under the sun of sages.

The state of permanent hallucination is death or abdication of consciousness, and one is then surrendered to all the chances comprised by the fatality of dreams. Every remembrance begets its own reflection, every evil desire creates an image, every remorse breeds a nightmare. Life becomes that of an animal, but of a peevish and tormented animal; the sense of morality and of time is alike absent; realities exist no longer; it is a general dance in the whirlpool of insensate forms. Sometimes an hour seems protracted over centuries, and again years may fly with an hour's swiftness.

Rendered phosphorescent by the Astral Light, our brains warm with

---

[1] "Change not the barbarous names of evocation," says one of the oracles attributed to Zoroaster, as we have seen, and the reason given is because of their "ineffable power". This was the true Zoroaster of Éliphas Lévi, and he was not, *ex hypothesi*, an exponent of Black Magic. "Barbarian words and signs unknown" are not less in favour with the so-called white variety.

[2] See my *Book of Ceremonial Magic*, pp. 100–102, for a study of this Grimoire.

innumerable reflections and images. We close our eyes, and it may happen that some brilliant, sombre or terrific panorama will unroll beneath our eyelids. He who is sick of a fever will scarcely close them through the night without being dazzled by an intolerable brightness. Our nervous system—which is a perfect electrical apparatus—concentrates the light in the brain, being the negative pole of that apparatus, or projects it by the extremities which are points designed for the circulation of our vital fluid. When the brain attracts powerfully some series of images analogous to any passion which has disturbed the equilibrium of the machine, the interchange of light stops, astral respiration ceases and the misdirected light coagulates, so to speak, in the brain. It comes about for this reason that the sensations of hallucinated persons are of the most false and perverse order. Some find enjoyment in lacerating the skin with thongs and in roasting their flesh slowly; others eat and relish things unfit for sustenance. Doctor Brierre de Boismont has collected a great series of instances, and many of them are extremely curious.[1] All excesses in life—whether through the misconstruction of good or through the non-resistance of evil—may overstimulate the brain and occasion the stagnation of light therein. Overweening ambition, proud pretence of sanctity, a continence full of scruples and desires, the indulgence of shameful passions notwithstanding repeated warnings of remorse —all these lead to syncope of reason, to morbid ecstasy, hysteria, vision, madness. The learned doctor goes on to observe that a man is not mad because he is subject to visions but because he believes in his visions rather than in ordinary sense. Hence it is obedience and authority that alone can save the mystics; if they have obstinate self-confidence there is no cure; they are excommunicated already by reason and by faith; they are the aliens of universal charity. They think themselves wiser than society; they dream of founding a religion, but they stand alone; they believe that they have secured for their private use the secret keys of life, but their intelligence is plunged already in death.

---

[1] The reference is to a work entitled *Des Hallucinations, ou Histoire raisonnée des Apparitions, des Visions, des Songes, de l'Extase, du Magnétisme et du Somnambulisme*. It was first published about 1850 and was of authority at its period. Its large array of materials will be always valuable. I believe that it was translated into English.

CHAPTER III

INITIATIONS AND ORDEALS

THAT which adepts have distinguished as the Great Work is not only the transmutation of metals but also and above all the Universal Medicine—that is to say, the remedy for all ills, including death itself. Now, the process which produces the Universal Medicine is the moral regeneration of man. It is that second birth alluded to by our Saviour in His discourse to Nicodemus, a doctor of the law. Nicodemus did not understand, and Jesus said: "Are you a master in Israel and know not these things?"—as if intending to intimate that they belonged to the fundamental principles of religious science, of which no professor could dare to be ignorant.[1]

The great mystery of life and its ordeals is represented in the celestial sphere and in the annual succession of the seasons. The four aspects of the sphinx correspond to these seasons and to the four elements. The symbolical figure on the shield of Achilles—according to the description of Homer—are analogous in their meaning to the Twelve Labours of Hercules. Like Hercules, Achilles must die, after having conquered the elements and even done battle with the gods. Hercules, on his part, triumphant over all the vices, represented by the monsters whom he fought, succumbs for a moment to love, the most dangerous of all. But he tears from his body the burning tunic of Dejanira, though the flesh comes with it from the bones; he leaves her guilty and vanquished, to die on his own part—but as one liberated and immortal.

Every thinking man is an Œdipus called to solve the enigma of the sphinx or, this failing, to die. Every initiate must become a Hercules, who, achieving the cycle of a great year of toil, shall, by sacrifices of heart and life, deserve the glory of apotheosis. Orpheus is not king of the lyre and of sacrifices till he has successively won and has learned how to lose Eurydice. Omphale and Dejanira are jealous of Hercules: one would debase him, the other yields to the counsels of an abandoned rival, and so is induced to poison him who has emancipated the world; but in the act she cures him of a far more fatal poison, which is her own unworthy love. The flame of the pyre purifies his too susceptible heart; he perishes in all his vigour and is seated victorious close to the throne of Jupiter. So also Jacob was not appointed the great patriarch of Israel till he had wrestled with an angel through the length of an entire night.

Ordeal is the great word of life, and life itself is a serpent which brings forth and devours unceasingly. We must escape from its folds; we must set our foot upon its head. Hermes duplicated the serpent, setting it against itself, and in an eternal equilibrium he converted it into the talisman of his power, into the glory of his caduceus.

[1] There is no need to say that the Second Birth, to which allusion is made by Christ, is not comprehended by any notion of a moral change, though such change is involved. Morality is the gate of spiritual life but is not its sanctuary.

The great ordeals of Memphis and Eleusis were designed to form kings and priests by entrusting science to strong and valiant men. The price of admission to such tests was the surrender of body, soul and life into the hands of the priesthood. The candidate descended thereafter through dark subterranean regions, wherein he traversed successively among flaming pyres, passed through deep and rapid floods, over bridges thrown across abysses, holding in his hand a lamp which must not be extinguished. He who trembled, he whom fear overcame, never returned to the light; but he who surmounted every obstacle intrepidly was received among the *mystæ*, which meant initiation into the Lesser Mysteries. He had yet to vindicate his fidelity and silence; it was only at the end of several years that he became an epopt, being a title equivalent to that of adept.[1]

Philosophy, in competition with the priesthood, imitated these practices, and put its disciples to the proof. Pythagoras exacted silence and abstinence for five years. Plato opened his schools to none but geometricians and those skilled in music; furthermore, he reserved part of his instruction to initiates, so that his philosophy had its mysteries.[2] He attributed the creation of the world to demons and represented man as the progenitor of all animals. But the demons of Plato signify the Elohim of Moses, being those powers by the combination and harmony of which the Supreme Principle created. When he represents beasts as begotten by humanity he means that they are the analysis of that living form, the synthesis of which is man. It was Plato who first proclaimed the divinity of the Word, and he appeared to foresee the approaching incarnation of this creative Word on earth; he proclaimed the sufferings and execution of the perfect just man, condemned by the iniquity of the world.

This sublime philosophy of the Word is part of the pure Kabalah, whence Plato was in no wise its inventor.[3] He makes no secret of this and

[1] The point which escapes in this synopsis of Egyptian initiation is that which distinguishes the official mysteries—like Masonry—from vital initiation, and I mention it here because there are memorials of Egyptian mysteries which suggest that they were no mere symbolical pageants but did communicate—to those who could receive—the life which is behind such symbolism.

[2] The analogy here instituted assumes in respect of the Greek mysteries that which has been implied previously regarding those of Egypt. The laws and by-laws of the schools of philosophy, whatever they exacted from pupils, were not imitations of the grades of initiation and advancement communicated in priestly sanctuaries, if there was mystic life in those sanctuaries. Even if they were merely pageants, the comparison does not obtain; for it is obvious that Pythagoras and Plato did not confer degrees by way of ritual. Matriculation and "the little go" are not ceremonial observances in the path of symbolism.

[3] The truth is that in so far as the Jewish Kabalah contains a *Logos* philosophy, so far it embodies confused reminiscences of Alexandrian schools of thought. Éliphas Lévi reminds one of Jacob Bryant, Davies and the respectable Mr. Faber, who explained the whole universe of history by the help of Shem, Ham and Japhet, the deluge and the Ark of Noah. He saw the Kabalah everywhere; had he spoken of a secret tradition subsisting in all times, of which Kabalism is a part in reflection, he would have been less confused and confusing; but he applied to the whole a term which is peculiar to a part. It is said in the *Zohar* that the Word which discovers unto us the supreme mysteries is generated by the union of light and darkness. Part I, fol. 32a. It is said also that the Word dwells in the superior heavens. Fol. 33. And there are other references

he proclaims that in any science only that must be received which is in harmony with eternal truths and with the oracles of God. Dacier, from whom this quotation comes, adds that "by these eternal truths Plato signified an ancient tradition which he supposes primeval humanity to have received from God and transmitted to later generations". It would be impossible to speak more clearly without actually naming the Kabalah: it is definition instead of name; in a sense, it is something more precise than the name itself.

Plato says otherwise that "the root-matter of this great knowledge is not to be found in books; we must seek in ourselves by means of deep meditation, discovering the sacred fire in its proper source.... This is why I have written nothing concerning these revelations and shall never even speak about them. Whosoever shall undertake to popularise them will find the attempt futile, for, except in the case of a very small number of men who have been endowed with understanding from God to discern these heavenly truths within themselves, it will render them contemptible to some, while filling others with vain and rash self-confidence, as if they were depositaries of marvels which they do not understand all the same."[1]

To the younger Dionysius he wrote: "I must bear witness to Archedemus concerning that which is far more precious, more divine by far, and that which you desire earnestly to know, having sent him to me expressly. He gives me to understand that in your view I have not explained to you sufficiently what I hold as to the nature of the First Principle. I can only write in enigmas, so that if my letter be intercepted on land or water, he who may read it shall understand nothing: all things encompass their king, from whom they draw their being, he being the source of all good things—second for those which are second and third for those which are third."

These few words are a complete summary of sephirotic theology.[2] The King is Ensoph—Supreme and Absolute Being. All radiates from this centre, which centre is everywhere, but we regard it after three especial manners and in three distinct spheres. In the Divine world, which is that of the First Cause, the King is one and first. In the world of science, which is that of secondary causes, the influence of the First Principle is felt, but is conceived only as first of the said causes. Therein the King manifests by the duad, which is the passive creating principle. Finally, in the third world, which is that of forms, he is revealed as perfect form, the incarnate Word, supreme goodness and beauty, created perfection.

---

[1] Dacier was a translator in the latter part of the eighteenth century, and his study on the *Doctrine of Plato* appeared in the third volume of a collection entitled *Bibliothèque des Anciens Philosophes*, which began publication in 1771.

[2] Those who may wish to be acquainted with the sources from which Lévi drew some of his materials may consult *Cælum Sephiroticum*, by J. C. Steebius, an old folio which appeared in 1679, as well as Reuchlin and Rosenroth. They will see how things change in his hands. According to the *Zohar*, *Ain Soph* reflects immediately into *Kether* on the path of manifestation. It is not correct to say that the king is *Ain Soph* in Kabalism and the letter of Plato is devoid of sephirotic analogies.

The King is therefore, at one and the same time, the first, second and third, seeing that He is all in all, centre and cause of all. Let us be silent on the genius of Plato, recognising only the exact knowledge of the initiate.

Let it therefore be said no longer that our great apostle St. John borrowed from the philosophy of Plato the prooemium of his gospel. It is Plato, on the contrary, who drew from the same sources as St. John; but he had not received that spirit which makes alive. The philosophy of him who expounded the greatest of human revelations might aspire towards the Word made man, but the gospel alone could give that Word to the world.

The Kabalah taught by Plato to the Greeks assumed at a later period the name of Theosophy and ended by embracing the whole of magical doctrine.[1] It is to this sum total of secret doctrine that all discoveries of research gravitated successively. The ambition was to pass from theory to practice and to find the realisation of words in works. The dangerous experiences of divination taught science how it might dispense with the priesthood; the sanctuary was betrayed, and men who had no mission dared to make the gods speak. It is for this reason that theurgy shared in the anathemas pronounced against Black Magic and was suspected of imitating its crimes because it could not exculpate itself from a share in its impiety. The evil of Isis is not lifted with impunity, and curiosity blasphemes faith when Divine things are concerned. "Blessed are those who have not seen and have believed," says the Great Master.

The experiments of theurgy and necromancy are always fatal for those who are abandoned to their practice. To set foot upon the threshold of the other world spells death, and it follows often in a strange and terrible manner. Vertigo supervenes, catalepsy and madness finish the work. It is unquestionable that in the presence of certain persons a disturbance takes place in the air, wainscots split, doors shake and creak. Fantastic signs and even stains, as of blood, seem to impress themselves on virgin-parchment or on linen. The nature of these signatures is always the same and they are classified by experts under the name of diabolical writings. The mere sight of such characters sends sufferers from magnetic hysteria into convulsions or ecstasy; they believe that they behold spirits, and Satan, or the genius of error, is transfigured for them into an angel of light. The pretended spirits require, as the condition of their manifestation, some kind of contact between the sexes, the putting of hand in hand, foot to foot, breathing face to face and even immodest embraces. Devotees are besotted by this kind of intoxication; they think that they are elected by God, that they are interpreters of heaven, and they regard obedience to the hierarchy in the light of fanaticism. They are the successors of the Indian race of Cain, victims of hasheesh and

[1] It must be said that the Greek word θεοσοφία did not pass into Latin in classical times and was unknown throughout the middle ages. As an illustration of its occult prevalence, I cannot trace that it was used by Paracelsus. In so far as it can be said to have become prevalent, it was in a mystic sense only, as in the proper use of words it could alone be. It was made familiar by Jacob Böhme.

fakirs. They profit by no warnings, and they perish by their own act and will.

To restore sufferers of this kind the Greek priests resorted to a species of homœopathy; they terrified the patients by exaggerating the disease itself, and for this purpose they put them to sleep in the cave of Trophonius.[1] The preparation for this experience was by fastings, lustrations and vigils; the patients were then taken down into the vault and shut up in total darkness. Intoxicating gases, like those in the Grotto of the Dog near Naples, filled the cavern, and the visionary was overcome speedily. Incipient asphyxia induced frightful dreams, from which the victim was rescued in time and carried forth palpitating all over, pale and with hair on end. In this condition he or she was seated on a tripod and prophetic utterances preceded complete awakening. Experiences of this sort so distracted the nervous system that their subjects never recalled them without trembling and in future did not dare to mention evocations or phantoms. Some of them never smiled again or felt the impulse of gaiety; the general impression was so melancholy that it passed into a proverb, and it was said of anyone who did not unbend: "He has slept in the cave of Trophonius."[2]

For the remanents of science and the recovery of its mysteries we must have recourse to the religious symbolism of antiquity rather than to the works of its philosophers. The priests of Egypt were better acquainted than ourselves with the laws of motion and of life. They could temper or promote action by reaction, and they foresaw without difficulty the realisation of effects the cause of which they had postulated. The pillars of Seth, Hermes, Solomon, Hercules symbolised in magical traditions this universal law of equilibrium, while the science of equilibrium led the initiates to that of universal gravitation about centres of life, heat and light. So in the Egyptian sacred calendars, where it is known that each month was placed under the protection of three decani or genii of ten days, the first decanate in the sign of Leo is represented by a human head with seven rays; the body has a scorpio-tail and the sign of Sagittarius is under the chin. Beneath the head is the name of IAO, and the figure was called Khnoubis, an Egyptian word which signifies gold and light. Thales and Pythagoras learned in the Egyptian sanctuaries that the earth gravitated round the sun, but they did not seek to publish the fact generally because it would have involved the revelation of a great temple-secret, being the dual law of attraction and radiation, of

---

[1] The classical authorities for the visitation of the cave of Trophonius include Pausanias of Cæsarea—who wrote the history of Greece—Cicero Pliny and Philostratus, not to mention the allusion found in the *Clouds* of Aristophanes. The account of Éliphas Lévi must be taken with certain reservations, but it is not a matter in which accuracy or its opposite is of any consequence outside scholarly research. There were various sacrifices and other ceremonies prior to the visitation, and the candidate for the experience usually descended alone. It is not, I think, on record that the effect of the visit was lasting.

[2] The actual formula seems to have been: "He has consulted the oracle of Trophonius."

fixity and movement, which is the principle of creation and the unfailing cause of life.[1] So also the Christian writer Lactantius, who had heard of this magical tradition, but as an effect in the absence of a cause, scoffed loudly at theurgical dreamers who believed in the motion of the earth and in antipodes, the result of which would be the fact that we walked on our heads with the feet upwards, though our heads appeared to be erect. Furthermore, as he added, with the logic of children, in such case we should infallibly fall head downwards through the heaven below us. So philosophers reasoned, while priests, without answering or even smiling at their blunders, continued to write in creative hieroglyphics concerning all dogmas, all forms of poetry and all secrets of truth.

In their allegorical description of Hades, the Greek hierophants concealed the palmary secrets of Magic. We find four rivers therein, even as in the Earthly Paradise, *plus* a fifth, which wound seven times round the others. There was a river of sorrows, and silence called Cocytus; there was a river of forgetfulness, or Lethe; and then there was a swift and irresistible river which carried all before it, flowing in an opposite course to yet another river of fire. The two last were named Acheron and Phlegethon, one being the negative and one the positive fluid, flowing eternally each in each. The black and icy waters of Acheron smoked with the warmth of Phlegethon, while the liquid flames of the latter were covered with thick vapours by the former. *Larvæ* and *lemures*, shadowy images of bodies which have lived and of those which have yet to come, issued from these vapours by myriads; but whether they drank or not from the flood of sorrows, all desired the waters of oblivion, to bring them youth and peace. The wise alone do not seek to forget, for memory is their reward already; so also they only are truly deathless, since they only are conscious of their immortality. The tortures of Tenarus are truly divine pictures of the vices and their eternal chastisement. The greed of Tantalus, the ambition of Sisyphus, will never be expiated, since they can never be satisfied. Tantalus is athirst in the water, Sisyphus rolls a stone towards the top of a mountain, hoping to take his seat thereon, but it falls back continually and drags him down into the abyss. Ixion, unbridled in licence, would have violated the queen of heaven and was scourged by infernal furies. He did not consummate his crime, for he embraced only a phantom. The phantom may have condescended in appearance to his love and may have ministered to his passion, but when he disowned duty, when his satisfaction was at the price of sacrilege, that which he thought was love proved hatred in a mask of flowers.

It is not from beyond the tomb, it is rather in life itself, that we must seek the mysteries of death. Salvation or condemnation begin here below, and this earth has also its heaven and hell. Virtue is ever rewarded, vice is ever punished; if the wealth of the wicked incline us at times to think that they enjoy impunity, that instrument of good and evil seeming to

---

[1] There is no question that, according to the *Zohar*, the sun is the centre of the planetary system, of which planets the earth is one.

be given them by chance, there is woe notwithstanding to the unjust, they may possess the key of gold, but for them it opens only the gate of the tomb and hell.

All true initiates have recognised the immense value of toil and suffering. A German poet tells us that sorrow is the dog of that unknown shepherd which leads the flock of humanity. Learn how to suffer and learn also to die—such are the gymnastics of eternity and such is the immortal novitiate. This is the moral lesson of Dante's *Divine Comedy*, and it was outlined in the allegorical Table of Cebes, which belongs to the time of Plato. An account of it has been preserved and many painters of the middle ages reconstructed the picture therefrom. It is at once a philosophical and magical monument, a perfect moral synthesis, and moreover the most audacious demonstration ever attempted of that Great Arcanum or Secret, the revelation of which must subvert heaven and earth. Our readers will unquestionably expect us to furnish its explanation, but he who has solved this enigma knows that it is inexplicable by its nature and is a sentence of death to those who take it by surprise, even as to those who reveal it.[1]

This secret is the royalty of the age and the crown of that initiates who is represented coming down as a victor from the mount of ordeal in the beautiful allegory of Cebes. The Great Arcanum has made him master of gold and light, which fundamentally are one thing; he has solved the quadrature of the circle; he directs perpetual motion; and he possesses the Philosophical Stone. Those who are adepts will understand me. There is neither interruption in the process of Nature nor a blank space in its work. The harmonies of heaven are in correspondence with those of earth, and eternal life fulfils its evolutions in accordance with the same laws which rule in the life of a day. The Bible says that God disposes all things according to weight, number and measure, and this luminous doctrine was also that of Plato. In the *Phædon* he represents Socrates as discoursing on the destinies of the soul in a manner which is quite in conformity with Kabalistical traditions. Spirits purified by trial are emancipated from the laws of weight, and they soar above the atmosphere of tears; others grovel in darkness and are those who manifest to the weak or criminal. All who are liberated from the miseries of material life come back no more to contemplate its crimes or share its errors: once is truly enough.

The care taken by the ancients over the burial of the dead protested strongly against necromancy, and those who disturbed the sleep of the grave were always regarded as impious. To call back the dead would condemn them to a second death, and the dread of earnest people, belonging to old religions, lest they should remain without burial after death,

---

[1] There is extraordinary confusion, at the least by way of expression, in this paragraph, which will inevitably create in the reader a notion that the work of Cebus was a picture. As a fact, it is a description of human life contained in a dialogue, to which the title of *Tabula* was given. It has been printed several times, and once, I believe, at Glasgow, in 1747.

was in view of the possibility that the corpse might be profaned by stryges and used in witchcraft. After death the soul belongs to God and the body to the common mother, which is earth. Woe to those who dare to invade these asylums. When the sanctuary of the tomb was disturbed, the ancients offered sacrifices to the angry *manes* and a holy thought lay at the root of this practice. As a fact, were it permitted anyone to attract, by means of conjurations, the souls floating in darkness but aspiring towards the light, such a person would be begetting retrograde and posthumous children, whom he must nourish with his own blood and with his own soul. Necromancers are makers of vampires, and they deserve no pity if they die devoured by the dead.

CHAPTER IV

THE MAGIC OF PUBLIC WORSHIP

FORMS are the product of ideas, and they in their turn reflect and reproduce ideas. So far as sentiments are concerned, these are multiplied by association in the union of those who share them, so that all are charged with the enthusiasm common to all. It comes about in this manner that if one or another individual be deceived easily on questions of the just and the beautiful, the people at large will, this notwithstanding, continue to exalt in their minds whatsoever things are sublime, and they will do it with a longing which is itself sublime. These two great laws of Nature were known to the ancient Magi and led them to see the necessity of a public worship which should be one in its nature, imposed on all, hierarchic and symbolic in character, like all religion, splendid as truth, rich and varied as Nature, starry as heaven, odoriferous as earth—a worship in fact of the kind established afterwards by Moses, realised in all its glory by Solomon, and, once again transfigured, centralised today in the great metropolis of St. Peter at Rome.

Humanity as a fact has never known more than one religion and one worship. This universal light has had its uncertain reflections and its shadows, but ever after the dark night of error we behold it emerge, one and pure like the sun.

The magnificence of the cultus is the life of religion, and if Christ chose poor ministers, His sovereign divinity did not demand poor altars. Protestants have failed to understand that ritual constitutes an instruction and that a sordid or negligible god must not be created in the imagination of the multitude. The English, who lavish so much wealth on their own homes, who also affect to prize the Bible highly, would find their particular churches exceedingly cold and bare if they remembered the unparalleled pomp of Solomon's Temple. But that which withers their forms of worship is the dryness of their own hearts; and with a cultus devoid of magic, splendour and pathos, how shall their hearts be ever informed with life? Look at their meeting-houses, which resemble town-halls, and look at those honest ministers—dressed like ushers or clerks—and who can do otherwise in their presence than regard religion as formalism and God as a justice of the peace?

Orthodoxy is the absolute character of Transcendental Magic. When truth is born into the world the star of science announces the fact to the Magi, and they come to adore the infant creator of futurity. Initiation is obtained by understanding in respect of the hierarchy, as also by the practice of obedience, and he who is initiated truly will never turn sectarian. The orthodox traditions were carried from Chaldea by Abraham; in combination with the knowledge of the true God, they reigned in Egypt at the period of Joseph. Koung-Tseu sought to establish them in China, but the imbecile mysticism of India, under the idolatrous form of the Fo cultus, was destined to prevail in that great empire. As by Abraham out of Chaldea, so was orthodoxy taken out of Egypt by Moses, and in the secret traditions of the Kabalah we find a theology at once complete, perfect, unique and comparable to our own at its grandest, when seen under the light of its interpretation by the fathers and doctors of the Church—a perfect whole, including lights which it is not given to the world yet to understand. The *Zohar*, which is the head and crown of the Kabalistic sacred books, unveils furthermore all depths and enlightens all obscurities of ancient mythologies and of sciences concealed in the sanctuaries of eld. It is true that we must know the secret of its meaning in order to make use of it, and it is further true that the keenest intellects which are not acquainted with the secret will find the *Zohar* beyond all understanding and even unreadable. It is to be hoped that careful students of our works on Magic will attain the secret for themselves, that they will come in their turn to decode and thus be able to read the book which explains so many mysteries.[1]

Initiation being the necessary consequence of that hierarchic principle which is the basis of realisation in Magic, it follows that the profane, after striving vainly to force the doors of the sanctuary, have been driven to raise altar against altar and to oppose ignorant disclosures of schism to the reticence of orthodoxy. Horrible histories were circulated concerning the Magi; sorcerers and vampires cast upon them the responsibility of their own crimes; they were represented as feasting on infants and drinking human blood. Such attacks of presumptuous ignorance against the prudence of science have invariably met with success sufficient to perpetuate their use. Has not some miserable creature set forth, in I know not what pamphlet, how he has heard with his own ears, and within the precincts of a club, the author of this book demanding the blood of the wealthy to make it into puddings for the nourishment of starving people? The more monstrous the calumny, the greater the impression that it produces in the minds of fools.

Those who slandered the Magi committed themselves the enormities of which they accused them and were abandoned to all the excesses of shameless sorcery. There was everywhere the rumour of apparitions and prodigies, and the gods themselves came down in visible forms to authorise orgies. The maniacal circles of pretended *illuminati* go back to the

---

[1] I have intimated elsewhere that the *Zohar* is in several respects a work of high entertainment, and that its reading is much more diverting than Arabian or Ambrosial Nights. But Éliphas Lévi is right in saying that it calls for some preliminary training. He does not quite mean, however, what I mean in making the suggestion. On the serious side the *Zohar* is assuredly a work of initiation and one of the great books of the world, though Sir John Lubbock and others of kindred enterprise did not happen to know of it. Lévi is substantially right also in saying that it requires a key, though his meaning is not expressed rightly. The explanation is that it is not a methodical system and presupposes throughout, on the part of its readers, an acquaintance with the tradition which it embodies in allusive form.

bacchantes who murdered Orpheus. Since the days of those fanatical and clandestine circles where promiscuity and assassination were combined with ecstasies and prayers, a luxurious and mystical pantheism increased continually. But the fatal destinies of this consuming and destroying dogma are recorded in one of the finest fables of Greek mythology. Certain pirates of Tyre surprised Bacchus in his sleep and carried him on board their vessel, thinking that the god of inspiration had so become their slave; but on a sudden, in the open sea, their ship was transfigured, the masts became vine-stocks, the rigging branches; satyrs were seen everywhere, dancing with lynxes and panthers; the crew were seized with frenzy, they felt themselves changed into goats and cast themselves into the sea. Bacchus subsequently landed in Bœotia and repaired to Thebes, the city of initiation, where he found that Pentheus had usurped the supreme power. The latter in his turn attempted to imprison the god, but the dungeon opened of itself and the captive came forth triumphant. Pentheus was enraged and the daughters of Cadmus, transformed into Bacchantes, tore him in pieces, thinking that they were immolating a young bull.[1]

Pantheism can never form a synthesis, but must be disintegrated by the sciences, which the daughters of Cadmus typify. After Orpheus, Cadmus, Œdipus and Amphiaraüs, the great fabulous symbols of magical priesthood in Greece are Tiresias and Calchas; but the first of these was an undiscerning or faithless hierophant. Meeting on a day with two interlaced serpents, he thought that they were fighting and separated them by a stroke of his wand. He did not understand the emblem of the caduceus, and hence sought to divide the forces of Nature, to separate science from faith, intelligence from love, man from woman. He mistook their union for warfare, wounded them in the act of separation, and so lost his own equilibrium. He became alternately male and female, but neither in a perfect way, for the consummation of marriage was forbidden him.[2] The mysteries of universal equilibrium and creative law are revealed fully herein. Generation is in fact a work of the human androgyne; in their division man and woman remain sterile, as religion without science, and, conversely, as mildness without force and force apart from mildness,

[1] It is difficult to say what authority was followed in producing this account. Pentheus was the second King of Thebes, succeeding Cadmus, who built the city. Bacchus was the son of Semele, the daughter of Cadmus, by Jupiter, but he was never a candidate for the Theban throne. The offence of Pentheus was not one of usurpation but of refusal to recognise the divinity of Bacchus. He was not torn to pieces by the daughters of Cadmus, but by a crowd of Bacchanals, among whom was his own mother. It is impossible to turn this story into an allegory of pantheism, as Lévi proceeds to do.

[2] The classical story is the very contrary of this. The effect of his experiments with the serpents was like that of passing through the foot of the rainbow; Tiresias was changed into a girl. He married in this form; but having met a second time with some other interlaced serpents, he again smote them and recovered his original sex. So far from being unable to consummate marriage in either case, he became an authority with the gods on the comparative extent of satisfaction attained by the two sexes in the act of sex.

justice in the absence of mercy and mercy divorced from justice. Harmony results from the analogy of things in opposition; they must be distinguished with a view to unite them and not separate, so that we may choose between them. It is said that man shifts incessantly from black to white in his opinions and ever deceives himself. It is so of necessity, for visible and real form is black and white; it manifests itself by an alliance of light and shadow which does not confuse them together. So are all contraries in Nature married, and he who would part them risks the punishment of Tiresias. Others say that he was smitten with blindness because he had surprised Minerva naked—that is to say, he had profaned the Mysteries. This is another allegory, but it is always the same thing symbolised.

Bearing, no doubt, this profanation in mind, Homer depicts the shade of Tiresias wandering in Cymmerian darkness and seeking amidst other hapless shades and larvæ to quench his thirst with blood when Ulysses consulted spirits, using a ceremonial which was magical and terrific after another manner than the contortions of our own mediums, or the harmless precipitated missives of our modern necromancers.

The priesthood is almost silent in Homer, for Calchas the diviner is neither a sovereign pontiff nor a great hierophant. He seems to be in the service of kings, with an eye to their possible wrath, and he dares not speak unwelcome truths to Agamemnon till he has besought the protection of Achilles. Thus he sows division between these chiefs and brings disasters on the army. All the narratives of Homer contain important and profound lessons, and he sought in the present case to impress upon Greece the need for divine ministry to be independent of temporal influences. The priestly caste should be responsible only to the supreme pontificate, and the high priest is incapacitated if one crown be wanting in his tiara. That he may be on equality with earthly sovereigns he must be himself a temporal king; he must be king in understanding and science, king also by his divine mission. Homer seems to tell us in his wisdom that failing such a priesthood there is something wanting to the equilibrium of empires.

Theoclymenes, another diviner, who appears in the Odyssey, fills almost the part of a parasite, purchasing a not too friendly hospitality from the suitors of Penelope by a useless warning and prudently withdrawing before the disturbance which he foresees.

There is a gulf between these good and bad fortune-tellers and the sibyls dwelling unseen in their sanctuaries, which are approached in fear and trembling. This notwithstanding, the successors of Circe yield only to daring; force or subtlety must be used to enter their retreat; they must be seized by the hair, threatened with the sword and dragged to the fatal tripod. Then, crimsoning and whitening by turn, shuddering and with hair on end, they utter disconnected words, escape in a fury, scribble on the leaves of trees detached sentences forming prophetic verses when collected, and casting these leaves to the wind, they shut themselves up in their refuge and ignore any further calls. The oracle thus produced had as many meanings as the modes of its possible combination varied. Had the leaves borne hieroglyphical signs instead of words the interpretations would have been multiplied further, while destiny could have been also consulted by their chance combination, a method followed subsequently in the divinations of geomancers by means of numbers and geometrical figures.[1] It is followed also at this day by adepts of cartomancy, who make use of the great magical Tarot alphabets, for the most part, without being acquainted with their values. In such operations accident only chooses the signs on which the interpreter depends for inspiration, and in the absence of exceptional intuition and second sight, the phrases indicated by the combinations of sacred letters or the revelations of the combined figures prophesy according to chance. It is insufficient to combine letters; one must know how to read. Cartomancy in its proper understanding is a literal consultation of spirits, without necromancy or sacrifices: but it postulates a good medium; it is otherwise dangerous and we do not recommend it to anyone. Is the memory of our bygone misfortunes not enough to embitter the sufferings of today, and must we then overload them with all the anxiety of the future, by partaking in advance of the catastrophes which it is impossible to avoid?

---

[1] The term "geometrical" scarcely applies to the figures of geomancy.

CHAPTER V

MYSTERIES OF VIRGINITY

THE Roman Empire was but the Greek in transfiguration. Italy was a Greater Greece, and when Hellenism had perfected its dogmas and mysteries, the education of the children of the wolf was the next task before it: Rome was already on the scene.

The particular feature of the initiation conferred on the Romans by Numa was the typical importance ascribed to woman, following the lead of Egypt, which worshipped the Supreme Divinity under the name of Isis. The Greek god of initiation is Iacchos, the conqueror of India, the splendid androgynous being wearing the horns of Ammon,[1] the Pantheus holding the sacrificial cup and pouring therefrom the wine of universal life—Iacchos, the son of thunder, the conqueror of tigers and lions. When the bacchantes dismembered Orpheus, the Mysteries of Iacchos were profaned; and under the Roman name of Bacchus he was only the god of intoxication. It was from Egeria, goddess of mystery and solitude, a sage and discreet divinity, that Numa sought his inspiration.

His devotion was rewarded; he was instructed by Egeria as to the honour which should be paid to the mother of the gods. Under this dedication he erected a circular temple beneath a cupola, and a fire was burnt therein which was never suffered to go out. It was maintained by four virgins, who were termed vestals, and so long as they were faithful to their trust they were surrounded with strange honours, while, on the other hand, their failure was punished with exceptional rigour. The maid's honour is that also of the mother, and the sanctity of every family depends on the recognition of virginal purity as a possible and glorious thing. Herein already woman is emancipated from the old bondage; she is no more an oriental slave, but a domestic divinity, guardian of the hearth, the honour of father and spouse. Rome in this manner became a sanctuary of morality, and on such condition was also queen of the nations and metropolis of the world.

The magical tradition of all ages attributes a certain supernatural and divine quality to the virgin state. Prophetic inspirations adorn it, while it is the hatred of innocence and virginity which prompted Göetic Magic to sacrifice children, whose blood was regarded notwithstanding as having a sacred and expiatory virtue. To withstand the allurement of generation is to graduate in the conquest of death, and supreme chastity was the most

---

[1] The Bacchus who was depicted with horns was the son of Jupiter and Proserpine. As regards the androgynous nature of Iacchos, I do not know Lévi's authority, but such a characteristic was ascribed to several deities, though sometimes against general likelihood. It was even said of Jupiter that he was a man but also an immortal maid.

glorious crown set before hierophants.[1] To expend life in human embraces is to strike roots in the grave. Chastity is a flower which is so loosely bound to earth that, when the sun's caresses draw it upwards, it is detached without effort and takes flight like a bird.

The sacred fire of the vestals was a symbol of faith and of pure love. It was an emblem also of that universal agent the terrible and electric nature of which Numa could produce and direct. If by culpable negligence the vestals allowed their fire to die out, it could only be rekindled by the sun's rays or by lightning. It was renewed and consecrated at the beginning of each year, a custom perpetuated and observed among us on Easter Eve.

Christianity has been wrongly accused of taking over all that was beautiful in anterior forms of worship; it is the last transfiguration of universal orthodoxy, and as such it has preserved whatsoever belonged to it, while rejecting dangerous practices and idle superstitions.

Furthermore, the sacred fire represented love of country and the religion of the hearth. To this religion, and to the inviolability of the conjugal sanctuary, Lucretia offered herself in sacrifice. Lucretia personifies all the majesty of ancient Rome; she could doubtless have escaped outrage by abandoning her memory to slander, but good repute is a *noblesse qui oblige*. In the matter of honour a scandal is more deplorable than an indiscretion. Lucretia raised her dignity as a virtuous woman to the height of the priesthood by suffering an assault so that she might expiate and avenge it afterwards. It was in memory of this illustrious Roman lady that high initiation in the cultus of the fatherland and the hearth was entrusted to women, men being excluded. It was for them to learn in this manner that true love is that which inspires the most heroic sacrifices. They were taught that the real beauty of man is heroism and grandeur; that the woman capable of betraying or forsaking her husband blasts both her past and future and is branded on the forehead with the ineffaceable stain of a retrospective prostitution, aggravated further by perjury. To cease loving him to whom the flower of her youth has been given is the greatest woe which can afflict the heart of a virtuous woman; but to publish it abroad is to falsify past innocence, to renounce probity of heart and integrity of honour; it is the last and most irreparable shame.

Such was the religion of Rome; to the magic of such a moral code she owed all her greatness, and when marriage ceased to be sacred in her eyes her decadence was at hand. In the days of Juvenal the mysteries of the *Bona Dea* are said to have been mysteries of impurity, which it may perhaps be possible to question, seeing that as women alone were admitted to these pretended orgies they must have betrayed themselves; but on the assumption that the charge is true, because anything seems possible after the reigns of Nero and Domitian, we can only conclude that the clean

---

[1] Lévi affirms elsewhere that the satisfaction of all the calls of sense is required for the work of philosophy. In the present place he confuses the issue by implying that chastity means either celibacy or the virgin state. Yet he did not fail to understand that the nuptial life is also a life of chastity; he speaks eloquently of the home and its sanctity, and he alludes elsewhere to the chaste and conjugal Venus.

reign of the mother of the gods was over and was giving place to the popular, universal and purer worship of Mary, the Mother of God.

Initiate of magical laws, and knowing the magnetic influences of communal life, Numa instituted colleges of priests and augurs, living under prescribed rules. This was the first idea of conventional institutions, which are one of the great powers of religion. Long anterior to this, the Jewish prophets were joined in sympathetic bonds, having prayer and inspiration in common. It would seem that Numa was acquainted with the traditions of Judea; his *flamines* and *salii* worked themselves into a state of exaltation by evolutions and dances recalling the performance of David before the ark. Numa did not establish new oracles intended to rival those of Delphos, but he instructed his priests especially in the art of auguries, which means that he acquainted them with a certain theory of presentiments and second sight, determined by secret laws of Nature. We despise nowadays the art of soothsaying and portents, because we have lost the profound science of light and the universal analogies of its reflections. In his charming tale of Zadig, Voltaire delineates, with light and unserious touch, a purely natural science of divination, but it is not for that less wonderful, presupposing as it does an exceptional fineness of observation and that power of deduction which escapes habitually the limited logic of the vulgar. It is said that Parmenides, the master of Pythagoras, having tasted the water of a certain spring, predicted an approaching earthquake. The circumstance is not extraordinary, for the presence of a bituminous and sulphureous flavour in water may well have advised the philosopher of subterranean activities in the district. Even the water itself may have been unusually disturbed. However this may be, the flight of birds is still considered premonitory of severe winters, and it may be possible to foresee some atmospheric influences by inspecting the digestive and respiratory apparatus of animals. Now, physical disturbances of the air have not infrequently a moral cause. Revolutions are translated therein by the phenomena of great storms; the deep breathing of nations moves heaven itself. Success proceeds coincidently with electric currents, and the hues of the living light reflect the motions of thunder. "There is something in the air," says the crowd, with its particular prophetic instinct. Soothsayers and augurs knew how to read the characters which the light inscribes everywhere and how to interpret the sigils of astral currents and revolutions. They knew why birds wing their flight in isolation or in flocks, under what influences they turn to North or South, to East or West, which is just what we cannot explain, though we scoff now at the augurs. It is so very easy to scoff and it is so difficult to learn thoroughly.

It was owing to such predetermined disparagement and to denial of what is not understood that men of parts, like Fontenelle, and men of learning, as Kircher, have written such intemperate things concerning the ancient oracles. Everything is craft and jugglery for strong minds of this order. They suppose automatic statues, concealed speaking-trumpets and artificial echoes in the vaults of every temple. Why this eternal slander of the sanctuary? Has there been nothing but roguery in the priesthoods? Would it have been impossible to find men of uprightness and conviction among the hierophants of Ceres or Apollo? Or were these deceived like the rest? And in such case how did it happen that the impostors continued their traffic for centuries without ever betraying themselves, individual rogues not being gifted with immortality? Recent experiments have shewn us that thoughts can be transferred, translated into writing and printed by the unaided force of the Astral Light. Mysterious hands still write on our walls, as at the feast of Belshazzar. Let us not forget the wise observation of a scholar who assuredly cannot be accused either of fanaticism or credulity: "Outside pure mathematics," said Arago, "he who pronounces the word 'impossible' is wanting in caution."

The religious calendar of Numa is based upon that of the Magi; it is a sequence of feasts and mysteries, recalling throughout the secret doctrine of initiates and perfectly adapting the public enactments of the *cultus* to the universal laws of Nature. Its arrangement of months and days has been preserved by the conservative influence of Christian regeneration. Even as the Romans under Numa, we still hallow by abstinence the days consecrated to the commemoration of birth and death; but for us the day of Venus is sanctified by the expiations of Calvary. The gloomy day of Saturn is that during which our incarnate God sleeps in His tomb, but He will rise up, and the life which He promises will blunt the scythe of Kronos. That month which Romans dedicated to Maia, the nymph of youth and flowers, the young mother who smiles upon the year's first-fruits, is consecrated by us to Mary, the mystical rose, the lily of purity, the heavenly mother of the Saviour. So are our religious observances ancient as the world, our feasts are like those of our forefathers, for the Redeemer of Christendom came to suppress none of the symbolic and sacred beauties of old initiation. He came, as He said Himself, in reference to the figurative Law of Israel, to realise and fulfil all things.

CHAPTER VI

SUPERSTITIONS

SUPERSTITIONS are religious forms surviving the loss of ideas. Some truth no longer known or a truth which has changed its aspect is the origin and explanation of all. Their name, from the Latin *superstes*, signifies that which survives; they are the dead remnants of old knowledge or opinion.

Ever governed by instinct rather than by thought, the common people cleave to ideas through the mediation of forms, and it is with difficulty that they modify their habits. The attempt to destroy superstitions impresses them always as an attack on religion itself, and hence St. Gregory, one of the greatest popes in Christendom, did not seek to suppress the old practices. He recommended his missionaries to purify and not destroy the temples, saying that "so long as a people have their old places of worship they will frequent them by force of habit and will thus be led more easily to the worship of the true God". He said also: "The Bretons have fixed days for feasts and sacrifices; leave them their feasts and do not restrain their sacrifices; leave them the joy of their festivals, but from the state of paganism draw them gently and progressively into the estate of Christ."

It came about in this manner that older pious observances were replaced by holy mysteries with scarcely a change of name. There was, for example, the yearly banquet called *Charistia*, to which ancestral spirits were invited, so making an act of faith in universal and immortal life. The Eucharist, or supernal *Charistia*, has replaced that of antiquity, and we communicate Easter by Easter with all our friends in heaven and on earth.[1] Far from maintaining the old superstitions by such adaptations, Christianity has breathed soul and life into the surviving signs of universal beliefs.

That science of Nature which is in such close consanguinity with religion, seeing that it initiates men into the secrets of Divinity, that forgotten science of Magic, still lives undivided in hieroglyphical signs and, to some extent, in the living traditions or superstitions which it has left outwardly untouched. For example, the observation of numbers and

---

[1] There were two pagan festivals which have a certain likeness between them: (a) *Charisia*, which was in honour of Aglaia, Thalia and Euphrosyne, the *Charites* or Graces. It was celebrated by dances at night, and the person who maintained the exercise longest was presented with a cake. (b) *Charistia*, a Roman festival, for the reconciliation of relations and friends, at which food was eaten. It could be wished for the perpetuity and catholicity of the sacraments that there were traces of a Eucharist in the Christian sense prior to Christian times.

days is a blind reminiscence of primitive magical dogma. As a day consecrated to Venus, Friday was always considered unlucky, because it signified the mysteries of birth and death. No enterprise was undertaken on Friday by the Jews, but they completed thereon the work which belonged to the week, seeing that it preceded the Sabbath, or day of compulsory rest. The number 13, being that which follows the perfect cycle of 12, also represents death, succeeding the activities of life; and in the Jewish *Symbolum* the article relating to death is numbered thirteen. The partition of the family of Joseph into two tribes brought thirteen guests to the first Passover of Israel in the Promised Land, meaning thirteen tribes to share the harvests of Canaan. One of them was exterminated, being that of Benjamin, youngest of the children of Jacob. Hence comes the tradition that when there are thirteen at table the youngest is destined to die quickly.[1]

The Magi abstained from the flesh of certain animals and touched no blood. Moses raised this practice into a precept, on the ground that it is unlawful to partake of the soul of animals, which soul is in the blood. It remains therein after their slaughter, like a phosphorous of coagulated and corrupted Astral Light, which may be the germ of many diseases. The blood of strangled animals digests with difficulty and predisposes to apoplexy and nightmare. The flesh of *carnivora* is also unwholesome on account of the savage instincts with which it has been associated and because it has already absorbed corruption and death.

"When the soul of an animal is separated violently from its body," says Porphyry, "it does not depart, but, like that of human beings which have died in the same way, it remains in the neighbourhood of the body. It is so retained by sympathy and cannot be driven away. Such souls have been seen moaning by their bodies. It is the same with the souls of men whose bodies have not been interred. It is to these that the operations of magicians do outrage, by enforcing their obedience, so long as the operators are masters of the dead body in whole or in part. Theosophers who are familiar with these mysteries, with the sympathy of animal souls for the bodies from which they are separated, and with their pleasure in approaching these, have rightly forbidden the use of certain meats, so that we may not be infected by alien souls.

Porphyry adds that prophecy may be acquired by feeding on the hearts of ravens, moles and hawks; here the Alexandrian theurgist betakes himself to the processes of the *Little Albert*, but though he lapses so quickly into superstition it is by entering a wrong path, for his point of departure was science.[2]

---

[1] It may be mentioned that 13 is also the number of resurrection, or birth into new life.

[2] The Grimoire mentioned under the name of *Little Albert* is called in the Latin edition *Alberti Parvi Lucii Libellus*, and is "a treasure of marvellous secrets." The original intention was to father it on *Albertus Magnus*, and in fact there is another collection which is known as the *Great Albert*. It is of similar value.

To indicate the secret properties of animals, the ancients said that at the epoch of the war of the giants, various forms were assumed by the gods with a view to concealment, and that they resumed these subsequently at pleasure. Thus, Diana changed into a she-wolf; the sun into a bull, lion, dragon and hawk; Hecate into a horse, lioness and bitch.

The name of *Pherebates* was, according to several theosophers, assigned to Proserpine because she lived upon turtle-doves, and these birds were the usual offering which the priestesses of Maïa made to that goddess, who is the Proserpine of earth, daughter of the fair Ceres, and foster-mother of the human race. The initiates of Eleusis abstained from domestic birds, fish, beans, peaches and apples; they abstained also from intercourse with a woman in child-bed, as well as during her normal periods. Porphyry, from whom this information is derived, adds as follows: "Whosoever has studied the science of visions knows that one must abstain from all kinds of birds in order to be liberated from the bondage of terrestrial things and find a place among the celestial gods." But the reason he does not give.

According to Euripides, the initiates of the secret cultus of Jupiter in Crete touched no flesh-meat; in the chorus addressed to King Minos, the priests in question are made to speak as follows: "Son of a Phœnician Tyrian woman, descendant of Europa and great Jupiter, King of the Isle of Crete, famous through an hundred cities, we come unto thee, forsaking temples built of oak and cypress fashioned with knives; leaders of a pure life, behold, we come. Since I was made a priest of Jupiter-Idæus, I take no part in the nocturnal feasts of Bacchanals, I eat no half-cooked meats; but I offer tapers to the mother of the gods. I am a priest among the Curetes clothed in white; I keep far from the cradles of men; I shun also their tombs; and I eat nothing which has been animated by the breath of life."

The flesh of fish is phosphorescent and hence is aphrodisiacal. Beans are heating and cause absence of mind. For every form of abstinence, including the most irregular forms, a deep reason, apart from all superstition, can probably be found. There are certain combinations of foods which are opposed to the harmonies of Nature. "Thou shalt not seethe the kid in his mother's milk," said Moses—a prescription which is touching as an allegory and wise on the ground of hygiene.

The Greeks, like the Romans, but not to the same extent, were believers in presages; it was good augury when serpents tasted the sacred offerings; it was favourable or the reverse when it thundered on the right or the left hand. There were presages in the ways of sneezing and in other natural weaknesses which may be left here to conjecture. In the "Hymn to Mercury", Homer narrates that when the god of thieves was still in his cradle he stole the oxen of Apollo, who took the youngster and shook him, to make him confess the larceny:

FORMATION AND DEVELOPMENT OF DOGMAS

Mercure s'avisant d'un étrange miracle,
De ses flancs courroucés fit entendre l'oracle;
Jusqu'au grand Apollon la vapeur en monta.[1]

It was all presage with the Romans—a stone against which the foot struck, the cry of a screech-owl, the barking of a dog, a broken vase, an old woman who was first to look at you. All such idle terrors had for their basis that grand magical science of divination which neglects no token but from an effect overlooked by the vulgar ascends through a sequence of interlinked causes. This science knows, for example, that those atmospheric influences which cause the dog to howl are fatal for certain sufferers, that the appearance and the wheeling of ravens mean the presence of unburied bodies—which is always of sinister augury; localities of murder and execution are frequented by these fowl. The flight of other birds prognosticates hard winters, while yet others, by their plaintive cries over the sea, give the signal of coming storms. On that which science discerns ignorance remarks and generalises; the first sees useful warnings everywhere; the other distresses and frightens itself at everything.

The Romans furthermore were great observers of dreams; the art of their interpretation belongs to the science of the vital light, to the understanding of its direction and reflections. Men versed in transcendental mathematics are well aware that there can be no image in the absence of light, be it direct, reflected or refracted; and by the direction of the ray, the return under the fold of which they know how to find, they arrive by an exact calculation, and invariably, at the source of light and can estimate its universal or relative force. They take into account also the healthy or diseased state of the visual mechanism, external or internal, and attribute thereto the apparent deformity of rectitude of images. For such persons dreams are a complete revelation, since dream is a semblance of immortality during that nightly death which we call sleep. In the dream-state we share in the universal life, unconscious of good or evil, time or space. We leap over trees, dance on water, breathe upon prisons and they fall; or, alternatively, we are heavy, sad, hunted, chained up—according to the

---

[1] I have suffered these lines to stand as they are given by Éliphas Lévi, following the French translation of Salomon Certon. Shelley, who rendered Homer's *Hymn to Mercury* into verse which is unworthy of his name, represented the Greek original by asterisks at this point, and I have taken a lesson from the counsel. Lévi gives some further lines—I scarcely know why, but they stand as follows in Shelley's version:

"Phœbus on the grass
Him threw, and whilst all that he had designed
He did perform—eager although to pass,
Apollo darted from his mighty mind
Towards the subtle babe the following scoff:—
'Do not imagine this will get you off,

" 'You little swaddled child of Jove and May!'
And seized him: 'By this omen I shall trace
My noble herds, and you shall lead the way.' "

state of our health and often that of our conscience. All this is useful to observe, and unquestionable, but what can be inferred therefrom by those who know nothing and are without the wish to learn?

The all-powerful action of harmony, in exalting the soul and giving it rule over the senses, was well known to the ancient sages; but that which they employed to soothe was wrested by enchanters to excite and intoxicate. The sorceresses of Thessaly and of Rome believed that the moon could be dragged from the sky by the barbarous verses which they recited and that it fell pale and bleeding to the earth. The monotony of their recitations, the sweep of their magical wands, their circumambulations about circles, magnetised, excited, and led them by stages to fury, to ecstasy, even to catalepsy itself. In this kind of waking state they fell into dream, saw tombs open, the air overcast by clouds of demons, the moon falling from heaven.

The Astral Light is the living soul of the earth, a material and fatal soul, controlled in its productions and movements by the eternal laws of equilibrium. This light, which environs and permeates all bodies, can also suspend their weight and make them revolve about a powerfully absorbent centre. Phenomena which have been so far insufficiently examined, though they are being reproduced in our own days, prove the truth of this theory. To the same natural law must be ascribed those magical whirlpools in the centre of which enchanters located themselves. It explains the fascination exercised on birds by certain reptiles and on sensitive natures by others which are negative and absorbent. Mediums are generally diseased creatures in whom the void opens and who thus attract the light, as abysses draw the water of whirlpools. The heaviest bodies can then be lifted like straws and are carried away by the current. Such negative and unbalanced natures, whose fluidic bodies are formless, can project their force of attraction, delineating by this means supplementary and fantastic members in the air. When the celebrated medium Home makes hands without bodies appear in his vicinity, his own hands are dead and frozen. It may be said that mediums are phenomenal beings in whom death struggles visibly against life. As much may be concluded in the case of enchanters, fortune-tellers, those with the evil eye and casters of spells. Consciously or unconsciously, they are vampires, who draw the life which they lack and thus disturb the balance of the light. When this is done consciously, they are criminals who should be punished, and when otherwise they are still exceedingly dangerous subjects, from whom delicate and nervous people should be carefully isolated.

Porphyry tells the following story in his life of Plotinus. "Among those who professed philosophy, there was a certain Olympius, who was of Alexandria and for a time disciple of Ammonius. He treated Plotinus with disdain, being ambitious to surpass him in repute. He sought also to injure him by magical ceremonies, but having found that the attempt re-acted on himself he admitted to his friends that the soul of Plotinus must be one of great power, since it could turn back on his enemies their own evil designs. Plotinus was conscious of the hostile attempts of Olympius, and there were times when he said suddenly: 'Now he is having convulsions.' This kind of thing being repeated, and finding that he was afflicted himself with the evils which he would have wrought on Plotinus, Olympius ceased to persecute."

Equilibrium is the great law of the vital light; projected with force and repelled by a nature more balanced than our own, it comes back upon ourselves with equal violence. Woe therefore to those who would employ natural powers in the service of injustice, since Nature is just and her reactions are terrible.

CHAPTER VII

MAGICAL MONUMENTS

WE have said that Egypt of old was itself a pantacle, and as much might be affirmed concerning the elder world at large. In proportion as the great hierophants were at pains to conceal their absolute science, they sought more and more to extend and multiply its symbols. The triangular pyramids, with their square bases, represented metaphysics grounded on the science of Nature; and the symbolical key of this science assumed the gigantic form of that wonderful sphinx which, in its age-long vigil at the foot of the pyramids, has hollowed for itself so deep a bed in the sand. Those seven great monuments called the wonders of the world were sublime commentaries on the pyramids and on the seven mysterious gates of Thebes. At Rhodes there was the Pantacle of the Sun, in which the god of light and truth was symbolised under a human form clothed with gold; he raised in his right hand the torch of intelligence and in his left held the shaft of activity. His feet were fixed on moles representing the eternal equilibrating forces of Nature, necessity and liberty, active and passive, fixed and volatile—in a word, the Pillars of Hercules. At Ephesus was the Pantacle of the Moon, which was the Temple of Diana Panthea, made in the likeness of the universe. It was a dome surmounting a cross, with a square gallery and a circular precinct recalling the shield of Achilles: The tomb of Mausoleus was the Pantacle of the Chaste and Conjugal Venus; in form it was after the manner of a *lingam*, having a square elevation and a circular precinct. In the middle place of the square rose a truncated pyramid, on which was a chariot with four horses, harnessed so as to form a cross. The Pyramids were the Pantacle of Hermes or of Mercury. The Olympian Jupiter was the Pantacle of that god. The walls of Babylon and the citadel of Semiramis were Pantacles of Mars. In fine, the Temple of Solomon—that universal and absolute pantacle destined to replace the others—was for the Gentile world the terrible Pantacle of Saturn.

The philosophical septenary of initiation, according to the mind of the ancients, may be summarised as three absolute principles, reducible to a single principle, and four elementary forms, which are one form only, the whole constituting an unity composed of form and idea. The three principles are as follows: (1) Being is being; in philosophy this signifies the identity of the idea and that which is, or truth; in religion it is the first principle, the Father. (2) Being is real; this means in philosophy the identity of knowledge and of that which is, or reality; in religion it is the Logos of Plato, the Demiourgos, the Word. (3) Being is logical; in philosophy this signifies the identity of reason and reality; in religion it is Providence, or

The Seven Wonders of the World

the Divine Action by which the good is realised, the mutual love of the true and the good, called the Holy Spirit in Christianity.

The four elementary forms were the expression of two fundamental laws: resistance and motion; the fixed state, or that inertia which resists, and active life, or the volatile; in other and more general terms, matter and spirit—matter being that nothingness which is formulated by passive affirmation, spirit being the principle of absolute necessity in that which is true. The negative action of material nothing on spirit was termed the evil principle; the positive action of spirit on this same nothingness, so that it might be filled with creation and with light, was called the good principle. To these conceptions there corresponded, on the one hand, humanity and, on the other, the rational and saving life, redeeming those who are conceived in sin—that is to say, in nothingness—because of their material generation.

Such was the doctrine of secret initiation, such the admirable synthesis that the spirit of Christianity came to vivify, enlightening by its splendour, establishing divinely by its dogma and realising by its sacraments. Under the veil which was intended to preserve it this synthesis has vanished. It is destined to be recovered by man in all its primitive beauty and all its material fecundity.

BOOK III

DIVINE SYNTHESIS AND REALISATION OF MAGIA BY THE CHRISTIAN REVELATION

ג—GIMEL

CHAPTER I

CHRIST ACCUSED OF MAGIC BY THE JEWS

AT the beginning of the Gospel according to St. John there is one sentence which is never uttered by the Catholic Church except in the bending of the knees; that sentence is: "The Word was made flesh." The plenary revelation of Christianity is comprised therein. So also elsewhere the Evangelist furnishes the criterion of orthodoxy, which is the confession of Jesus Christ manifested in flesh—that is to say, in visible and human reality.

After emblazoning in his visions the pantacles and hieroglyphs of esoteric science; after exhibiting wheels revolving within wheels; after picturing living eyes turning to all the spheres; after deploying the beating wings of the four mysterious living creatures—Ezekiel, the most profound Kabalist of the ancient prophets, beholds nothing but a plain strewn with dry bones. At his word they are covered with flesh and so is form restored to them. A pitiful beauty invests these remnants of death, but that beauty is cold and lifeless. Of such were the doctrines and mythologies of the elder world, when a breath of love descended upon them from heaven. Then the dead shapes rose up; the wraiths of philosophy gave place to men of true wisdom; the Word was incarnate and alive; it was no longer the day of abstractions but one of reality. That faith which is proved by works replaced the hypotheses which ended in nothing but fables. Magic was transformed into sanctity, wonders became miracles, the common people —excluded by ancient initiation—were called to the royalty and priesthood of virtue. Realisation is thus of the essence of Christian religion, and its doctrine gives a body even to the most obvious allegories. The house of the young man who had great possessions is still shewn in Jerusalem, and it might be in no sense impossible for careful research to discover a lamp which, by a similar tradition, once belonged to one of the foolish virgins. Such ingenuous credulities are fundamentally not very dangerous; indeed they prove only the living and realising power of the Christian faith. The Jews accused that faith of having materialised belief and idealised earthly things. In our *Doctrine and Ritual of Transcendental Magic* we have recited the scandalous parable of the *Sepher Toldos Jeshu* which was invented to support the accusation. It is related in the *Talmud* that Jesus ben Sabta, or the son of the divorced woman, having studied profane mysteries in Egypt, set up a false stone in Israel and led the people into idolatry. It was acknowledged notwithstanding that the Jewish priesthood did wrong when it cursed him with both hands, and it is in this connection that we find in the *Talmud* one beautiful precept which is destined hereafter to unite Christendom and Israel: "Never curse with both hands, so that one of them may always be free to forgive and to bless." As a fact, the priesthood was guilty of injustice towards that peace-bringing Master who counselled his disciples to obey the constituted hierarchy. "They are in the seat of Moses," the Saviour said; "Do therefore that which they tell you but not as they do themselves." On another occasion he commanded ten lepers to shew their persons to the priests, and they were cured on the road. What touching abnegation in the Divine Worker of miracles, Who thus ascribed to His most deadly enemies the very honour of His miracles! For the rest, were those who accused Christ of setting up a spurious corner-stone acquainted themselves with the true one? Had not the Jews in the days of the Pharisees lost the science of that which is at once the corner-stone, the cubic stone, the philosophical stone—in a word, the fundamental stone of the Kabalistic Temple, square at the base and triangular above like the pyramids? By impeaching Jesus as an innovator did they not proclaim that they had themselves forgotten antiquity? Was not that light which Abraham saw and rejoiced extinguished for the unfaithful children of Moses, and was it not recovered by Jesus, Who made it shine with a new splendour? To be quite certain on the subject, the Gospel and *Apocalypse* of St. John must be compared with the mysterious doctrines of the *Sepher Yetzirah* and *Zohar*. It will then be realised that Christianity, so far from being a heresy in Israel, was the true orthodox tradition of Jewry, while it was the Scribes and Pharisees who were sectarians. Furthermore, Christian orthodoxy is proved by the consent of the world at large and by the suspension of the sovereign priesthood, together with the perpetual sacrifice, in Israel—the two indisputable marks of a true religion. Judaism without a temple, without a High Priest and without a sacrifice survives only as a dissident persuasion; certain persons are still Jews, but the Temple and Altar are Christian.

There is a beautiful allegorical exposition in the apocryphal gospels of this criterion of certitude in respect of Christianity: its evidence is that of realisation. Some children were amusing themselves by fashioning birds of clay, and among them was the child Jesus. Each little artist praised his own work, and only Jesus said nothing; but when He had moulded His birds, He clapped His hands, telling them to fly, and they flew. So did Christian institutions shew their superiority over those of the ancient world; the latter are dead, but Christianity is alive. Considered as the fully realised and vital expression of the Kabalah—that is to say, of primitive tradition—Christianity is still unknown, and hence that Kabalistic and prophetic book called the *Apocalypse* yet remains to be

DIVINE SYNTHESIS AND REALISATION OF MAGIA

explained, being incomprehensible without the Kabalistic Keys. The traditional interpretation was long preserved by the Johannites, or disciples of St. John; but the Gnostics intervened—to the total confusion and loss of everything, as will be made clear at a later stage.[1]

We read in the Acts of the Apostles that St. Paul at Ephesus collected all the books which treated of things curious and burnt them in public. The reference is no doubt to the old Göetic texts, or works of necromancy. The loss is regrettable assuredly, since even from the memorials of error there may shine some rays of truth, while information may consequently be derived which will prove precious to science.[2] It is a matter of general knowledge that at the advent of Christ Jesus the oracles were silenced everywhere, and a voice went wailing over the sea, crying: "Great Pan is dead." A pagan writer, who takes exception to the report, declares on his own part that the oracles did not cease, but in a little while no one was found to consult them. The rectification is valuable, for such an attempted justification is more conclusive than the pretended calumny. Much the same thing should be said concerning the works of wonder, which fell into contempt in the presence of real miracles. As a fact, if the higher laws of Nature are obedient to true moral superiority, miracles become supernatural like the virtues which produce them. This theory detracts nothing from the power of God, while the fact that the Astral Light is obedient to the superior Light of Grace signifies in reality for us that the old serpent of allegory places its vanquished head beneath the foot of the Queen of Heaven.

---

[1] We shall meet with this sect accordingly, and it will be found that the present remark is either (a) not intended to justify the alleged traditional interpretation or (b) that the initial reference has to be qualified by its subsequent extension. Johannite Christianity has been the subject of much romancing among the exponents of High-Grade Masonry. Woodford's *Cyclopædia of Freemasonry* identifies its followers with Nazarenes and Nasarites, and adds that they regarded St. John the Baptist as "the only true prophet". One order of Templar Masonry, which is now extinct, seems to have claimed connection with the Johannite sect.

[2] I have quoted elsewhere the previous remark of the author on the same subject as a curious example of how things are apt to strike a French exponent of occultism at different periods of time and in other states of emotion. "St. Paul burnt the books of Trismegistus"—not Göetic texts or works of necromancy; "Omar burned the disciples of Trismegistus (?) and St. Paul. O persecutors! O incendiaries! O coffers! When will you finish your work of darkness and destruction!" This is from the *Rituel de la Haute Magie*, p. 337.

CHAPTER II

THE WITNESS OF MAGIC TO CHRISTIANITY

MAGIC, being the science of universal equilibrium and having the truth, reality and reason of being for its absolute principle, accounts for all the antinomies and reconciles all actualities which are in conflict one with another by the one generating principle of every synthesis—that harmony results from the analogy of opposites. For the initiate of this science religion is not in doubt because it exists, and we do not deny what is. Being is being—אהיה אשר אהיה. The apparent opposition of religion and reason is the strength of both, establishing each in its distinct domain and fructifying the negative side of each by the positive side of the other: as we have just said, it is the attainment of agreement by the correspondence between things that are contrary. The cause of all religious errors and confusions is that, in ignorance of this great law, it has been sought to make religion a philosophy and philosophy in its turn a religion, subjecting matters of faith to the processes of science, which is no less ridiculous than the subjection of science to the blind obedience of faith. It is no more the province of a theologian to affirm a mathematical absurdity or reject the demonstration of a theorem than it is the province of a man of learning, in the name of science, to oppose or maintain the mysteries of dogma.

If we inquire of the Academy of Sciences whether it is mathematically true that there are Three Persons in one God and whether, on the basis of physiology, it can be certified that Mary, the Mother of God, was conceived immaculate, the Academy of Sciences will decline to judge thereon, and it will be right. Scholarship has no title to pronounce, as the questions belong to the realm of faith. An article of faith is believed or is not believed, but in either case it is not a matter of discussion: it is of faith precisely because it eludes examination by science.

When Joseph de Maistre assures us that one of these days we shall speak in terms of wonder about our actual stupidity, he is referring, no doubt, to those people of pretended strong mind who daily inform us that they will believe in the truth of a dogma when it has been proved scientifically. This is equivalent to saying that they will believe when nothing is left for believing, when dogma as such is destroyed, having become a scientific theorem. It is another way of suggesting that we shall confess to the infinite when it has been explained, determined, circumscribed, defined, or, in a word, changed into the finite. We will believe in the infinite when we are quite certain that it does not exist; we will admit the immensity of the ocean when we see it put into bottles. But then, my friends, that which has been proved to you and brought within your comprehension is henceforth a matter of knowledge and not of faith. On the other hand, if you are informed that the Pope has decided that two and two are not four and that the square of the hypotenuse is not equal to the squares drawn on the two other sides of a right-angled triangle, you would be justified in replying that the Pope has not so decided because he has no title; these things do not concern him and he may not meddle therein. Here a disciple of Rousseau will exclaim that this is all very well, but the Church does require us to believe in things which are in formal opposition to mathematics. All mathematical science tells us that the whole is greater than the part; this notwithstanding, when Jesus Christ communicates with his disciples, He must hold His entire body in His hand and put His head in His own mouth. The miserable pleasantry in question occurs textually in Rousseau. It is easy to answer that the sophist is confounding science with faith and the natural order with that which is supernatural or divine. Were it claimed by religion that in the communication of the Eucharist our Saviour had two natural bodies of the same form and size, and that one was eaten by the other, science would be entitled to protest. But religion lays down that the body of the Master is divinely and sacramentally contained under the natural sign or appearance of a fragment of bread. Once more, it is a question of believing or not believing: whosoever reasons thereon, and discusses the thing scientifically, deserves to be classed as a fool.[1]

Truth in science is proved by exact demonstrations; truth in religion is proved by unanimity of faith and holiness of works. We have authority in the Gospel to recognise that he who could say to the paralytic "Take up thy bed and walk" had the right to forgive sins. Religion is true if it is the realisation of perfect morality. Works are the proof of faith. It is permissible to ask science whether Christianity has constituted a vast association of men for whom the hierarchy is a principle, obedience the rule and charity a law. If science answers, on the basis of historical documents, that this is the case but that the association of Christians has failed in the matter of charity, then I take it at its own word, which admits the existence of charity, since it recognises that there can be deficiency therein. Charity is at once a great word and a great thing; it is a word which did not exist prior to Christianity and that which it stands for is the sum total of religion. Is not the spirit of charity the Divine Spirit made visible on earth? Has not this Spirit manifested its sensible existence by acts, institutions, monuments and by immortal works? To be brief, we do not understand how a sceptic, who is a man of good faith, can see a daughter of St. Vincent de Paul without wishing to kneel and pray. The

---

[1] In his *Fundamental Philosophy*, James Balmes seeks to shew that the Eucharistic Mystery, understood in the literal sense of transubstantiation, is not absurd in itself—that is to say, is not intrinsically contradictory. To establish that it is, one must demonstrate: (a) that to abstract passive sensibility from matter is to destroy the principle of contradiction; (b) that the correspondences between our sense organs and objects are intrinsically immutable; (c) that it is absolutely necessary for impressions to be transmitted to the sensitive faculties of the soul by those organs and that they can never be transmitted otherwise. See Book III, *Extension and Space*, c. 33, *Triumph of Religion*. I make this citation because it seems to me that Éliphas Lévi acted incautiously in debating the observation of Rousseau.

spirit of charity—this indeed is God; it is immortality in the soul; it is the hierarchy, obedience, the forgiveness of injuries, the simplicity and integrity of faith.

The separated sects are death-struck at the root because in separating they were wanting in charity, while in trying to reason on faith they were wanting in simple good sense. It is in the sects that dogma is absurd because it is pseudo-reasonable. As such it must be a scientific theorem or nothing. Now, in religion we know that the letter kills and that the spirit alone gives life; but what is the spirit in question unless it be that of charity? The faith which moves mountains and withstands martyrdom, the generosity which gives all, the eloquence which speaks with the tongue of men and angels—all this, says St. Paul, is nothing without charity. He adds that knowledge may vanish away and prophecy may cease, but charity is eternal. Charity and its works—hereof is the reality in religion: now, true reason never denies reality, for it is the demonstration of that being which is truth. It is in this manner that philosophy extends a hand to religion, but without ever wishing to usurp its domain, and, on this condition, religion blesses, encourages and enlightens philosophy by its loving splendours. Charity is the mysterious bond which, according to the dream of Greek initiates, must reconcile Eros and Anteros. It is that coping of the door of Solomon's Temple which unites the two pillars *Jachin* and *Boaz*; it is the common guarantee between rights and duties, between authority and liberty, between the strong and weak, between the people and the government, man also and woman. It is the divine sentiment which is requisite for life in human science; it is the absolute of good, as the triple principle Being-Reality-Reason is the absolute of the true. These elucidations have been necessary for the proper interpretation of that beautiful symbol of the Magi adoring the Saviour in the manger. The kings are three—one white, one tawny and one black; they offer gold, frankincense and myrrh. The reconciliation of opposites is expressed by this double triad, and it is precisely that which we have just been seeking to explain. Christianity, as expected by the Magi, was in effect the consequence of their secret doctrine; but this Benjamin of ancient Israel caused, by the fact of its birth, the death of its mother. The Magic of Light, that of the true Zoroaster, of Melchisedek and Abraham, came to an end with the advent of the Great Fulfiller. Henceforth, in a world of miracles, mere prodigies could be nothing more than a scandal and magical orthodoxy was transfigured into the orthodoxy of religion. Those who dissented could be only *illuminati* and sorcerers; the very name of Magic could be interpreted only according to its evil sense, and it is under this inhibition that we shall follow hereafter its manifestations through the centuries.

The first arch-heretic mentioned in the traditions of the Church was Simon the Magician; his legend embodies a multitude of marvels; it is an integral part of our subject and we shall endeavour to separate its basis from the cloud of fables by which it is surrounded. Simon was by nationality a Jew and is believed to have been born in the Samaritan town of

DIVINE SYNTHESIS AND REALISATION OF MAGIA

Gitton.[1] His master in Magic was a sectarian named Dositheus, who gave out that he was sent by God and was the Messiah foretold by the prophets.[2] Under his tuition Simon not only acquired the illusory arts but also certain natural secrets which belong really to the tradition of the Magi. He possessed the science of the Astral Fire and could attract great currents thereof, making himself seem impassible and incombustible. He had also the power to rise and remain in the air. Feats of this kind have been performed frequently, in the absence of science and, so to speak, accidentally, by enthusiasts intoxicated with Astral Light, as for example the convulsionaries of St. Médard; and the phenomena recur at the present day in the mediumistic state. Simon magnetised at a distance those who believed in him and appeared to them under various figures. He produced images and visible reflections—e.g. everyone, on a certain occasion, thinking that they could see fantastic trees in a bare country. Moreover, objects which are normally inanimate were moved in his vicinity, as furniture is now moved within the atmosphere of Home, the American; and, finally, when he intended to enter or leave a house the doors creaked, shook and ended by opening of their own accord.

Simon performed these wonders before the chief people of Samaria, and as his actual achievements were in due course exaggerated, the thaumaturgist passed for a divine being. It came about also that as he owed his power to states of excitement by which reason is disturbed, so he came to regard himself as such an exceptional being that he did not hesitate to claim divine honours and dreamed modestly of usurping the worship of the whole world. His crises or ecstasies produced extraordinary physical results. Sometimes he appeared pale, withered, broken, like an old man at the point of death; sometimes the luminous fluid revitalised his blood, so that his eyes shone, his skin became smooth and soft, and he appeared regenerated and renewed suddenly. The Easterns have great capacity for the amplification of wonders; they claimed to have seen Simon passing from childhood to decrepitude and again at his will returning from decrepitude into childhood. His miracles were noised abroad everywhere, till he became not only the idol of Jewish Samaria but also of the neighbouring countries.

However, the worshippers of marvels are generally hungry for new emotions and they did not fail to get weary of that which at first had astonished them. The Apostle St. Philip having reached Samaria, to preach the gospel therein, a new current of enthusiasm was thus started, with the result that Simon lost all his prestige. He was conscious, moreover, that his abnormal states had ceased—as he thought through loss of power; he believed that he was surpassed by magicians more learned than himself, and the course which he took was to attach himself to the apostles in the hope of studying, discovering or buying their secret.

[1] The place of his birth is uncertain; Cyprus is one of the alternatives.
[2] This is Dositheus of Samaria, who was contemporary with Christ. There is an account of him by St. Epiphanius and he is also mentioned by Photius.

Simon was certainly not an initiate of Transcendental Magic, which would have told him that wisdom and sanctity are needful for those who would direct the secret forces of Nature without being broken thereby; that to play with such terrible weapons without understanding them was the act of a fool; and that swift and terrible death awaits those who profane the Sanctuary of Nature. Simon was consumed by an unquenchable thirst, like that of a drunkard; the suspension of his ecstasy was the loss of all his happiness, and made ill by past excesses, he thought to regain health in renewed intoxication. One does not willingly come back to the state of a simple mortal after posing as a god. To recover that which he had lost Simon submitted therefore to all the rigours of apostolic austerity; he watched, he prayed, he fasted, but the wonders did not return. Then he reflected that between Jews it might be possible to reach an understanding, and he offered money to St. Peter. The chief of the apostles drove him indignantly away; and he who received so willingly the contributions of his disciples was now at the end of his resources; he abandoned forthwith the society of men who had shewn such disinterestedness, and with the money which St. Peter disdained he purchased a female slave named Helena.[1]

Mystical vagaries are always akin to debauch. Simon became passionately enamoured of his servant; that passion, at once weakening and exalting, restored his cataleptic states and the morbid phenomena which he termed his gifts of wonders. A mythology full of magical reminiscences, combined with erotic dreams, issued fully armed from his brain; he undertook pilgrimages like the apostles, carrying Helena with him, dogmatising and shewing himself to those who were willing to worship and doubtless also to pay him.

According to Simon, the first manifestation of God was by means of a perfect splendour which produced its reflection immediately. He was himself this sun of souls and the reflection was Helena, whom he affected to call Selene, being the name of the moon in Greek. Now the moon of Simon came down at the beginning of the ages on that earth which the magus had mapped out in his perpetual dreams. There she became a mother, impregnated by the thought of his sun, and she brought into the world angels, whom she reared by herself without speaking of them to their father. The angels rebelled against her and imprisoned her in a mortal body. It was then that the splendour of God was compelled to descend in its turn that it might redeem Helena, and so the Jew Simon was manifested on earth. There he had to overcome death and carry his Helena through the air, followed by the triumphant choir of the elect, while the rest of mankind was abandoned on earth to the eternal tyranny of the angels. Thus the arch-heretic, imitating Christianity but in the reverse sense, affirmed the eternal reign of revolt and evil, represented the world as

[1] It is, I believe, one of the Christian apologists who mentions that Helen was found by Simon in a house of ill-fame at Tyre. It is said otherwise that she was Helen of Troy in a previous incarnation.

DIVINE SYNTHESIS AND REALISATION OF MAGIA

created or at least completed by demons, destroyed the order and the hierarchy, to pose alone with his concubine as the way, the truth and the life. Here was the doctrine of Antichrist, and it was not to perish with Simon, for it has been perpetuated to our own days. Indeed prophetic traditions of Christianity speak of his transitory reign and triumph to come as heralding the most terrible calamities. Simon claimed the title of saint and, by a curious coincidence, the chief of a modern Gnostic sect which recalls all the sensuous mysticism of the first arch-heretic—the inventor of the "free woman"—is also named Saint-Simon. Cainism is the name which might be given to all the false revelations issued from this impure source. They are dogmas of malediction and of hatred against universal harmony and social order; they are disordered passions affirming licence in the place of duty, sensual love instead of chaste and devoted love, the prostitute in place of the mother, and Helena, concubine of Simon, in place of Mary, the mother of the Saviour.

Simon became a notoriety and repaired to Rome, where the emperor, attracted by all extraordinary spectacles, was disposed to welcome him: this emperor was Nero. The illuminated Jew astonished the crowned fool by a trick which is common in jugglery. He was decapitated, but afterwards saluted the emperor, his head being restored to his shoulders. He caused furniture to move and doors to open; in a word, he acted as a veritable medium and became sorcerer-in-ordinary at the orgies of Nero and the banquets of Trimalcyon. According to the legend-makers, it was to rescue the Jews of Rome from the doctrine of Simon that St. Peter himself visited that capital of the world. Nero, by means of his inferior spies, was informed speedily that a new worker of Israelitish wonders had arrived to make war on his own enchanter, and he resolved to bring them together for his amusement. Petronius and Tigellinus were perhaps at this feast.[1]

"May peace be with you," said the prince of apostles on entering. "We have nothing to do with your peace," answered Simon. "It is by war that truth is discovered. Peace between adversaries is the victory of one and the defeat of the other."

St. Peter answered: "Why do you reject peace? The vices of men have created war, but peace ever abides with virtue."

"Virtue is power and skill," said Simon. "For myself I face the fire, I rise in the air, I restore plants, I change stones into bread; and you, what do you do?"

"I pray for you," said St. Peter, "that you may not perish the victim of your enchantments."

"Keep your prayers; they will not ascend to heaven as quickly as myself."

And behold the magician passing out by a window and rising in the air outside. Whether this was accomplished by means of some aërostatic

---

[1] Because they were both favourites of Nero, or because the reference to a feast reminded Éliphas Lévi of the celebrated Banquet in the *Satyricon* of Petronius Arbiter. Sophronius Tigellinus was one of Nero's ministers.

apparatus concealed under his long robes or whether he was lifted up, like the convulsionaries of Paris the Deacon, owing to an exaltation of the Astral Light, we are unable to say; but during this phenomenon St. Peter was praying on his knees, and Simon fell suddenly with a great cry, to be raised with his thighs broken. Nero imprisoned St. Peter, who seemed a far less diverting magician than Simon; the latter died of his fall. The whole of this history, which belongs to the popular rumours of the period, is now relegated, though perhaps wrongly, to the region of apocryphal legends.[1] On such account it is not less remarkable or less worthy to be preserved.

The sect of Simon did not end with himself, and his successor was one of his disciples, named Menander.[2] He did not pose as a god, being contented with the role of a prophet; but when he baptised proselytes, a visible fire came down upon the water. He also promised immortality of soul and body as the result of this magical immersion, and in the days of St. Justin, there were still followers of Menander who firmly believed themselves immortal. The deaths which occurred among them by no means disabused the others, for those who died were excommunicated forthwith, on the ground that they had been false brethren. For these believers death was an actual apostasy and their immortal ranks were filled up by enrolling new proselytes. Those who understand the extent of human folly will not be surprised to hear that in this present year, being 1858, there exists in America and France a fanatical sect in continuation of that of Menander.[3]

The qualification of magician added to the name of Simon rendered Magic a thing of horror to Christians; but they did not on this account cease to honour the memory of the Magi-Kings who adored the Saviour in His cradle.

---

[1] The dispute between St. Peter and Simon the Magician is not a matter of popular rumour; it is a methodical account contained in one of the forged *Recognitions* ascribed to St. Clement. It will be understood that the version presented by Éliphas Lévi is decorated by his own imagination. It seems generally regarded as certain that Simon visited Rome to enrol disciples, and there is the authority of Eusebius for some kind of meeting with St. Peter.

[2] It might be more accurate to say that there were many successors, of whom Menander was the chief. So also there were many Simonian sects, including the school which followed Dositheus, described by Lévi and others as the master of Simon. Menander claimed to be the envoy of the Supreme Power of God.

[3] They were not included at the period—about 1865—in *La France Mystique* of Erdan, though it contained *choses inouies*; and they are not found among *les petites religions de Paris* at the present day, though it contains a Gnostic church confessing to a hierarchic government and, I believe, with an authorised branch at San Francisco —perhaps less *in partibus infidelium* than is the sect in its own country.

Disputation between Simon the Magician and St. Peter and St. Paul

CHAPTER III

THE DEVIL

BY its clear formulation of concepts respecting the Divine, Christianity leads us to the understanding of God as the most absolute and the most purest love, while it defines, not less clearly, the spirit which is opposed to God, the spirit of revolt and hatred: hereof is Satan. But this spirit is not a personality and is not to be regarded as a kind of black god: it is a perversity which is common to all extralineal intelligences. "My name is legion," says Satan in the Gospel, "for we are many." The birth of intelligence may be compared to the Star of the Morning, and, after it has shone for an instant, if it fall of its own accord into the void of darkness we may apply to it that apostrophe which was uttered by Isaiah to the king of Babylon: "How art thou fallen from heaven, O Lucifer, Son of the Morning?" But does this mean that the celestial Lucifer, the Morning Star of intelligence, has been changed into a brand of hell? Can the name of "Light-bearer" be applied justly to the angel of trespass and of darkness? We think not, more especially if it be understood, as we understand, who have the magical tradition behind us, that the hell personified by Satan, and symbolised by the old serpent, is that central fire which encompasses the earth, consuming all that it produces and devouring its own tail, like the serpent of Kronos—in a word, that Astral Light of which the Almighty spoke to Cain when He said, "If thou doest evil, sin shall be straightway at thy gates"—that is to say, disorder will take possession of all thy senses; "yet unto thee I have made subject the lust of death, and it is for thee to rule it."[1]

The royal and almost divine personification of Satan is a blunder which goes back to the false Zoroaster or, otherwise, to the sophisticated doctrine of the later and materialistic Magi of Persia; it was they who represented the two poles of the intellectual world as deities, making a divinity out of passive force in contradistinction to that force which is active. We have indicated that the same grave error was made by Indian mythology. Ahriman, or Siva, is the father of the demon, as the latter is understood by superstitious makers of legend, and hence it was said by our Saviour, "The devil is a liar like his father." On this question the Church rests satisfied with the Gospel texts and has published no dogmatic decisions, having the definition of the devil as their object. Good Christians avoid even naming him, while religious moralists recommend the faithful

[1] I have given Lévi's version literally without pretending to account for it. In the authorised version the passage reads: "If thou doest not well, sin lieth at the door. And unto thee shall be his desire, and thou shalt rule over him." Genesis iv, 7.

DIVINE SYNTHESIS AND REALISATION OF MAGIA

to take no concern regarding him, seeking to resist his arts by thinking only of God. We cannot but admire this wise reserve on the part of priestly teaching. Why indeed should the light of doctrine be reflected on him who is intellectual obscurity and darkest night of the heart? Let the spirit which would distract us from the knowledge of God remain unknown by us. It is assuredly not of our intention to perform what the Church has omitted; we certify on such a subject only as to the secret instruction of initiates in the occult sciences. They have said that the Great Magical Agent—accurately termed Lucifer because it is the vehicle of light and the receptacle of all forms—is a mediating force diffused throughout creation; that it serves for creation and destruction; that the fall of Adam was an erotic intoxication which made his race subject to that fatal light; that all amorous passion which invades the senses is a whirlpool of this light, seeking to draw us down into the gulf of death; that madness, hallucinations, visions, ecstasies, constitute an exceedingly dangerous exaltation of this interior phosphorus; finally, that the light in question is of the nature of fire, that it is warming and vivifying in its prudent use, but that it burns, dissolves and destroys in its excess. Over this light man is called, on the one hand, to assume a sovereign empire, so earning his immortality, but, on the other, he is menaced by the intoxication, absorption and eternal destruction thereof. In its devouring, avenging and fatal aspect the Astral Light may be called the fire of hell, the serpent of legend, while the tormented sin which abounds therein, the tears and the gnashing of teeth on the part of the abortions that it consumes, the phantom of life which escapes them and seems to insult their misery—all this may be termed the devil or Satan. Among the pomps and works of hell may be included, in fine, those actions, those illusionary images of pleasure, wealth and glory which are misdirected by the vertigo of this light.

Father Hilarion Tissot regards certain nervous diseases which are accompanied by hallucinations and delirium as diabolical possessions, and, understood in the sense of the Kabalists, he is right assuredly. Whatsoever delivers our soul to the fatality of vertigo is truly infernal, since heaven is the eternal reign of order, intelligence and liberty. The possessed people of the Gospel fled away from Jesus Christ; the oracles were silenced in the presence of the apostles; while those who are prey to the disease of hallucination have ever manifested an invincible repugnance for initiates and sages. The suspension of oracles and obsessions proved the triumph of human liberty over fatality. When astral diseases reappear, it is an ominous sign of spiritual enervation, and manifestations of this kind are followed invariably by fatal disorders. The disturbances here referred to continued till the French Revolution, and the fanatics of Saint-Médard were the prophets of its sanguinary calamities. The famous criminologist Torreblanca, who had gone to the root of Diabolical Magic, described accurately all the phenomena of astral disturbance when classifying the works of the dæmon. Here are some extracts from the 15th chapter of his work on *Operative Magic*:[1] (1) The demon is endeavouring continually to lead us into error. (2) He deludes the senses by disturbing the imagination, though he cannot change its nature. (3) When things abnormal are manifested to the eye of man, an imaginary body assumes shape in the mind, and so long as that phantom remains therein the phenomena continue. (4) The demon destroys equilibrium in the imagination by a disturbance of the vital functions, whether by irregularity in health or actual disease. (5) When some morbid cause has destroyed this equilibrium, and that also of reason, waking dream becomes possible and that which has no existence assumes the semblance of reality. (6) The mental perception of images in this manner makes sight unworthy of trust. (7) Visions are bodied forth, but they are merely thought-forms. (8) The ancients distinguished two orders of disease, one of them being the perception of imaginary forms, which was termed frenzy, and the other corybantism, or the hearing of voices and other sounds which have no existence.

It follows from these statements, which are curious in several respects, that disease is attributed by Torreblanca to the demon, who indeed is disease itself, with which we should agree entirely—if permitted by dogmatic authority. The recurring efforts of the Astral Light to disintegrate and absorb entities are part of its nature; its ceaseless currents have a wearing effect like water and it consumes even as fire, for it is the very essence and dissolving force of fire. The spirit of perversity and the love of destruction which characterise those whom it governs are instincts of this force. They are further consequent on the suffering of the soul, which is conscious of incomplete life and feels torn in opposite directions. The soul yearns to make an end of itself, yet fears to die alone, and therefore would include all creation in its destruction. Such astral perversity assumes frequently the form of the hatred of children; an unknown power impels certain subjects to kill them, and imperious voices seem to demand their death. Dr. Brierre de Boismont cites terrible examples of this mania, recalling the crimes of Papavoine and Henriette Cornier.

Sufferers from astral perversion are malevolent, and they are jealous at the joy of others; they are especially inimical to hope, and even when offering consolation they choose the most desperate and heartrending figures of speech. The explanation is that their life is synonymous with suffering and that they have been whirled into the dance of death. It is, moreover, astral perversion and the lust of death which abuses the act of generation, leading to its perversion or dishonour by sacrilegious mockeries and shameful pleasantries. Obscenity is a blasphemy against life. Each of these vices is personified by a black idol or by a demon, which is the negative and distorted reflection of the divinity who com-

[1] I suppose that reference is intended to *Epitome Delictorum, sive de Magia, in qua aperta vel occulta invocatio Dæmonum*, etc., 4to. I have no record of the first edition, but it was reprinted at Leyden in 1679.

municates life; these are idols of death. Moloch is the fatality which devours infants. Satan and Nisroch are gods of hatred, fatality and despair. Astarte, Lilith, Nehamah, Ashtaroth are idols of debauchery and abortion. Adramelech is the god of murder, while Belial is that of eternal revolt and anarchy. Such are the monstrous conceptions of reason, when it pauses on the verge of extinction and slavishly worships its destroyer, so that it may reach the end of its torment by the destroyer absorbing it. According to the Kabalists, the true name of Satan is that of Jehovah reversed, for Satan is not a black god but the negation of Deity. He is the personification of atheism and idolatry. The devil is not a personality for initiates but a force created with a good object, though it can be applied to evil: it is really the instrument of liberty. They represented this force, which presides over physical generation, under the mythological figure of the horned god Pan, and hence comes the goat of the Sabbath, brother of the old serpent, the light-bearer or phosphorus, converted by poets into the false Lucifer of legend.

CHAPTER IV

THE LAST PAGANS

THE eternal miracle of God is the unchangeable order of His providence in the harmonies of Nature; prodigies are derangements and are attributable only to degeneration in the creature. Divine miracle is thus a providential reaction for the restoration of the broken order. When Jesus cured the possessed He calmed them and suspended the marvels which they produced; when the apostles subdued the exaltation of the pythonesses they put an end to divination. The spirit of error is a spirit of agitation and subversion; the spirit of truth brings tranquillity and peace in its path. Such was the civilising influence of Christianity at its dawn; but those passions which are friends of disturbance did not, without a struggle, leave it in possession of the palm of easy victory. Expiring polytheism drew powers from the Magic of the old sanctuaries; to the mysteries of the Gospel it still opposed those of Eleusis. Apollonius of Tyana was set up as a parallel to the Saviour of the world, and Philostratus undertook to construct a legend on the subject of this new deity. Thereafter came the Emperor Julian, who would have been himself deified if the javelin which slew him had not also struck the last blow at Cæsarian idolatry. The enforced and decrepit rebirth of a religion which was dead in its forms was a literal abortion, and Julian, who attempted it, was doomed to perish with the senile offspring which he strove to bring into the world.

This notwithstanding, Apollonius and Julian were two curious, even great, personalities, and their history is epoch-making in the annals of Magic. Allegorical legends were in fashion at that period. Those who were masters embodied their doctrine in their personality, and those who were initiated disciples wrote fables which combined the secrets of initiation. The history of Apollonius by Philostratus, too absurd if it be taken literally, becomes memorable when its symbolism is examined according to the data of science. It is a kind of pagan gospel, opposed to that of Christianity; it is a secret doctrine at large, and we are in a position to reconstruct and explain it.

In the third book of Philostratus, the initial chapter contains an account of Hyphasis, a wonderful river which rises in a certain plain and is lost in unapproachable regions. That river represents magical knowledge, which is simple in its first principles but difficult to deduce accurately in respect of final consequences.[1] Philostratus tells us in this connection that marriages are not fruitful unless consecrated by the balsam of trees

[1] It has to be observed that the Hyphasis was a certain river of India which is assigned by tradition as the boundary of Alexander's conquests. Had Éliphas Lévi been acquainted with this fact he might have allegorised with success thereon.

DIVINE SYNTHESIS AND REALISATION OF MAGIA

which grow on the banks of Hyphasis. The fish of this river are sacred to Venus; their crest is blue, the scales are of many colours and their tail is golden: they can raise the tail at will. In the river there is also an animal resembling a white worm, the stewing of which produces an inflammable oil that can be kept in glass only. The animal is reserved only for the king's service, as it has power to overthrow walls. When the grease of it is exposed to the air it ignites, and there is then nothing in the whole world with which the flame can be extinguished.

By the fish of the river Hyphasis Apollonius signifies universal configuration which magnetic experiments have recently proved to be blue on one side, golden on that which is opposite and of many colours at the centre. The white worm is the Astral Light, which resolves into oil when condensed by a triple fire, and such oil is the Universal Medicine. It can only be contained by glass, this being a non-conductor for the Astral Light, its porousness being inappreciable. This secret is reserved to the king, which means an initiate of the first order, for it is truly concerned with a force by which cities can be destroyed. Some important secrets are here indicated with great clearness.

In the next chapter Philostratus speaks of unicorns and says that the horn of these animals can be fashioned into drinking-cups which are a safeguard against all poisons. The single horn of the symbolical creature represents hierarchic unity, and hence Philostratus adds, on the authority of Damis, that the cups in question are also exclusive to kings. "Happy," says Apollonius, "is he who is never intoxicated but in drinking out of such a goblet."

Damis narrates further that Apollonius met with a woman who was white from feet to breasts but black in the upper region. His disciples were alarmed at the prodigy, but the master gave her his hand, for he knew her. He told them that she was the Indian Venus, whose colours are those of the bull Apis, adored by the Egyptians. This harlequin female is magical science, the white limbs—or created forms—of which reveal the black head, or that supreme cause which is unknown to man at large. But Philostratus and Damis knew, and it was under emblems like these that they gave expression in concealment to the doctrine of Apollonius. The secret of the Great Work is contained in the fifth to the tenth chapters of this third book, and the form of symbolism adopted is that of dragons defending the entrance to a palace of the wise.[1] There are three species of dragons—dwellers respectively of marshes, plains and mountains. The mountain is Sulphur, the marsh Mercury and the plain is the Salt

[1] It is noticeable that the alchemists of past centuries, who were so apt to see the Hermetic Mystery at large in all literature, and who fathered many mythical treatises on the great and the holy men of old, are silent regarding Apollonius. I am far from admitting the interpretation of Éliphas Lévi, as Philostratus belongs to the dawn of the third century, when alchemy may be said to have been unborn; but I am sure that if the early expositors had known the life of Apollonius they might almost have suspected something. Even the Abbé Pernety missed the obvious opportunity in his discourse on the Hermetic significance of the Greek and Egyptian fables.

of the Philosophers. The dragons of the plain are pointed on the back, like a saw-fish, referring to the acid potency of salt. Those of the mountains have golden scales and a golden beard, while the sound of their creeping movement is like the tinkling of copper. In their head is a stone by which all miracles can be worked. They bask on the shores of the Red Sea and they are caught by the help of a red cloth embroidered with golden letters; on these enchanted letters they lay their head and fall asleep, and they are then decapitated with an axe. Who does not recognise here the Stone of the Philosophers, the Magistery at the Red and the famous regimen of fire, represented by golden letters? Under the name of Citadel of the Wise, Philostratus goes on to describe the Athanor as a hill surrounded by a mist but open on the southern side. It has a well four paces in breadth, from which an azure vapour rises, drawn up by the warmth of the sun and displaying all colours of the rainbow. The bottom of the well is sanded with red arsenic. In its vicinity is a basin filled with fire, and thence rises a livid flame, odourless and smokeless, and never higher or lower than the basin-edge. There are also two reservoirs of black stone, in one of which rain is stored and in the other wind. The rain-cistern is opened when there is excessive drought and then clouds come forth which water the whole country. It would be difficult to describe more exactly the Secret Fire of the Philosophers and that which they term their *Balneum Mariæ*. It follows from this account that the ancient alchemists employed electricity, magnetism and steam in their Great Work.

Philostratus speaks subsequently of the Philosophical Stone itself, which he calls indifferently a Stone and Light. "The profane are not permitted to discover it, because it vanishes if not laid hold of according to the processes of the Art. It is the wise only who, by means of certain verbal formulæ and rites, can attain the *Pantarba*. This is the name of the Stone, which at night has the appearance of fire, being flaming and sparkling, while in the day it dazzles by its brightness. This light is a subtle matter of admirable virtue, for it attracts all that is near it.[1]

The above revelation concerning the secret doctrines of Apollonius proves that the Philosophical Stone is no other than an universal magnet, formed of the Astral Light condensed and fixed about a centre. It is an artificial phosphorus containing the concentrated virtues of all generative heat, and the multitude of allegories and traditions extant concerning it are as testimonies to its certain existence.[2]

The entire life of Apollonius, as recorded by Philostratus, following Damis the Assyrian, is a tissue of apologues and parables, the concealed doctrine of great masters of initiation being written in this manner at the period, as already intimated. We know therefore why the recital embodies

---

[1] It must be remembered that the Stone in symbolism is far older than the particular symbol which is called the Philosophical Stone, or Stone of Alchemy.
[2] The last statement obtains in respect of the Mystic Stone, as understood, for example, by Zoharic writers.

fables, and underneath the text of these fables we should expect to find, and may even look to understand, the secret knowledge of the hierophants.

His great science and conspicuous virtues notwithstanding, Apollonius was not a successor in the hierarchic school of the Magi. His initiation had India as its source and he was addicted to the enervating practices of the Brahmins; further, he preached rebellion and regicide openly: he was a great character in a wrong path. The figure of the Emperor Julian seems more poetic and beautiful than that of Apollonius; he maintained on the throne of the world all the austerity of a sage; and he sought to transpose the young sap of Christianity into the enfeebled body of Hellenism. He was a noble maniac, guilty only of too much devotion to the associations of the fatherland and the images of its ancestral gods. As a counterpoise to the realising efficacy of Christian doctrine he called Black Magic to his aid and plunged into darksome evocations, following the lead of Jamblichus and Maximus of Ephesus. But the gods whom he desired to resuscitate in their youth and beauty appeared before him cold and decrepit, shrinking from life and light, and ready to fly before the sign of the cross.

The closing had been taken in full according to the grade of Hellenism, and the Galilean had conquered. Julian died like a hero, without blaspheming Him who overcame, as it had been falsely pretended.[1] Ammianus Marcellinus portrays his last moments at length: they were those of a warrior and philosopher. The maledictions of Christian sacerdotalism echoed long over his tomb; has not the Saviour, that lover of noble souls, pardoned adversaries less interesting and less generous than the unfortunate Julian?

On the death of this emperor, Magic and idolatry were involved in one and the same universal reprobation. At this time there came into existence those secret associations of adepts, to which Gnostics and Manicheans gravitated at a later period. The societies in question were the depositaries of a tradition of errors and truths admixed; but they transmitted, under the seal of terrific pledges, the Great Arcanum of ancient omnipotence, together with the ever frustrated hopes of extinct worships and fallen priesthoods.

---

[1] The introduction to the *Dogme de la Haute Magie* says: (*a*) That Julian was one of the illuminated and an initiate of the first order; (*b*) That he was a Gnostic allured by the allegories of Greek polytheism; (*c*) That he had the satisfaction of expiring like Epaminondas with the periods of Cato.

CHAPTER V

LEGENDS

THE strange narratives embodied in the *Golden Legend*, howsoever fabulous they may be, are referable notwithstanding to the highest Christian antiquity. They are parables rather than histories; the style is simple and Eastern, like that of the Gospels; and their traditional existence proves that a species of mythology had been devised to conceal the Kabalistic mysteries of Johannite initiation. The *Golden Legend* is a Christian Talmud expressed in allegories and apologues. Studied from this point of view, the newer in proportion as it is more ancient, the work will become of real importance and highest interest.[1] One of the narratives in this Legend so full of mysteries characterises the conflict of Magic and dawning Christianity in a manner which is equally dramatic and startling. It is like an outline in advance of Chateaubriand's *Martyrs* and the *Faust* of Goethe combined.

Justina was a young and lovely pagan maiden, daughter of a priest of the idols, after the manner of Cymodoce. Her window opened on a court which gave upon the Christian church, so that she heard daily the pure and recollected voice of a deacon reading the holy Gospels aloud. The unknown words touched and stirred her heart, so deeply indeed that when her mother remarked one evening how grave she seemed, and sought to be the confidant of her preoccupations, Justina fell at her feet and said, "Bless me, my mother, or forgive me: I am a Christian." The mother wept and embraced her, after which she returned to her husband and related what she had heard. That night in their sleep the parents were both visited by the same dream. A divine light descended upon them, a sweet voice called them and said: "Come unto me, all ye that are afflicted, and I will comfort you. Come, ye beloved of my father, and I will give unto you the kingdom which has been prepared for you from the beginning of the world."

The morning dawned; father and mother blessed their daughter. All three were enrolled among the catechumens and, after the usual probation, they were admitted to Holy Baptism. Justina returned white and radiant from the church, between her mother and aged father, when two forbidding men, wrapped in their mantles, passed as Faust and Mephistopheles going by Margaret: they were Cyprian the magician and his disciple Acladius. They stopped, dazzled by the apparition, but Justina went on without seeing them and reached home with her family.

[1] The *Golden Legend* was compiled about 1275 by Jacobus de Voragine, Archbishop of Genoa. His authorities were (*a*) Eusebius, (*b*) St. Jerome, (*c*) legendary matter. I am sure that Kabalistic mysteries and Johannite initiation must look elsewhere for their records. The suggestion, however, is not worth debating.

DIVINE SYNTHESIS AND REALISATION OF MAGIA

The scene now changes and we are in the laboratory of Cyprian. Circles have been traced, a slaughtered victim still palpitates by a smoking chafing-dish; the genius of darkness stands in the presence of the magician, saying: "Thou hast called me; I come. Speak: what dost thou require?"—"I love a virgin."—"Seduce her."—"She is a Christian." —"Denounce her."—"I would possess and not lose her: canst thou aid me?"—"I tempted Eve, who was innocent and conversed daily with God Himself. If thy virgin be Christian, know that it is I who caused Jesus Christ to be crucified."—"Thou wilt deliver her into my hands, therefore." —"Take this magical unguent, and anoint the threshold of her dwelling: the rest concerns me."

And now Justina is asleep in her small and simple room, but Cyprian is at the door murmuring sacrilegious words and performing horrible rites. The demon creeps to the pillow of the young girl and instils voluptuous dreams full of the image of Cyprian, whom she seems to meet again on issuing from the church. This time, however, she looks at him; she listens, while the things which he whispers fill her heart with trouble. But she moves suddenly, she awakes and signs herself with the cross. The demon vanishes and the seducer, doing sentinel at the door, waits vainly through the whole night.

On the morrow he renews his evocations and loads his infernal accomplice with bitter reproaches. The latter confesses his inability, is driven forth in disgrace, and Cyprian invokes a demon of superior class, who transforms himself by turns into a young girl and a beautiful youth, tempting Justina by advice as well as caresses. She is on the point of yielding, but her good angel helps her; she joins inspiration to the sign of the cross and expels the evil spirit. Cyprian thereupon invokes the king of hell and Satan arrives in person. He visits Justina with all the woes of Job and spreads a frightful plague through Antioch; the oracles, at his instigation, declare that it will cease only when Justina shall satisfy Venus and love, who are alike outraged. Justina, however, prays in public for the people, and the pest ceases. Satan is baffled in his turn; Cyprian compels him to acknowledge the omnipotence of the sign of the cross and defies him by making it on his own person. He abjures Magic, becomes a Christian, is consecrated bishop and meets with Justina in a convent. They love now with the pure and lasting love of heavenly charity; persecution befalls both; they are arrested together, put to death on the same day and ratify in the breast of God their mystical and eternal marriage.[1]

According to the legend, St. Cyprian was Bishop of Antioch, but ecclesiastical history says that his seat was that of Carthage. It matters little, for the rest, whether the personalities are the same; the one belongs to poetry, while the other is a father and martyr of the Church.

---

[1] In the *Golden Legend* the story is entitled "Of St. Justina", whose festival is on September 26. St. Cyprian, Bishop of Carthage, is entirely distinct from the Cyprian of legend.

THE HISTORY OF MAGIC

There is extant among the old Grimoires a prayer attributed to the St. Cyprian of legend, who is possibly the holy Bishop of Carthage: its obscure and figurative expressions may have given credit to the idea that prior to his conversion he was addicted to the deadly practices of Black Magic. It may be rendered thus.

"I, Cyprian, servant of our Lord Jesus Christ, have prayed unto God the Father Almighty, saying: Thou art the strong God, my God omnipotent, dwelling in the great light. Thou art holy and worthy of praise, and Thou hast beheld in the old days the malice of Thy servant and the iniquities into which I was plunged by the wiles of the demon. I was ignorant of Thy true name; I passed in the midst of the sheep and they were without a shepherd. The clouds shed no dew on earth; trees bare no fruit and women in labour could not be delivered. I bound and did not loose; I bound the fishes of the sea, and they were captive; I bound the pathways of the sea, and many evils did I encompass. But now, Lord Jesus Christ, I have known Thy Holy Name, I have loved Thee, I am converted with my whole heart, my whole soul and all my inward being. I have turned from the multitude of my sins, that I may walk in Thy love and follow Thy commandments, which are henceforth my faith and my prayer. Thou art the Word of truth, the sole Word of the Father, and I conjure Thee now to break the chain of clouds and send down on Thy children Thy goodly rain like milk, to set free the rivers and liberate those who swim, as also those which fly. I conjure Thee to break all the chains and remove all the obstacles by the virtue of Thy Holy Name."

The antiquity of this prayer is evident and it embodies most remarkable reminiscences of primitive types belonging to Christian esotericism during the first centuries of this era.

The qualification of "Golden" given to the fabulous legend of allegorical saints is a sufficient indication of its character. Gold, in the eyes of initiates, is condensed light; the sacred numbers of the Kabalah were called golden; the moral instructions of Pythagoras were contained in *Golden Verses*; and for the same reason that mysterious work of Apuleius in which an ass has an important role, is called the *Golden Ass*.

The Christians were accused by Pagans of worshipping an ass, and the slander in question is not of their own devising; it is referable to the Jews of Samaria, who expressed Kabalistic ideas on the Divinity by means of Egyptian symbols. Intelligence was represented in the symbol of a magical star, venerated under the name of *Rempham*; science was depicted by the emblem of *Anubis*, the latter name being altered into *Nibbas*; whilst vulgar faith or credulity appeared in the likeness of *Thartac*, a god represented holding a book, wearing a mantle and having the head of an ass.[1] According to the Samaritan doctors, Christianity was the reign of *Thartac*, or blind faith and vulgar credulity set up as an universal oracle, superior to understanding and knowledge. This is why,

[1] This pictorial sign appears in an old Grimoire.

DIVINE SYNTHESIS AND REALISATION OF MAGIA

in their intercourse with Gentiles and when they heard themselves identified by these with Christians, they protested and begged not to be confounded with the worshippers of an ass's head. The pretended revelation diverted the philosophers, and Tertullian mentions a Roman caricature, extant in his days, which exhibited *Thartac* in all his glory, identified as the god of Christianity, much to the amusement of Tertullian, though he was the author of that famous aphorism: *Credo quia absurdum*.[1]

The Golden Ass of Apuleius is the occult legend of *Thartac*. It is a magical epic and a satire against Christianity, which the author had doubtless professed for a period, or so at least he appears to intimate under the allegory of his metamorphosis into an ass. The story of the work is as follows. Apuleius was travelling in Thessaly, the country of enchantments. He received hospitality at the house of a man whose wife was a sorceress, and he seduced the servant of his hostess, thinking to obtain in this manner the secrets of her mistress. The maid promised to deliver to her lover a concoction by means of which the sorceress changed herself into a bird, but she made a mistake in the box and Apuleius was transformed into an ass. She could only console him by saying that to regain his proper form it would be sufficient to eat roses, the rose being the flower of initiation. The difficulty at the moment being to find roses in the night, it was decided to wait till the morrow and the servant therefore stabled the ass, but only for it to be taken by robbers and carried off. There was little chance now of coming across roses, which are not intended for asses, and gardeners chased away the animal with sticks.

During his long and sad captivity he heard the history of Psyche related, that marvellous and symbolical legend which was like the soul and poetry of his own experience. Psyche desired to take by surprise the secrets of love, as Apuleius sought those of Magic; she lost love and he the human form. She was an exiled wanderer, living under the wrath of Venus, and he was the slave of thieves. But after having journeyed through hell, Psyche was to return into heaven, and the gods took pity on Lucius. Isis appeared to him in a dream and promised that her priest, warned by a revelation, would give him roses during the solemnities of her coming festival. That festival arrived, and Apuleius describes at great length the procession of Isis; the account is valuable to science, for

---

[1] With this reverie of Éliphas Lévi on the subject of the mystic ass let us compare another which is of an entirely different order, though it belongs to the same category. (1) It is recorded by Josephus that a certain Jew named Onias obtained leave from Ptolemy Philometor to build a temple in honour of God at a certain place in Arabia which was subsequently called Onium, after the founder. (2) This Onium was not Heliopolis, as supposed commonly. (3) The Temple at Onium, on account of a similitude of sound, was connected with the Greek word ονος, signifying Ass. (4) The Greeks in consequence believed themselves to have discovered the secret object of Jewish worship, being the animal in question. (5) It was asserted that there was an ass's head in the vestibule of every Jewish temple. (6) As the Greeks did not closely distinguish between Jews and Christians, the ass came also to be called the god of the Christians.—Jacob Bryant: *Analysis of Antient Mythology*, 3rd edition, vol. vi, pp. 82 *et seq*.

it gives the key of Egyptian mysteries. Men in disguise come first, carrying grotesque animals; these are the vulgar fables. Women follow strewing flowers and bearing on their shoulders mirrors which reflect the image of the great divinity. So do men go in front and formulate dogmas which women embellish, reflecting unconsciously the higher truths, owing to their maternal instincts. Men and women came afterwards in company as light-bearers; they represented the alliance of the two terms, the active and passive generators of science and life.[1] After the light came harmony, represented by young musicians, and, in fine, the images of gods, to the number of three, followed by the grand hierophant, carrying, instead of an image, the symbol of great Isis, being a globe of gold surmounted by a Caduceus. Lucius Apuleius beheld a crown of roses in the hands of the high priest; he approached and was not repulsed; he ate the roses and was restored to human shape.

All this is learnedly written and intermingled with episodes which are now heroic and again grotesque in character, as befitted the double nature of Lucius and the ass. Apuleius was at once the Rabelais and Swedenborg of the old world at the close of the epoch.

The great masters of Christianity either failed or refused to understand the mysticism of the *Golden Ass*. St. Augustine in the *City of God* asks in the most serious manner whether one is to believe that Apuleius was metamorphosed literally into an ass and seems disposed to admit the possibility, but only as an exceptional phenomenon—from which nothing follows as a consequence. If this be an irony on his part, it must be allowed that it is cruel, but if it be ingenuousness . . . However, St. Augustine, the acute rhetorician of Madaura, was scarcely given to being ingenuous.

Blind and unfortunate indeed were those initiates of the Antique Mysteries who ridiculed the ass of Bethlehem without perceiving the infant God Who shone upon the peaceful animals in the stable—the Child on whose forehead reposed the conciliating star of all the past and future. Whilst philosophy, convicted of impotence, offered insult to victorious Christianity, the fathers of the Church assumed all the magnificence of Plato and created a new philosophy based upon the living reality of the Divine Word, ever present in His Church, reborn in each of its members and immortal in humanity. It would be a greater dream of pride than that of Prometheus, were it not at the same time a doctrine which is all abnegation and all devotion, human because it is divine and divine because it is human.

---

[1] The commentary of the *Zohar* on Genesis ii, 22, says that the words "which the Lord God had taken from man" signify that the Tradition has issued from the Written Doctrine. The words "and brought him to man" indicate that the Traditional Law must not remain isolated: it can only exist in union with the Written Law. Part I, fol. 48b. It follows, and is made plain elsewhere, that man is the Written Law and woman the Secret Doctrine.

CHAPTER VI

SOME KABALISTIC PAINTINGS AND SACRED EMBLEMS

IN obedience to the Saviour's formal precept, the primitive Church did not expose its Most Holy Mysteries to the chance of profanation by the crowd. Admission to Baptism and the Eucharist was in virtue of progressive initiations; the sacred books were also held in concealment, their free study and, above all, interpretation being reserved to the priesthood. Moreover, images were fewer and less explicit in character. The feeling of the time refrained from reproducing the figure of Christ Himself, and the paintings on the catacombs were, for the most part, Kabalistic emblems. There was the Edenic Cross with the four rivers, where harts came to drink; the mysterious fish of Jonah was replaced frequently by a two-headed serpent; a man rising from a chest recalls pictures of Osiris.[1] All these allegories at a later period fell under proscription, owing to the Gnosticism which misapplied them, materialising and debasing the holy traditions of the Kabalah.

The name of Gnostic was not always rejected by the Church. Those fathers whose doctrine was allied to the traditions of St. John frequently made use of this title to designate the perfect Christian. Apart from the great Synesius, who was a finished Kabalist but of questionable orthodoxy, St. Irenæus and St. Clement of Alexandria applied it in this sense. The false Gnostics were all in revolt against the hierarchic order, seeking to level the sacred science by its general diffusion, to substitute visions for understanding, personal fanaticism for hierarchic religion, and especially the mystical licence of sensual passions for that wise Christian sobriety and obedience to law which are the mother of chaste marriages and saving temperance.

The induction of ecstasy by physical means and the substitution of somnambulism for sanctity—these were the invariable tendency of those Cainite sects which perpetuated the Black Magic of India. The Church could do no less than condemn them energetically, and it did not swerve from its mission; it is only regrettable that the good grain of science often suffered when the spade was driven and the flame kindled in fields overgrown by tares.

Enemies of generation and the family, the false Gnostics sought to insure sterility by increasing debauch; their pretence was to spiritualise matter, but actually they materialised spirit, and this in the most repulsive manner. Their theology abounds in the copulation of Eons and in volup-

---

[1] In one of the pictorial symbols of Alchemy the head of the winged solar man is represented rising from a chest. It is a recurring image.

tuous embraces.[1] Like the Brahmans, they worshipped death under the symbol of the *lingam*; their creation was an infinite onanism and their redemption an eternal abortion.

Looking to escape from the hierarchy by the help of miracle—as if miracle apart from the hierarchy proved anything but disorder or rascality, the Gnostics, from the days of Simon Magus, were great workers of prodigies. Substituting the impure rites of Black Magic for the established worship, they caused blood to appear instead of the Eucharistic wine and substituted cannibal communions for the peaceful and pure supper of the Heavenly Lamb.[2] The arch-heretic Marcos, a disciple of Valentinus, said Mass with two chalices; he poured wine into the smaller and on pronouncing a magical formula the larger vessel was filled with a liquor like blood, which swelled up seething. He was not a priest, and he sought to prove in this manner that God had invested him by a miraculous ordination.[3] He incited all his disciples to perform the same marvel in his presence. It was women more especially whose success was parallel to his own, but when they passed subsequently into convulsions and ravishment, Marcos breathed upon them, communicating his own mania, so that they covenanted to forget for his sake, and for that of religion, not only all prudence but all decency.

Such intervention of women in the priesthood was always the dream of false Gnostics, for in so equalising the sexes they introduced anarchy into the family and raised a stumbling-block in the path of society. Maternity is the true priesthood of women; modesty is the ritual of the fireside and the religion thereto belonging. This the Gnostics failed to understand, or they understood it too well rather, and in misguiding the sacred instincts of the mother they cast down the barrier which stood between them and complete liberty for their desires.[4]

The sorry candour of lewdness was not, however, a gift possessed by all. On the contrary, the Montanists, among other Gnostics, exaggerated morality in order to make it impracticable. Montanus himself, whose acrid

[1] It is obvious that Éliphas Lévi pictures only the dark side of Gnosticism; he says nothing and perhaps knew nothing of the higher aspects. His stricture on the copulation of Eons reads strangely for a defender of Kabalism, seeing that the *Zohar* abounds in similar images.

[2] This statement requires to be checked by a French authority of the period, with whom Éliphas Lévi could not fail to be acquainted. I refer to Jacques Matter and his *Histoire Critique du Gnosticisme*, a second and enlarged edition of which was published in 1843. According to the testimony of this writer: (a) Some Gnostics rejected the Eucharist entirely; (b) Those who preserved it never taught the real communication of man in the flesh and blood of the Saviour; (c) for them it was an emblem of their mystic union with a being belonging to the Pleroma; (d) The wonderworking Eucharist was particular to Marcos, but according to St. Irenæus it was the result of trickery; (e) He filled chalices with wine and water, pronounced over them a formula of his own, and caused these liquids to appear purple and ruby in colour. *Op. cit.*, vol. ii, pp. 344–346.

[3] This assertion is merely a matter of inference.

[4] The materials here embodied come direct from Matter, and the last sentence is almost in his own words. The earlier writer says that he caused women to bless the chalice. Nothing is said as to the intervention of men, other than Marcos, in the celebration.

doctrines inveigled the paradoxical and extremist genius of Tertullian, was given over, with Priscilla and Maximilla, his prophetesses, or—as we should now say—his somnambulists, to all the boundless licentiousness of frenzy and ecstasy. The natural penalty of such excesses was not wanting to their authors; they ended in raving madness and suicide.

The doctrine of the Marcosians was a profound and materialised Kabalah; they dreamed that God had created everything by means of the letters of the alphabet; that these letters were as so many divine emanations, having the power of generating beings; that words were all-powerful and worked wonders virtually, as also in literal reality.[1] All this is true in a certain sense, but not in that of the Marcosian heresy. The heretics in question supplemented actualities by hallucinations and believed that they went invisible because they were transported mentally where they wished in the somnambulistic state. In the case of false mystics, life and dream are frequently so confused together that the predominant dream-state invades and submerges reality: it is then uttermost rule of folly. The natural function of imagination is to evoke images and forms, but in a condition of abnormal exaltation it can also exteriorise forms, as proved by the phenomena of monstrous pregnancies and a host of analogous facts which official science would do more wisely to study rather than deny stubbornly. Of such are the disorderly creations which religion brands justly under the name of diabolical miracles, and of such were those of Simon, the Menandrians and Marcos.

In our own days a false Gnostic named Vintras, at present a refugee in London, causes blood to appear in empty chalices and on sacrilegious hosts. The unhappy being then passes into ecstasies, after the manner of Marcos, prophesies the downfall of the hierarchy and the coming triumph of a pretended priesthood, given up to unrestricted intercourse and unbridled love.[2]

After the protean pantheism of the Gnostics came the dualism of Marcos, formulating as religious dogma the false initiation prevalent among the pseudo-Magi of Persia. The personification of evil produced a God in competition with God Himself, a King of Darkness as well as a King of Light, and there is referable to this period that pernicious doctrine of the ubiquity and sovereignty of Satan against which we register our most energetic protest. We make no pretence in this place of denying

[1] The dream ascribed to Marcos and his followers is that, however, of the *Zohar*, the opening section of which describes the letters of the Hebrew alphabet as coming before God in succession, praying to be used in the work of creation which was about to begin. They were set aside in their turn for the reason applying to each, with the exception of *Beth*, which was taken as the basis of the work, while *Aleph* was installed as the first of all the letters, the Master of the Universe affirming that His own Divine Unity was in virtue of this letter. The meaning was that *Aleph* corresponds to the No. 1. This, says the *Zohar*, with ingenuous subtlety, is why the two first words of Scripture have *Beth* as their initial and the two next words have *Aleph*.—*Zohar*, Part I, fols. 2b–3b.

[2] It will be seen in a later section that this charge against Vintras rests upon the evidence of persons expelled from the sect which he founded, and, so far as I am aware, it has not been put forward seriously.

or affirming the tradition concerning the fall of angels, deferring herein, as in all that concerns faith, to the supreme and infallible decisions of the Holy, Catholic, Apostolic and Roman Church. But assuming that the fallen angels had a leader prior to that apostasy, the event in question could not do otherwise than precipitate them into total anarchy, tempered only by the inflexible justice of God. Separated from that Divinity which is the source of all power, and more guilty by far than the others, the prince of angels in rebellion could be nothing but the last and most impotent of all outcasts.

But if there be a force in Nature which attracts those who forget God towards sin and death, such force is no other than the Astral Light, and we do not decline to recognise it as an instrument in subservience to fallen spirits. We shall recur to this subject, prepared with a complete explanation, so that it may be intelligible in all its bearings and all its orthodoxy.[1] The revelation of a great secret of occultism thus effected will make evident the danger of evocations, all curious experiences, abuses of magnetism, table-turning and whatever connects with wonders and hallucinations.

Arius had prepared the way for Manicheanism by his hybrid creation of a Son of God distinct from God Himself. It was equivalent to the hypothesis of dualism in Deity, inequality in the Absolute, inferiority in Supreme Power, the possibility of conflict between the Father and the Son, and even its necessity. These considerations, and the disparity between the terms of the divine syllogism, make inevitable the rejection of the notion. Is there any question whether the Divine Word can be good or evil—can be either God or the devil? But this was the great dilemma involved by the addition of a diphthong to the Greek word $ομουσιος$, by which it was changed to $ομοιουσιος$. In declaring the Son consubstantial with the Father, the Council of Nicæa saved the world, though the truth can be realised only by those who know that principles in reality constitute the equilibrium of the universe.

Gnosticism, Arianism, Manicheanism came out of the Kabalah misconstrued. The Church was therefore right in forbidding to its faithful the study of a science so dangerous; the keys thereof should be reserved solely to the supreme priesthood. The secret tradition would appear as a fact to have been preserved by sovereign pontiffs, at least till the papacy of Leo III, to whom is attributed an occult ritual said to have been presented by him to the Emperor Charlemagne. It contains the most secret characters of the Keys of Solomon. This little work, which should have been kept in concealment, came into circulation later on, necessitating its condemnation by the Church, and it has passed consequently into the domain of Black Magic. It is known under the name of the *Enchiridion*

---

[1] The question, however, stood over until the appearance of *La Clef des Grands Mystères*, a considerable part of which is embodied in the digest of Lévi's writings which I published long since as *The Mysteries of Magic*. The Astral Light is explained as "magnetised electricity"—as already quoted.

DIVINE SYNTHESIS AND REALISATION OF MAGIA

of Leo III, and we are in possession of an old copy which is exceedingly rare and curious.[1]

The loss of the Kabalistic keys could not entail that of the infallibility of the Church, which is ever assisted by the Holy Spirit, but it led to great obscurity in exegesis, the sublime imagery of Ezekiel's prophecy and the Apocalypse of St. John being rendered completely unintelligible. May the lawful successors of St. Peter accept the homage of this book and bless the labours of their humblest child, who, believing that he has found one of the keys of knowledge, comes to lay it at the feet of those who alone have the right to open and to shut the treasures of understanding and of faith.

---

[1] In my *Book of Ceremonial Magic* I have given full opportunities for the judgment of this so-called occult ritual, which should certainly have been kept in concealment, or better still allowed to perish, not on account of its secrets but because it is in all respects worthless, and its ascription to Leo III an insult to that pontiff.

CHAPTER VII

PHILOSOPHERS OF THE ALEXANDRIAN SCHOOL

On the eve of its extinction the school of Plato diffused a great light at Alexandria; but, victorious after three centuries of warfare, Christianity had assimilated all that was permanent and true in the doctrines of antiquity. The last adversaries of the new religion attempted to check the progress of men who were alive by galvanising mummies. The time had come when the competition could be taken seriously no longer, and the pagans of the school of Alexandria, unwillingly and unconsciously, were at work on the sacred monument raised by the disciples of Jesus of Nazareth to confront all the ages. Ammonius Saccas, Plotinus, Porphyry, Proclus are great names in the annals of science and virtue; their theology was elevated, their doctrine moral, their own manners were austere. But the chief and most touching figure of this epoch, the brightest star in the whole constellation, was Hypatia, the daughter of Theon—that virginal and learned girl whose understanding and virtues would have taken her to the baptismal font, but she died a martyr for liberty of conscience when they attempted to drag her thereto. Synesius of Cyrene was trained at the school of Hypatia; he became Bishop of Ptolemais, and was one of the most instructed philosophers as well as the best Christian poet of the early centuries. It was he who remarked that the common people always despised things which are of easy understanding and that what they require is imposture. When it was proposed to confer on him episcopal dignity, he wrote thus in a letter to a friend: "The mind which is drawn to wisdom and to the contemplation of truth at first hand is forced to disguise it, so that it may be rendered acceptable to the multitude. There is a real analogy between light and truth, as between our eyes and ordinary understandings. The sudden communication of a light too brilliant dazzles the material eye, and rays that are moderated by shadow are more serviceable to those whose sight as yet is feeble. So, in my opinion, fictions are necessary for the people, truth being harmful to those who are not strong enough to contemplate it in all its splendour. If, therefore, the ecclesiastical laws permit reserve in judgment, and allegory in mode of expression, I can accept the dignity which is offered me; the condition is, in other words, that I shall remain a philosopher at home, though I shall tell apologues and parables in public. What can there be in common, as a fact, between the vulgar crowd and sublime wisdom? Truth must be kept in secret; the multitude need instruction proportioned to their imperfect reason."

It is regrettable that Synesius should write in this strain, as nothing can be more impolitic than to let a reservation appear when one is entrusted with public teaching. As a result of similar indiscretions, there is the common remark of today that religion is necessary for the people; the

DIVINE SYNTHESIS AND REALISATION OF MAGIA

question is for what people, seeing that no one will tolerate inclusion in this category when understanding and morality are involved.

The most remarkable work of Synesius is a treatise on dreams, in which he unfolds the purest Kabalistic doctrines and appears as a theosophist whose exaltation and obscure style have rendered suspect of heresy; but he had neither the obstinacy nor the fanaticism of sectarians. He died as he had lived—in the peace of the Church, confessing his doubts frankly but submitting to hierarchic authority; his clergy and his flock asked nothing better at his hands. According to Synesius, the state of dream proves the individuality and immaterial nature of the soul, which in this condition creates for itself a heaven, a country, palaces shining with light, or otherwise darksome caverns—according to its inclinations and desires. Moral progress may be estimated by the tendency of dreams, for in these free will is suspended, while fancy is abandoned entirely to the dominant instincts. Images are produced in consequence as a reflection or shadow of thought; presentiments take bodily shape; memories are intermingled with hopes. The book of dreams is inscribed sometimes with radiant and sometimes with dark characters, but accurate rules can be established by which they may be decoded and read. Jerome Cardan wrote a long commentary on the treatise of Synesius and may even be said to have completed it by a dictionary of all dreams, having their explanation attached. The whole is to be distinguished entirely from the little books of colportage, and it really claims a serious place in the library of occult science.[1]

A certain section of criticism has ascribed to Synesius those remarkable works which appear under the name of Dionysius the Areopagite; in any case, these are regarded as apocryphal and belonging to the brilliant period of the school of Alexandria. They are monuments of the conquest of higher Kabalism by Christianity, and they are intelligible only for those who have been initiated therein. The chief treatises of Dionysius are on Divine Names and the Celestial and Ecclesiastical Hierarchies. The first explains and simplifies all mysteries of rabbinical theology. According to the author, God is the infinite and indefinable principle; in Himself He is one and inexpressible, but we ascribe to Him names which formulate our own aspirations towards His divine perfection.[2] The sum of these names

---

[1] It is laid down in the work of Synesius (a) that chastity and temperance are indispensable for the knowledge of divination by dreams; (b) that these being granted, divination by dreams is both valuable and simple; (c) that all things past, present and future convey their images to us; (d) that there is no general rule of interpretation; (e) that each should make his divinatory science for himself, by noting his dreams. The philosopher gives some account of the profit which he had derived personally from a study of the images of sleep. Divination also preserved him from the ambushes laid by certain magicians, so that he suffered no harm at their hands.

[2] Éliphas Lévi's knowledge of the works attributed to Dionysius is doubtless derived from the translation of Monsignor Darboy, Archbishop of Paris, which appeared in 1845. There is an elaborate introduction designed to establish the authenticity of the texts and this is excellent, at least for its period, as a piece of special pleading. The reader who refers to the treatise on Divine Names need not be distressed when he finds that it embodies no mysteries of rabbinical theology. To

and their relation with numbers constitute that which is highest in human thought; theology is less the science of God than that of our most sublime yearnings. The degrees of the spiritual hierarchy are afterwards established on the primitive scale of numbers, governed by the triad. The angelical orders are three, and each order contains three choirs. It is on this model that the hierarchy should be established on earth, and the Church is its most perfect type: therein are princes, bishops, and lastly simple ministers. Among the princes are cardinal-bishops, cardinal-priests and cardinal-deacons. Among prelates there are arch-bishops, simple bishops and suffragans. Among ministers there are rectors or vicars, simple priests and those who hold the diaconate. The progression to this holy hierarchy is by three preparatory degrees, being the sub-diaconate, minor orders and clerkship. The functions of all correspond to the angels and the saints; they are to glorify the threefold Divine Names, in each of the Three Persons, because the Undivided Trinity is adored in its fulness in each of the Divine Hypostases. This transcendental theology was that of the primitive church, and possibly it is attributed to St. Dionysius only in virtue of a tradition which goes back to his and the apostolic times, much as the rabbinical editors of the *Sepher Yetzirah* attributed that text to the patriarch Abraham, because it embodies the tradition perpetuated from father to son in the family of this patriarch. However it may be, the books of St. Dionysius are precious for science; they consecrate the mystical marriage of antique initiation with the gospel of Christianity, uniting a perfect understanding of supreme philosophy with a theology which is absolutely complete and in all things above reproach.

---

many of us at the present day the most important of the Dionysian writings is that on Mystical Theology, which is omitted in the enumeration of Lévi and not perhaps unnaturally, as it is a *pelagus divinitatis* over which he would not have ventured to sail.

Hermetic Magic

BOOK IV

MAGIC AND CIVILISATION

ד—DALETH

CHAPTER I

MAGIC AMONG BARBARIANS

BLACK Magic retreated before the light of Christianity, Rome was conquered by the cross, and prodigies took refuge in that dark circle with which the barbarous provinces enringed the new Roman splendour. Among a large number of extraordinary phenomena there is one which was verified in the reign of the Emperor Hadrian. At Tralles, in Asia, a young and noble girl named Philinnium, originally of Corinth and daughter of Demostrates and Charito, was captivated by Machates, a youth of mean condition. Marriage was impossible, for, as it has been said, Philinnium was noble, moreover, an only daughter and a rich heiress. Machates was a man of the people and kept a tavern. The passion of Philinnium was increased by difficulties; she escaped from her father's home and took refuge with Machates. An illicit intercourse began and continued for six months, when the girl was discovered by her parents, rescued by them and sequestered carefully. Measures were now projected for leaving the country and removing her to Corinth; but Philinnium, who had visibly wasted since separation from her lover, was seized thereupon with a languishing disorder, neither smiling nor sleeping, and refusing all nourishment. It came to pass, in fine, that she died. The parents then relinquished their determination to depart and purchased a vault, where the young girl was deposited, clothed in her richest garments. The sepulchre was situated in an enclosure belonging to the family and no one entered therein after the burial, for pagans did not pray at the tombs of the departed. The noble family were so anxious to avoid all scandal that all the arrangements took place in secret, and Machates had no idea as to what had become of his mistress. But on the night following the entombment, when he was about to retire, the door opened slowly and, coming forward with lamp in hand, he beheld Philinnium magnificently apparelled, but pallid, cold and fixing him with a dreadful stare in the eyes. Machates ran to meet her, took her in his arms, asked a thousand questions amidst as many caresses, and they passed the night together. Before daybreak Philinnium rose up and disappeared, while her lover was still plunged in profound sleep.

Now, the girl had an old nurse who loved her tenderly and wept bitterly at her loss. She may have been an accomplice in her misconduct, and since the burial of her beloved, being unable to sleep, she rose frequently at night in a kind of delirium and wandered round the dwelling of Machates. It came about in this manner that a few days after the episode just narrated she observed a light in the young man's chamber; drawing nearer and looking through the chinks of the door, she recognised Philinnium seated beside her lover, looking at him in silence and yielding to his embraces. In a state of distraction the poor woman ran back to awaken the mother and give account of what she had seen. It was regarded at first as the raving of a visionary, but in the end, persuaded by her entreaties, the mother rose and repaired to the house of Machates. All were asleep therein and there was no answer to knocking. The lady looked through the chinks of the door; the lamp was extinguished, but a moonbeam lighted the chamber and the mother saw on a chair the draperies of her daughter and could distinguish two persons asleep in the bed. She was seized with fright, returned home trembling, not daring to visit the sepulchre of her child, and passed the rest of the night in agitation and tears. On the morrow she sought the lodging of Machates and questioned him gently. The young man confessed that Philinnium visited him every night. "Why refuse her to me?" he said to the mother. "We are affianced before the gods." Then opening a coffer he shewed Charito the ring and girdle of her daughter, adding: "She gave me these last night, pledging me never to belong to anyone but her; seek therefore to separate us no longer, since we are united by a mutual promise."

"Will you therefore in your turn go to the grave in search of her?" said the mother. "Philinnium has been dead for these four days, and it is doubtless a sorceress or a stryge who has assumed her likeness to deceive you. You are the spouse of death, your hair will whiten tomorrow, and the day after you also will be buried. In this manner do the gods avenge the honour of an outraged family."

Machates turned white and trembled at this language; he began to fear on his own part that he was the sport of infernal powers; he begged Charito to bring her husband that evening, when he would hide them near his room, and at the time of the phantom's arrival would give a signal to warn them of the fact. They came, and at the allotted hour came also Philinnium to Machates, who was in bed, but fully clothed and only pretending to sleep. The girl undressed and placed herself beside him; Machates gave the signal; the parents entered with torches and uttered a great cry on recognising their daughter. Philinnium, with pallid face, rose from the bed to her full height, and said in a hollow and terrible voice: "O my father and my mother, why have you been jealous of my happiness and why have you pursued me even beyond the grave? My love had compelled the infernal gods; the power of death was suspended; three days only and I should have been restored to life. But your cruel curiosity makes void the miracle of Nature; you are killing me a second time."

After these words she fell back, an inert mass, upon the bed; her countenance faded; a cadaverous odour filled the chamber; and there was nothing now but the disfigured remains of a girl who had been five days dead. On the morrow the whole town was in commotion over this prodigy. People crowded to the amphitheatre, where the history was recounted in public, and the crowd then visited the mortuary vault of Philinnium. There was no sign of her presence, but they came upon an iron ring and a gilded cup, which she had received as presents from Machates. The corpse was in the room of the tavern, but the young man had vanished. The diviners were consulted and they directed that the remains should be interred without the precincts of the town. Sacrifices were offered to the Furies and to the terrestrial Mercury; the celestial *manes* were conjured and there were offerings to Jupiter Hospitalis.

Phlegon, a freedman of Adrian, who was the ocular witness of these facts, and relates them in a private letter, adds that he had to exercise his authority to calm a place disturbed by so extraordinary an event, and he finishes his story with the following words: "If you think fit to inform the emperor, let me know, that I may send some of those who have been witnesses of these things." The history of Philinnium is therefore well authenticated. A great German poet[1] has made it the subject of a ballad which everyone knows under the title of the *Bride of Corinth*. He supposes that the girl's parents were Christians, and this gives him the opportunity to make a powerful poetic contrast between human passions and the duties of religion. The mediaeval dæmonographers have not failed to explain the resurrection, or possibly the apparent death, of the young Greek lady as a diabolical obsession. On our own part, we recognise an hysterical coma accompanied by lucid somnambulism: the father and mother of Philinnium killed her by their rough awakening, and public imagination exaggerated all the circumstances of this history.[2]

The terrestrial Mercury, to whom sacrifices were ordained by diviners, is no other than the Astral Light personified. It is the fluidic genius of the earth, fatal for those who arouse it without knowing how to direct; it is the focus of physical life and the magnetised receptable of death. This blind

[1] Goethe.
[2] This explanation is not in accordance with the recorded facts, for which Phlegon and Proclus are the authorities. The works of Phlegon were published at Leyden in 1620, under the editorship of Meursius, and again in 1775 at Halle, by Franzius; they contain the story of Philinnion—as the name is spelt by Phlegon. Machates was a foreign friend of Demostratus from Pella, not an innkeeper. Philinnion appeared to him after her death in the house of his parents and declared her love. Her intercourse with Machates was discovered accidentally by a servant, and the *dénouement* is much as it is given in the present place. Philinnion said, however, that she acted with the consent of the gods. Éliphas Lévi accounts for his discrepancies by an appeal to the narratives of French dæmonographers, but he makes no references by which we can check him. He states, however, that they are answerable for the alleged fact that Machates was the keeper of a tavern. The date of the actual occurrence is the reign of Philip II of Macedon, and the "emperor" referred to should be King Philip. Lévi confuses the date of Phlegon (Hadrian's reign) with the date of the incident. Phlegon was merely a collector of curious stories, and could not, of course, have witnessed an incident which took place 500 years before his birth!

force, which the power of Christianity enchained and cast into the abyss, meaning into the centre of the earth, made its last efforts and manifested its final convulsions by monstrous births among barbarians. There is scarcely a district in which the preachers of the gospel did not have to contend with animals in hideous forms, being incarnations of idolatry in its death-throes. The *vouivres, graouillis, gargoyles, tarasques* are not allegorical only; it is certain that moral disorders produce physical deformities and do, to some extent, realise the frightful forms attributed by tradition to demons. The question arises whether those fossil remains from which Cuvier built up his mammoth monsters belong really in all cases to epochs preceding our creation. Is also that great dragon merely an allegory which Regulus is represented as attacking with machines of war and which according to Livy and Pliny lived on the borders of the river Bagrada? His skin, which measured 120 feet, was sent to Rome and was there preserved until the period of the war with Numantia. There was an ancient tradition that when the gods were angered by extraordinary crimes they sent monsters upon earth, and this tradition is too universal not to be founded upon actual facts; it follows that the stories concerning it belong more frequently to history than mythology.

In all memorials of barbarian races, at that epoch when Christianity conquered them with a view to their civilisation, we find (a) the last traces of high magical initiation spread formerly throughout the world, and (b) proofs of the degeneration which had befallen such primitive revelation, together with the idolatrous vileness into which the symbolism of the old world had lapsed. In place of the disciples of the Magi, diviners, sorcerers and enchanters reigned everywhere; God was forgotten in the deification of men. The example was given by Rome to its various provinces, and the apotheosis of the Cæsars familiarised the whole world with the religion of sanguinary deities. Under the name of Irminsul the Germans worshipped and sacrificed human victims to that Arminius or Hermann who caused Augustus to mourn the lost legions of Varus. The Gauls referred to Brennus the attributes of Taranis and of Teutas, burning in his honour colossi built of rushes and filled with Romans. Materialism reigned everywhere, idolatry being synonymous therewith, as is also the superstition which is ever cruel because it is always base.

Providence, which predestined Gaul to become the most Christian land of France, caused, however, the light of eternal truths to shine forth therein. The original Druids were true children of the Magi, their initiation deriving from Egypt and Chaldea, or in other words, from the purest sources of primitive Kabalah.[1] They adored the Trinity under the names of Isis or Ilesus, being supreme harmony; Belen or Bel, meaning the Lord in Assyrian and having correspondence with the name Adonai; Camul or

[1] It will be understood at the present day that this is reverie and only serves to remind us that Aristotle ascribed the philosophy of Greece to a source in Gaul, while it is affirmed by Clement of Alexandria that Pythagoras derived therefrom. It is thought now, on the other hand, that Druidism in its later developments may have been influenced not only by Greek but also by Phœnician ideas.

Camael, a name which personifies divine justice in the Kabalah.[1] Beneath this triangle of light they postulated a divine reflection, also consisting of three personified emanations, being: Teutas or Teuth, identical with the Thoth of the Egyptians, and the Word or formulated Intelligence; then Strength and Beauty, the names of which varied like the emblems. Finally they completed the sacred septenary by a mysterious image representing the progress of dogma and its developments to come. The form was that of a young girl, veiled and bearing an infant in her arms; they dedicated this symbol to the virgin who shall bear a child.[2]

The ancient Druids lived in strict abstinence, preserved the deepest secrecy concerning their mysteries, studied the natural sciences, and only admitted new adepts after prolonged initiations. There was a celebrated Druidic college at Autun, and, according to Saint-Foix, its armorial bearings still exist in that town. They are azure, with serpents argent couchant, surmounted by mistletoe, garnished with acorns vert, to distinguish it from other mistletoe, it being the oak and not the mistletoe which naturally bears the acorns. Mistletoe is a parasitic plant which has fruit particular to itself.[3]

The Druids built no temples but worked the rites of their religion on dolmens and in forests. The mechanical means by which they raised such colossal stones to form their altars is even now a matter of speculation. These erections are still to be seen, dark and mysterious, under the clouded sky of Armorica. The old sanctuaries had secrets which have not come down to us. The Druids taught that the souls of ancestors watched over children; that they were made happy by their glory and suffered in their shame; that protecting genii overshadowed trees and stones of the fatherland; that the warrior who died for his country expiated all his offences, fulfilled his task with dignity, was elevated to the rank of a genius and exercised henceforth the power of the gods. It followed that for the Gauls patriotism itself was a religion; women and even children carried arms, if necessary, to withstand invasion. Joan of Arc and Jeanne Hachette of Beauvais only carried on the traditions of those noble daughters of the Gauls. It is the magic of remembrances which cleaves to the soil of the fatherland.

The Druids were priests and physicians, curing by magnetism and charging amulets with their fluidic influence. Their universal remedies were mistletoe and serpents' eggs, because their substances attract the

[1] In Druidic mythology Belen, otherwise Heol, was the sun-god; Camael was god of war. The highest divinity is believed to have been that Esus who is mentioned by Lucan. He is represented by the circle, as a sign of infinity, and all fate was beneath him. The most important goddess was Keridwen, who presided over wisdom. The conclusion of Lévi's enumeration is like the beginning—a dream.

[2] A note by Éliphas Lévi says that a Druidic statue was found at Chartres, having the inscription: VIRGINI PARITURÆ. It is curious that Druidic inscriptions should be in the Latin tongue.

[3] It was supposed to increase the species by preventing sterility, and it was dignified by other ascribed virtues; it was the ethereal tree and the growth of the high summit. It was included among the ingredients of the mystical cauldron of Keridwen, in which genius, inspiration and serenity were said to dwell.

Astral Light in an especial manner.[1] The solemnity with which mistletoe was cut down drew upon this plant the popular confidence and rendered it powerfully magnetic. It came about in this manner that it worked marvellous cures, above all when it was fortified by the Druids with conjurations and charms. Let us not accuse our forefathers of over-great credulity herein; it may be that they knew that which is lost to us. The progress of magnetism will some day reveal to us the absorbing properties of mistletoe: we shall then understand the secret of those spongy growths which draw the unused virtue of plants and become surcharged with tinctures and savours. Mushrooms, truffles, gall on trees and the different kinds of mistletoe will be employed with understanding by a medical science which will be new because it is old. We shall cease to ridicule Paracelsus, who collected moss (*usnea*) from the skulls of hanged men; but one must not move quicker than science, which recedes that it may advance the farther.

---

[1] The same occult importance attaches to this statement as to another in the *Dogme et Rituel*, where Éliphas Lévi, explaining the superstitions of the past, affirms for those who can suffer it that the toad is not poisonous but is a sponge for poisons. I suppose, however, it is obvious that if "popular confidence" can render mistletoe magnetic, popular distrust may instil poison into toads.

CHAPTER II

INFLUENCE OF WOMEN

In imposing upon woman the severe and tender duties of motherhood Providence has entitled her to the protection and respect of man. Made subject by Nature itself to the consequence of affections which are her life, she leads her masters by the chains which love provides, and the more fully that she is in conformity with the laws which constitute and also defend her honour the greater is her sway, and the deeper that respect which belongs to her in the sanctuary of the family. To revolt is for her to abdicate, and to tempt her by a pretended emancipation is to recommend her divorce by condemning her beforehand to sterility and disdain. Christianity alone has the power to emancipate woman by calling her to virginity and the glory of sacrifice. Numa foresaw this mystery when he instituted the vestals; but the Druids forestalled Christianity by giving ear to the inspirations of virgins and paying almost divine honours to the priestesses of the island of Sayne.

In Gaul women did not prevail by their coquetry and their vices, but they ruled by their counsels; apart from their concurrence, neither peace nor war was made; the interests of the hearth and family were thus pleaded by mothers and the national pride shone in the light of justice when it was tempered by the maternal love of country.

Chateaubriand calumniated Velleda by representing her as yielding to the love of Eudorus; she lived and died a virgin. When the Romans invaded Gaul she was already advanced in years and was a species of *Pythia* who prophesied amidst great solemnities and whose oracles were preserved with veneration. She was clothed in a long black vestment, having no sleeves; her head was covered by a white veil, which came down to her feet; she wore a vervain crown, and a sickle was placed in her girdle; her sceptre was in the form of a distaff; her right foot was shod with a sandal and her left foot wore a kind of *chaussure à poulaine*. At a later period the statues of Velleda were taken for those of Berthe *au grand pied*. The High Priestess bore, as a fact, the insignia of the protecting divinity of the female Druids; she was Hertha, or Wertha, the youthful Gaulish Isis, the Queen of Heaven, the virgin who must bring forth a child. She was depicted with one foot on the earth and the other on the water, because she was queen of initiation and presided over universal science. The foot set upon the water was usually supported by a ship, analogous to the bark or conch of the ancient Isis. She held the distaff of the Fates wound about with a thread, part black, part white, because she presided over all forms and symbols, and it was she who wove the vestment of ideas. She was also given the allegorical form of the syrens, half woman and half fish, or the torso of a beautiful girl whose legs were serpents, signifying the flux of things and the analogical alliance of opposites in the manifestation of all occult forces of Nature. Under this last form Hertha took the name of Melusine or Melosina, the musician, the singer—that is to say, the syren who reveals harmonies. Such is the origin of the legends concerning Queen Bertha and the fairy Melusine. The latter came, it is said, in the eleventh century to a lord of Lusignan; she was loved by him, and their espousals took place on the condition that he did not seek to penetrate certain mysteries of her existence. That promise was given, but jealousy begat curiosity and led to perjury. He spied upon Melusine and surprised her in one of her metamorphoses, for once every week the fairy resumed her serpent-legs. He uttered a cry which was answered by one far more despairing and terrible. Melusine disappeared, but still returns, making lamentation whenever a member of the house of Lusignan is at the point of death.[1] The legend is imitated from the fable of Psyche and refers, like this, to the dangers of sacrilegious initiations, or profanation of the mysteries of religion and of love; it is borrowed from the traditions of the ancient bards and derives evidently from the learned school of the Druids. The eleventh century took possession of it and brought it into prominence, but it existed from the far past.[2]

In France it would seem that inspiration was attributed more especially to women; elves and fairies preceded saints, and the French saints have almost invariably something of the fairy character in their legend. St. Clothilde made us Christians and St. Geneviève kept us French, repelling —by the force of her virtue and her faith—the threatening invasion of Attila. Joan of Arc is, however, rather of the fairy family than the hierarchy of holy women; she died like Hypatia, the victim of marvellous natural gifts and the martyr of her generous character. We shall speak of her later on. St. Clothilde still performs miracles along the countryside. At Andelys we have seen a crowd of pilgrims thronging about a *piscina* in which the statue of the saint is immersed annually, and according to popular belief the first diseased person who goes down into the water subsequently is cured at once. Clothilde was a woman of action and a great queen, but she went through many sorrows. Her elder son died after his baptism, and the fatality was ascribed to witchcraft; the second fell ill and reached the point of death. The fortitude of the saint did not yield, and Sicambre, when standing one day in need of more than human

---

[1] The floating traditions and *chansons* concerning Melusine were collected by Jean d'Arras into a beautiful romance of chivalry at the close of the fourteenth century.
[2] Whether this hypothesis of antiquity is warranted or not, the fact that it is adopted should have prevented Éliphas Lévi from characterising the romance of Melusine as an imitation of the fable of Psyche: it is obviously the reverse side. The allegory in the latter case is that of the assumption of the soul by the Divine Spirit, so that all which is capable of redemption in our human nature, its emotion, its desire and its love, may enter into the glorious estate of the mystic marriage. The allegory in the former case is that of the union instituted between the psychic part and all that is of earth in our nature; but this earth is not capable of true marriage, and whereas the other experiment ends in the world of unity, this terminates, as it can only, in that of separation.

courage, remembered the God of Clothilde. She became a widow after converting and practically founding a great kingdom, and she saw the two children of Clodomir butchered practically under her eyes. In such sorrows do queens on earth resemble the Queen of Heaven.[1]

After the great and brilliant figure of Clothilde, history presents us with a hideous offset in the baleful personality of Fredegonde, the woman whose glance was witchcraft, the sorceress who slew princes. She accused her rivals of Magic and condemned them to tortures which she alone merited. Chilperic had one remaining son by his first wife; this young prince, who was named Clovis, was attached to a daughter of the people whose mother passed for a sorceress. Mother and daughter were both accused of disturbing the reason of Clovis by means of philtres and with murdering the two children of Fredegonde by magical spells. The unhappy women were arrested; the daughter, Klodswinthe, was beaten with rods, her beautiful hair cut off, and this was hung by Fredegonde on the door of the prince's chamber. Subsequently Klodswinthe was brought up for sentence. Her firm and simple answers astonished the judges, and the chronicle says that it was proposed to submit her to the test of boiling water. A consecrated ring was placed in a tub set over a great fire and the accused, clothed in white, after having confessed and communicated, had to plunge her arm in the tub in search of the ring. Her unchanged features made everyone cry out that a miracle had taken place, but there was another cry, which was one of reprobation and horror, when the unhappy child drew forth her arm frightfully burnt. She then asked permission to speak and said to her judges and the people: "You demanded a miracle from God to establish my innocence. God is not to be tempted, and He does not suspend the laws of Nature in response to the caprice of men; but He gives strength to those who believe in Him, and for me has performed a greater wonder than that which He refused to you. This water has burned me, yet have I plunged my whole arm into it and have brought forth the ring. I have neither cried, whitened, nor quivered under this horrible torture. Had I been a magician, as you say, I should have resorted to witchcraft so that I might not be burnt; but I am a Christian and God has given me grace to prove it by the constancy of martyrs." Such logic was not of the kind that they understood at that barbarous epoch; Klodswinthe was sent back to prison, there to await execution; but God took pity upon her, and the chronicle from which the account is drawn says that He called her to Himself. If it be a legend only, it must be allowed that it is beautiful and deserves to be kept in memory.

Fredegonde lost one of her victims but not the other two. The mother was put to the torture and, overcome by her sufferings, she confessed whatever was required, including the guilt of her daughter and the complicity of Clovis. Armed with these admissions, Fredegonde obtained the surrender of his son by the ferocious Chilperic. The young prince was arrested and stabbed in prison, Fredegonde declaring that he had escaped

---

[1] See Jules Garinet: *Histoire de la Magie en France*, 1818, pp. 11, 12.

from remorse by suicide. The corpse of the unhappy Clovis was shewn to his father, with the dagger still in the wound. Chilperic looked on coldly; he was entirely under the rule of Fredegonde, who dishonoured him with effrontery among the officers of the palace, taking so little pains at concealment that the evidence was before his eyes, almost despite himself. Instead of slaying the queen and her accomplices, he departed on a hunt in silence. He might have concluded to suffer the outrage, through his fear of displeasing Fredegonde, but the latter was ashamed on his account, and did him the honour of believing in his wrath, that she might have a pretext for his assassination. He had glutted her with crimes and meanness: she killed him out of disgust.

Fredegonde, who destroyed on the pretext of sorcery the women whose sole guilt was to have displeased her, experimented herself in Black Magic and protected some of those whom she thought were skilled therein. Ageric, bishop of Verdun, had a pythoness arrested who made a great deal of money by recovering stolen objects and identifying the thieves; she was probably a somnambulist. The woman was examined, but the demon refused to go out of her as long as she was chained; if the pythoness were left in a church, unguarded and unwatched, he agreed to leave her. They fell into the trap; it was the woman herself who went out, to take refuge with Fredegonde, who hid her in the palace and ended by saving her from being further exorcised, as also probably from the stake. On this occasion therefore she did good without meaning it, yet it was rather through her pleasure in evil.[1]

---

[1] The story of Fredegonde and her connection with sorcery is told by Gregory of Tours, but Éliphas Lévi derived it from Jules Garinet, already cited. The particulars concerning Klodswinthe appear to be his own invention, of which her imputed discourse bears all the marks.

CHAPTER III

THE SALIC LAWS AGAINST SORCERERS

UNDER the rule of the first French kings, the crime of Magic did not entail death save for those of exalted position, while there were some who were proud to die for an offence by which they were raised above the vulgar crowd and became formidable even in the sight of kings. There was the general Mummol, for example, who, on the rack by the orders of Fredegonde, declared that he experienced nothing, who provoked more frightful tortures and died braving the executioners, while the latter were moved to forgive him at the sight of such extra-natural fortitude.[1]

Among the Salic laws, supposed to have been enacted in 474, and attributed to Pharamond by Sigebert, the following ordinances are found:

"If anyone shall testify that another has acted as a *héréburge* or *strioporte*—titles applied to those who carry the copper vessel to the spot where the vampires perform their enchantments—and if he shall fail to convict him, he shall be condemned hereby to a forfeit of 7500 *deniers*, being 180½ *sous*. . . . If anyone shall charge a free woman as a vampire or as a prostitute, and shall fail to prove his words, he shall forfeit 2500 *deniers*, being 62½ *sous*. . . . If a vampire shall devour a man and be found guilty, she shall forfeit 8000 *deniers*, being 200 *sous*."

It will be seen that in those times cannibalism was possible on terms and, moreover, that the market-price of human flesh was not at a premium. It cost 180½ *sous* to slander a man, but for a modicum above that sum he could be killed and eaten, which was at once more honest and thorough. This remarkable legislation recalls an equally curious Talmudic recital, being one which was interpreted after a memorable manner by the famous Rabbi Jechiel in the presence of a certain queen who is not named in the book.[2] It was most likely Queen Blanche, for Rabbi Jechiel lived in the reign of St. Louis. He had been called upon to answer the objections of a converted Jew named Douin, who had received at baptism the Christian name of Nicholas. After various discussions on texts of the Talmud they came to the following passage: "If anyone shall offer any blood of his children to Moloch, let him die the death." The Talmud annotates thus: "He therefore who shall offer not a modicum of blood alone by the whole blood and the whole flesh of his children, does not come under the judgment of the law and no penalty is declared against him." Those who took

---

[1] See Garinet, *Histoire de la Magie en France*, pp. 14–16, and Th. de Cauzons, *La Magie et la Sorcellerie en France*, vol. ii. p. 100. The original authority is again Gregory of Tours: *Histoire des France*, Book VI, c. 35. The account of Lévi is rather incorrect, for after unheard-of tortures, the life of Mummol was spared, but he died on the way to Bordeaux. It does not appear that he defied his executioners and the renewed torture was ordained by Chilperic.

[2] The work in question is called *Acta Disputationis cum quodam Nicolai*.

part in the debate clamoured at a construction which passed all understanding: some laughed in pity, some quivered with indignation. Rabbi Jechiel could scarcely obtain a hearing, and when he succeeded at last there was every mark of disfavour, to indicate that he was condemned beforehand.

"With us," said he, "the penalty of death is an atonement and consequently a reconciliation, not an act of vengeance. All who die by the law of Israel die in the peace of Israel; they partake of peace in death, and they sleep with their fathers. No malediction descends with them into the grave; they abide in the immortality of the House of Jacob. Death is therefore a crowning grace; it is the cure of a poisoned wound by the hot iron. But we do not apply the iron to those who are past cure; we have no jurisdiction over those the extent of whose transgression has cut them off for ever from Israel. Such are as now dead, and it is not therefore for us to shorten the term of their reprobation on earth: they are delivered over to the wrath of God. Man is warranted to wound only that he may heal, and we do not apply remedies to those who are beyond recovery. The father of a family punishes only his children and is content to shut the door against strangers. Those great criminals upon whom our law pronounces no sentence are thereby excommunicated for ever, which is a penalty greater than death."

The explanation of Rabbi Jechiel is admirable and breathes all the patriarchal genius of ancient Israel. Truly the Jews are our fathers in science, and if we—in place of their persecution—had sought to understand them, they would not have been at this day so far alienated from our faith.

The above Talmudic tradition shews the Jewish antiquity of belief in the immortality of the soul.[1] What is this reintegration of the guilty in the family of Israel by an expiatory death unless it be a protest against death itself and a sublime act of faith in the perpetuity of life? Comte Joseph de Maistre understood this doctrine well when he raised the executioner's sanguinary mission into a kind of peculiar priesthood. The anguish of punishment supplicates, said this great writer, and blood in his outpouring still remains a sacrifice. Were capital punishment other than a plenary absolution it would be nothing but retaliation on murder; the man who suffers his sentence fulfils all his penance and enters by death into the immortal society of the children of God.

The Salic laws were those of a people still in the state of barbarity, where everything is redeemed by a ransom, as in time of war. Slavery still obtained and human life had a debatable and relative value. That must be always purchasable which there is a right to sell, and only money is due for the destruction of an object which has a price in money. That one

[1] A story of the days of St. Louis is obviously not Talmudic and the antiquity of the idea of immortality among the Jews fortunately rests on a better foundation than this. The criticism exposes the carelessness of Lévi if he is regarded as a man of learning. Some will think that he traded on the ignorance of his readers.

efficacious legislation of the period was that of the Church, and its councils took the most stringent measures against the vampires and poisoners who went under the name of sorcerers. The Council of Agde in Lower Languedoc, held in 506, pronounced excommunication against them. The first Council of Orléans, convened in 541, condemned divinatory operations; that of Narbonne, in 589, not only visited sorcerers with the greater excommunication but ordained that they should be sold as slaves for the benefit of the poor. The same council decreed public whipping for *amatores diaboli*—meaning, no doubt, those who were concerned about him, feared him, evoked him and attributed to him power which was in any wise like that of God.[1] We offer our congratulations sincerely to the disciples of M. le Comte de Mirville that they did not live in such days.

While these events were passing in France an Eastern visionary was engaged in founding a religion which was also an empire. Was Mahomet an impostor or was he hallucinated? For the Moslems he is still a prophet, and for Arabic scholars the Koran will be always a masterpiece. An unlettered man, a simple camel-driver, he created notwithstanding the most perfect literary monument of his country. His success might pass as miraculous, and the martial fervour of his successors threatened for a moment the liberty of the whole world. But the day came when Asia broke under the iron hand of Charles Martel. That rough soldier tarried little for prayer when there was fighting to be done; when he wanted money he looted monasteries and churches, and even sold ecclesiastical benefices to his warriors. As the priesthood, for these reasons, could not suppose that his arms were blessed by God, his victories were ascribed to Magic. Indeed, religious feeling was so stirred up against him that St. Eucher, the venerable Bishop of Orléans, learned in a vision from an angel that the saints whose churches he had spoliated or profaned forbade him to enter into heaven, and even disinterred his body, which they plunged with his soul in the abyss. St. Eucher communicated the revelation to Boniface, Bishop of Mayence, and to Fulfvad, arch-chaplain of Pepin the Short. The tomb of Charles Martel was opened, the body proved to be missing, the inner side of the stone was blackened as if by burning, a foul smoke exhaled and a great serpent came out. An authentic report of the opening was sent by Boniface to Pepin the Short and Carloman, who were the sons of Charles Martel, praying them to take warning by the dreadful example and to respect holy things. Yet there was little of that virtue on the part of those who violated the grave of a hero on the faith of a dream, and attributed a destruction which had been completely and rapidly accomplished by death itself to the work of hell.[2]

Some extraordinary phenomena, occurring publicly in France, characterised the reign of Pepin the Short. The air seemed to be alive with

---

[1] What was actually intended by the expression *amatores diaboli* should have been perfectly well understood by Éliphas Lévi. It corresponds to the legends concerning *incubi* and *succubi*. For a specific example see Brierre de Boismont, *Des Hallucinations*, pp. 151 *et seq.*

[2] The story comes from Gregory of Tours.

human shapes; heaven reflected illusory scenes of palaces, gardens, tossing waves, ships in full sail and hosts in battle array. The atmosphere was like a great dream, and the details of these fantastic pageants were visible to everyone. Was it an epidemic attacking the organs of vision or an aerial perturbation projecting illusions on condensed air? Was it not more probably a general delusion occasioned by some intoxicating and pestilential effluvium diffused throughout the atmosphere? The likelihood of the latter explanation is increased by the fact that these visions provoked the populace, who in their imagination beheld sorcerers in the clouds scattering unwholesome powders and poisons with open hands. The country was smitten with sterility, cattle died, and the mortality extended also to human beings.

The occurrences offered an opportunity to circulate a story, the success and credit of which was in proportion to its extravagance. At that time the famous Kabalist Zedekias[1] had a school of occult science, where he taught not indeed the Kabalah but the entertaining speculations arising thereform and forming the exoteric part of a science which has been ever hidden from the profane. With mythology of this kind Zedekias diverted the minds of his hearers. He told how Adam, the first man, originally created in an almost spiritual estate, abode above our atmosphere, in a light which gave birth at his pleasure to the most wonderful vegetation. He was served by choirs of beautiful beings, fashioned in the likeness of male and female, of whom they were animated reflections, formed from the purest substance of the elements. They were sylphs, salamanders, undines and gnomes; but in his unfallen condition Adam reigned over the gnomes and undines only by the agency of the salamanders and sylphs, who alone had the power of ascending to his aerial paradise.

There was nothing to equal the felicity of our first parents amidst the ministry of the sylphs; they were perishable spirits, but they had incredible skill in building and weaving the light, causing it to flower in a thousand forms, more varied than the most brilliant and fruitful imagination can now conceive. The earthly paradise—so named because it reposed upon the earthly atmosphere—was therefore a domain of enchantments. Adam and Eve slept in palaces of pearls and sapphires; roses sprang up around them and formed a carpet for their feet; they glided over waters in sea-shells drawn by swans; birds communed with them in delicious speech of music; flowers stooped to caress them. But all this was lost by the fall, which cast our progenitors down to earth, and the material bodies which clothed them henceforth are those skins of beasts mentioned in the Bible. They were alone and naked, where no one obeyed their caprice of thought. They forgot their life in Eden, or viewed it only as a dream seen through the glass of memory. But the realms of paradise still and for ever extend above the earthly atmosphere, inhabited by sylphs and salamanders, who are thus constituted guardians of man's domain, like mourn-

[1] The account of Zedekias and the atmospheric marvels is taken from Garinet, pp. 34 *et seq.*

ful retainers still in the house of a master whose return they expect no more.

Imaginations were fired by these astonishing fictions when the visions of the air began to be seen in the full light of day. They signified unquestionably the descent of sylphs and salamanders in search of their former masters. Voyages to the land of sylphs were talked of on all sides, as we talk at the present day of animated tables and fluidic manifestations. The folly took possession even of strong minds, and it was time for an intervention on the part of the Church, which does not relish the supernatural being hawked in the public streets, seeing that such disclosures, by imperilling the respect due to authority and to the hierarchic chain of instruction, cannot be attributed to the spirit of order and light. The cloud-phantoms were therefore arraigned and accused of being hell-born illusions, while the people—anxious to get something into their hands—began a crusade against sorcerers. The public folly turned to a paroxysm of mania; strangers in country places were accused of descending from heaven and were killed without mercy; imbeciles confessed that they had been abducted by sylphs or demons; others who had boasted like this previously either would not or could not unsay it; they were burned or drowned, and, according to Garinet, the number who perished throughout the kingdom almost exceeds belief.[1] It is the common catastrophe or dramas in which the first parts are played by ignorance or fear.

Such visionary epidemics recurred in the reigns following, and all the power of Charlemagne was put in action to calm the public agitation. An edict, afterwards renewed by Louis the Pious, forbade sylphs to manifest under the heaviest penalties. It will be understood that in the absence of the aerial beings the judgment fell upon those who made a boast of having seen them, and hence they ceased to be seen. The ships in air sailed back to the port of oblivion, and no one claimed any longer to have journeyed through the blue distance. Other popular frenzies replaced the previous mania, while the romantic splendours of the great reign of Charlemagne furnished the makers of legends with new prodigies to believe and new marvels to relate.

---

[1] See pp. 34–37 of his History. But the account in Garinet is derived from the *Cinquième Entretien* in the romance entitled *Le Comte de Gabalis*.

CHAPTER IV

LEGENDS OF THE REIGN OF CHARLEMAGNE

CHARLEMAGNE is the real prince of enchantments and the world of faërie; his reign is like a solemn and brilliant pause between barbarism and the middle ages; while he himself is a grand and majestic apparition, recalling the magical pageant of Solomon's sway: he is at once a resurrection and a prophecy. In him the Roman empire, overleaping Frankish and Gaulish origins, reappeared in all its splendour; in him also, as in a symbol, evoked and manifested by divination, there is delineated beforehand the perfect empire of the ages of mature civilisation, the empire crowned by priesthood and establishing its throne beside the altar.

The era of chivalry and the marvellous epos of romances begin with Charlemagne; the chronicles of his period are like the *Four Sons of Aymon*, or *Oberon, King of Faerie*. Birds utter speech and direct the French army when the path has been lost in the forest; brazen colossi appear in midocean and indicate to the emperor a free way eastward. Roland, first of the paladins, wields a magic sword, baptised like any Christian and bearing the name of Durandal; the hero addresses this sword, which seems to understand him, and nothing can resist its supernatural onset. Roland has also an ivory horn, contrived so skilfully that the lightest breath wakens a response within it, and that answer is heard for twenty leagues around, causing even mountains to quiver. When the paladin falls at Roncesvàlles, overwhelmed rather than conquered, even then he uprises like a giant beneath some avalanche of trees and rolling rocks; he winds his horn, and the Saracens take refuge in flight. Charlemagne, at a distance of more than ten leagues, hears the signal and would speed to his aid, but he is prevented by the traitor Ganelon, who has sold the French army to the barbaric horde. Finding himself abandoned, Roland for the last time embraces his Durandal, and then, summoning all his strength, strikes it with both hands against a mountain block, hoping to shatter the weapon, lest it fall into the hands of infidels; but the block itself is cloven, the sword is not even indented. Hereat Roland clasps it to his breast and yields up his spirit with so high and proud a mien that the Saracens do not dare to approach, but, still shaking, direct a cloud of arrows against their conqueror, who is no more. To be brief, Charlemagne, bestowing a throne upon the papacy and receiving from its hands the empire of the world in return, is the most imposing of all personalities in French history.

We have spoken of the *Enchiridion*—that minute work which combines the most secret symbols of the Kabalah with the most beautiful Christian prayers. Occult tradition[1] attributes its composition to Leo III and affirms that it was presented by this pontiff to Charlemagne, as the most

[1] It is not in reality an occult tradition; it is simply the unauthorised claim of the Grimoire

precious of all offerings. Any king who owned it and knew how to use it worthily could become master of the world. This tradition is not perhaps to be cast aside lightly.

It assumes (1) the existence of a primitive and universal revelation, explaining all Secrets of Nature and harmonising them with the Mysteries of Grace, conciliating reason with faith, since both are daughters of God and concur to illuminate intelligence by their double life. (2) The necessity —which imposes itself—of concealing this revelation from the multitude, lest the same be abused by those who do not understand it, and lest they turn against faith not only the power of reason but that of faith itself, to the confusion of reason, which is never too well within the comprehension of the vulgar. (3) The existence of a secret tradition, reserving the knowledge of these mysteries for the sovereign priesthood and the temporal masters of the world. (4) The perpetuity of certain signs or pantacles, expressing the said mysteries in a hieroglyphical manner which is understood only by adepts.[1]

The *Enchiridion*, from this point of view, should be regarded as a collection of allegorical prayers and its secret Kabalistic pantacles are keys thereto. Some of the chief figures may be described as follows. The first, which appears on the cover of the work itself, represents a reversed equilateral triangle inscribed within a double circle. The two words, which are written within the triangle in the form of a cross, are *Elohim* and *Tzabaoth*, meaning the God of armies, the equilibrium of natural forces and the harmony of numbers.[2] On the three sides of the triangle are the three great names—*Jehovah, Adonai, Agla*; above the name of Jehovah is the Latin word *Formatio*; above that of Adonai is *Reformatio*; and above Agla is *Transformatio*. Thus creation is ascribed to the Father, redemption or reform to the Son, and sanctification or transmutation to the Holy Spirit—in consonance with the mathematical laws of action, reaction and equilibrium. Furthermore, Jehovah is to be understood as the genesis and formation of dogma in accordance with the elementary significance of the four letters comprised in the sacred Tetragram; *Adonai* is the realisation of this dogma in human form—that is to say, in the Lord manifest, who is Son of God or perfect man;[3] and *Agla*, as we have explained fully else-

---

[1] It should be mentioned that this enumeration of assumptions expressed or implied in the claims of occult tradition, by the hypothesis of its present exponent, has nothing to do with the *Enchiridion*, which makes only two claims, and these are particular to itself. They are (a) that it was sent to Charlemagne by Pope Leo and (b) that certain prayers, which rank as its chief feature, possess mysterious power. The suggestion of Lévi's next paragraph notwithstanding, there is no other point of view from which the book can be regarded.
[2] It is said elsewhere by Éliphas Lévi that the *Enchiridion* has never been published with its true figures, and one is led to suppose that a more important MS. copy may have been in his possession. The plates which he describes belong to a printed edition, but there are no particulars concerning it. Most of the symbols are perfectly well known otherwise, and I have given them in the *Book of Ceremonial Magic*, where they were taken from examples with which I am acquainted. Some of them correspond to the description of Lévi.
[3] *Adonai*, according to the *Zohar*, is one of the titles of *Shekinah*.

where, expressed the synthesis of all dogma and all Kabalistic science, seeing that the hieroglyphics of which this name is formed exhibit in a clear manner the triple secret of the Great Work.[1]

The second pantacle is a head, having three faces, crowned by a tiara and issuing from a vessel filled with water. Those who are initiated into the mysteries of the *Zohar*[2] will understand the allegory which is presented by this head. The third pantacle is the double triangle, known as the Star of Solomon. The fourth is the Magical Sword, bearing the device—*Deo duce, comite ferro*: it is an emblem of the Great Arcanum and the omnipotence of the adept. The fifth is the problem of the human form attributed to the Saviour, as resolved by the number forty. It is the theological number of the *Sephiroth* multiplied by that of natural realities.[3] The sixth is the pantacle of the spirit, represented by bones, duplicating the letter E and the mystic Tau, or T. The seventh and most important is the Great Magical Monogram, interpreting the keys of Solomon, the Tetragram, the sign of the *Labarum*, and the master-word of adeptship.[4] This pantacle is read by its revolution wheelwise and is pronounced Rota, Taro or Tora. The letter A is frequently replaced in this seal by the number one, which is its equivalent. The pantacle in question contains also the form and value of the four hieroglyphical emblems of the Tarot suits—being the Wand, Cup, Sword and Denier. These elementary hieroglyphics recur everywhere on the sacred monuments of Egypt; while Homer also depicts them on the shield of Achilles, placing them in the same order as the author of the *Enchiridion*. The proofs of these explanations, if offered in the present place, would divert us from our immediate subject and would, moreover, demand a special study which we hope to undertake and make public at some future time.[5]

The magical sword or dagger depicted in the *Enchiridion* seems to

[1] He has said elsewhere (a) that to pronounce the word *Agla* Kabalistically is to undergo all the trials of initiation and fulfil all its works; (b) that the occult forces which comprise the empire of Hermes are obedient to him who can pronounce, according to science, the incommunicable name of *Agla*; (c) and that its letters represent (1) unity, (2) fecundity, (3) the perfect cycle and (4) the expression of the synthesis.

[2] He means that it symbolises the Creative Intelligence rising over the waters of creation. It is not, strictly speaking, Zoharic symbolism, but it corresponds to his own construction of one of the sections, namely the *Book of Concealment*.

[3] It is more especially a Rosicrucian number, and its importance in Kabalism arises from its frequent recurrence in the scriptures of the Old Testament. When the days of the greater exile draw to their close, and judgment is coming upon all the peoples and all the kings of the world who have oppressed Israel, it is said that a pillar of fire shall be raised from earth to heaven and shall be visible to everyone for a period of forty days. The King Messiah will leave that place which is called the Bird's Nest in the Garden of Eden and will manifest in the land of Galilee. At the end of the forty days a splendid star of all colours will appear in the East, etc. *Zohar*, Part II, fol. 7b.

[4] A reference to Plate III in the *Book of Ceremonial Magic* will shew that the emblem in question is not the Labarum. For a design which is intended to represent the latter, see Plate IV, Fig. 2. There is really no connection between the Sigils of the *Enchiridion* and the text of the work.

[5] Éliphas Lévi wrote and published much after the *History of Magic*, but the intention here expressed did not pass into realisation

have been the particular symbol of the Secret Tribunal, or Company of Free Judges. It is in the form of a cross and is concealed or enveloped by the device which surrounds it. God alone wields it, and he who strikes therewith is responsible to none for his actions. As such, it is terrible in its menace and so also in its privilege. We know that the Vehemic dagger smote in the dark those who were guilty, their crime itself often remaining unknown. What are the facts respecting this appalling justice? The answer involves an excursion into realms of shadow which history has failed to enlighten and recourse to traditions and legends for light which science cannot give.

The Free Judges were a secret association opposed, but in the interests of order and of government, to anarchic and revolutionary societies which were secret in like manner. We know that superstitions die hard and that degenerated Druidism had struck its roots deeply in the savage lands of the North. The recurring insurrections of Saxons testified to a fanaticism which was (a) always turbulent, and (b) incapable of repression by moral force alone. All defeated forms of worship—Roman paganism, Germanic idolatry, Jewish rancour—conspired against victorious Christianity. Nocturnal assemblies took place; thereat the conspirators cemented their alliance with the blood of human victims; and a pantheistic idol of monstrous form, with the horns of a goat, presided over festivals which might be called *agapæ* of hatred. In a word, the Sabbath was still celebrated in every forest and wild of yet unreclaimed provinces. The adepts who attended them were masked and otherwise unrecognisable; the assemblies extinguished their lights and broke up before daybreak; the guilty were to be found everywhere, and they could be brought to book nowhere. It came about therefore that Charlemagne determined to fight them with their own weapons.

In those days, moreover, feudal tyrants were in league with sectarians against lawful authority; female sorcerers were attached to castles as courtesans; bandits who frequented the Sabbaths divided with nobles the bloodstained loot of rapine; feudal courts were at the command of the highest bidder; and the public burdens weighed with all their force only on the weak and poor. The evil was at its height in Westphalia,[1] and faithful agents were despatched thither by Charlemagne entrusted with a secret mission.[2] Whatsoever energy remained among the oppressed, whosoever still loved justice, whether among the people or among the nobility, were drawn by these emissaries together, bound by pledges and vigilance in common. To the initiates thus incorporated they made known the full

---

[1] At the period in question Westphalia comprehended the region between the Rhine and the Weser. Its southern boundary was the mountains of Hesse; its northern the district of Friesland, which at that time extended from Holland to Schleswig.
[2] No secret mission in the sense intended by Éliphas Lévi was ever entrusted by Charlemagne. He had overcome the Saxons of Westphalia after a thirty years' war had enforced the religion of the conqueror upon them, and had established a Frankish system of government therein.

powers which they carried from the emperor himself, and they proceeded to institute the Tribunal of Free Judges.[1]

They were a kind of secret police, having the right of life and death. The mystery which surrounded their judgments, the swiftness of their executions, helped to impress the imagination of people still in barbarism. The Holy Vehm assumed gigantic proportions; men shuddered in describing apparitions of masked persons, of summonses nailed to the doors of nobles in the very midst of their watch-guards and their orgies, of brigand chiefs found dead with the terrible cruciform dagger in their breasts and on the scroll attached thereto an extract from the sentence of the Holy Vehm. The Tribunal affected most fantastic forms of procedure: the guilty person, cited to appear at some discredited cross-road, was taken to the assembly by a man clothed in black, who bandaged his eyes and led him forward in silence. This occurred invariably at some unseemly hour of the night, for judgment was never pronounced except at midnight. The criminal was carried into a vast underground vault, where he was questioned by one voice.[2] The hoodwink was removed, the vault was illuminated in all its depth and height, and the Free Judges sat masked and wearing black vestures. The sentences were not capital invariably, for those who judged were familiar with the circumstances of the crime, though nothing transpired concerning them, as death would have overtaken the revealer instantly.[3] Sometimes these formidable assemblies were so crowded that they were comparable to an army of avengers; one night the emperor himself presided over the Secret Tribunal, and more than one thousand Free Judges sat in a circle round him.[4] In the year 1400 ten thousand members existed in Germany. People with a bad conscience suspected their own relations and friends. William of Brunswick is reported to have said on a certain occasion: "If Duke Adolphus of Schleswig should pay me a visit, I must infallibly hang him, as I do not wish to be hanged." Frederick of Brunswick, a prince of the same family, who was emperor for a moment, refused to obey a citation of the Free Judges, and from that time forward he went armed from head to foot and surrounded

---

[1] The origin of the Secret Tribunal is clouded, like all the history of its period, but it is quite certain that it is referable to the middle of the thirteenth century. It should be added that Éliphas Lévi was by no means author of the Charlemagne hypothesis, which had been advanced many years previously. The competitive views are numerous. It will be seen directly that a document of the Tribunal claims that it originated in the days of Charlemagne, supposing that it has been quoted correctly. Jules Garinet supported the claim without showing any knowledge on the subject.

[2] The meetings of the Tribunal were frequently held in the town-house and the castle, sometimes in the market-place, and on rare occasions in churchyards. There is only one record concerning a session underground. The general place was under trees in the open air.

[3] An accused person had the right to conduct his own defence, or he could bring an advocate with him. There were also certain circumstances under which there was the right of appeal.

[4] The evidence is wanting for this extraordinary statement. Éliphas Lévi seems to have been under the impression that the Tribunal was like a Masonic Grand Lodge, with one mode and place of meeting. It was naturally composed of many tribunals and met, as we have seen, in all kinds of places.

by guards. One day, however, he fell a little apart from his suite and had occasion to loosen some part of his armour. He did not return and his guards entered the copse where he had sought retirement for a moment. The unfortunate man was in the act of expiring, with the dagger of the Holy Vehm in his body and his sentence attached to the weapon. Looking round in all directions, they could distinguish a masked man retreating at a slow pace, but no one dared to follow him.

The Code of the Vehmic Court was found in the ancient archives of Westphalia and has been printed in the *Reichstheater* of Müller, under the following title: "Code and Statutes of the Holy Secret Tribunal of Free Counts and Free Judges of Westphalia, established in the year 772 by the Emperor Charlemagne and revised in 1404 by King Robert, who made those alterations and additions requisite for the administration of justice in the tribunals of the illuminated, after investing them with his own authority."

A note on the first page forbade any profane person to glance at the book under penalty of death. The word "illuminated", here given to the associates of the Secret Tribunal, unfolds their entire mission: they had to track down in the shadows those who worshipped the darkness; they counterchecked mysteriously those who conspired against society in favour of mystery; but they were themselves the secret soldiers of light, who cast the light of day on criminal plottings, and it is this which was signified by a sudden splendour illuminating the Tribunal when it pronounced sentence.

The public provisions of the law under Charlemagne authorised this holy war against the tyrants of the night. The records may be consulted to ascertain the penalties inflicted on sorcerers, diviners, enchanters, *noueurs d'aiguilette*, and those who administered poison in the guise of love-philtres. The same laws made it penal to trouble the air, raise tempests construct characters and talismans, cast lots, practise witchcraft and magical charms, whether on men or cattle. Sorcerers, astrologers, diviners, necromancers, occult mathematicians are declared execrable and made subject to punishment in the same way as thieves and assassins. Such severity will be understood by recalling all that has been said on the horrible rites of Black Magic and its infant sacrifices. The danger must have been grave indeed when its repression assumed forms at once so severe and numerous.

Another institution which is referable to the same root was that of knight-errantry. The knights-errant were a species of Free Judges who appealed to God and their spears against all the oppressions of castellans and all the malice of necromancers. They were armed missionaries, who protected themselves with the sign of the cross and then clove miscreants asunder; after such manner did they earn the remembrance of some noble dame, sanctifying love by the martyrdom of a life which was one of utter self-devotion. We are far removed already from those pagan courtesans to whom slaves were offered in sacrifice and for whom the conquerors of the ancient world burnt cities. For the ladies of Christendom other sacrifices were requisite; life must have been risked in the cause of the weak and oppressed, captives must have been set free, punishment meted out to the profaners of holy affections; and then those lovely and white ladies, whose skirts were embroidered with heraldic badges; whose hands were pale and delicate; those living madonnas, proud as lilies, who came back from church, with Books of Hours under their arms and rosaries at their girdles, would remove a veil broidered with gold or silver and give it as a scarf to the knight who knelt before them, praying to them and dreaming of God. Let us forget Eve and her errors; they are forgiven a thousand times, and are more than atoned for by this ineffable grace of the noble daughters of Mary.

CHAPTER V

MAGICIANS

THAT fundamental dogma of transcendental science which consecrates the eternal law of equilibrium attained its plenary realisation in the constitution of the Christian world. Two living pillars—the Pope and Emperor—supported the structure of civilisation. But the empire suffered partition when it slipped from the feeble hands of Louis the Pious and Charles the Bald. The temporal power, abandoned to the chances of conquests or intrigue, lost the providential unity which kept it in harmony with Rome. The Pope had often to intervene as grand justiciary and, at his proper risk and peril, he restrained the ambitions and audacity of many competitive sovereigns.

Excommunication was at that time a terrible penalty, for it was sanctioned by universal belief, and it produced phenomena which awed the crowd, being mysterious effects of the magnetic current of condemnation. There is the example of Robert the Pious, who, having incurred this terrible penalty by an unlawful marriage, became the father of a monstrous child, similar to those effigies of demons which mediæval art represented in such ridiculous aspects of deformity. The melancholy fruit of a forbidden union bore witness at least to the tortured conscience and frightful dreams by which the mother was possessed. Robert accepted the event as a proof of the wrath of God and submitted to the papal judgment. Renouncing a marriage which the Church declared incestuous, he repudiated Bertha to espouse Constance of Provence, and it remained for him to recognise in the questionable morals and arrogant character of his new bride a second chastisement of heaven.

The makers of chronicles at the period were enamoured of diabolical legends, but their records exhibit more of credulity than of good taste. Every monkish malady, every unhealthy nightmare of nuns, is looked upon as a case of veridic apparition. The result is repellent phantasmagoria, stupid allocutions, impossible transfigurations, to which the artistic spirit of Cyrano de Bergerac is the one thing wanting to render them entertaining creations. From the reign of Robert to that of St. Louis there is nothing, however, which seems to deserve recounting.[1]

The famous Rabbi Jechiel, great Kabalist and truly remarkable physician, lived in the reign of St. Louis. All that is told of his lamp and magical nail goes to prove that he had discovered electricity, or was at

[1] That this statement is amply justified may be seen by a reference to *La Magie et la Sorcellerie en France*, by T. De Cauzons, a work of considerable research published within the last few years in 4 vols. The section entitled *La Magie sous les premiers Capétiens* is a record of trivialities concerning diabolical manifestations and can have been included only for the sake of chronological completeness.

least acquainted with its most important uses.[1] Ancient as that of Magic, the knowledge of this force was transmitted as one of the keys of the greater initiation. When the night came a radiant star appeared in the lodging of Jechiel, the light being so brilliant that no eye could gaze thereon without being dazzled, while the beam that it darted was tinted with rainbow colours. It was never known to fail and it was never replenished with oil or other combustible substance extant at that time. When importunity or ill-intentioned curiosity sought to intrude on Jechiel by knocking persistently at his door, the Rabbi struck a nail fixed in his cabinet, producing simultaneously a blue spark on the head of the nail and the door-knocker. The ill-advised person was shaken in such a manner that he cried for mercy, believing that the earth was opening under his feet. One day a hostile mob swarmed about the entrance, uttering murmurs and menaces, while they stood with interlaced arms to resist the commotion and supposed quaking of the ground. The boldest among them plied furiously at the knocker, but Jechiel pressed his nail; in a moment the assailants were tumbled one over another and fled crying out like people who have been burnt. They were quite sure that the earth had opened and swallowed them as far as the knees; they knew not how they got out; but nothing would persuade them to return and renew the attack. The sorcerer thus earned quietude by the terror which he diffused.

St. Louis, great Catholic as he was, was also a great king, and wishing to know Jechiel, he summoned him to his court,[2] had several conversations with him, was satisfied fully by his explanations, protected him from his enemies, and during the rest of his life ever failed to testify esteem for him and to act benevolently towards him.

Albertus Magnus lived at the same period, and he still passes among the people as grand master of all magicians.[3] Historians of the time affirm that he possessed the Philosophic Stone,[4] and that after studying for thirty years he had succeeded in solving the problem of the android—in other words, that he had fabricated an artificial man who was endowed with life and speech, who could, in fact, answer questions with such precision and subtlety that St. Thomas Aquinas, infuriated at being unable to silence the image, broke it with a blow of his stick. Such is the popular fable; let us now see what it signifies.

The mystery of the formation of man and of his primitive appearance on earth have continually absorbed seekers after the problems of Nature. Man, as a fact, appears last in the world of fossils, and the Mosaic days

---

[1] The story of Rabbi Jechiel's device of self-protection is told by Bartolocci, *s.v.* R. Jechiel de Parisio, in the *Magna Bibliotheca Rabbinica*, vol. iii, pp. 834, 835. It is on the authority of R. Ghedalia ben David Iacchiia. But although Jechiel is supposed to have been a magician there was neither electricity nor magic in his process, only a kind of trap at his own door step or threshold.

[2] It so happens that he went to see him and fell into the trap of the Jew. Garient is the authority for the imaginary visit to the court of St. Louis. He follows Sauval.

[3] This paragraph is adapted from Garinet, *Hist. de la Magie en France*, p. 76.

[4] Many treatises on alchemy have been fathered on Albertus Magnus, including *Libellus de Alchymia* and *Concordantia Philosophorum*.

of creation have deposited their successive remains, bearing witness that those days were in reality long periods of time. How then was humanity formed? Genesis testifies that God made Adam from the slime of the earth and breathed into his nostrils the breath of life—a statement the truth of which we do not question for a moment; but we repudiate notwithstanding the heretical and anthropomorphic idea of a Deity moulding clay with His fingers. God, being a pure spirit, has no hands, and He causes His creatures to develop one from another by the power which He has imparted to Nature. If, therefore, the Lord made Adam from the dust of the earth, we must understand that man came out of that earth under the Divine Influence and yet after a natural manner. The name Adam in Hebrew signifies red earth,[1] but what is this earth actually? It is that which the alchemists sought, and it follows that the Great Work was not the secret of metallic transmutation—a trivial and accessory result—but the universal secret of life.[2] It was the quest for the middle point of transformation, at which light becomes matter and condenses into an earth containing within itself the principle of motion and of life. It was the generalisation of the phenomenon which tinges the blood red by the creation of those innumerable corpuscles which are magnetic even as the worlds and are alive like animals. For disciples of Hermes the metals were the coagulated blood of earth, passing, like that of man, from white to black and from black to crimson, following the work of the light.[3] To set this fluid in motion by means of heat and impart thereto the tingeing fructification of light by the aid of electricity—such was the first part of the work of wisdom. The end was more arduous and sublime; it was a question of recovering the adamic earth, which is the coagulated blood of the vital earth; and the supreme dream of philosophers was to accomplish the work of Prometheus by imitating the work of God—that is to say, by producing a man who should be the child of science, as Adam was child of divine omnipotence. The dream was insensate perhaps, and yet it was sublime.

Black Magic, which ever apes the Magic of Light, but takes it, as it were, backwards, was also concerned with the android, that it might be used as an instrument of passion and an oracle of hell. For this object it was requisite to outrage Nature and obtain a species of venomous fungus, full of concentrated human malice—the living realisation of all crime. For this reason magicians sought the mandragore beneath a gibbet from which some corpse was suspended; they caused it to be torn up by a dog tied to the plant, a mortal blow being inflicted on the animal. The eradication was effected by the convulsions of the agonised beast; the dog's

---

[1] According to the *Zohar*, Adam was formed of earth brought from the four quarters, and this is really an allusion to the symbolic correspondence between the parts of his personality and the four elements of ancient physics.

[2] The universal secret which was sought by mystic Alchemy was more truly that of the life of life; it was the quest of transmutation in God.

[3] The thesis of physical Alchemy was that Nature always intended to produce gold but was thwarted by the impurity of the *media* amidst which she worked under the earth. The inferior metals resulted. The end of Hermetic art was to complete the design of Nature and raise what is base to perfection.

soul passed into the plant and also attracted thereto that of the hanged man. Enough of these horrors and absurdities; those who are curious in such knowledge may consult the common Grimoire known along the countryside under the name of *Little Albert*. They will find further the method of making a mandragore in the form of a cock with a human face. Stupidity and impiety vie one with another in all such processes, for Nature cannot be outraged wilfully without at the same time reversing the laws of reason.

Albertus Magnus was neither infanticide nor deicide; he was neither guilty of the crime of Tantalus nor that of Prometheus; but he had succeeded in creating and arming at all points that purely scholastic theology, outcome of the categories of Aristotle and the sentences of Peter Lombard, that logic of syllogism consisting of argumentation in place of reasoning and of finding an answer for everything by subtleties concerning the terms. It was less a philosophy than a philosophical automaton, replying in an arbitrary manner and unrolling its theses like the revolution of machinery. It was in no sense the human *logos*, but the unvaried cry of a mechanism, the inanimate speech of an android. It was the fatal precision of machinery, in place of the free application of rational necessities. St. Thomas Aquinas,[1] with one blow, shattered this scaffolding of words when he proclaimed the eternal empire of reason in that magnificent sentence which has been cited already so often: "A thing is not just because God wills it, but God wills it because it is just." The approximate consequence of this proposition, in arguing from the greater to the lesser, was: A thing is not true because Aristotle has said it, but Aristotle could not say it reasonably unless it were true. Seek first therefore truth and justice, and the science of Aristotle shall be added unto you. Aristotle, galvanised by scholasticism, was the veritable android of Albertus Magnus, while the master's wand of St. Thomas Aquinas was the doctrine of the *Summa Totius Theologiæ*, a masterpiece of power and reason which will again be studied in our theological schools when it is proposed to return seriously to sane and healthy subjects.[2]

As for the Philosophical Stone bequeathed by St. Dominic[3] to Albert and by the latter to St. Thomas Aquinas, we must understand it as the philosophical and religious basis of ideas prevalent at the period. Had St. Dominic been able to accomplish the Great Work he would have secured for Rome that empire of the world about which he was so jealous for the Church, and would have diverted the fire which consumed so many heretics to the heating of his own crucibles. St. Thomas changed all that he touched into gold, but this is a figure of speech only, gold being in this case an emblem of truth.

---

[1] St. Thomas Aquinas wrote eight treatises on alchemy, if the ascriptions of the literature could be trusted. They are of the same authenticity as those of Albertus Magnus

[2] The study in question was enjoined in a particular manner by Leo XIII.

[3] I do not know or have forgotten how this legend originated, but in any case no works on transmutation have been imputed to St. Dominic, which leads me to think that the story of his adeptship did not attain any considerable currency.

It is opportune at this point to say a few further words concerning that Hermetic science cultivated from the first Christian centuries by Ostanes, Romarius, Queen Cleopatra, the Arabian Geber, Alfarabius and Salmanas, by Morien, Artephius and Aristeus.[1] Understand in an absolute manner, this science may be called the Kabalah in realisation, or the Magic of Works. It has therefore three analogous degrees—religious realisation, philosophical realisation and physical realisation. The first is the solid basis of empire and priesthood; the second is the establishment of an absolute doctrine and an hierarchic instruction; the last is the discovery and application, within the measures of the Microcosm or lesser world, of that creative law which peoples incessantly the greater universe. The law in question is one of movement combined with substance, of the fixed with the volatile, humid with solid. Its principle is divine impulsion, its instrument the universal light—ethereal in the infinite, astral in stars and planets, metallic, specific or mercurial in metals, vegetable in plants vital in animals, magnetic or personal in men.

This light is the quintessence of Paracelsus and is either latent or active in all created substances. Such quintessence is the true elixir of life, and it is extracted from earth by cultivation; from metals by incorporation, rectification, exaltation and synthesis; from plants by distillation and coction; from animals by absorption; from men by generation; from the air by respiration. In this sense we are told by Aristeus that air must be derived from air; by Khunrath that living mercury must be obtained from the perfect man formed by the androgyne; by practically all the sages, that the medicine of metals must be derived from metals and that this medicine—though fundamentally one in all kingdoms—is graduated and specified according to forms and species. Its use is threefold—by sympathy, repulsion or equilibrium. The graduated quintessence was only the auxiliary of forces; the medicine of each kingdom must be derived from the kingdom itself, with the addition of basic mercury—terrestrial or mineral—and of synthetic living mercury, or human magnetism.

Such is the rapid and summary sketch of this science, which is vast and profound as the Kabalah, mysterious as Magic, real as the exact sciences, but too long and too often discredited by the frustrated greed of false adepts and by the obscurities with which true sages have surrounded their theories and their processes.

---

[1] A fragment of Ostanes is included in the Byzantine collection of ancient alchemists. Romarius should read Comarius, whose tract in the same collection is supposed to be addressed to Cleopatra. Salmanas wrote on the fabrication of artificial pearls and was supposed to be an Arab. A treatise on weights and measures is attributed to Cleopatra, and there are also some Latin forgeries. The other names are well known in the literature of Alchemy

CHAPTER VI

SOME FAMOUS PROSECUTIONS

THE societies of the elder world perished through the materialistic egoism of castes, becoming petrified on their own part, isolating the common people in a hopeless reprobation and reserving the reins of power to a small number of the elect, so that it was deprived of that circulation which is the principle of progress, motion and life. Power without antagonism, without competition and hence without control, proved fatal to the sacerdotal royalties. The republics, on the other hand, perished by the conflict of liberties which, in the absence of all duty, hierarchially and highly sanctioned, are speedily converted into so many tyrannies in rivalry with one another. To find a stable point between these two abysses, the idea of Christian hierophants was to create a society pledged to self-sacrifice by solemn vows, protected by severe rules, recruited by initiation, and, as sole depositary of the great religious and social secrets, making kings and pontiffs without being itself exposed to the corruptions of empire. Such was the secret of that kingdom of Christ Jesus which, without being of this world, ruled over all its grandeurs. The same idea presided over the establishments of the great religious orders which were so often at war with secular authorities, whether ecclesiastical or civil. A similar realisation was also dreamed by dissident sects of Gnostics and Illuminati, which claimed to pin their faith on the primitive Christian tradition of St. John. A time came when this dream was an actual menace for the Church and the State, when a rich and dissolute Order, initiated into the mysterious doctrines of the Kabalah,[1] seemed ready to turn on legitimate authority, on the conservative principles of the hierarchy, menacing the entire world with a gigantic revolution. The Templars, whose history is understood so little, were the terrible conspirators in question, and it is time at length to reveal the secret of their fall, so absolving the memory of Clement V and Philip the Fair.

In 1118 nine crusading knights, then in the East—among whom was Geoffrey de Saint-Omer and Hugh de Payens—dedicated themselves to religion, placing their vows in the hands of the patriarch of Constantinople, which seat had always been hostile, secretly or openly, to that of Rome since the days of Photius. The avowed object of the Templars was to protect Christians on pilgrimage to the holy places; their concealed end was to rebuild the Temple of Solomon on the model foreshewn by Ezekiel. Such a restoration, predicted formally by Judaising mystics of the first Christian centuries, had become the secret dream of the Eastern patriarchs.

[1] This must be understood in the general sense of the Secret Tradition perpetuated in various forms through Christian times. The Templars had no concern in the secret schools of Jewry. On the basis of the official process which resulted in their condemnation, they have been accused of Black Magic, Sorcery and of entering into a league with the Order of Assassins.

So rebuilt and consecrated to the Catholic worship, the Temple of Solomon would have been in effect the metropolis of the universe. East would prevail over West and the patriarchs of Constantinople would seize the papacy.[1]

To explain the name of Templars adopted by this military Order, historians assume that Baldwin II, King of Jerusalem, gave them a house in the vicinity of the Temple of Solomon. But they are guilty of a serious anachronism, since at that period the edifice in question had not only ceased to exist, and not only was there no stone of Zerubbabel's Second Temple left upon another, but it would have been difficult to indicate the site on which they stood. It is to be concluded that the House allotted to the Templars by Baldwin was not situated in the vicinity of Solomon's Temple but of that place on which these secret and armed missionaries of the Eastern patriarch designed to rebuilt it.

The Templars took for their scriptural models the military Masons of Zerubbabel, who worked with sword in one hand and trowel in the other.[2] Hence sword and trowel became their insignia when at a later period, as we shall see, they concealed themselves under the name of Masonic Brothers. The trowel of the Templars is fourfold; the triangular blades are disposed in the form of a cross, constituting a Kabalistic pantacle known as the Cross of the East.[3]

The inmost thought of Hugh de Payens, in establishing his Order, was not precisely to serve the ambition of the patriarchs of Constantinople. At that period there was a sect of Christian Johannites in the East who claimed to be alone initiated into the inner mysteries of the Saviour's religion; they claimed also to know the true history of Jesus Christ. Adopting some part of the Jewish traditions and Talmudic accounts, they regarded the facts in the Gospels as allegories, of which St. John had the key. The proof was his saying that if all things done by Jesus were recorded, "I suppose that even the world itself could not contain the books that should be written." They held that such a statement would be ridiculous exaggeration unless it referred to allegory and legend, which can be varied and prolonged to infinity. As to the actual historical facts, the Johannites recounted what follows.

A young girl of Nazareth, named Miriam, betrothed to a young man of her own tribe, named Jochanan, was surprised by a certain Pandira, or Panther, who entered her chamber in the garb and under the name of her lover and by force fulfilled his desires. Jochanan, becoming acquainted

[1] I have dealt with the claims of this speculation in my *Secret Tradition in Freemasonry*, vol. i, pp. 300 *et seq*.

[2] The reference is really to the fourth chapters of the apocryphal *Book of Nehemiah* which is the *Second Book of Esdras*, and to the Masons of Nehemiah, not of Zerubbabel. The latter was concerned with the building of the Second Temple and the former with that of the walls about Jerusalem. Half of the young men did the work of restoring the fortifications and half stood in readiness to fight. The builders also were girded with a sword about the reins. The sword in one hand and trowel in the other is a symbolical expression.

[3] It is obvious that the arrangement of four triangular blades in a cruciform pattern would constitute an ordinary Maltese cross or cross of the Knights of St. John. This was an Assyrian emblem in pre-Christian times.

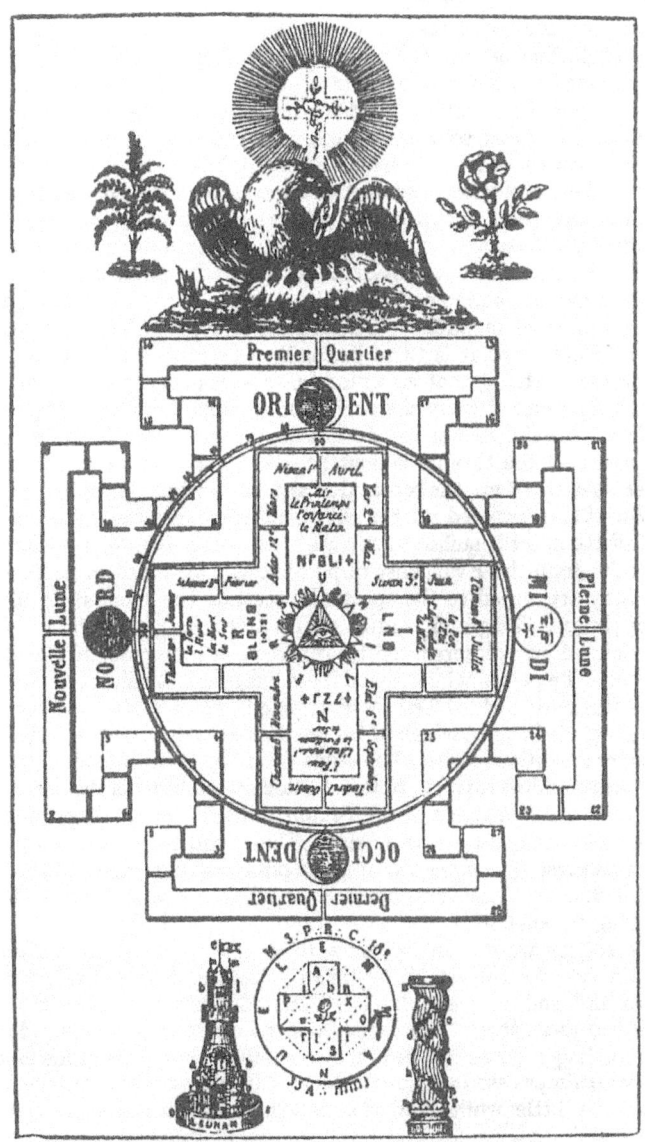

The Philosophical Cross, or Plan of the Third Temple

with her misfortune, left her without compromising her because as a fact she was innocent; and the girl was delivered of a son, who received the name of Joshua or Jesus. The infant was adopted by a Rabbi named Joseph, who carried him into Egypt, where he was initiated into the secret sciences, and the priests of Osiris, recognising that he was the true incarnation of Horus so long promised to the adepts, consecrated him sovereign pontiff of the universal religion. Joshua and Joseph returned to Judea, where the knowledge and virtue of the young man excited very soon the envy and hatred of the priests, who one day reproached him publicly with the illegitimacy of his birth. Joshua, who loved and venerated his mother, questioned his master and learned the whole history respecting the crime of Pandira and the misfortunes of Miriam. His first impulse was to deny her in public when he said in the middle of a marriage-feast: "Woman, what is there in common between you and me?" But afterwards, realising that an unfortunate woman must not be punished for having suffered what she could not prevent, he cried: "My mother has in no wise sinned, nor has she lost her innocence; she is virgin and yet is mother: let the twofold honour be paid to her. As for me, I have no father on earth; I am the son of God and humanity."

We will not proceed further with a fiction so distressing to the hearts of Christians; let it suffice to say that the Johannites went so far as to make St. John the Evangelist responsible for this spurious tradition and that they attributed to the apostle in question the foundation of their secret church. The grand pontiffs of this sect assumed the title of Christ and claimed an uninterrupted transmission of powers from the days of St. John. The person who boasted these imaginary privileges at the epoch of the foundation of the Temple was named Theoclet. He was acquainted with Hugh de Payens, whom he initiated into the mysteries and the hopes of his supposititious church;[1] he seduced him by ideas of sovereign priesthood and supreme royalty; in fine, he designated him his successor. Thus was the order of Knights of the Temple tainted from the beginning with schism and conspiracy against kings. These tendencies were wrapped in profound mystery, for the Order made profession externally of the uttermost orthodoxy. The chiefs alone knew whither it was tending, the rest following in good faith.

To acquire wealth and influence, to intrigue on the basis of these and at need fight for the establishment of Johannite dogma—such were the means and end proposed by the initiated brethren. "Observe," they argued to themselves, "the papacy and rival monarchies engaged in the work of haggling, selling one another, falling into corruption and tomorrow perhaps destroying one another. All this indicates heritage for the Temple; a little while, and the nations will demand sovereigns and

---

[1] The blasphemous fiction is well known and its root is in the *Sepher Toldos Jeshu*; it is inaccurate to call it a tradition; more properly it is a lying invention. I have failed to discover a source for the Theoclet story, but it is barely possible that it may have risen up within the circle of Fabré Palaprat's *Ordre du Temple*.

pontiffs from among us; we shall be the equilibrium of the universe, arbiters and masters of the world."

The Templars had two doctrines; one was concealed and reserved to the leaders, being that of Johannism;[1] the other was public, being Roman Catholic doctrine. They deceived in this manner the enemies that they hoped to supplant. The Johannism of the adepts was the Kabalah of the Gnostics, but it degenerated speedily into a mystic pantheism carried even to idolatry of Nature and hatred of all revealed dogma. For their better success, and in order to secure partisans, they fostered the regrets of every fallen worship and the hopes of every new cultus, promising to all liberty of conscience and a new orthodoxy which should be the synthesis of all persecuted beliefs. They went even so far as to recognise the pantheistic symbolism of the grand masters of Black Magic, and the better to isolate themselves from obedience to a religion by which they were condemned beforehand, they rendered divine honours to the monstrous idol Baphomet,[2] even as of old the dissenting tribes had adored the Golden Calf of Dan and Bethel. Certain monuments of recent discovery and certain precious documents belonging to the thirteenth century offer abundant proof of all that is advanced here. Other evidences are concealed in the annals and beneath the symbols of Occult Masonry.

With the seeds of death sown in its very principle, and anarchic because it was heretical, the Order of Knights of the Temple had conceived a great work which it was incapable of executing, because it understood neither humility nor personal abnegation. For the rest, the Templars, being in most cases without education and capable only of wielding the sword successfully, possessed no qualification for overruling or for binding at need that queen of the world called public opinion. Hugh de Payens did not possess the depth of view which distinguished at a later period the military founder of a militia not less formidable to kings. The Templars were Jesuits who failed. Their principle was to become rich in order to purchase the world, and, as a fact, they so became, for in 1312 they possessed in Europe alone more than 9000 manors. Wealth was also the rock on which they broke; they became insolent and permitted their disdain for the religious and social institutions which they hoped to upset to appear in public. Everyone knows the answer of Richard Cœur de Lion to the confidential priest who had said to him: "Sire, you have three daughters who cost you dearly and of whom it would be to your

---

[1] In the year 1844 Jacques Matter made a special study of the accusations against Knights Templar in his *Histoire Critique du Gnosticisme*, vol. iii, pp. 315 *et seq*. He states that the alleged preference of the Templars for St. John's Gospel is nowhere attested by the history of the Order. They were not therefore tinctured by remanents of Paulician Gnosticism, as it is not likely that they would be.

[2] Elsewhere Éliphas Lévi says: (*a*) That the hypothetical idol Baphomet was a symbolical figure representing the First Matter of the *Magnum Opus*, which is the Astral Light; (*b*) That it signified further the god Pan, which may be identified with "the Christ of dissident sacerdotalism"; (*c*) That the Baphometic head is "a beautiful allegory which attributes to thought alone the first and creative cause"; and finally, (*d*) That it is "nothing more than an innocent and even a pious hieroglyph".

great advantage if you were set free: they are ambition, avarice and luxury." . . . "That is true," said the king. "Well, well, let us marry them. I give ambition to the Templars, avarice to the monks and luxury to the bishops. I am certain in advance of the consent of all the parties."

The ambition of the Templars proved fatal to themselves; their projects were divined and anticipated. Pope Clement V and King Philip the Fair gave the signal to Europe, and the Templars, caught, so to speak, in a net, were arrested, disarmed and cast into prison. Never was a *coup d'état* accomplished with such appalling uniformity. The entire world was dumbfounded and awaited the strange revelations of a prosecution which was to echo down through the ages. But it was impossible to unveil before the people the plan of the Templar conspiracy; to do so would have initiated the multitude into secrets reserved for masters. Recourse was had therefore to the charge of Magic, for which accusers and witnesses were both forthcoming. The Templars, in the ceremony of their reception, spat upon the image of Christ, denied God, gave obscene kisses to the Grand Master, adored a brazen head with carbuncles for eyes, held commune with a great black cat and had intercourse with female demons. Such are the items put forward seriously in the act of indictment. The end of this drama is familiar; Jacques de Molay and his companions perished in the flames, but before dying the grand master of the Temple organised and instituted Occult Masonry. Within the walls of his prison he founded four Metropolitan Lodges—at Naples for the East, Edinburgh for the West, Stockholm for the North and Paris for the South. The Pope and King perished speedily in a strange and sudden manner.[1] Squin de Florian, the accuser-in-chief of the Order, was assassinated. In breaking the sword of the Templars it was converted into a dagger and their proscribed trowels henceforth were utilised only in the erection of tombs. Let them pass at this point into darkness, wherein they took refuge while maturing their vengeance. We shall see them reappear at the great epoch of the Revolution and we shall recognise them by their signs and by their works.

The greatest magical prosecution to be found in history, after that of the Temple, was the trial of a maid who was, moreover, almost a saint. The Church, in this case, has been accused of subservience to the base resentment of a vanquished party, and it has been asked earnestly what anathemas of the Chair of St. Peter fell upon the assassins of Joan of Arc.[2]

---

[1] The suggestion is that they were summoned by Jacques de Molay to appear before the Divine Tribunal within a year and a day, there to answer for their injustice, and that they died within the time mentioned, which does not happen to be true.

[2] The revision of the process which condemned the Maid of Orléans was begun by Charles VII himself in 1449. In 1552 twelve articles were drawn up, designed to exhibit its illegality and injustice. For political reasons, meaning the relations between France and England, the mother and brothers of Joan were made plaintiffs at Rome, and Pope Calixtus V appointed a commission. In 1456 the commission pronounced its judgment, reversing and annulling the first process on the ground of roguery, calumny, injustice, contradictions and manifest error in fact and law.—*La Magie et la Sorcellerie en France*, vol. ii, pp. 514–518.

MAGIC AND CIVILISATION

To those who are really unacquainted, it may be said at once that Pierre Cauchon, the unworthy Bishop of Beauvais, struck suddenly with death by the hand of God, was excommunicated after death by Callixtus IV, his remains being taken from consecrated ground and cast into the public sewers. It was not therefore the Church which judged and condemned the Maid of Orléans, but a bad priest and an apostate.

Charles VII, who gave up this noble girl to her destroyers, fell afterwards into the hands of an avenging providence; he died of self-starvation, through dread of being poisoned by his own son. Fear is the torment of the base. The king in question gave up his life to a courtesan, and for her he burdened with debt a kingdom which had been saved to him by a virgin. Courtesan and virgin have been celebrated by our national poets—Agnes Sorel by Béranger and Joan of Arc by Voltaire.

Joan perished in her innocence, but the laws against Magic were vindicated soon after in the case of one who was chief among the guilty. The personage in question was one of the most valiant captains under Charles VII, but the services which he rendered to the state could not counterbalance the extent and enormity of his crimes. All tales of ogres and Croquemitaine were realised and surpassed by the deeds of this fantastic scoundrel, whose history has remained in the memory of children under the name of Blue Beard. Gilles de Laval, Lord of Raiz, had indeed so black a beard that it seemed to be almost blue, as shown by his portrait in the Salle des Maréchaux, at the Museum of Versailles. A Marshal of Brittany, he was brave because he was French; being rich, he was also ostentatious; and he became a sorcerer because he was insane.[1]

The mental derangement of the Lord of Raiz was manifested in the first instance by sumptuous devotion and extravagant magnificence. When he went abroad he was preceded invariably by cross and banner; his chaplains were covered with gold and vested like prelates; he had a college of little pages or choristers, who were always richly clothed. But day by day one of these children was called before the marshal and was seen no more by his comrades; a newcomer succeeded him who disappeared, and the children were sternly forbidden to ask what became of the missing ones or even refer to them among themselves. The children were obtained by the marshal from poor parents, whom he dazzled by his promises, and who were pledged to trouble no further concerning their offspring—these, according to his stories, being assured a brilliant future.

The explanation is that, in his case, seeming devotion was the mask and safeguard of infamous practices. Ruined by imbecile prodigality, the marshal desired at any cost to create wealth. Alchemy had exhausted his last resources and loans on usurious terms were about to fail him; he determined therefore to attempt the last and most execrable experiments of Black Magic, in the hope of obtaining gold by the aid of hell. An

---

[1] It has been suggested that the charge of sorcery covered a political conspiracy for his destruction and was of the same value as the same charge in respect of the Knights Templar.

apostate priest of the diocese of Saint-Malo, a Florentine named Prélati, and Sillé,[1] who was the marshal's steward, became his confidants and accomplices. He had espoused a young woman of high birth[2] and kept her practically shut up in his castle at Machecoul, which had a tower with the entrance walled up. A report was spread by the marshal that it was in a ruinous state and no one sought to penetrate therein. This notwithstanding, Madame de Raiz, who was frequently alone during the dark hours, saw red lights moving to and fro in this tower; but she did not venture to question her husband, whose bizarre and sombre character filled her with extreme terror.

On Easter Day in the year 1440[3] the marshal, having communicated solemnly in his chapel, bade farewell to the lady of Machecoul, telling her that he was departing to the Holy Land; the poor creature was even then afraid to question, so much did she tremble in his presence; she was also several months in her pregnancy. The marshal permitted her sister to come on a visit as a companion during his absence. Madame de Raiz took advantage of this indulgence, after which Gilles de Laval mounted his horse and departed. To her sister Madame de Raiz communicated her fears and anxieties. What went on in the castle? Why was her lord so gloomy? What signified his repeated absences? What became of the children who disappeared day by day? What were those nocturnal lights in the walled-up tower? These and the other problems excited the curiosity of both women to the utmost degree.[4] What, all the same, could be done? The marshal had forbidden them expressly even to approach the tower, and before leaving he had repeated this injunction. It must assuredly have a secret entrance, for which Madame de Raiz and her sister Anne proceeded to search through the lower rooms of the castle, corner by corner and stone after stone. At last, in the chapel, behind the altar, they came upon a copper button, hidden in a mass of sculpture. It yielded under pressure; a stone slid back and the two curiosity-seekers, now all in a tremble, distinguished the lowermost steps of a staircase, which led them to the condemned tower.

At the top of the first flight there was a kind of chapel, with a cross upside down and black candles; on the altar stood a hideous figure, no doubt representing the demon. On the second floor they came upon furnaces, retorts, alembics, charcoal—in a word, all the apparatus of alchemy. The third flight led to a dark chamber, where the heavy and fetid atmosphere compelled the young women to retreat. Madame de Raiz came into collision with a vase, which fell over, and she was conscious that her robe and feet were soaked with some thick and unknown liquid. On returning to

[1] Francesco Prelati seems to have been a magician by profession, and as regards Gilles de Sillé, it is said otherwise that he was a priest of St. Malo.
[2] This was Catherine de Thouars, and it was to her that the bulk of his fortune was due. He is said to have been one of the richest nobles in Europe.
[3] It will be understood that what follows is merely romantic narrative. See *Gilles de Rais, dit Barbe Bleue*, by Bossard et Maulde.
[4] The account at this point represents the admixture of the Blue-Beard or folk element and may be read in conjunction with Perrault.

the light at the head of the stairs she found that she was bathed in blood.

Sister Anne would have fled from the place, but in Madame de Raiz curiosity was even stronger than disgust or fear. She descended the stairs, took a lamp from the infernal chapel and returned to the third floor, where a frightful spectacle awaited her. Copper vessels filled with blood were ranged the whole length of the walls, bearing labels with a date on each, and in the middle of the room there was a black marble table, on which lay the body of a child murdered quite recently. It was one of these basins which had fallen, and black blood had spread far and wide over the grimy and worm-eaten wooden floor.

The two women were now half dead with terror. Madame de Raiz endeavoured at all costs to efface the evidence of her indiscretion. She went in search of a sponge and water, to wash the boards; but she only extended the stain and that which at first seemed black became all scarlet in hue. Suddenly a loud commotion echoed through the castle, mixed with the cries of people calling to Madame de Raiz. She distinguished the awe-striking words, "Here is Monseigneur come back." The two women made for the staircase, but at the same moment they were aware of the trampling of steps and the sound of other voices in the devil's chapel. Sister Anne fled upwards to the battlement of the tower; Madame de Raiz went down trembling and found herself face to face with her husband, in the act of ascending, accompanied by the apostate priest and Prélati.

Gilles de Laval seized his wife by the arm and without speaking dragged her into the infernal chapel. It was then that Prélati[1] observed to the marshal: "It is needs must, as you see, and the victim has come of her own accord." . . . "Be it so," answered his master. "Begin the Black Mass." . . . The apostate priest went to the altar, while Gilles de Laval opened a little cupboard fixed therein and drew out a large knife, after which he sat down close to his spouse, who was now almost in a swoon and lying in a heap on a bench against the wall. The sacrilegious ceremonies began.

It must be explained that the marshal, so far from taking the road to Jerusalem, had proceeded only to Nantes, where Prélati lived; he attacked this miserable wretch with the uttermost fury and threatened to slay him if he did not furnish the means of extracting from the devil that which he had been demanding for so long a time. With the object of obtaining delay, Prélati declared that terrible conditions were required by the infernal master, first among which would be the sacrifice of the marshal's unborn child after tearing it forcibly from the mother's womb. Gilles de Laval made no reply but returned at once to Machecoul, the Florentine sorcerer and his accomplice the priest being in his train. With the rest we are acquainted.

[1] It does not appear that Francesco Prélati and Gilles de Sillé were brought to account subsequently.

Meanwhile, Sister Anne, left to her own devices on the roof of the tower and not daring to come down, had removed her veil, to make signals of distress at chance. They were answered by two cavaliers accompanied by a posse of armed men, who were riding towards the castle; they proved to be her two brothers, who, on learning the spurious departure of the marshal for Palestine, had come to visit and console Madame de Raiz. Soon after they arrived with a clatter in the court of the castle, whereupon Gilles de Laval suspended the hideous ceremony and said to his wife: "Madame, I forgive you, and the matter is at an end between us if you do now as I tell you. Return to your apartment, change your garments and join me in the guest-room, whither I am going to receive your brothers. But if you say one word, or cause them the slightest suspicion, I will bring you hither on their departure; we shall proceed with the Black Mass at the point where it is now broken off, and at the consecration you will die. Mark where I place this knife."

He rose up, led his wife to the door of her chamber and subsequently received her relations and their suite, saying that his lady was preparing herself to come and salute her brothers. Madame de Raiz appeared almost immediately, pale as a spectre. Gilles de Laval never took eyes off her, seeking to control her by his glance. When her brothers suggested that she was ill, she answered that it was the fatigue of pregnancy, but added in an undertone, "Save me; he seeks to kill me." At the same moment Sister Anne rushed into the hall, crying: "Take us away; save us, my brothers: this man is an assassin!"—and she pointed to Gilles de Laval. While the marshal summoned his people, the escort of the two visitors surrounded the women with drawn swords; and the marshal's people disarmed instead of obeying him. Madame de Raiz, with her sister and brothers, gained the drawbridge and left the castle.

On the morrow, Duke John V invested Machecoul, and Gilles de Laval, who could count no longer on his men-at-arms, yielded without resistance.[1] The parliament of Brittany had decreed his arrest as a homicide, the ecclesiastical tribunal preparing in the first place to pronounce judgment upon him as heretic, sodomite and sorcerer. Voices of parents, long silenced by terror, rose upon all sides, demanding their missing children: there was universal dole and clamour throughout the province. The castles of Machecoul and Chantocé were ransacked, resulting in the discovery of two hundred skeletons of children; the rest had been consumed by fire.

Gilles de Laval appeared with supreme arrogance before his judges.[2] To the customary question, "Who are you?" he answered: "I am Gilles de Laval, Marshal of Brittany, Lord of Raiz, Machecoul, Chantocé and other fiefs. And who are you that dare to question me?" He was answered,

[1] He was really cited to appear before Jean de Malestroit, Bishop of Nantes and Chancellor of Brittany. He obeyed this summons.
[2] The records say that he was insolent at the beginning but soon changed his methods, and the confession which he made involved two of his servants, named Henri and Poitou.

"We are your judges, magistrates of the Ecclesiastical Court."—"What, you my judges! Go to, I know you well, my masters. You are simoniacs and obscene fellows, who sell your God to purchase the joys of the devil. Speak not therefore of judging me, for if I am guilty, it is you, who owed me good example, that are my instigators."—"Cease your insults, and answer us."—"I would rather be hanged by the neck than reply to you. I am surprised that the president of Brittany suffers your acquaintance with matters of this kind. You question that you may gain information and afterwards do worse than you have done."

But this haughty insolence was demolished by the threat of torture.[1] Before the Bishop of Saint-Brieuc and the President Pierre de l'Hôpital, Gilles de Laval made confession of his murders and sacrileges. He pretended that his motive in the massacre of children was an execrable delight which he sought during the agony of these poor little beings. The president found it difficult to credit this statement and questioned him anew. "Alas," said the marshal abruptly, "you torment both yourself and me to no purpose."—"I do not torment you," replied the president, "but I am astonished at your words and dissatisfied. What I seek and must have is the pure truth." The marshal answered: "Verily there was no other cause What more would you have? Surely I have admitted enough to condemn ten thousand men."

That which Gilles de Laval shrank from confessing was that he sought the Philosophical Stone in the blood of murdered children, and that it was covetousness which drove him to this monstrous debauchery. On the faith of his necromancers he believed that the universal agent of life could be suddenly coagulated by the combined action and reaction of outrage on Nature and murder. He collected afterwards the iridescent film which forms on blood as it turns cold;[2] he subjected it to various fermentations, digested the product in the philosophical egg of the athanor, combining it with salt, sulphur and mercury. He had doubtless derived his recipe from some of those old Hebrew Grimoires which, had they been known at the period, would have been sufficient to call down on Jewry at large the execration of the whole earth. Persuaded, as they were, that the act of human impregnation attracts and coagulates the Astral Light in its reaction by sympathy on things subjected to the magnetism of man, the Israelitish sorcerers had plunged into those enormities of which Philo accuses them, as quoted by the astrologer Gaffarel.[3] They caused trees to

[1] It was the servants of Gilles de Rais who accused him under torture.
[2] This explanation is absolutely supposititious, there being no tittle of evidence for the existence of such a process in the records of Black Magic. It is of course possible that some readers may ascribe secret sources of information to Éliphas Lévi. Speaking generally, Black Magic and the synonymous white variety were concerned little enough in alchemical processes, good or bad. Their amateurs and adepts sought enrichment by the discovery of buried treasures with the assistance of demons; they sought also to communicate with evil spirits who could bring gold and precious stones from the mines, or who could themselves accomplish transmutation.
[3] It is just to say that Gaffarel wrote in defence of the Jews and to clear them of many accusations besides those made by Philo. His thesis was that many things were falsely imposed upon them.

be grafted by women, who inserted the graft while a man performed on their persons those acts which are an outrage to Nature. Wherever Black Magic is concerned the same horrors recur, for the spirit of darkness is not one of invention.

Gilles de Laval was burned alive in the *pré de la Magdeleine*, near Nantes; he obtained permission to go to execution with all the pageantry that had accompanied him during life, as if he wished to involve in the ignominy of his punishment the ostentation and cupidity by which he had been so utterly degraded and lost so fatally.[1]

---

[1] His fate was shared by the servants already mentioned, who are said to have been his accomplices.

CHAPTER VII

SUPERSTITIONS RELATING TO THE DEVIL

WE have borne witness to the sobriety of decisions pronounced by the Church respecting the genius of evil; she has recommended her children not to be in fear concerning him, not to be preoccupied about him and not even to pronounce his name. This notwithstanding, the propensity of diseased imaginations and weak minds towards the monstrous and the horrible lent, during the evil days of the middle ages, a formidable importance and most portentous forms to the darksome being who deserves nothing but oblivion, because he has rejected truth and light for ever. This seeming realisation of the phantom expressing perversity was an incarnation of human frenzy; the devil became the nightmare of cloisters, the human mind fell a prey to its own fear and, though supposed to be reasonable, trembled at the chimeras which it had evoked. A black and deformed monster spread its bat-wings between heaven and earth, to prevent youth and life from trusting in the promises of the sun and the still peace of the stars. This harpy of superstition poisoned all things with its breath, infected all by its contact. There was dread over eating and drinking lest the eggs of the reptile should be swallowed; to look upon beauty was to court perhaps an illusion begotten of the monster; to laugh suggested the sneer of the eternal tormentor as a funereal echo; to weep pictured him insulting the mourner's tears. The devil seemed to keep God imprisoned in heaven while he imposed blasphemy and despair upon men on earth.

Superstitions lead quickly into absurdity and mental alienation; nothing is more deplorable and more irksome than the multitudinous accounts with which popular writers on the history of Magic have burdened their compilations. Peter the Venerable beheld the devil leering in lavatories; another maker of chronicles recognised him under the form of a cat, which, however, resembled a dog and skipped like a monkey; a certain lord of Corasse was served by an imp named Orthon, which appeared as a sow, but exceedingly emaciated and indeed almost fleshless. The prior of St. Germain des Prés, named William Edeline, testifies that he saw him in the form of a sheep which, as it seemed to him, must be kissed below the tail, as a mark of reverence and honour.

Wretched old women confessed that he had been their lover; the marshal Trivulce died of terror, while protecting himself by cut and thrust against the devils swarming in his room. Hundreds of wretched idiots and fools were burnt on admitting their former commerce with the malignant spirit; rumours of *incubi* and *succubi* were heard on all sides; judges deliberated gravely on revelations which should have been referred to doctors; moreover, they were actuated by the irresistible pressure of public opinion, and indulgence towards sorcerers would have exposed magistrates themselves to all the popular fury. The persecution of fools made folly contagious and the maniacs tore one another to pieces; people were beaten to death, burnt by slow fire, plunged into icy water in the hope of compelling them to break the spells which they had cast, while justice intervened only to complete on the stake what had begun in the blind rage of the multitude.

In recounting the history of Gilles de Laval we have indicated sufficiently that Black Magic may be not only a real crime but the gravest of all offences; unfortunately the method of the times confused the diseased with malefactors and punished those who should have been cared for with patience and charity.

At what point does man's responsibility begin and at what point does it end? The problem is one which may well disturb frequently the virtuous depositories of human justice. Caligula, son of Germanicus, appeared to have inherited all the virtues of his father, but his reason was distracted by poison and he became the terror of the world. Was he in reality guilty, and ought not his crimes to be laid at the doors of those base Romans who obeyed instead of imprisoning him?

Father Hilarion Tissot, who has been mentioned previously, goes further than ourselves and would include even voluntary crime in the category of madness, but unfortunately he explains madness itself as obsession of the evil spirit. We might ask this good ecclesiastic what he would think of the father of a family who after shutting his door on a wastrel known to be capable of every kind of evil, should give him leave to frequent, advise, abduct and obsess his own little children? Let us therefore admit, so as to be truly Christian, that the devil, whomsoever he may be, obsesses only those who give themselves voluntarily to him, and that such are responsible for everything which he may prompt them to do, even as a drunken man is held liable rightly for the disorders of which he may be guilty under the influence of drink. Drunkenness is a transient madness and madness is a permanent intoxication; both are caused by a phosphoric congestion of the cerebral nerves, which destroys our etheric equilibrium and deprives the soul of its instrument of precision. The spiritual and personal soul then resembles Moses bound and swaddled in his cradle of rushes, and abandoned to the rocking of the Nile waters. It is carried away by the fluidic and material soul of the world, that mysterious water over which the Elohim brooded when the Divine Word was formulated by the luminous sentence: "Let there be light."

The soul of the world is a force which tends automatically to equilibrium; either will must predominate over it or it conquers the will. It is tormented by any incomplete life, as if this were a monstrosity, and it strives therefore to absorb intellectual abortions. Hence maniacs and hallucinated people experience an irresistible yearning for destruction and death; annihilation seems to them a blessing, and they would not only attain death on their own part but would delight in witnessing that of others. They realise that life is escaping them; consciousness stings and goads them to despair; their very existence is a perception of death, and it is hell-torment. One hears an imperious voice commanding him to kill his son in the cradle. He struggles, he weeps, he flees, but ends by taking a hatchet and slaying the child. Another, and this terrible story is a thing of recent occurrence, is driven by voices crying for hearts; he beats his parents to death, opens their breasts, tears out their hearts and begins to devour them. Whosoever of his free will is guilty of an evil action offers by that fact an earnest to eternal destruction and cannot foresee whither this fatal bargain will lead him.

Being is substance and life; life manifests by movement; movement is perpetuated by equilibrium; equilibrium is therefore the law of immortality. Conscience is the awareness of equilibrium, which is equity and justice. All excess, when it is not mortal, is corrected by an opposite excess; it is the eternal law of reaction; but if excess subverts all equilibrium it is lost in the outer darkness and becomes eternal death.

The soul of the earth carries with it in the vertigo of astral movement all which offers no resistance in virtue of the equilibrated forces of reason. Wherever an imperfect and ill-formed life manifests, this soul directs its energies to destroy it, just as vitality pours in to heal wounds. Hence the atmospheric disorders which occur in the nieghbourhood of certain diseased persons, hence fluidic commotions, the automatic movement of tables, levitations, stone-throwing, and the visible and tangible projection of astral hands and feet by obsessed persons. It is Nature at work on a cancer which it is trying to extirpate, on a wound which it seeks to close, or on some vampire whose death is desired, that it may revert to the common source of life.

The spontaneous movement of inert objects can result only from the operation of forces which magnetise the earth; a spirit, or in other words a thought, can raise nothing in the absence of a lever. Were it otherwise, the—so to speak—infinite toil of Nature for the creation and perfecting of organs would be without an object. If the spirit freed from the senses could render matter obedient to its will, the illustrious dead would be the first to manifest in accordance with order and harmony, but in place of this there are only incoherent and feverish activities produced about diseased and capricious beings. These are irregular magnets which derange the soul of the earth; but when the earth is in delirium through the eruption of such abortive beings, it is because it is passing through a crisis on its own part, and through one which will end in violent commotions.

There is extraordinary puerility in some who pass for serious. There is, for example, the Marquis de Mirville,[1] who refers all inexplicable phenomena to the devil. But, my dear sir, if the devil could intervene in

---

[1] The Marquis Eudes de Mirville wrote *Des Esprits et de leurs Manifestations Fluidiques devant la Science Moderne*, 1858, and other large books, which were highly recommended by ecclesiastical authority of the day. He saw the intervention of Satanism everywhere in psychic and occult phenomena. Remove the personality of Satan and Éliphas Lévi says exactly the same thing

the natural order, would he not demolish everything? By the hypothesis concerning his character, scruples could scarcely influence him. You will reply that God's power restrains, and that it does or does not is obvious; but on the first supposition the devil is rendered impotent, while on the second it is he who is master. M. de Mirville might say further that God suffers him a little while. Does he mean just enough to deceive poor men, just enough to puzzle their heads, so wooden already—as is known? In this alternative it is no longer the devil who is master; it is rather God Who is— but no, one dares not continue: to go further would be to blaspheme.

We do not understand properly the harmonies of being, which follow an ordered sequence, as the illustrious maniac Fourier well said. The spirit acts upon spirits by means of the Word; matter receives the imprints of spirit and communicates therewith by means of a perfect organism. Harmony in forms is related to harmony in ideas, and the light is the common mediator. Light is spirit and life; it is the synthesis of colours, the accord of shadows, the harmony of forms; and its vibrations are living mathematics. But darkness and its phantastic illusions, the phosphorescent errors of slumber and words spoken in delirium—all these create nothing, realise nothing and in a word do not exist. Such things belong to the limbus of life, are vapours of astral intoxication and delusions of tired eyes. To follow these will o' the wisps is to walk in a blind alley; to believe in their revelations is to worship death: such is Nature's testimony.

Incoherence and abuse are the only messages of table-turning; they are echoes of the low-life deeps of thought, absurd and anarchic dreams, words which the scum of the people make use of to express defiance. There is a book by Baron de Guldenstubbé,[1] who pretends to conduct a correspondence with the outer world. He has had answers, and such answers— obscene sketches, despairing hieroglyphics and the following Greek signature, πνεῦμα θάνατος, which may be translated "spirit of death". Such is the last word of the phenomenal revelations according to American doctrine; such is doctrine itself in separation from sacerdotal authority and in the attempt to establish it independently of hierarchic control. The reality and importance of the phenomena, the good faith of those who believe them, are in no sense denied; but we must warn all who are concerned against the dangers to which they are liable if they do not prefer the spirit of wisdom, communicated divinely and hierarchically to the Church, before all these disorderly and obscure messages, in which the fluidic soul of the earth reflects automatically the mirage of intelligence and the dreams of slumbering reason.

---

[1] The reference is to *La Réalité des Esprits et le Phénomène Merveilleux de leur Écriture Directe*. It appeared in 1857 and is a very curious collection of materials. Long after, or in 1875, the same writer published *La Morale Universelle*, which seems to be a plea for secular education.

BOOK V

THE ADEPTS AND THE PRIESTHOOD

ה—HE

CHAPTER I

PRIESTS AND POPES ACCUSED OF MAGIC

WE have explained that owing to the profanations and impieties of Gnostics the Church proscribed Magic. The condemnation of the Knights Templar completed the rupture, and from this time forward, compelled to seek concealment and plan revenge in the shadows, Magic ostracised the Church in turn. More prudent·than those arch-heretics who opposed altar to altar in public day, and thus entailed denunciation and the headsman's axe on themselves, the adepts dissimulated their resentment as well as their doctrines. They bound themselves together by dreadful oaths and, realising the importance of first securing a favourable view at the tribunal of public opinion, they turned back on their accusers and judges the sinister rumours by which they were pursued themselves and denounced the priesthood to the people as a school of Black Magic.

So long as his convictions and beliefs are not rooted in the irremovable foundations of reason, man ardently and indifferently desires both truth and falsehood; on either side he finds that there are cruel reactions. Who shall put an end to this warfare? Only the spirit of Him who has said: "Render not evil for evil, but overcome evil by good."

The Catholic priesthood has been charged with the spirit of persecution, though its mission is that of the good Samaritan, for which reason it superseded the unpitying Levites, who continued their way without extending compassion to him who had fallen among thieves. It is in the exercise of humanity that priests prove their Divine consecration. Hence it is a supreme injustice to cast upon sacerdotalism at large the crimes of certain men who are unfortunately sealed with the priesthood. For a man, as such, it is always possible to be wicked; but a true priest is, on the contrary, always charitable. Now, the false adept did not look at the question from this standpoint;[1] for them the Christian priesthood was made void and was hence an usurping power since the proscription of the Gnostics. What, said they, is a hierarchy whose degrees are no longer regulated by conscience?

[1] The reader should understand that Éliphas Lévi is only giving expression to a point of view; it must not be supposed that there were adepts—either true or false—who said or thought the things which are here set down at the period in question, or indeed at any other period.

The same ignorance of the Mysteries and the same blind faith drive into the same fanaticism or the same hypocrisy the prime leaders and lowest ministers of the sanctuary. The blind are leaders of the blind. The supremacy between equals is no longer anything but the result of intrigue and chance. The pastors consecrate the sacred elements with a gross and disordered faith; they are jugglers in bread and eaters of human flesh; they are no longer thaumaturgists, but sorcerers. Such was the sectarian verdict. To support the calumny they invented fables, affirming, for example, that the popes had been given over to the spirit of darkness ever since the tenth century. The learned Gerbert, who was crowned as Sylvester II, made confession—as it is said—to this effect on his death-bed. Honorius III, being he who confirmed the Order of St. Dominic and preached the Crusades, was himself an abominable necromancer, author of a Grimoire which still bears his name and is reserved exclusively to priests. The same false adepts paraded and commented on this Grimoire, seeking in such manner to turn against the Holy See the most terrible of all popular prejudices at that period—the mortal hatred of those who, wrongly or rightly, passed publicly for sorcerers.

Some malevolent or credulous historians have favoured these lying inventions. Thus Platina, a scandalous chronicler of the papacy, reproduces from Martinus Polonius the calumnies against Sylvester II. According to this fable, Gerbert, who was proficient in mathematical science and the Kabalah, performed an evocation of the devil and required his assistance to attain the pontificate. The fulfilment of his ambition was not only promised by the demon but it was affirmed further that he should not die except at Jerusalem, to which place it will be understood readily that the magician determined inwardly that he would never go. He became pope as promised, but on a certain day, when he was saying Mass in a church at Rome, he felt seriously ill, and remembering suddenly that the chapel wherein he was officiating was dedicated to the Holy Cross of Jerusalem, he realised what had come to pass. He caused a bed to be put up in the chapel and, summoning his cardinals, confessed publicly that he had engaged in commerce with demons. He ordained further that his dead body should be placed upon a chariot of green wood and should be drawn by two virgin horses, one black and the other white; that they should be started on their course but neither led nor driven; and that his remains should be interred wherever a halt was made. The chariot proceeded in this manner across Rome and stopped in front of the Lateran. Loud cries and groans were heard for a few moments, after which there was silence and the burial took place. So ends a legend the proper place of which is in the hawker's chap-books.

Martinus Polonus, on the faith of whom Platina repeats such reveries, had borrowed them on his own part (a) from a certain Galfridus and (b) from Gervaise, a maker of chronicles, whom Naudé terms "the greatest forger of fables and the most notorious liar that ever took pen in hand". From sources of similar value the protestants have derived a scandalous and obviously apocryphal story concerning a pretended Pope Joan, who was also a sorceress, as we have all heard: indeed she is one to whom books on Black Magic are still attributed. We have glanced at a memoir of this female pope by a protestant historian and have taken note of two very curious engravings contained therein. They are assumed to be portraits of the heroine but are in reality ancient Tarots, representing Isis crowned with a tiara. It is well known that the hieroglyphic figure on the second Tarot card is still called the female pope, being a woman wearing a tiara on which are the points of the crescent moon, or the horns of Isis. One example in the protestant book is even more remarkable: the hair of the figure is long and scanty; there is a solar cross on the breast; she is seated between the two pillars of Hercules; and behind her flows the ocean, with lotus-flowers blooming on the surface of the water. The second portrait represents the same divinity, with attributes of the sovereign priesthood and holding her son Horus in her arms. As Kabalistic documents the two pictures are of singular value, but they are little to the purpose of those who are concerned with Pope Joan.

To dispose of the accusation of sorcery in respect of Gerbert, supposing that it could be taken seriously, it would be enough to mention that he was the most learned man of his century, and having been preceptor of two sovereigns he owed his election to the gratitude of one of his august pupils. He had extraordinary proficiency in mathematics, and his knowledge of physics may have exceeded that of his epoch;—in a word, he was a man of universal erudition and great ability, as the letters which he left bear witness, though he was not a denouncer of kings like the terrible Hildebrand. He chose to instruct princes rather than excommunicate them, and enjoying the favour of two French kings and three emperors, he had no need, as Naudé has judiciously pointed out, to sell himself to the devil for the archbishoprics of Rheims and Ravenna, or for the papacy in succession to these. It is true that he attained the successive positions, to some extent in spite of his merit; it was an age when able politicians were taken for possessed people and those who were learned for enchanters. Gerbert was not only a great mathematician, as we have said, and a distinguished astronomer, but he excelled also in mechanics, and—according to William of Malmesbury—he erected at Rheims such wonderful hydraulic machines that the water itself executed symphonies and played most enchanting airs. Moreover, according to Ditmare, he adorned the town of Magdebourg with a clock which registered all the motions of heaven and the times when the stars rose and set. Finally, by the evidence of Naudé,[1] whom we cite once again with pleasure, he made "that test of brass which was devised so ingeniously that the before-mentioned William of Malmesbury was himself deceived thereby and referred it to Magic. Further, Onuphrius states that he saw in the Farnese library a learned book on geometry composed by this same Gerbert; and for myself I

[1] See Gabriel Naudé: *Apologie pour les Grands Hommes faussement accusés de la Magie.*

estimate that, without adjudicating on the opinion expressed by Ertordiensis and some others, who regard him as the maker of timepieces and of arithmetic as these exist now among us, all these evidences are sufficiently valid to warrant the conclusion that those who had never heard of cube, parallelogram, dodecahedron, almicantar, valsagora, almagrippa, cathalzem and other names, familiar enough in these days to such as understand mathematics, conceived that they were those of the spirits invoked by Gerbert and that such a multitude of things so rare could not emanate from a single personality in the absence of extraordinary advantages, from the possession of which it followed therefore that he must have been a magician."

To indicate the lengths of impertinence and bad faith reached by makers of chronicles, it remains to say that Platina[1]—that maliciously naïve echo of all Roman pasquinades—affirms that the tomb of Sylvester II itself turned sorcerer, weeping prophetically at the approaching downfall of each pope and that the reprobate bones of Gerbert shook and rattled together when one of them was about to die. An epitaph engraved on the tomb lends colour to these wonders—so adds unblushingly the librarian of Sixtus IV. Such are the proofs which pass among historians as sufficient to certify the existence of a curious historical document. Platina was librarian of the Vatican; he wrote his history of the popes by order of Sixtus IV; he wrote also at Rome, where nothing could be easier than to verify the truth or falsehood of such an assertion, which, notwithstanding the pretended epitaph, never existed outside the imagination of the authors from whom Platina borrowed with incredible lack of caution[2]— a circumstance which moves justly the indignation of honest Naudé, whose further remarks shall follow: "It is a pure imposture and manifest falsehood, both in respect of the experience—being the pretended prodigies at the tomb of Sylvester II—the same having never been witnessed by anyone—and of the alleged inscription on the tomb, that inscription—as it exists really—having been composed by Sergius IV and so far from supporting the supposed magical fables, is, on the contrary, one of the most excellent testimonies that could be desired to the good life and integrity of Sylvester. It is truly a shameful thing that so many catholics should be abettors of a slander concerning which Marianus Scotus, Glaber, Ditmare, Helgandus, Lambert and Herman Contract, who were his contemporaries, make no mention."

Proceeding now to the Grimoire of Honorius, it is to the third bearer of that name, or to one of the most zealous pontiffs of the 13th century, that this impious book is attributed. Assuredly Honorius III was eminently likely to be hated by sectarians and necromancers, and well might they seek to dishonour him by representing him as their accomplice.

---

[1] Bartholemæus Platina was assistant librarian of the Vatican, and his *Opus in Vitas Summorum Pontificum* appeared at Venice in 1479, two years before his death.

[2] "Let the popes see to it," he remarks, according to a Note of Lévi; "it is they who are concerned in the question."

Occult Seals and Primitive Egyptian Tarots

Censius Savelli, crowned pope in 1216, confirmed that Order of Saint Dominic which proved so formidable to Albigensians and Vaudois—those children of Manicheans and sorcerers. He established also the Franciscans and Carmelites, preached a crusade, governed the Church wisely and left many decretals. To charge with Black Magic a pope so eminently catholic[1] is to cast similar suspicion on the great religious orders which he instituted, and the devil thereby could scarcely fail to profit.

Some old copies of the Grimoire of Honorius bear, however, the name of Honorius II, but it is impossible to make a sorcerer of that elegant Cardinal Lambert who, after his promotion to the sovereign pontificate, surrounded himself either with poets, to whom he gave bishoprics for elegies—as in the case of Hildebert, Bishop of Mans—or with learned theologians, like Hugh de Saint-Victor. But it so happens that the name of Honorius II is for us a ray of light pointing to the true author of the frightful Grimoire in question.[2] In 1061, when the empire began to take umbrage against the papacy and sought to usurp the sacerdotal influence by fomenting troubles and divisions in the sacred college, the bishops of Lombardy, impelled by Gilbert of Parma, protested against the election of Anselm, Bishop of Lucca, who had been raised to the papal chair as Alexander II. The Emperor Henry IV took the part of the dissentients and authorised them to elect another pope, promising to support them. They chose Cadulus, or Cadalus, an intriguing Bishop of Parma, a man capable of all crimes and a public scandal in respect of simony and concubinage. He assumed the name of Honorius II and marched at the head of an army against Rome. He was defeated and condemned by all the prelates of Germany and Italy. Returning to the charge, he gained possession of part of the Holy City and entered St. Peter's; he was expelled and took refuge in the Castle of St. Angelo, whence he obtained leave to retire only on the payment of a heavy ransom. It was then that Otho, Archbishop of Cologne, the Emperor's envoy, dared to reproach Alexander II in public for having usurped the Holy See; but a monk named Hildebrand took up the cause of the lawful pontiff with such force of eloquence that the Emperor drew back in confusion and asked pardon for his own criminal attempts. The Hildebrand in question was already in the sight of providence that fulminating Gregory VII who was to come and who thus inaugurated the work of his life. The anti-pope was deposed by the Council of Mantua and Henry IV obtained his pardon. Cadalus returned into obscurity, and it is then probably that he decided to become

[1] Éliphas Lévi, in his defence of the Catholic Religion, by which he means that of Rome, reminds one of Talleyrand proceeding to consecrate and entreating his familiars about him not to make him laugh: in the symbolic language of the man in the street, his tongue is so evidently in his cheek. An open enemy of Rome would think twice before saying that the pope who authorised the instruments which were used in the execrable massacres of Albigensians and Vaudois was "so eminently catholic".
[2] I refer the readers of this section to my *Book of Ceremonial Magic*, where the content and history of this Grimoire are considered with special reference to the criticism of Éliphas Lévi.

the high priest of sorcerers and apostates, in which capacity, and under the name of Honorius II, he composed the Grimoire that passes under this name.[1]

What is known of the anti-pope's character lends colour to an accusation of the kind; he was daring in the presence of the weak, grovelling in that of the strong, debauched and intriguing, devoid of faith and morals, seeing nothing in religion but an engine of impunity and rapine. For such a person the Christian virtues were obstacles, and faith in the clergy was a difficulty which had to be overcome; he would therefore make priests after his own heart, or capable, that is to say, of all crimes and sacrileges. Now, this would seem to have been the purpose in chief of the Grimoire called that of Honorius.

The work in question is not without importance for those who are curious in the science. It appears at first sight to be a mere tissue of revolting absurdities,[2] but for those who are initiated in the signs and secrets of the Kabalah, it is literally a monument of human perversity, for the devil appears therein as an instrument of power.

To utilise human credulity and to turn the bugbear which dominates it to the account of the adept and his caprices—such is the secret of the work. It aspires to make darkness darker before the eyes of the multitude by usurping the torch of science, which at need, and in bold hands, may become that of butchers and incendiaries. To identify faith with servitude, reserving power and liberty for oneself, is indeed to imagine the reign of Satan on earth, and it should not be surprising if the authors of such a conspiracy against public good sense and religion should hope to manifest and, in a sense, to incarnate on earth the fantastic sovereign of the evil empire.

The doctrine of this Grimoire is the same as that of Simon and the majority of the Gnostics: it is the substitution[3] of the passive for the active principle. A pantacle which forms a frontispiece to the work gives expression to this doctrine, being passion as predominant over reason, sensualism deified and the woman in priority to the man, a tendency which recurs in all antichristian mystic systems. The crescent moon of Isis occupies the centre of the figure and it is encompassed by three triangles, one within another. The triangle is surmounted by a *crux ansata* with double cross-bar. It is inscribed within a circle and within the space formed by the three

---

[1] I have mentioned in the *Book of Ceremonial Magic* that the first edition of the *Grimoire of Honorius* is referred to 1629, being about 900 years after the death of its alleged author. I have also referred it to its proper source in the *Sworn Book of Honorius*, which belongs to the fourteenth century. The Honorius here in question was the spokesman of magicians assembled at a mythical place. He is described as the son of Euclid and Master of the Thebans.

[2] This is another way of stating that it is precisely of the same character as the *Key of Solomon the King*, the *Keys of Rabbi Solomon* and the *Magical Elements of Peter de Abano*, which correspond to the description given.

[3] The Grimoire is, on the contrary, a Ritual for the evocation of evil spirits, and, granting only the legality of this operation, it is conformable in all respects to the doctrine of the Latin Church. Now, it is idle to say that this Church substitutes the passive for the active principle, the cultus of the Blessed Virgin notwithstanding.

segments of the circle there is on one side the sign of the spirit and the Kabalistic seal of Solomon, on the others the magic knife and the initial letter of the binary, below a reversed cross forming the figure of the lingam, and the name of God אל= AL, also reversed. About the circle is written: "Obey your superiors and be subject unto them, for they will see that you do."[1]

Rendered into a symbol or profession of faith, this pantacle is therefore textually as follows:—Fatality reigns by virtue of mathematics, and there is no other God than Nature. Dogmas are aids to sacerdotal power and are imposed on the multitude to justify sacrifices. The initiate is above any religion and makes use of all, but that which he says is the antithesis of that which he believes. The law of obedience prescribes and does not explain; initiates are made to command and those who are profane to obey.

All who have studied the occult sciences know that the old magicians never expressed their doctrine in writing but formulated it by the symbolical characters of pantacles. On the second page of the book there are two circular magical seals. In the first is the square of the Tetragram with an inversion and substitution of names. Instead of אהיה= EIEIE; יהוה = JEHOVAH; אדני =ADONAI; אגלא= AGLA—the four sacred words signifying:[2] The Absolute Being is Jehovah, the Lord in Three Persons, God and the hierarchy of the Church, the author of the Grimoire has substituted יהוה, JEHOVAH; אדני, ADNI; דראר, D'RAR; אהיה, EIEIE—which signifies: Jehovah, the Lord, is none other than the fatal principle of eternal rebirth, personified by this same rebirth in the Absolute Being.

About the square within the circle is the name of Jehovah in its proper form, but also reversed; on the left is that of Adonai and on the right are the three letters אחו, ACHV, followed by two points, the whole meaning: Heaven and hell are each the reflection of each; that which is above is as that which is below; God is humanity—humanity being expressed by the letters ACHV, which are the initials of Adam and Eve.[3]

On the second seal is the name אראריתא, ARARITA, and below it is ראש, RASH, encircling twenty-six Kabalistic characters. Below the seal are ten Hebrew letters, given in the following order: יב מבהברדרר The whole is a formula of materialism and fatality, which is too long, and, it may be, too perilous for explanation in this place. The prologue of the Grimoire comes next in order and may be given at full length.[4]

[1] I am not acquainted with this frontispiece, but I have seen a copy having a design on the title-page representing the sun within an inverted triangle.
[2] This exegesis is personal to Éliphas Lévi and has no authority in Kabalism, as there is no need to say, seeing that the Secret Tradition in Jewry did not maintain the hierarchy of the Latin Church. In the *Zohar*, Adonai is a title of *Shekinah*, as already stated.
[3] On the assumption of course that the letter *Aleph* stands for *Adam*, while *Cheth* and *Vau* are the first letters in the name of *Eve*. The interpretation throughout is of the same value and Éliphas Lévi was not more serious in expressing it than I am in translating it. The *Grimoire of Honorius* is no such abyss of decorative philosophical iniquity.
[4] I have used the translation made from the Grimoire itself, published in my *Book of Ceremonial Magic*, p. 107.

THE ADEPTS AND THE PRIESTHOOD

"The Holy Apostolic Chair, unto which the Keys of the Kingdom of Heaven are given by those words that Christ Jesus addressed to St. Peter: I give unto thee the Keys of the Kingdom of Heaven, and unto thee alone the power of commanding the Prince of Darkness and his angels, who, as slaves to their master, do owe him honour, glory and obedience, by virtue of those other words of Christ Jesus, addressed to Satan himself: Thou shalt worship the Lord thy God, and Him only shalt thou serve—hence by the power of these Keys the Head of the Church has been made the Lord of hell. But seeing that until this present the Sovereign Pontiffs have alone had the charge of evoking and commanding spirits, His Holiness Honorius II, being moved by his pastoral care, has desired benignly to communicate the science and power of evocations and of empire over spirits to his venerable Brethren in Jesus Christ, with the conjurations which must be used in such case; now therefore the whole is contained in the Bull which here follows."

Here in all truth is the pontificate of hell, that sacrilegious priesthood of anti-popes which Dante seems to stigmatise in the raucous cry uttered by one of his princes of perdition: *Pope Satan, Pope Satan; Aleppe*. Let the legitimate pontiff continue as prince of heaven; it is enough for the anti-pope Cadalus to be the sovereign of hell. "Be He the God of good, for god of evil am I; we are divided, but my power is equal."

The Bull of the infernal pontiff follows,[1] and the mystery of darksome evocations is expounded therein with a terrific knowledge concealed under superstitious and sacrilegious forms. Fastings, watchings, profanation of mysteries, allegorical ceremonies and bloody sacrifices are combined with artful malice. The evocations are not deficient in poetry or in enthusiasm, mingled with horror. For example, the author ordains that an operator should rise at midnight on the Thursday in the first week of evocations, should sprinkle his room with holy water and light a taper of yellow wax—prepared on the previous day and pierced in the form of a cross. By the uncertain light of this candle he must enter a church alone and read the Office of the Dead in a low voice, substituting in place of the ninth lesson at Matins the following rhythmic invocation which is here translated from the Latin, preserving its strange form and its refrains, which recall the monotonous incantations of old-world sorcerers:

> O Lord, deliver me from the infernal terrors,
> Exempt my spirit from sepulchral larvæ;
> To seek them out I shall go down to their hell unaffrighted:
> I shall impose my will for a law upon them.

---

[1] It affirms that the power to command demons is resident in the Seat of Peter and then proceeds to communicate that power by dispensation to "venerable brethren and dear sons in Jesus Christ", being those comprised in the ranks of the ecclesiastical hierarchy.

I will call upon night and its darkness to bring forth splendour:
Rise up, O Sun; and, Moon, be thou white and brilliant;
To the shades of hell I will speak and confess no terror:
I shall impose my will for a law upon them.

Dreadful in aspect are they, their forms in appearance fantastic:
I will that the demons shall once again become angels.
Whence to their nameless distortion I speak, never fearing:
I shall impose my will for a law upon them.

These shades are illusions evoked by the eye affrighted;
I and I only can heal their loveliness blasted,
And into the deeps of hell I plunge unaffrighted:
I shall impose my will for a law upon them.[1]

After many other ceremonies there comes the night of evocation. In a sinister place, in the light of a fire kindled with broken crosses, a circle is traced with the embers of a cross, reciting while so doing a magical hymn containing versicles of several psalms. It may be rendered as follows:[2]

"O Lord, the king rejoices in Thy power; let me finish the work of my birth. May shadows of evil and spectres of night be as dust blown before the wind. . . . O Lord, hell is enlightened and shines in Thy presence; by Thee do all things end and all begin by Thee: JEHOVAH, TSABAOTH, ELOHIM, ELOI, HELION, HELIOS, JODHEVAH, SHADDAI. The Lion of Judah rises in His glory; He comes to complete the victory of King David. I open the seven seals of the dread book. Satan falls from heaven, like summer lightning. Thou hast said to me: Be far from thee hell and its tortures; they shall not draw to thy pure bodies. Thine eyes shall withstand the gaze of the basilisk; thy feet shall walk fearlessly on the sap; thou shalt take up serpents, and they shall be conquered by thy smile; thou shalt drink poisons, and they shall in nowise hurt thee. ELOHIM, ELOHAB, TSABAOTH, HELIOS, EHYEH, EIEAZEREIE, O THEOS, TSEHYROS. The earth is the Lord's and the fulness thereof; He hath established it over the gaping abyss. Who shall go up unto the mountain of the Lord? The innocent of hands and clean of heart; he who hath not held truth in captivity, nor hath received it to let it remain idle; he who hath conceived the height in his soul and hath not sworn by a lying word. The same shall receive strength for his domain, and hereof is the infinite of human birth, generation by earth and fire, the divine bringing forth of those who seek God. Princes of Nature, enlarge your doors; yoke of heaven, I lift thee. Come to me, ye

---

[1] It must be explained that the oration in the Grimoire is not rhythmic, but the "when I shall impose my will upon them" recurs several times, literally or in substance. In this manner Éliphas Lévi gets the refrain of his verses: *Je leur imposerai ma volonté pour loi*. His metrical rendering is well conceived and executed.

[2] I have rendered in prose that which is given by Lévi in verse, which is anything but in the words of the Ritual. Compare my translation of the prayer taken from the Grimoire in the *Book of Ceremonial Magic*, pp. 280–282.

holy cohorts: behold the King of glory. He hath earned his name; he holds in his hand the seal of Solomon. The master hath broken the black bondage of Satan and hath led captivity captive. The Lord alone is God, and He only is King. To Thee only be glory, O Lord; glory and glory to Thee."[1]

One seems to hear the sombre puritans of Walter Scott or Victor Hugo accompanying, with fanatic psalmody, the nameless work of sorcerers in *Faust* or *Macbeth*.

In a conjuration addressed to the shade of the giant Nimrod, the wild huntsman who began the Tower of Babel, the adept of Honorius menaces that ancient reprobate with the riveting of his chains and with torture increased daily, should he fail in immediate obedience to the will of the operator. It is the sublimity of pride in delirium, and this anti-pope, who could only understand a high priest as a ruler of hell, seems to yearn after the usurped and mournful right of tormenting the dead eternally, as if in revenge for the contempt and rejection of the living.

---

[1] The Ritual proceeds to the conjuration of the Kings presiding in the four quarters of heaven and the evil angels who rule over the days of the week.

CHAPTER II

APPEARANCE OF THE BOHEMIAN NOMADS

AT the beginning of the fifteenth century hordes of unknown swarthy wanderers began to spread through Europe.[1] Sometimes denominated Bohemians, because they claimed to come from Bohemia, sometimes Egyptians, because their leader assumed the title of Duke of Egypt, they exercised the arts of divination, larceny and marauding. They were nomadic tribes, bivouacking in huts of their own construction; their religion was unknown; they gave themselves out to be Christians; but their orthodoxy was more than doubtful. Among themselves they practised communism and promiscuity, and in their divinations they made use of a strange sequence of signs, allegorical in form, and depending from the virtues of numbers. Whence came they? Of what accursed and vanished world were they the surviving waifs? Were they, as superstitious people believed, the offspring of sorceresses and demons? What expiring and betrayed Saviour had condemned them to roam for ever? Was this the family at large of the Wandering Jew, or the remnants of the ten tribes of Israel, lost sight of in captivity and long enchained by Gog and Magog in unknown regions? Such were the doubting questions at the passage of these mysterious strangers, who seemed to retain only the superstitions and vices of a vanished civilisation. Enemies of toil, they respected neither property nor family; they dragged their women and children after them; they pestered the peace of honest house-dwellers with their pretended divinations. However all this may be, their first encampment in the vicinity of Paris is told by one writer as follows:

"In the next year, 1427, on the Sunday after the middle of August, being the 17th of the month, there came to the environs of Paris twelve so-called penitentiaries—a duke, earl and ten men, all on horses, saying that they were good Christians, originally of Lower Egypt. They stated further that in former times they were conquered and turned to Christianity, those refusing being put to death, while those who consented to baptism were left as rulers of the country. Some time subsequently the Saracens invaded them, and many who were not firm in the faith made no attempt to withstand or defend their country, as in duty bound, but submitted, became Saracens and abjured our Saviour. The Emperor of Germany, the King of Poland and other rulers, having learned that the people renounced their faith so easily, becoming Saracens and idolaters, fell upon them and conquered them again easily. It appeared at first as if they had the intention to leave them in their country, so that they might be led back to Christianity, but, after deliberation in council, the emperor

[1] The presence of the gipsies in Europe can be traced prior to the fifteenth century.

and the rest of the kings ordained that they should never own land in their native country without the consent of the Pope, to obtain which, they must journey to Rome. Thither they proceeded in a great body, the young and the old, involving great suffering for the little ones. They made confession of their sins at Rome, and the Pope, after considering with his advisers, imposed on them, by way of penance, a seven years' wandering through the world sleeping in no bed. He ordained further that every bishop and croziered abbot should give them, once and for all, ten livres of the Tours currency as a contribution towards their expenses. He presented them with letters to this effect, gave them his benediction, and for five years they had been wandering through the world.

"Some days afterwards, being the day of the martyrdom of St. John the Baptist, or August 29, the general horde followed and were not permitted to enter within Paris, but were lodged at the Chapelle St. Denis. They numbered about 120 persons, including women and children. They stated that when they left their own country they consisted of one thousand or twelve hundred souls; the others had died on the road, their king and queen among them; the survivors were still expecting to become possessors of worldly goods, for the holy father had promised them good and fertile lands when their penance was finished.

"While they were at the chapel there was never so great a crowd at benediction, for the people flocked to see them from St. Denis, Paris, and the suburbs. Their children, both boys and girls, were the cleverest tricksters. Nearly all had their ears pierced and in each ear were one or two silver rings, which they said were a sign of good birth in their own country; they were exceedingly dark and with woolly hair. The women were the ugliest and blackest ever seen; their faces were covered with sores, their hair was black as the tail of a horse, their clothes consisted of an old *flaussoie* or *schiavina* tied over the shoulder by a cord or morsel of cloth, and beneath it a poor shirt. In a word, they were the most wretched creatures who had ever been seen in France, within the memory of the oldest inhabitant. Their poverty notwithstanding, they had sorceresses among them who inspected the hand, telling what had happened to the person consulting them in their past life and what awaited them in the future. They disturbed the peace of households, for they denounced husband to wife and wife to husband. And, what was still worse, while talking to people about their magic art they managed to fill their purses by emptying those of their hearers. One citizen of Paris who gives account of these facts adds that he himself talked to them three or four times without losing a halfpenny; but this is the report of the people everywhere, and the news reached the bishop of Paris, who went thither taking a Minorite friar called the little Jacobin, and he, by the bishop's command, preached a great sermon and excommunicated all, male and female, who had told fortunes and all who had shewn their hands. The horde was ordered away and departed accordingly on September 8, proceeding towards Pontoise."

It is not known whether they continued their journey North of the capital, but their memory has survived in a corner of the Department du Nord. "As a fact, in a wood near the village of Hamel, five hundred feet from a druidic monument consisting of six stones, there is a fountain which is called the Sorcerer's Kitchen, and it is there, according to tradition, that the *Cara Maras* rested and quenched their thirst. Now these were assuredly the *Caras'mar*, namely the Bohemians, or wandering sorcerers and diviners, to whom ancient Flemish charters granted the right to be fed by the inhabitants."

They left Paris, but others came in their place, so that France was exploited as much as other countries. There is no record of their landing in England or in Scotland, but before very long the latter kingdom numbered more than one hundred thousand.[1] They were called *seard* and *caird*, as much as to say artisans, craftsmen, for the Scots word is derived from the Sanskrit k+r, whence comes the verb to do, the *Ker-aben* of the gipsies and the Latin *cerdo* or bungler, which they are not. If there was no trace of them at the same period in northern Spain, where the Christians took refuge against the Moslem domination, it was doubtless because the Arabs in the South were more to their liking; however, under John II the gipsies refuge against the Moslem domination, it was doubtless because the Arabs were clearly distinguished from these latter, though no one knew whence they came. To sum up, it came about that, from the time in question forward, they were generally known over the whole European continent. One of the bands of king Sindel appeared at Ratisbon in 1433, while Sindel himself, accompanied by his reserve, camped in Bavaria in 1439. He seemed to have come from Bohemia, for the Bavarians, unaware that in 1433 the tribe had given themselves out as Egyptians, termed them Bohemians, under which name they reappeared in France and so have been known therein. Willy-nilly, they were tolerated. Some perambulated the mountains, seeking gold in the rivers; some forged shoes for horses and chains for dogs; others—more marauders than pilgrims—crept about, ferreting everywhere, and everywhere thieved and pilfered. A few of them, weary of shifting and fixing their tents continually, came to a stand and hollowed out hovels, square huts of four to six feet, underground, and covered with a roof of green branches, the ridge of which, set across two stakes, in the form of a Y, rose scarcely more than two feet above the soil. It was in this den, of which little more than the name has remained in France, that the whole family was huddled together pell-mell. In such a lodging, with no opening but the door and a hole for the smoke, the father hammered, the children—crouched round the fire—blew the bellows and the mother boiled the pot, which contained only the spoil of poaching. Among old clothes, a bridle and a knapsack hung from long wooden nails, with no other furniture than an anvil, pincers and hammer—there met credulity and love, maid and knight, lady of the manor and page. There they shewed their bare white hands to the penetrating glance of the sibyl; there love was purchased, happiness was sold, and lying found its recom-

[1] The authority of George Borrow is quoted for this statement

pense. Thence came mountebanks and cardsharpers, the star-spangled robe and peaked hat of the magician, the vagrants and their slang, street dancers and daughters of joy. It was the kingdom of idleness and *trupherie*, of Villon manners and free meals. They were people who were continually busy in doing nothing, as a simple story-teller of the middle ages terms it. A scholar who is equally modest and distinguished, M. Vaillant, author of a history of the *Rom-Muni*, or Bohemians, some of whose pages we have cited, gives no more flattering portrait, though he ascribes to the gipsies great importance in the sacerdotal history of the ancient world. He recounts how these strange protestants of primitive civilisation, travelling through the ages with a malediction on their foreheads and rapine in their hands, excited curiosity at first, then mistrust, finally proscription and hatred on the part of mediæval Christians. It will be readily understood what dangers might attach to this people without a fatherland, parasites of the whole world and citizens of nowhere. They were Bedouins who perambulated empires like deserts; they were nomadic thieves who gilded about everywhere and remained nowhere. It came to pass speedily that the people regarded them as sorcerers, even as demons, casters of lots, stealers of children, and there was some ground for all this. Moreover, the nomads began to be accused everywhere of celebrating frightful mysteries in secret; they were held responsible for all unknown murders, for all mysterious abductions, as the Greeks of Damascus accused the Jews of killing one of their fraternity and drinking his blood. It was affirmed that they preferred boys and girls from twelve to fifteen years old. Here was an effectual way to ensure that they should be held in horror and avoided by the young; but it was odious all the same, for the child and the common people are only too credulous, while a fear begets hatred, so also it tends to breed persecution. It was this which came to pass; they were not only avoided and fled from, but they were refused fire and water; Europe became like India in their respect and every Christian was a Brahman armed against them. In some countries, if a young girl approached one of them to give alms out of charity, her distracted governess would warn her to beware, for the gipsy was a *katkaon*, an ogre, who would suck her blood when she was asleep in the night. The girl drew back trembling. If a boy passed near enough for his shadow to fall on the wall near which they were seated, and where perhaps a whole gipsy family was eating or basking in the sun, his master would cry: "Keep off, child; these vampires will steal your shadow and your soul will dance at their Sabbath through all eternity." So did Christian hatred resuscitate the *lemures* and goblins, the vampires and ogres, as a ground of their impeachment. "They were descended from Mambres, whose miracles competed against those of Moses; they were sent by the king of Egypt to spy everywhere on the children of Israel and render their lot intolerable; they were the murderers made use of by Herod to exterminate the first-born of Bethlehem; they were pagans indeed, for others, but they did not understand a single word of Egyptian, their language comprising, on the contrary, a good deal of

Hebrew, and they were therefore the refuse of that abject race who slept in the tombs of Judea after devouring the corpses which they contained; they were otherwise those miscreant Jews who were tortured, chased and burned in 1348 for having poisoned our wells and cisterns, and they had returned once again to the work. As a final alternative, whether Jews or Egyptians, Essenians or Chusians, Pharaohnians or Caphtorians, Assyrian Balistari or Philistines of Canaan, they were renegades, and it was testified in Saxony, France and everywhere that they were fit only for burning and hanging."

The proscription which came upon them fell also on that strange book in which they used to consult destiny and to obtain oracles. Its coloured cards bearing incomprehensible figures are undoubtedly the monumental summary of all ancient revelations, the key to Egyptian hieroglyphics, the keys also of Solomon, the primeval scriptures of Enoch and Hermes. The author to whom we refer gives proof here of uncommon sagacity, speaking of the Tarot as a man who as yet does not understand it perfectly but has made it a profound study. What he says is as follows:

"The form, disposition, arrangement of these tablets, and of the figures which they depict, though considerably modified by time, are so manifestly allegorical, while the allegories correspond so closely to the civil, philosophical and religious doctrine of antiquity, that one is compelled to regard them as a synthesis of the matter of faith among ancient peoples. We have sought to make evident already that the Tarot is a deduction from the sidereal *Book of Enoch*, who is Henochia; that it is modelled on the astral wheel of Athor, who is As-taroth; that, like the Indian Ot-tara, which is the polar bear or Arc-tura in the northern hemisphere, it is the force major (*tarie*), on which rests the solidity of the world and the sidereal firmament of earth. Consequently, like the polar Bear, which is regarded as the chariot of the sun, the chariot of David and Arthur, it is the Greek fortune, the Chinese destiny, the Egyptian hazard, the lot of the Romanies; and that, in their unceasing revolution about the polar Bear, the stars pour down on earth those auspices and fatalities, that light and shadow, cold and heat, whence flow the good and evil, the love and hatred which make up human happiness.

"If the origin of this book is so lost in the night of time that no one knows where or when it was invented, everything leads us to believe that it is of Indo-Tartaric origin and that, variously modified among ancient nations, according to the phases of their doctrines and the characteristics of their wise men, it was one of their books of occult science, possibly even one of their sibylline books. We have sufficiently indicated the road by which it has reached us; we have seen that it must have been known to the Romans and that it came to them not only from the first days of the empire but of the Republic itself, by the intervention of those numerous strangers of Eastern origin, who were initiated into the mysteries of Bacchus and of Isis and who brought their knowledge to the heirs of Numa."

THE ADEPTS AND THE PRIESTHOOD

Vaillant does not say that the four hieroglyphical signs of the Tarot—being Wands, Cups, Swords and Deniers, or golden circles—are found in Homer, sculptured on the shield of Achilles; but according to him: "the Cups are the arcs or arches of time, the vessels or ships of heaven. The Deniers are the constellations, fixed and movable stars. The Swords are fires, flames, rays; the Wands are shadows, stones, trees, plants. The Ace of Cups is the vase of the universe, the arch of celestial truth, the principle of earth. The Ace of Deniers is the sun, the great eye of the world, the sustenance and element of life. The Ace of Swords is the spear of Mars, whence come wars, misfortunes and victories. The Ace of Wands is the serpent's eye, the pastoral crook, the cowherd's goad, the club of Hercules, the emblem of agriculture. The two of Cups is the cow, Io or Isis, and the bull Apis or Mnevis. The three of Cups is Isis, the moon, lady and queen of night. The three of Deniers is Osiris, the sun, lord and king of day. The nine of Deniers is the messenger Mercury, or the angel Gabriel. The nine of Cups is the gestation of good destiny, whence comes happiness."

Finally, M. Vaillant tells us that there is a Chinese diagram consisting of characters which form great oblong compartments, of equal size and precisely that of the Tarot cards. These compartments are arranged in six perpendicular columns, the first five consisting of fourteen compartments each, making seventy in all; whilst the sixth is only half filled and contains seven compartments. Moreover, this diagram is formed after the same combination of the number seven; each complete column is of twice seven or fourteen compartments, while the half column contains seven compartments. It is so much like the Tarot that the four suits of the latter occupy the four first columns; in the fifth column are the twenty-one trumps, while the seven remaining trumps are in the sixth column, the last representing the six days constituting the week of creation. Now, according to the Chinese, this diagram goes back to the first epoch of their empire, being the drying up of the waters of the deluge by IAO. The conclusion is, therefore, that this is either the original Tarot or a copy thereof; that in any case the Tarot is anterior to Moses, is referable to the beginning of the ages, or the epoch of the formulation of the Zodiac; and that its age is consequently six thousand six hundred years.[1]

"Such is the Romany Tarot from which by transposition the Hebrews have made the word *Torah*, signifying the Law of Jehovah. So far, then, from being a game, as it is at the present day, it was a book, and a serious book, the book of symbols and of emblems, of analogies or the relations between stars and man; the book of destiny, by the aid of which the sorcerer unveiled the mysteries of fortune. Its figures, their names, their number, and the oracles drawn from these made it naturally regarded by Christians as the instrument of a diabolical art, a work of Magic. It will be hence understood with what severity they proscribed it, the moment it became known to them by that abuse of confidence which the rashness of

[1] Long before Vaillant, this Chinese inscription was described by Court de Gebelin who also believed that it was a form of the Tarot

the *Sagi* committed on public credulity. In this manner, faith being lost in its message, the Tarot became a game, while its pictures underwent modification according to the taste of nations and the successive spirit of centuries.[1] It is to the work in this trivial form that we owe our modern playing cards, the combinations of which are comparable to those of the Tarot in the same way as the game of draughts is comparable to the game of chess. It follows that the origin of cards is attributed wrongly to the reign of Charles VI, and it may be noted further that the initiates of the Order of the Belt, established before 1332 by Alphons XI, king of Castile, pledged themselves not to play cards. Le Sage tells us that, in the days of Charles V, St. Bernard of Sienna condemned cards to be burnt and that they were then called *triumphales* after the game of triumph played in honour of the victorious Osiris or Ormuzd, represented by one of the Tarot cards. Furthermore, that king himself proscribed cards in 1369, and the reason that little Jean de Saintré was honoured by his favour was because he did not play. In those days cards were termed *Naipes* in Spain and *Naibi* in Italy, the *Naibi* being she-devils, sibyls and pythonesses."

M. Vaillant, from whom we have been again quoting, considers therefore that the Tarot has been modified and altered, which is true for the German examples bearing Chinese figures, but not for those of Italy, which have only been altered in details, nor for those of Besancon, in which traces remain of primitive Egyptian hieroglyphics. In the *Doctrine and Ritual of Transcendental Magic* we have shewn how untowards in their results were the labours of Etteilla or Alliette in respect of the Tarot. This illuminated hairdresser, after working for thirty years, only succeeded in producing a bastard set, the Keys of which are transposed, so that the numbers no longer answer to the signs. In a word, it is a Tarot suited to Etteilla and to the measure of his intelligence, which was not of great extent.

We are scarcely in agreement with M. Vaillant when he suggests that the gipsies were the lawful proprietors of this key to initiations. They owed it doubtless to the infidelity or imprudence of some Kabalistic Jew. The gipsies originated in India, or their historian has at least shown the likelihood of this theory. Now the extant Tarot is certainly that of the gipsies and has come to us by way of Judea. As a fact, its keys are in correspondence with the letters of the Hebrew alphabet, and some of its figures reproduce even their forms. What then were the gipsies? As a poet has said: They were the debased remnant of an ancient world; they were a sect of Indian Gnostics, whose communion caused them to be proscribed in every land; as they may be said to admit practically, they are profaners of the Great Arcanum, overtaken by a fatal malediction. A horde misled

[1] If certain beautiful Tarot cards preserved in the Bibliothèque du Roi and at the Musée Carrer are the work of Jacques Gringonneur, which is disputed, as we have seen, then the Tarot is first heard of in 1393, and as it was in 1423 that St. Bernardin of Sienna preached against playing cards, which were no doubt Tarots, it is probable that they were put to the same use at the earlier date that they were put to at the later.

by some enthusiastic fakir, they had become wanderers through the world, protesting against all civilisations in the name of a pretended natural law which dispensed them from almost every duty. Now the law which seeks to prevail in violation of duty is aggression, pillage and rapine; it is the hand of Cain raised against his brother, and society in defending itself seems to be avenging the death of Abel.

In 1840 certain mechanics of the Faubourg St. Antoine, weary, as they put it, of being hoodwinked by journalists and of serving as tools for the ambition of ready speechmakers, resolved to found and to edit a journal of pure radicalism and of logic apart from evasion or circumlocution. They combined therefore and deliberated for the firm establishment of their doctrines; they took as their basis the republican device of liberty, equality and the rest. But liberty seemed to them incompatible with the duty of labour, equality with the law of property, and they therefore decided on communism. One of them, however, pointed out that in communism the sharpest would preside over the division and would get the lion's share; it was decreed thereupon that no one should have the right to intellectual superiority. But it was further remarked that even physical beauty might constitute an aristocracy, so they decreed that there should be an equality in ugliness. Finally, as those who till the ground are yoked to the ground, it was settled that true communists could not follow agriculture, must have only the world for their fatherland and humanity itself for their family, whence it became them to have recourse to caravans and go round the world eternally. We are not relating a parable; we have known those who were present at the convention in question and we have read the first number of their journal, which was entitled *The Humanitarian* and was suppressed in 1841. As to this, the press reports of the period may be consulted. Had the journal continued and had the incipient sect recruited proselytes for the Icarian emigration, as the old attorney Cabet was doing at the same period, a new race of Bohemians would have been organised, and vagabondage would have counted one race the more.

CHAPTER III

LEGEND AND HISTORY OF RAYMUND LULLY

WE have explained that the Church proscribed initiation because it was indignant at the profanations of the Gnosis. When Mohammed armed Eastern fanaticism against faith he opposed savage and warlike credulity to the piety which is ignorant but which prays. His successors set foot in Europe and threatened to overrun it speedily. The Christians said: Providence is chastising us; and the Moslems answered: Fatality is on our side.

The Jewish Kabalists, who were in dread of being burnt as sorcerers in countries called catholic, sought an asylum among the Arabs, for these in their eyes were heretics but not idolaters. They admitted some of them to a knowledge of their mysteries, and Islam, which had already conquered by force, was before long in a position to hope that it might prevail also by science over those whom educated Araby termed in its disdain the barbarians of the West. To onslaughts of physical force the genius of France opposed the strokes of its own terrific hammer. Before the flowing tide of Mohammedan armies a mail-clad finger had traced a clear line and a mighty voice of victory cried to the flood: Thou shalt go no further. The genius of science raised up Raymund Lully, and he reclaimed the heritage of Solomon for that Saviour Who was the Son of David; it was he who for the first time called the children of blind faith to the splendours of universal knowledge. The pseudo-scholars, and the people who are wise in their own conceit, continue to speak with scorn of this truly great man; but the popular instinct has avenged him. Romance and legend have taken up his story, with the result that he is pictured as one impassioned like Abelard, initiated like Faust, an alchemist even as Hermes, a man of penitence and learning like St. Jerome, a rover after the manner of the Wandering Jew, a martyr in fine like St. Stephen, and one who was glorious in death almost as the Saviour of the world.

Let us make our beginning with the romance: it is one of the most touching and beautiful that have come within our knowledge.

On a certain Sunday, in the year 1250, a beautiful and accomplished lady, named Ambrosia di Castello, originally of Genoa, went, as she was accustomed, to hear mass in the church of Palma, a town in the island of Majorca. A mounted cavalier of distinguished appearance and richly dressed, who was passing at the time in the street, noticed the lady and pulled up as one thunderstruck. She entered the church, quickly disappearing in the shadow of the great porch. The cavalier, quite unconscious of what he did, spurred his horse and rode after her into the midst of the affrighted worshippers. Great was the astonishment and scandal. The cavalier was well known; he was the Seigneur Raymund Lully, Seneschal of the Isles and Mayor of the Palace. He had a wife and three children, while Ambrosia di Castello was also married and enjoyed, moreover, an irreproachable reputation. Raymund Lully passed therefore for a great libertine. His equestrian entrance into the church of Palma was noised over the whole town, and Ambrosia, in the greatest confusion, sought the advice of her husband. He was apparently a man of sense, and he did not consider his wife insulted because her beauty had turned the head of a young and brilliant nobleman. He proposed that Ambrosia should cure her admirer by folly as grotesque as his own. Meanwhile, Raymund Lully had written already to the lady, to excuse, or rather to accuse himself still further. What had prompted him, he said, was "strange, supernatural, irresistible". He respected her honour and the affections which, he knew, belonged to another; but he had been overwhelmed. He felt that his imprudence required for its expiation high self-devotion, great sacrifices, miracles to be accomplished, the penitence of a Stylite and the feats of a knight-errant.

Ambrosia answered: "To respond adequately to a love which you term supernatural would require an immortal existence. If this love be sacrificed heroically to our respective duties during the lives of those who are dear to each of us, it will, beyond all doubt, create for itself an eternity at that moment when conscience and the world will permit us to love one another. It is said that there is an elixir of life; seek to discover it, and when you are certain that you have succeeded, come and see me. Till then, live for your wife and your children, as I also will live for the husband whom I love; and if you meet me in the street make no sign of recognition."

It was evidently a gracious *congé*, which put off her lover till Doomsday; but he refused to understand it as such, and from that day forth the brilliant noble disappeared to make room for the grave and thoughtful alchemist. Don Juan had become Faust. Many years passed away; the wife of Raymund Lully died; Ambrosia di Castello in her turn became a widow; but the alchemist appeared to have forgotten her and to be absorbed only in his sublime work.

At length, one day, the widow being alone, Raymund Lully was announced, and there entered the apartment a bald and emaciated old man, who held in his hand a phial filled with a bright and ruddy elixir. He advanced with unsteady step, seeking her with his eyes. The object which they sought was before them, but he did not recognise her, who in his imagination had remained always young and beautiful.

"It is I," she said at length. "What would you with me?"

At the accents of that voice, the alchemist startled violently; he recognised her whom he had thought fondly to find unchanged. Casting himself on his knees at her feet, he offered her the phial, saying: "Take it, drink it, it is life. Thirty years of my own existence are comprised in it; but I have tried it, and I know that it is the elixir of immortality."

"What," asked Ambrosia, with a sad smile, "have you yourself drunk it?"

"For two months," replied Raymund, "after having taken a quantity of the elixir equal to that which is contained here, I have abstained from all other nourishment. The pangs of hunger have tormented me; but not only have I not died, I am conscious within me of an unparalleled accession of strength and life."

"I believe you," said Ambrosia; "but this elixir, which preserves existence, is powerless to restore lost youth. My poor friend, look at yourself," and she held up a mirror before him.

Raymund Lully recoiled, for it is affirmed by the legend that he had never surveyed himself in this manner during the thirty years of his labours.

"And now, Raymund," continued Ambrosia, "look at me," and she unbound her hair, which was white as snow; then, loosening the clasps of her robe, she exposed to him her breast, which was almost eaten away by a cancer. "Is it this," she asked piteously, "which you wish to immortalise?"

Then, seeing the consternation of the alchemist, she continued: "For thirty years I have loved you, and I would not doom you to a perpetual prison in the body of an infirm old man; in your turn, do not condemn me. Spare me this death which you term life. Let me suffer the change which is necessary before I can live again truly: let us renew our nature with an eternal youth. I have no wish for your elixir, which prolongs only the night of the tomb: I aspire to immortality."

Raymund Lully thereupon cast down the phial, which was broken on the ground.

"I deliver you," he said, "and for your sake I remain in prison. Live in the immortality of heaven, while I am condemned for ever to a living death on this earth."

Then, hiding his face in his hands, he went away weeping. Some months after, a monk of the Order of St. Francis assisted Ambrosia di Castello in her last moments. This monk was the alchemist, Raymund Lully. The romance ends here and the legend follows. This legend merges several bearers at different periods of the name Raymund Lully into a single personality, and thus endows the repentant alchemist with a few centuries of existence and expiation. On the day when the unfortunate adept should have expired naturally, he experienced all the agonies of dissolution; then, at the supreme crisis, he felt life again take possession of his frame, like the vulture of Prometheus resuming its banquet. The Saviour of the world, Who had stretched forth His hand towards him, returned sorrowfully into heaven, and Raymund Lully found himself still on earth, with no hope of dying.

He betook himself to prayer, and devoted his existence to good works; God granted him all graces save that of death, but of what profit are the others in the absence of that which should complete and crown them all? One day the Tree of Knowledge was shewn to him, laden with its luminous fruits; he understood being and its harmonies; he divined the Kabalah; he established the foundations and sketched the plan of a universal science, from which time he was saluted as the illuminated doctor. So did he obtain glory, that fatal recompense of toil which God, in His mercy, seldom confers upon great men till after their death, because it intoxicates and poisons the living. But Raymund Lully, who could not by death give place to the glory after, might have occasion to fear that it would perish before himself, and meanwhile it could seem to him only a derision of his immortal misfortune.

He knew how to make gold, so that he might purchase the world and all its kingdoms, yet he could not assure to himself the humblest tomb. He was the pauper of immortality. Everywhere he went begging for death, and no one was able to give it him. The courtly nobleman had become an absorbed alchemist, the alchemist a monk; the monk became preacher, philosopher, ascetic, saint, and, last of all, missionary. He engaged hand to hand with the learned men of Arabia; he battled victoriously against Islamism, and had everything to fear from the fury of its professors. Everything to fear—this means that he had something to hope, and that which he hoped for was death.[1]

He engaged a young Arab of the most fanatical class as his attendant, and posed before him as the scourge of the religion of Mohammed. The Arab assassinated his master, which was what he expected; but Raymund Lully did not die; it was the assassin that he would have forgiven who killed himself in despair at his failure, so that conscience had an added burden instead of deliverance and peace.

He was scarcely cured of his wounds when he embarked for Tunis, in which place he preached Christianity openly; but the Bey in admiration of his learning and his courage protected him against the madness of the crowd and caused him to re-embark with all his books. Before long he returned to the same parts, preaching at Bone, Bougia and other African towns; the Moslems were stupefied and feared to lay hands upon him. In the end he revisited Tunis and collecting the people in the streets, he proclaimed that, though driven from the place, he had come back to confound the impious doctrines of Mohammed and to die for Jesus Christ. This time there was no protection possible, the enraged people hunted him, a veritable insurrection broke out; he fled, to encourage them further; already he was broken by many blows, pouring with blood, covered with wounds; and yet he continued to live. He sank finally, buried—literally speaking—under a mountain of stones.

On the same night, says the legend, two Genoese merchants, Steven Colon and Louis de Pastorga, sailing over the open sea, beheld a great light shining from the port of Tunis. They changed their course and, approaching the shore, discovered a mound of stones, which diffused far and near this miraculous splendour. They landed in great astonishment and finally discovered the body of Raymund Lully, mangled but still

[1] The romantic history of Raymund Lully on which Éliphas Lévi worked was written by Jean Marie de Vernon.

breathing. He was taken on board the ship and carried to Majorca, where in sight of his native land the martyr was permitted to expire. God set him free by a miracle and his penance was so finished.

Such is the odyssey of the fabulous Raymund Lully; let us come now to the historical realities.

Raymund Lully, the philosopher and adept, being the one who deserved the title of illuminated doctor, was the son of that seneschal of Majorca who was made famous by his ill-starred passion for Ambrosia di Castello.[1] He did not discover the elixir of immortality, but he made gold in England for King Edward III, and this gold was called *aurum Raymundi*. There are extant certain very rare coins which are called *Raymundins* by experts. Louis Figuier identifies these with the rose-nobles which were struck during the reign in question,[2] and suggests, a little frivolously, that the alchemy of Raymund Lully was only a sophistication of gold which would be difficult to detect at a period when chemical processes were much less perfect than they are at the present day. This notwithstanding, he recognises the scientific importance of Lully and gives his judgment concerning him as follows:

"Raymund Lully, whose genius embraced all branches of human knowledge, and who brought together in the *Ars Magna* a vast system of philosophy, summarising the encyclopædic principles of science as it then stood, could not fail to bequeath a valuable heritage to chymists. He perfected and described carefully various compounds which are used widely in chemistry; we owe him the preparation of carbonate of potassium by means of tartar and by wood ashes, the rectification of spirits of wine, the preparation of essential oils, the cuppellation of silver, and the preparation of sweet mercury."[3]

Other scientists, feeling sure that the rose-nobles were pure as gold, have speculated that, having regard to the very imperfect processes of practical chemistry during the middle ages, such transmutations as those of Raymund Lully, and indeed other adepts, were merely the separation

---

[1] What is certain historically is as follows: (*a*) That the story of Ambrosia di Castello, so far as regards its root-matter, concerns the original and only Raymund Lully, who was the author of the *Ars Magna*; (*b*) That it is in all probability fictitious; (*c*) That it has been decorated and dramatised by Éliphas Lévi, who has done his work admirably; (*d*) That concerning the father of the illuminated doctor we know only that he was a great soldier; (*e*) That the author of the alchemical treatises was not the author of the *Ars Magna*; (*f*) That the alchemical writer is said to have been (1) another Raymund Lully, which, I think, means only that he assumed the name in order to father his works upon a celebrated person, and (2) a proselyte of the gate, being a person who becomes a Jew, but this is manifestly contradicted by the evidence of the alchemical texts; (*g*) That when the works of Raymund Lully were collected, at the end of the eighteenth century, into eight enormous folio volumes, we find, as I have said elsewhere, a third Raymund Lully, who was a mystic; but as to his real identity we know nothing.

[2] Rose Nobles were replaced by Angels in 1465, *temp.* Edward IV.

[3] Louis Figuier wrote occult romances under the guise of history, and did not know what he was talking about in respect of the *Ars Magna*. There is no reason to suppose that it had even passed through his hands. It was otherwise as regards the little alchemical texts; and there is no reason to question what he says concerning them.

of the gold found in silver mines, and purified by means of antimony, which is actually indicated, in a great number of Hermetic symbols, as the efficient and chief element in the Powder of Projection.[1] We agree with them that chemistry was non-existent at the period in question, and we may add that it was created by adepts or rather that the adepts, while keeping to themselves those synthetic secrets which were the treasure of the magical sanctuaries, instructed their contemporaries as to some of the analytical processes. These were afterwards perfected, but they have not as yet led men of science to reach that ancient synthesis which constitutes Hermetic philosophy, in the proper sense of the term.

In this philosophical *Testament*, Raymund Lully has set forth all the principles of this science, but in a veiled manner, following the practice and indeed the duty of adepts. He also composed a *Key* to the *Testament* mentioned, and finally a *Key* to the *Key*, or, more definitely, a codicil, which is in our opinion the most important of his writings on alchemy. Its principles and modes of procedure have nothing in common either with the sophistication of pure metals or with the separation of alloys. As a theory, it is in conformity with the principles of Geber and as a practice with those of Arnaldus de Villanova; in respect of doctrine it is in conformity with the most exalted ideas of the Kabalah. Those earnest minds who refuse to be discouraged by the discredit into which ignorance brings the great things should study Kabalistically the codicil of Raymund Lully, if they seek to carry on that research of the absolute which was followed by the greatest men of genius in the elder world.[2]

The whole life of this pre-eminent adept, the first initiate after St. John who was devoted to the hierarchic apostolate of holy orthodoxy—his entire life, we repeat, was passed in pious foundations, in preachings, in immense scientific labours. Thus, in 1276, he established at Palma a college of Franciscans dedicated to the study of Oriental languages, and Arabic especially, with the object of refuting the works of Mohammedan doctors and of preaching the Christian faith among the Moors. John XXI confirmed this institution by a pastoral letter dated from Viterbo on December 16, in the first year of his pontificate.

From 1293 to 1311 Lully solicited and obtained from Pope Nicholas IV and from the kings of France, Sicily, Cyprus and Majorca the establishment of many other colleges for the same purpose. Wherever he went he gave instructions in his Great Art, which is a universal synthesis of human knowledge, and has as its prime object the institution of one

---

[1] The story of a transmutation performed by someone called Raymund Lully in England depends from the alchemical texts mentioned, and is therefore no evidence and from a forged Testament of John Cremer, who called himself Abbot of Westminster, but no person of this name filled the office in question, either at the supposed period or any other.

[2] The tracts extant under the name of the alchemical Raymund Lully are enumerated by Lenglet du Fresnoy in connection with those attributed to the author of the *Ars Magna*. Mangetus printed sixteen in his *Bibliotheca Chemica Curiosa*, 1702. The *Codicillus, Vade Mecum,* or *Cantilena* is a considerable work, divided into 74 chapters.

language among men as also one mode of thought. He visited Paris and there astonished the most learned doctors; afterwards he crossed over to Spain, tarried at Complute, where he founded a central academy for the study of languages and sciences. He reformed a number of convents, went on to Italy and recruited soldiers for a new military order, the institution of which he advocated at the very Council of Vienna which condemned the Templars. The catholic science and the true initiation of St. John were intended thereby to rescue the protecting sword of the Temple from faithless hands. The great ones of this world derided poor Raymund Lully, and yet in their own despite they did all that he desired. This illuminated personality, termed by derision Raymund the Fantastic, seems to have been pope of popes and king of kings; he was poor as Job and gave alms to sovereigns; he was called a fool, and he was of that order of folly which confounds sages. The greatest politician of the period, Cardinal Ximenes, whose mind was as vast as it was serious, never spoke of him except as the divine Raymund Lully and the most enlightened doctor. He died in 1314, according to Genebrard, or in 1315, according to the author of the preface to the *Meditations* of the Hermit Blaquerne. He was eighty years old, and the end of his toilsome and holy existence came on the Festival of the martyrdom of St. Peter and St. Paul.[1]

A disciple of the great Kabalists, Raymund Lully sought to establish an absolute and universal philosophy by substituting for the conventional abstractions of systems a fixed notion of natural actualities and by substituting a simple and natural mode of expression for the ambiguous terms of scholasticism. He condemned the definitions of the scholars at his period because they perpetuated disputes by their inexactitude and amphibology. According to Aristotle, man is a reasonable animal, but it may be replied that he is not an animal and is only rarely reasonable. Moreover, the words "animal" and "reasonable" cannot be brought into harmony; a fool, in this sense, would not be a man, and so forth. Raymund Lully defined things by their right names and not by their synonyms or approximations; afterwards he explained the names by etymology. To the question—What is man?—he would therefore reply that the word, in its general acceptation, signified the state of being human, but taken in a particular acceptation it designates the human personality. What, however, is this human personality? Originally, it is the personality which God made by breathing life into a body compounded of earth (*humus*); literally, it is you, it is I, it is Peter, Paul, and so on. Those who were accustomed to scientific jargon protested to the illuminated doctor that anyone could talk like this; that on the basis of such a method the whole world might pose as learned; and that popular common sense would be preferred before the doctrine of academies. "That is just what I wish," was the answer of Raymund Lully in his great simplicity. Hence the reproach of puerility made against his enlightened theory; and puerile

[1] The reader may consult at this point my study of the life and writings of Raymund Lully in the *Lives of Alchemystical Philosophers*, pp. 68–88.

it was in a sense, but with the puerility of His counsel, Who said, "Except ye become as one of these little ones, ye shall not enter into the Kingdom of heaven." Is not the Kingdom of Heaven also that of science, seeing that the celestial life of God and men is but understanding and love?

The design of Raymund Lully was to set the Christianised Kabalah against the fatalistic *magia* of the Arabs, Egyptian traditions against those of India, the Magic of Light against Black Magic. He testified that, in the last days, the doctrines of Antichrist would be a materialised realism and that there would be a recrudescence of all the monstrosites of evil Magic. Hence he sought to prepare minds for the return of Enoch, or otherwise for the final revelation of that science the key of which is in the hieroglyphical alphabets of Enoch. This harmonising light of reason and faith is to precede the Messianic and universal reign of Christianity on earth. So was Lully a great prophet for true Kabalists and seers, while for sceptics who at least can respect exalted characters and noble aspirations he was a sublime dreamer.

CHAPTER IV

ON CERTAIN ALCHEMISTS

NICHOLAS FLAMEL belongs to alchemy exclusively, and he enters into our consideration only because of the hieroglyphical book of Abraham the Jew, in which the scrivener of the rue Saint-Jacques-la-Boucherie found the absolute keys of the Great Work. This book was founded on the Keys of the Tarot and was simply a hieroglyphical and Hermetic commentary on the *Sepher Yetzirah*. We find as a fact, by the description of Flamel himself, that the leaves were twenty-one in number, making twenty-two with the title,[1] and that they were divided into three septenaries, having a blank leaf at every seventh page. Let us here bear in mind that the Apocalypse, that sublime Kabalistic and prophetic summary of all occult types, also divided its symbols into three septenaries, between each of which there is silence in heaven, thus instituting a striking analogy with the uninscribed leaf in the mystic book of Flamel.[2] The septenaries of the Apocalypse are (*a*) seven seals to open, meaning seven mysteries to be learned and seven difficulties to be overcome; (*b*) seven trumpets to sound, being seven utterances to understand; (*c*) seven vials to empty, which signify seven substances which must be volatilised and fixed.

In the work of Flamel the first seventh leaf has as its hieroglyphical character the wand of Moses overcoming the serpents brought forth by the magicians of Pharaoh. They are seen devouring one another, and the figure as a whole is analogous to the Victor of the Tarot, yoking to his cubic chariot the white and black sphinxes of Egyptian Magic. The symbol in question corresponds to the seventh dogma in the creed of Maimonides: we acknowledge but one prophet, who is Moses. It represents the unity of science and the work; it represents further the Mercury of the Wise, which is formed by the dissolution of composites and by the reciprocal action of the Sulphur and Salt of metals.

The emblem on the fourteenth page was the Brazen Serpent set upon a cross. The cross represents the marriage of the purified Sulphur and Salt, as also the condensation of the Astral Light. The fourteenth Trump card in the Tarot depicts an angel, who is the spirit of the earth, mingling the liquids in two ewers, one of gold and one of silver. It is the same symbol formulated after another manner. On the 21st leaf of Flamel's book there was the type of space and universal life, represented

---

[1] There is no reference to a title in the original text.
[2] It is stated once only in the Apocalypse that "there was silence in heaven about the space of half an hour". See Chapter VIII, verse 1.

by a desert with springs of water and serpents gliding hither and thither.[1] In the Tarot, space is typified by the four signs allocated to the cardinal points of heaven, and life is represented by a naked girl dancing in a circle. Flamel does not specify the number of springs and serpents, but the former would probably be four, springing from one source, as in the Pantacle of Eden; the serpents would be four, seven, nine or ten.

On the fourth leaf was the figure of Time, preparing to cut off the feet of Mercury. Close by was a rose-tree in blossom, the root being blue, the stem white, the leaves red, and the flowers golden.[2] The number four is that of elemental realisation. Time is atmospheric nitre; his scythe is the acid which is extracted from this nitre, and the Mercury is fixed thereby, being transformed into salt. The rose-tree represents the Work and the successive colours which characterise its stages: it is the mastery passing through the black, white and red aspects, out of which gold is produced as a blossom that buds and unfolds.

The number five is that of the Great Mystery, and on the fifth page blind men were represented digging up the ground round the rose-tree in search of the grand agent which is present everywhere. Some others, who were better advised, were weighing a white water, resembling a solidified air.[3] On the reverse side of this page was the massacre of the innocents, with the sun and moon descending to bathe in their blood. This allegory, which is the literal secret of Hermetic art, has reference to that process of taking air into air, as Aristeus[4] puts it; or, to speak intelligible language, of using air as force, expanding it by means of Astral Light, just as water is changed into steam by the action of fire. This can be accomplished by the aid of electricity, magnets and a powerful projection of the operator's will, when directed by science and good intent. The children's blood represents that essential light which is extracted by philosophical fire from elementary bodies. When it is said that the sun and moon come down to bathe, the meaning is that the silver therein is tinctured into gold, and that the gold acquires a grade of purity by which its sulphur is transformed into the true Powder of Projection.

We are not writing a treatise on alchemy, although this science is really Transcendental Magic put into operation; we reserve its revelations and wonders for other special and more extended works.

Popular tradition affirms that Flamel did not die and that he buried

---

[1] The *Book of Nicholas Flamel* describes the symbols as follows: (1) A Wand and serpents devouring one another; (2) a Cross, on which a serpent was crucified; (3) Deserts, in the midst of which were many fair fountains, whence issued a number of serpents that glided here and there.

[2] Mercury and Saturn—as Flamel supposed them to be—were depicted on the obverse side of this leaf and the symbolic flower was on the reverse side. It is not said to be a rose, but simply a fair flower. The rose-tree was on the obverse side of the fifth leaf.

[3] The original has no reference to solidified air.

[4] Otherwise Arisleus, who figures prominently in the discourses of the *Turba Philosophorum*.

a treasure under the tower of Saint-Jacques-la-Boucherie. According to illuminated adepts, this treasure, contained in a cedar box covered with plates of the seven metals, was the original copy of the famous book attributed to Abraham the Jew, with commentaries in the writing of Flamel and sufficient specimens of the Powder of Projection to transmute the sea into gold, supposing that the sea were Mercury.

After Flamel came Bernard Trevisan, Basil Valentine and other famous alchemists. The twelve Keys of Basil Valentine are at once Kabalistic, magical and Hermetic. Then in 1480 appeared Trithemius, who was the master of Cornelius Agrippa and the greatest dogmatic magician of the middle ages. Trithemius was an abbot of the Order of St. Benedict, of irreproachable orthodoxy and unimpeachable conduct. He was not so imprudent as to write openly on occult philosophy, like his venturesome disciple Agrippa. All his magical works turn on the art of concealing mysteries, while his doctrine was expressed in a pantacle, after the manner of true adepts. This pantacle is excessively rare, and is found only in a few manuscript copies of his tract *De Septem Secundeis*. A Polish gentleman and man of exalted mind and noble heart, Count Alexander Branistki possesses a curious example which he has kindly shewn to us. The pantacle consists of two triangles joined at the base, one white and the other black. At the apex of the black triangle there is a fool crouching, who turns his head with difficulty and gazes awe-struck into the triangle, where his own likeness is reflected. On the apex of the white triangle stands a man in the prime of life, armed as a knight, having a steady glance and an attitude of strong and peaceful command. In this triangle are inscribed the letters of the divine Tetragram. The natural and exoteric sense of the emblem may be explained by an aphorism as follows: The wise man rests in the fear of the true God, but the fool is overwhelmed by the terror of a false god made in his own image. By meditating on the pantacle as a whole, and thereafter on its constituents successively, the adepts, however, will find therein the last word of Kabalism and the unspeakable formula of the Great Arcanum. In other words, it is the distinction between miracles and prodigies, the secret of apparitions, the universal theory of magnetism and the science of all mysteries.

Trithemius composed a history of Magic, written entirely in pantacles under the title: *Veterum Sophorum Sigilla et Imagines Magicæ*. In his *Steganography* and *Polygraphy* he gives the key to all occult writings and explains in veiled terms the real science of incantations and evocations. Trithemius is in Magic the master of masters, and we have no hesitation in proclaiming him the most wise and learned of adepts.

It is otherwise with Cornelius Agrippa, who was a seeker all his life and attained neither science nor peace. His books are full of erudition and assurance; he was himself of an independent and fantastic character, so it came about that he passed for an abominable sorcerer and was persecuted by the priesthood and princes. In the end he wrote against the sciences which had failed to bring him happiness, and he died in misery and abandonment.

We now come to the mild and pleasing figure of that learned and sublime Postel, who is known only by his over-mystical love for an elderly but illuminated woman. There is something far different in Postel from the disciple of Mother Jeanne, but vulgar minds prefer to disparage rather than to learn and have no wish to see anything better in him. It is not for the benefit of these that we propose to make known the genius of William Postel.

He was the son of a poor peasant, belonging to the district of Barenton in Normandy; by force of perseverance and much sacrifice he contrived to teach himself and became the most learned man of his time; but poverty pursued him always and want occasionally compelled him to sell his books. Full of resignation and sweetness, he worked like a labouring man to win a morsel of bread and then went back to his studies. He acquired all known languages and sciences of his period; he discovered rare and priceless manuscripts, including the apocryphal gospels and the *Sepher Yetzirah*; he initiated himself into the mysteries of the transcendental Kabalah,[1] and in his simple admiration for that absolute truth, for that supreme reason of all philosophies and dogmas, it was his ambition to reveal it to the world. He therefore spoke the language of mysteries openly and wrote a book entitled the *Key of Things kept Secret from the Foundation of the World*.[2] He dedicated this work to the fathers assembled at the Council of Trent, entreating them to enter the path of conciliation and universal synthesis. No one understood him; some accused him of heresy and the most moderate were contented to say that he was a fool.

The Trinity, according to Postel, made man in Its image and Its likeness. The human body is dual and its triadic unity is through the union of the two halves. The human soul is also dual; it is *animus* and *anima*, or intellect and emotion; it has also two sexes, the male being resident in the head and the female in the heart. Redemption in its completion must also be dual in humanity; the mind by its purity makes good the errors of the heart, and then the generosity of the heart must rescue the egoistic barrenness of the brain. Christianity, from Postel's standpoint, has been so far understood only by the reasoning mind and has not entered into the heart. The Word has been made man, but the world will be saved when the Word shall have been made woman. The sublime grandeurs of the spirit of love will be taught by the maternal genius of religion, and then reason will be harmonised with faith, because it will comprehend, interpret and restrain the sacred excesses of devotion.

Observe, he remarks, how religion is understood by the majority of

[1] There is an old story that he translated the *Sepher Ha Zohar* into Latin, but the manuscript has never been found.
[2] It was first published at Basle and afterwards at Amsterdam in 1646. In 1899 the second edition was rendered into French. It deserves and will repay careful reading from the mystic point of view.

Christians; it is only as an ignorant and persecuting partiality, a superstitious and stupid stubbornness, and fear—base fear—above all. Why is this? Because those who profess it have not the woman-heart, because they are foreign to the divine enthusiasms of that mother-love which explains all religion. The power that has invaded the brain and binds the spirit is not that of the good, understanding and long-suffering God; it is of the wicked, imbecile and cowardly Satan. It comes about in this manner that there is far more fear of the devil than love for the Divine. The frozen and shrivelled brain weighs on the dead heart like a tombstone. What an awakening will it be for understanding, what a rebirth for reason, what a victory for truth, when the heart shall be raised by grace! Why am I the first and almost the only person to comprehend this, and what can one who has attained resurrection perform alone among the dead, who can hear nothing? Come therefore and come quickly, O mother-spirit, who appeared to me at Venice in the soul of a virgin inspired by God; descend and teach the women of the new world their redeeming mission and their apostolate of holy and spiritual life.

It is a fact that Postel owed these noble inspirations to a pious woman named Jeanne, whose acquaintance he had made at Venice. He was the spiritual adviser of this elect soul and was drawn into the current of mystic poetry which eddied about her. When he administered the Eucharist to her she became radiant and transfigured in his eyes, and although she was more than fifty years old the poor priest confesses innocently that he would have taken her for less than fifteen: so did the sympathy of their hearts transform her in his eyes. One must have followed the life of asceticism to understand such celestial hallucinations and lyrical puerilities, such a mystic marriage between two virginal beings, such extraordinary enthusiasms of love in two pure souls. In her he discerned the living spirit of Jesus Christ by which the world would be regenerated. I have seen, says he, this light of the heart which will drive the hideous spectre of Satan from all minds; it is no chimera of my dreams; she has appeared in the world, has taken flesh in a maid, in whom I have hailed the mother of the world to come. This is analysing rather than translating Postel, but the rapid abridgment of his sentiments and language will make plain that he spoke figuratively, and, as maintained by the learned Jesuit Desbillons in his notice on the life and works of Postel, that nothing was further from his thoughts than to represent, as some have pretended, a second incarnation of divinity in this poor hospital sister who had only drawn him by the brightness of her humble virtues. We are utterly certain that all those who have slandered and ridiculed Postel are not worth one Mère Jeanne.

The mystical relations of Postel and the nun continued for about five years, at the end of which time she died, assuring her confessor that she would never be parted from him but would help him when freed from the bond of material life. "She kept her promise," says Postel; "she has been with me at Paris, has enlightened me with her own light and has harmonised my reason and my faith. Two years after her ascent into heaven her spiritual body and substance descended into me and permeated sensibly my whole body, so that it is she rather than myself who lives in me." After this experience Postel always regarded himself as a risen being and signed himself *Postellus Restitutes*. As a matter of fact, one curious result followed: his white hair became again black, his wrinkles disappeared and the ruddy colour of youth was assumed by his countenance, previously made thin and pallid by his austerities and vigils. His derisive biographers assert that he dyed his hair and painted his face; it was insufficient to picture him as a fool, and so out of his noble and generous character they produced a juggler and charlatan. Assuredly the imbecility or bad faith of cold and sceptic minds, when they pass judgment on enthusiastic hearts, is more wonderful than the eloquent unreason of the latter.

"It has been imagined," writes Father Desbillons, "and is still, I understand, believed that the regeneration supposed to have been accomplished by Mother Jeanne is the foundation of his system; it had however been completely developed before he was aware of her existence, and he never departed from it, unless indeed he did so a few years before his death. It had come into his mind that the evangelical reign of Jesus Christ, established by the Apostles, could be no longer maintained among Christians or propagated among infidels unless enforced by the light of reason. To this principle, which affected him personally, he added another, being the destination of the King of France to universal monarchy. The way of the Second Advent must be prepared by conquest of hearts and conviction of minds, that there may be henceforth but one faith and Jesus Christ reigning over the whole world in the person of a single king and in virtue of one law." According to Father Desbillons, this proves that Postel was mad. Mad for having thought that religion should reign over minds by the supreme reason of its doctrine, and that the monarchy, to be strong and permanent, should bind hearts together by the victories of public prosperity under the dominion of peace. Mad for having believed in the coming of that kingdom about which we say daily—His kingdom come. Mad because he believed in reason and justice on earth. Well, well, they spoke truly; poor Postel was mad. The proof of his madness is that he wrote, as already said, to the Fathers of the Council of Trent, entreating them to bless the whole world and to launch anathemas against no one. As another example, he tried to convert the Jesuits and cause them to preach universal concord among men—peace between sovereigns, reason among priests, and goodness among the princes of this world. In fine, as a last and supreme madness, he neglected the benefits of this world and the favour of the great, lived always humbly and in poverty, possessed nothing but his knowledge and his books, and desired nothing but truth and justice. May God give peace to the soul of poor William Postel.

He was so mild and so good that his ecclesiastical superiors took pity upon him and, thinking probably, as was said later on of La Fontaine, that he was more silly than wicked, they were contented with shutting him up in his convent for the rest of his days. Postel was grateful for the quiet thus ensured towards the close of life, and he died peaceably, retracting everything that his superiors required. The man of universal concord could not be an anarchist; he was before all things the sincerest of catholics and humblest of Christians. The works of Postel will be rediscovered one of these days and will be read with wonder.

Let us pass to another maniac who was called Theophrastus Aureolus Bombast and was known in the World of Magic under the famous name of Paracelsus. There is no need to recapitulate what has been said concerning this master in our *Doctrine and Ritual of Transcendental Magic*, but something may be added on the occult medicine restored by Paracelsus. This truly Universal Medicine is based upon a spacious theory of light, called by adepts fluid or potable gold. Light, that creative agent, the vibrations of which are the movement and life of all things; light, latent in the universal ether, radiating about absorbing centres, which, being saturated thereby, project movement and life in their turn, so forming creative currents; light, astralised in the stars, animalised in animals, humanised in human beings; light, which vegetates in plants, glistens in metals, produces all forms of Nature and equilibrates all by the laws of universal sympathy—this is that light which exhibits the phenomena of magnetism, divined by Paracelsus, which tinctures the blood, being released from the air as it is inhaled and discharged by the hermetic bellows of the lungs. The blood then becomes a true elixir of life, wherein ruby and magnetic globules of vital light float in a slightly gilded fluid. These globules are actual seeds, ready to assume all forms of that world whereof the human body is an abridgment. They can become rarefied and coagulated, so renewing the humours which circulate in the nerves and in the flesh encompassing the bones. They radiate outside, or rather, in rarefying, they are drawn by the currents of light and circulate in the astral body—that interior and luminous body which is dilated by the imagination of ecstatics, so that their blood sometimes colours objects at a distance when these have been penetrated and identified with the astral body. In a special work on occult medicine that which is stated here will be proved, however strange and paradoxical it may seem at first sight to men of science.[1] Such were the bases of medicine as put forward by Paracelsus; he cured by sympathy of light; he administered medicaments not to the outward material body, which is entirely passive, which can be rent and cut up without feeling anything when the astral body has withdrawn, but to the inward medium, to that vehicle which is the source of sensations. The quintessence of these he renewed by sympathetic quintessences. For example, he healed wounds by applying powerful reactives to the spilt blood, thus sending back its physical soul and purified sap to the body. To cure a diseased limb he made a limb of

[1] This promise represents another unfulfilled intention of Éliphas Lévi.

The Seven Planets and their Genii

wax and, by will-power, transferred thereto the magnetism of the diseased limb. Then he treated the wax with vitriol, iron and fire, thus reacting by imagination and magnetic correspondence on the sick person himself, to whom the limb of wax had become an appendix and supplement. Paracelsus knew the mysteries of blood; he knew why the priests of Baal made incisions with knives in their flesh, and then brought down fire from heaven; he knew why orientals poured out their blood before a woman to inspire her with physical love; he knew how spilt blood cries for vengeance or mercy and fills the air with angels or demons. Blood is the instrument of dreams and multiplies images in the brain during sleep, because it is full of the Astral Light. Its globules are bisexual, magnetised and metalled, sympathetic and repelling. All forms and images in the world can be evoked from the physical soul of blood.

"At Baroche," says the estimable traveller Tavernier,[1] "there is a first-class English house, which I reached on a certain day with the English president, on my way from Agra to Surat. There came also certain jugglers, asking leave to exhibit some of their professional skill, and the president was curious to see it. In the first place they lighted a great fire, at which they heated iron chains, then wound them about their bodies and pretended that they were suffering in consequence, but no harm followed. They next took a morsel of wood, set it in the ground and asked one of the spectators to choose what fruit he liked. His choice fell upon mangoes, and thereupon one of the performers put a shroud about him and squatted on the ground five or six times. I had the curiosity to ascend to an upper room, where I could see through a fold in the sheet what was being done by the man. He was actually cutting the flesh under the arm-pits with a razor, and rubbing the wood with his blood. Each time he rose up the wood grew visibly; on the third occasion there were branches and buds thereon, on the fourth the tree was covered with leaves, and on the fifth it was bearing flowers.

"The English president had brought his chaplain from Amadabat to baptise a child of the Dutch commander, the president acting as godfather. The Dutch, it should be mentioned, do not have chaplains except where soldiers and merchants are gathered together. The English clergyman began by protesting that he could not consent to Christians assisting at such spectacles, and when he saw how the performers brought forth from a bit of dry wood, in less than half an hour, a tree of four or five feet in height, having leaves and flowers as in springtime, he felt it his duty to put an end to the business. He announced therefore that he would not administer communion to those who persisted in witnessing such occurrences. The president was thus compelled to dismiss the jugglers."

Dr. Clever de Maldigny, to whom we owe this extract, regrets that

---

[1] See *Les Six Voyages de Jean Baptiste Tavernier, en Turquie, en Perse et aux Indes*, Paris, 1676. There were five French editions, and the work was also translated into English.

the growth of the mangoes was thus stopped abruptly, but he does not explain the occurrence. To our mind it was a case of fascination by the magnetism of the radiant light of blood, a phenomenon of magnetised electricity, identical with that termed palingenesis, by which a living plant is made to appear in a vessel containing ashes of the same plant long since perished.

Of such were the secrets known by Paracelsus, and it was in the application of these hidden natural forces to purposes of medicine that he made at once so many admirers and enemies. For the rest, he was by no means a simple personality like Postel; he was naturally aggressive and of the mountebank type; so did he affirm that his familiar spirit was hidden in the pommel of his great sword, and never left his side. His life was an unceasing struggle; he travelled, debated, wrote, taught. He was more eager about physical results than moral conquests, and while first among practical magicians he was last among adepts of wisdom. His philosophy was one of sagacity and, on his own part, he termed it *philosophia sagax*.[1] He divined more than anyone without knowing anything completely. There is nothing to equal his intuitions, unless it be the rashness of his commentaries. He was a man of intrepid experiences, intoxicated with his own opinions, his own talk, intoxicated otherwise on occasion, if we may believe some of his biographers. The works which he has left are precious for science, but they must be read with caution. He may be called the divine Paracelsus, understood in the sense of diviner; he is an oracle, but not a true master. He is great above all as a physician, for he had found the Universal Medicine. This notwithstanding, he could not prolong his own life, and he died, while still young, worn out by work and by excesses.[2] He left behind him a name shining with fantastic and ambiguous glory, due to discoveries by which his contemporaries failed to profit. He had not uttered his last word, and is one of those mysterious beings of whom it may be said, as of Enoch and St. John: He is not dead, and he will come again upon earth before the last day.

---

[1] This is really the title of a particular treatise, but as it is exceedingly long and may be said to be *de omnibus rebus*, it may not be taken unjustly to represent his philosophy at large.
[2] The latest and most successful apologist of Paracelsus says that the charge of intemperance was invented by his enemies. See the *Life of Paracelsus*, by Miss Anna M. Stoddart, 1911.

CHAPTER V
SOME FAMOUS SORCERERS AND MAGICIANS

AMIDST a great multiplicity of commentaries and studies on the work of Dante, no one, that we are aware, has signalised its characteristic-in-chief. The masterpiece of the glorious Ghibelline is a declaration of war against the papacy by a daring revelation of mysteries. The epic of Dante is Johannite and Gnostic; it is a bold application of Kabalistic figures and numbers to Christian dogmas, and is further a secret negation of the absolute element therein; his visit to the supernatural worlds takes place like an initiation into the Mysteries of Eleusis and Thebes. He is guided and protected by Virgil amidst the circles of the new Tartarus, as if the tender and melancholy prophet of the destinies of the son of Pollio were, in the eyes of the Florentine poet, the illegitimate yet true father of the Christian epic. Thanks to the pagan genius of Virgil, Dante emerges from that gulf above the door of which he had read the sentence of despair; he escapes by standing on his head, which means by reversing dogma. So does he ascend to the light, using the demon himself, like a monstrous ladder; by the force of terror he emerges from terror, from the horrible by the power of horror. He seems to testify that hell is without egress for those only who cannot go back on themselves; he takes the devil against the grain, if I may use so familiar an expression, and attains emancipation by audacity.[1] This is truly protestantism surpassed, and the poet of Rome's enemies has already divined Faust ascending to heaven on the head of the defeated Mephistopheles. Observe also that the hell of Dante is but a negative purgatory, by which is meant that his purgatory seems to take form in his hell, as if in a mould; it is like the lid or stopper of the gulf, and it will be understood that the Florentine titan in scaling Paradise meant to kick purgatory into hell.[2]

His heaven is composed of a series of Kabalistic circles divided by a cross, like the pantacle of Ezekiel; in the centre of this cross a rose

[1] Éliphas Lévi, who rather misquotes Dante, held that he had performed the same kind of mental pilgrimage, and had escaped in the same manner—by reversing dogma. He says elsewhere: "It was after he had descended from gulf to gulf and from horror to horror to the bottom of the seventh circle of the abyss . . . that Dante . . . rose consoled and victorious to the light. We have performed the same journey, and we present ourselves before the world with tranquillity on our countenance and peace in our heart . . . to assure mankind that hell and the devil . . . and all the rest of the dismal phantasmagoria are a nightmare of madness."

[2] The interpretation of the *Divine Comedy* as embodying an act of war against the papacy was begun by Gabriele Rossetti, about 1830, in his *Disquisitions on the Anti-Papal Spirit which produced the Reformation*. For the obscure and dubious tenets to which Éliphas Lévi gives the name of Johannite, he substitutes the doctrines of Albigenses and Waldenses. The same thesis, taken over from its Italian deviser, was maintained in the same interest by Eugène Aroux, firstly in *Les Mystères de la Chevalerie*, and afterwards in the great body of annotation attached to his translation of Dante. The latter work appeared in 1856. The interpretation of Lévi is a variant of that of Aroux. The disquisitions of the French writer are a fountain of joy for criticisms. He produced yet another monument, being *Dante Hérétique, Revolutionnaire et Socialiste*, 1854. He was a devoted member of the Latin Church, though I think that there would have been joy among the faithful had his books been burnt at Rome.

blossoms, thus for the first time manifesting publicly and almost explaining categorically the symbol of the Rosicrucians. We say for the first time because William of Lorris, who died in 1260, five years before the birth of Dante, did not complete the *Romance of the Rose*, his mantle falling upon Clopinel some fifty years later. It will be discovered with a certain astonishment that the *Romance of the Rose* and the *Divine Comedy* are two opposite forms of a single work—initiation by independence of spirit, satire on all contemporary institutions and an allegorical formula of the grand secrets of the Brotherhood of the Rosy Cross.

These important manifestations of occultism coincide with the fall of the Templars, since Jean de Meung, or Clopinel, a contemporary of Dante in the old age of the latter, flourished during his best years at the court of Philip the Fair. The *Romance of the Rose* is the epic of old France, a profound work in a trivial form, a revelation of occult mysteries as instructed as that of Apuleius. The roses of Flamel, Jean de Meung and Dante belong to the same bush.

A genius like Dante could not be an arch-heretic. Great men give an impetus to intelligence, and the impetus takes effect subsequently in activities which are startled by restless mediocrities. It may have been that Dante was never read—and he would assuredly not have been understood—by Luther. This notwithstanding, the mission of the Ghibellines, made fruitful by the potent thought of the poet, raised up the empire against the papacy by slow degrees; it was continued from century to century under various names, and in the end it made Germany protestant. It was certainly not Luther who produced the Reformation; it was the latter which took possession of Luther and impelled him forward. This square-shouldered monk could boast only obstinacy and daring, but he was the needful instrument for revolutionary ideas. Luther was the Danton of anarchic theology; superstitious and rash, he believed that he was obsessed by the devil; it was the devil who dictated his arguments against the Church, made him declaim, spout nonsense, and above all things write. The inspiring genius of all the Cains asked nothing at that time but ink, preassured that, given this fluid flowing from the pen of Luther, there would be presently a sea of blood. Luther was conscious of the fact, and he hated the devil because he was another master; one day he threw the ink-horn at his head, as if to satiate him by the violent libation. The episode recalls that jocular regicide who daubed his accomplices with ink when he signed the death-warrant of Charles I.

The device of Luther was, "Turk rather than papist"; and as a fact protestantism at its root is, like Islamism, simple Deism organised into a conventional cultus, or if it differs therefrom it is only by its remnants of catholicism imperfectly effaced. From the standpoint of the negation of catholic dogma, the protestants are Moslems with a few superstitious the more and a prophet the less.

Men renounce God less unwillingly than they give up the devil, as the apostates of all times have proved abundantly. Speedily subdivided by anarchy, the disciples of Luther had but one bond of belief in common; all had faith in Satan, and this spectre, magnifying in proportion as their spirit of revolt took them the farther from God, reached terrible proportions at last. Carlostad, archdeacon of Würtemberg, being one day in the pulpit, saw a black man enter the temple, take a seat in front of him and stare at him with dreadful fixity through the entire length of his sermon. He became anxious, left the pulpit and questioned the assistants; but no one had seen the phantom. Carlostad returned home in a state of dismay; he was met by the youngest of his sons, who said that a stranger in black had inquired for him and promised to return in three days. There was no room for doubt in the mind of the hallucinated archdeacon; that stranger was the spectre of his vision. A fever was brought on by his terror; he retired to bed and died before the third day.

These unhappy heretics were afraid of their own shadows; their consciences had remained catholic and consigned them to hell without pity. Walking one evening with his wife Catherine de Bora, Luther looked up to heaven, which was bright with stars, and said in an undertone, as he sighed deeply: "Ah, beautiful sky, which I shall never see!"—"What!" exclaimed his wife. "Do you then think that you are condemned?" Luther answered: "Who knows whether God will not punish us for having been unfaithful to our vows?" Supposing that Catherine, seeing his lack of self-confidence, had cursed and left him, it may be that the reformer, overcome by the Divine Warning, would have recognised his criminal offence in betraying that Church which was his first spouse and would have turned weeping towards the cloister which he had left wilfully. But God, Who withstands the proud, doubtless found him unworthy of this saving affliction. The sacrilegious comedy of Luther's marriage was the providential punishment of his pride, and as he remained obstinate in his sin, that punishment was always with him and derided him to the end. He died between the devil and his wife, appalled at the one and exceedingly embarrassed by the other.

Corruption and superstition are well paired together. The epoch of the dissolute Renaissance, equally persecuting and credulous, was certainly not that of the second birth of reason. Catherine de' Medici was a sorceress, Charles IX consulted necromancers, Henry III played at devotion and debauch. It was the heyday then of astrologers, though a few of them were tortured from time to time, to make them change their predictions. There were, moreover, the court sorcerers, who dabbled a little in poisoning and deserved the hangman's rope. *Trois-Échelles*, the magician of Charles IX, was a juggler and rogue; one day he made confession to the King and his misdeeds were not peccadilloes; the King forgave him, but promised his cure on the gallows if he had a relapse; he did relapse, and was hanged in due course.[1]

[1] The authority is the demonographer Bodin. Trois-Échelles confessed to the King that he had given himself over to a spirit who enabled him to perform prodigies. He was forgiven on condition that he denounced others who were guilty of sorcery. It is supposed that his subsequent condemnation was the consequence of new operations on his own part.

THE ADEPTS AND THE PRIESTHOOD

When the League vowed the death of the weakly and miserable Henri III it had recourse to witchcraft and Black Magic. L Étoile[1] declares that a wax image of the King was set on the altars where priests of the League said Mass, and that the image was stabbed with a knife during a prayer embodying maledictions and anathemas. When the King failed to die with sufficient celerity, it was concluded that he was also a sorcerer. Pamphlets were published representing Henri III as holding conventions where the crimes of Sodom and Gomorrah were but the prelude of more frightful and unheard- of outrages. Included among the King's minions there was said to be one who was the devil in person, and young virgins were abducted and prostituted by force to Beelzebub.[2] The people believed these fables, and a fanatic was found at last to execute the threats of sorcery. Jacques Clément suffered from visions and imperious voices, which commanded him to kill the King; he sought regicide like a martyr and died laughing like the heroes of Scandinavian mythology. Scandal-mongering chronicles have pretended that a great lady of the court supplemented the inspirations of the monk's solitude by the magnetism of her caresses; but the anecdote is wanting in probability. It was the monk's continence which promoted his exaltation, and had he begun to lead the blind life of passion an unsatiable appetite for pleasure would have possessed his entire nature and he would not have been willing to die.

Whilst religious wars incarnardined the world, secret illuministic associations, which were nothing but theurgic and magical schools, were incorporated in Germany. The most ancient of these seems to have been that of the Rosicrucians, whose symbols go back to the times of the Guelphs and the Ghibellines, as we see by the allegories in the poem of Dante and by the emblems in the *Romance of the Rose*.

The rose, which from all times has been the type of beauty, life, love and pleasure, expressed mystically the secret thought of all protests manifested at the Renaissance.[3] It was the flesh in rebellion against the oppression of spirit; it was Nature testifying that, like grace, she was a daughter of God; it was love refusing to be stifled by the celibate; it was life in revolt against sterility; it was humanity aspiring towards natural religion, full of reason and love, founded on the revelations of the harmony of being, of which the rose, for initiates, was the living floral symbol. It is in truth a pantacle; the form is circular, the leaves of the corolla are heart-shaped and rest harmoniously on one another; its tint offers the most harmonious shades of the primitive colours; its calyx is of purple

---

[1] That is, Pierre de l'Étoile. See *Véritable Fatalité de Saint Cloud*, art. 8.
[2] This account is drawn from Garinet, who cites two pamphlets of the period: (A) *Les Sorcelleries de Henri de Valois, et les Oblations qu'il faisait au Diable dans le Bois de Vincennes*, 1589; (B) *Remonstrances à Henri de Valois sur les choses horribles envoyées par un enfant de Paris*, 1589.
[3] Compare Aroux: *La Comédie de Dante*, vol. ii, p. 33 of his *Clef de la Comédie*. The Rose is "the Albigensian Church and its doctrines . . . transformed into a mystic flower". Hence the immense vogue of the romance of William of Lorris, despite the anathemas of Gerson.

and gold. We have seen that Flamel, or rather the *Book of Abraham the Jew*, represents it as the hieroglyphical sign of the fulfilment of the Great Work.[1] Here is the key to the romance of Clopinel and William de Lorris. The conquest of the rose was the problem offered by initiation to science, whilst religion was at work to prepare and to establish the universal, exclusive and final triumph of the Cross.

The problem proposed by high initiation was the union of the Rose and the Cross, and in effect occult philosophy, being the universal synthesis, must take into account all phenomena of being. Considered solely as a physiological fact, religion is the revelation and satisfaction of a need of souls. Its existence as a fact is scientific, and to deny it would be a denial of humanity itself. No one has invented it; like laws and civilisations, it is formed by the necessities of moral life. From this merely philosophical and restrained standpoint, religion must be regarded as fatal if one explains all by fatality, and as Divine if one confesses to a Supreme Intelligence as the mainspring of natural laws.[2] Hence it follows that the characteristic of every religion, properly so called, being to depend directly from Divinity by a supernatural revelation—no other mode of transmission poviding a sufficient sanction of dogma—it must be concluded that the true natural religion is religion that has been revealed; this is to say, it is natural to adopt a religion only on the understanding that it has been revealed, every true religion exhorting sacrifices, and man having neither the power nor right to impose the same on his fellow creatures, outside and especially above the ordinary conditions of humanity.

Proceeding from this strictly rational principle, the Rosicrucians were led to respect the dominant hierarchic and revealed religion. They could be therefore no more the enemies of the papacy than of legitimate monarchy, while if they conspired against popes and kings, it was because they considered these or those personally as apostates in respect of duty and supreme abettors of anarchy.[3] What in fact is a despot—whether spiritual or temporal—but a crowned anarchist? It is possible to explain in this manner the protestantism and even radicalism of certain great

---

[1] The words of Flamel are as follows: "On the fifth leaf was a fair rose-tree, flowered, in the midst of a garden, growing up against a hollow oak, at the foot whereof bubbled forth a fountain of pure white water, which ran headlong down into the depths below. Yet it passed through the hands of a great number of people who digged in the earth, seeking after it, but, by reason of their blindness, none of them knew it, except a very few, who considered its weight." *Le Livre de Nicolas Flamel.*

[2] It will be seen that this is the counter-thesis to the explanation of the spiritual world by means of natural law; it is the explanation of the natural world by means of spiritual law. So also Eliphas Lévi is right when he goes on to affirm in substance that the religion of supernatural grace is the font of natural religion. It is in the light of the instituted sacraments that we find the hidden grace of those in Nature.

[3] "We do now securely call the Pope Antichrist, which was formerly a capital offence. . . . We do hereby condemn the East and the West, meaning the Pope and Mahomet. . . . He (the Pope) shall be torn in pieces with nails, and a final groan shall end his ass's braying. . . . The judgment due to the Roman impostor who now poureth his blasphemies with open mouth against Christ. . . . The mouth of this viper shall be stopped." See *Confessio Fraternitatis,* R.C., 1616.

THE ADEPTS AND THE PRIESTHOOD

adepts, who were assuredly more catholic than some popes and more monarchic than some kings—of certain eccentric adepts, such as Henry Khunrath and the true *illuminati* of his school.

By all but those who have made a particular study of the occult sciences, Khunrath is practically unknown; he is a master notwithstanding, and one of the first rank. He is a sovereign prince of the Rosy Cross, worthy in all respects of this scientific and mystical title.[1] His pantacles are splendid as the light of the *Book of Splendour*, called *Zohar*; they are learned as Trithemius, precise like Pythagoras, complete in their disclosure of the Great Work as the book of Abraham and Nicholas Flamel.

Khunrath, who was chemist and physician, was born in 1502, and he was forty-two years old when he attained transcendent theosophical initiation.[2] The *Amphitheatre of Eternal Wisdom*, which is the most remarkable of his works, was published in 1598, for the approbation of the Emperor Rudolph annexed thereto was dated on June 1 of the year in question.[3] Though professing a radical protestantism, the author claims loudly the titles of catholic and orthodox; he testifies that he possesses, but keeps secret as he ought, a key to the Apocalypse, which key is one and threefold, even as universal science. The division of the work is sevenfold, and through these sections are distributed the seven degrees of initiation into transcendental philosophy. The text is a mystical commentary on the oracles of Solomon,[4] and the work ends with a series of synoptic schedules which are the synthesis of Magic and the occult Kabalah—so far as concerns that which can be made public in writing. The rest, being the esoteric and inexpressible part of the science, is formulated in magnificent pantacles carefully designed and engraved. These are nine in number, as follows: (1) The dogma of Hermes; (2) Magical realisation; (3) The path of wisdom and the initial procedure in the work; (4) The Gate of the Sanctuary enlightened by seven mystic rays; (5) A Rose of Light, in the centre of which a human figure is extending its arms in the form of a cross; (6) The magical laboratory of Khunrath, demonstrating the necessary union of prayer and work; (7) The absolute synthesis of science; (8) Universal equilibrium; (9) A summary of Khunrath's personal doctrine, embodying an energetic protest

---

[1] The Masonic title of Sovereign Princes Rose-Croix ascribed in France to the members of the Eighteenth Degree, under the obedience of the Ancient and Accepted Scottish Rite, has been changed in England to Excellent and Perfect Princes. The old Rosicrucian title was that of *Frater*, and the head of the Order was termed *Imperator*.

[2] I have let this date stand, as it is difficult to say what Éliphas Lévi is driving at. Khunrath was born in 1559 or 1560, and he died early in the seventeenth century.

[3] This is a mistake. The *Amphitheatrum* appeared in 1609, the licence having been obtained previously.

[4] The work contains (*a*) 365 versicles drawn from *Proverbs* and the apocryphal *Book of Wisdom*, the Latin Vulgate being printed side by side with a new translation by Khunrath. These versicles are divided into seven grades. (*b*) An interpretation at length of each versicle. (*c*) An introduction to the first engraved plate; (*d*) to the second; (*e*) to the third; (*f*) to the fourth; and (*g*) an epilogue or conclusion to the whole work.

against all his detractors.[1] It is a Hermetic pantacle surrounded by a German caricature, full of liveliness and ingenuous choler. The philosopher's enemies are depicted as insects, zanies, oxen and asses, the whole being decorated with Latin legends and gross German epigrams. Khunrath is shewn on the right in the garb of a citizen, and on the left in that of his student's apartment; in both he makes faces at his adversaries. As a townsman he is armed with a sword and tramples on the tail of a serpent; as a student he is carrying a pair of tongs and is crushing the serpent's head. In public he demonstrates and at home instructs, but, as indicated by his gestures, the truth is the same always and expressed with disdain for the impure breath of his adversaries. The latter notwithstanding is so pestilential that the birds of heaven fall dead at their feet. This exceedingly curious plate is wanting in many copies of the work.

The book as a whole contains all mysteries of the highest initiation. As the title announces, it is Christo-Kabalistic, Divine-magical, physico-chemical, threefold-one, and universal. It is a true manual of Transcendental Magic and Hermetic Philosophy. A more complete and perfect initiation cannot be found elsewhere, unless indeed it is in the *Sepher Yetzirah* and *Zohar*. In the four important corollaries which follow the explanation of the third figure, Khunrath establishes: That the cost of accomplishing the Great Work (apart from the operator's maintenance and personal expenses) should not exceed the sum of thirty thalers. He adds, "I speak with authority, having learned from one who had knowledge; those who expend more deceive themselves and waste their money." It follows that either Khunrath had not himself composed the Philosophical Stone or did not wish to admit it for fear of persecution. He proceeds to establish the duty of the adept not to devote more than the tenth part of his wealth to his personal use, the rest being consecrated to the glory of God and works of charity. Finally, he affirms that the mysteries of Christianity and Nature interpret and illuminate one another, and that the future reign of Messiah will rest on the dual foundation of science and faith. The oracles of the Gospel being thus confirmed by the book of Nature, it will be possible to convince Jews and Mohammedans regarding the truth of Christianity on the grounds of science and reason, so that—with the help of Divine Grace—they will be converted infalliby to the religion of unity. He ends with this maxim: "The seal of Nature and of Art is simplicity."

Contemporary with Khunrath there was another initiated doctor, Hermetic philosopher and disciple of Paracelsian medicine; this was

[1] Éliphas Lévi has misplaced most of the plates, and it is difficult to follow his descriptions. No. 1 is the laboratory and oratory of the adept. No. 2 is apparently that which he calls the Path of Wisdom. No. 3 is the Philosophical Stone. No. 4 is that which Lévi describes as the Dogma of Hermes, because the sentences of the Emerald Tablet are inscribed on a Rock of Ages or Mountain of Initiation. No. 5 is the Gate of the Sanctuary, but it is enlightened by three rays. No. 6 is that which Lévi terms a Rose of Light, but it is really the sun with Christ in the centre. Nos. 7 and 9 correspond to the descriptions given; but No. 8 is scarcely a doctrine of equilibrium: it is the doctrine of regeneration through Christ, in Whom the law is fulfilled.

THE ADEPTS AND THE PRIESTHOOD

Oswald Crollius, author of the *Book of Signatures, or True and Vital Anatomy of the Greater and Lesser World*.[1] The preface to this work is a sketch of Hermetic philosophy, exceedingly well done; Crollius seeks to demonstrate that God and Nature have, so to speak, signed all their works, that every product of a given natural force bears the stamp of that force printed in indelible characters, so that he who is initiated in the occult writings can read, as in an open book, the sympathies and antipathies of things, the properties of substances and all other secrets of creation. The characters of different writings were borrowed primitively from these natural signatures existing in stars and flowers, on mountains and the smallest pebble. The figures of crystals, the marks on minerals, were impressions of the thought which the Creator had in their formation. The idea is rich in poetry and grandeur, but we lack any grammar of this mysterious language of worlds and a methodical vocabulary of this primitive and absolute speech. King Solomon alone is credited with having accomplished the dual labour; but the books of Solomon are lost. The enterprise of Crollius was not a reconstitution of these, but an attempt to discover the fundamental principles obtaining in the universal language of the creative Word.

It was recognised on these principles that the original hieroglyphics, based on the prime elements of geometry, corresponded to the constitutive and essential laws of forms, determined by alternating or combined movements, which, in their turn, were determined by equilibratory attractions. Simples were distinguished from composites by their external figures; and by the correspondence between figures and numbers it became possible to make a mathematical classification of all substances revealed by the lines of their surfaces. At the root of these endeavours, which are reminiscences of Edenic science, there is a whole world of discoveries awaiting the sciences. Paracelsus had divined them, Crollius indicates them, another who shall follow will realise and provide the demonstration concerning them. What seemed the folly of yesterday will be the genius of tomorrow, and progress will hail the sublime seekers who first looked into this lost and recovered world, this Atlantis of human knowledge.

The beginning of the seventeenth century was the great epoch of alchemy; it was the period of Philip Muller, John Torneburg, Michael Maier, Ortelius, Poterius, Samuel Norton, Baron de Beausoleil, David Planis Campe, Jean Duchesne, Robert Fludd, Benjamin Mustapha, D'Espagnet, the Cosmopolite—who is in the first rank—de Nuisement, who translated and published the Cosmopolite's writings, John Baptist van Helmont, Eirenæus Philalethes, Rodolph Glauber, the sublime shoemaker Jacob Böhme.[2] The chief among these initiates were devoted

---

[1] The *Basilica Chymica* was translated into French by J. Marcel de Boulene and published at Lyons in 1624. It was reprinted at Paris in 1633. The third part is the *Book of Signatures*. The Latin edition appeared at Frankfort in 1608.

[2] Some of these names are exceedingly obscure, and no importance attaches to their literary remains. Philip Muller wrote *Miracula et Mysteria Medico-Chymica*, 1614. It was printed eight times at various places. Of John Torneburg I have no record.

to the researches of Transcendental Magic, but they concealed most carefully that detested name under the veil of Hermetic experiments. The Mercury of the Wise which they desired to discover and hand on to their disciples was the scientific and religious synthesis, the peace which abides in the sovereign unity. The mystics themselves were but blind believers in the true *illuminati*, while illuminism, properly so called, was the universal science of light.

In the spring of 1623 the following strange proclamation was placarded through the streets of Paris: "We who are the authorised messengers of the Brothers of the Rosy Cross, making visible and invisible sojourn in this town, by the grace of the Most High, towards Whom the hearts of sages turn, do give instruction, without external means, in speaking the language of the countries wherein we dwell,[1] and do rescue men who are our fellow-workers from terror and from death. If anyone shall seek us out of mere curiosity, he will never communicate with us; but if he be actuated by an earnest desire to be inscribed on the register of our fraternity, we, who are discerners of thoughts, will make manifest to such an one the truth of our promises, so only that we do not disclose the place of our abode, since thought in its union with the firm will of the reader shall be sufficient to make us known to him and him likewise to us."

Public opinion took hold of this mysterious manifesto, and if anyone asked openly who were those Brothers of the Rosy Cross, an unknown personage would perchance take the inquirer apart, and say to him gravely:[2] "Predestined to the reformation which must take place speedily in the whole universe, the Rosicrucians are depositaries of supreme wisdom, and as undisturbed possessors of all gifts of Nature, they can dispense these at pleasure. In whatsoever place they may be, they know all things which are going on in the rest of the world better than if they were present amongst them; they are superior to hunger and thirst and have neither age nor disease to fear. They can command the most powerful spirits and genii. God has covered them with a cloud to protect them from their enemies, and they cannot be seen except by their own consent—had anyone eyes more piercing than those of the eagle. Their general assemblies are held in the pyramids of Egypt; but, even as the rock whence issued the spring of Moses, these pyramids proceed with them into the desert and will follow them until they enter the Promised Land."

Ortelis was commentator on Sendivogius; Michael Paterius or Potier was the author of ten alchemical tracts, but I have never heard that they were in estimation among lovers of the art. The Baron de Beausoleil was still more voluminous and is better known. The works of David de Planis Campe were collected into a folio in 1646; he is regarded as an alchemical dreamer. Duchesne was *Sieur de la Violette*, and his writings are in six volumes. Benjamin Mustapha, or rather Mussaphia, wrote on potable gold. The other names are known to science as, Lévi would express it, and are famous therein.

[1] The sum of this intimation is a little obscure. See my *Real History of the Rosicrucians*, pp. 388-390, for various versions of the proclamation.

[2] I have been unable to find the authority for this discourse, as a whole, but some fragments of it are cited by Gabriel Naudé.

CHAPTER VI

SOME MAGICAL PROSECUTIONS

THE Greek author of the allegorical Tablet of Cebes gives expression to this admirable conclusion: "There is one only real good to be desired, and this is wisdom; there is but one evil to fear, and it is madness." Moral evil, wickedness and crime are indeed and literally mania. Father Hilarion Tissot has therefore our heartfelt sympathy when he proclaims without ceasing in his extravagantly daring pamphlets that in place of punishing criminals we must take them under our charge and cure them. But, sympathy notwithstanding, reason rises in protest against excessively charitable interpretations of crime, the consequence of which would be to destroy the sanction of morality by disarming law. We liken mania to intoxication, and seeing that the latter is nearly always voluntary, we applaud the wisdom of judges who punish the misdemeanours and crimes committed in the state of drunkenness, not regarding the voluntary loss of reason as an excuse. There may come even a day when the self-induced condition will be counted as an aggravating circumstance and when the intelligent being who by his own act sets himself outside reason will find that he is also outside the pale of law. Is not law the reason of humanity? Woe to him who gets drunk, whether with wine, pride, hatred, or even love. He becomes blind, unjust, the sport of circumstance; he is a walking scourge and living fatality; he may slay or violate; he is an unchained fool, and let him be denounced as such. Society has the right of self-defence; it is more than a right, it is duty, for society has children.

These reflections are prompted by the magical prosecutions of which we have to give some account. The Church and Society have been too often charged with the judicial murder of fools. We admit that the sorcerers were fools, but theirs was the folly of perversity. If some innocent but diseased persons have perished among them, these things are misfortunes for which neither Society nor the Church can be held responsible. Every man who is condemned according to the laws of his country and the judicial forms of his time is condemned justly, his possible innocence being henceforth in the hands of God: before men he is and must remain guilty.

In a remarkable romance, called *The Sorceresses' Sabbath*,[1] Ludwig Tieck depicts a holy woman, a poor old creature outworn by macerations, mentally enfeebled by fasts and prayers, who, being full of horror at sorcerers, yet disposed by excess of humility to accuse herself of all crimes, ends in believing that she is a witch, confesses it, is convicted by error and prejudgment, and finally is burnt alive. What would such a history prove, supposing that it were true? Neither more nor less than the possibility of

---
[1] There does not appear to be a story with this title either in *The Phantasus* or elsewhere in the works of Tieck.

a judicial blunder. But if such mistakes are possible in fact they cannot be so in equity, or what would become of human justice? Socrates condemned to death might have had recourse to flight and his own judges would have furnished the means, but he respected the laws and resolved therefore to die.

The severity of certain sentences must be blamed to the laws and not the tribunals of the middle ages. Was Gilles de Laval, whose crimes and their punishment have been narrated, condemned unjustly, and must he be absolved as a fool? Were those horrible imbeciles innocent who composed philtres from the fat of little children? Moreover, Black Magic was the general mania of this unfortunate epoch. By their incessant application to questions of sorcery the very judges occasionally ended by thinking that they also had committed the same crimes The plague became epidemic in many localities and executions seemed to multiply the guilty.

Demonographers like Delancre, Delrio, Sprenger, Bodin, and Torreblanca give reports of many prosecutions, the details of which are equally tedious and revolting. The condemned creatures were mostly hallucinated and idiotic, but they were wicked in their idiocy and dangerous in their hallucination. Erotic passion, greed and hatred were the chief causes which brought about disorder in their reason: they were indeed capable of anything. Sprenger says that sorceresses were in league with midwives to secure dead bodies of new-born children. The midwives killed these innocents at the very moment of their birth, driving long needles into the brain. The babe was said to have been still-born and was buried as such; on the night following, the stryges dug up the ground and removed the corpse, which they stewed in a pan with narcotic and poisonous herbs, afterwards distilling this human gelatine. The liquor did duty as an elixir of long life, and the solid part—pounded and incorporated with soot and the grease of a black cat—was used for magical rubbing. The stomach turns with loathing at such abominable revelations, and pity is silenced by anger; but when one refers to the trials themselves, sees the credulity and cruelty of judges, the lying promises of mercy employed to extract admissions, the atrocious tortures, obscene examinations, shameful and ridiculous precautions, and finally the public execution, with the derisive ministrations of a priesthood which surrendered to the secular arm and asked mercy on those whom it had just condemned to death, amidst all this chaos one is forced to conclude that religion alone rests holy, but that human beings are all and equally either idiots or scoundrels.

In the year 1598 a priest of Limousin, named Pierre Aupetit, was burned alive for ridiculous confessions extracted from him by torture.[1] In 1599 a woman named Antide Collas was burned at Dole because there was something abnormal in her sexual conformation, and it was regarded as explicable only by a shameful intercourse with Satan. Repeatedly put to the torture, stripped, scrutinised by doctors and judges, overwhelmed

[1] See Pierre De Lancre: *Tableau de l'Inconstance des Démons*, Book VI., Discourse 4. But Éliphas Lévi seems to have followed the summary account of Garinet.

with shame and suffering, the unfortunate being confessed everything that she might somehow end it all.¹ Henri Boguet, judge of Saint-Claude, relates how he caused a woman to be tortured as a sorceress because there was a piece missing from the cross of her rosary, and it was a certain sign of witchcraft in the view of this ferocious maniac. A child of twelve years, brought up by the inquisitors, accused his own father of taking him to the Sabbath. The father died in prison as the result of his sufferings, and it was proposed to burn the boy, which was opposed by Boguet—who made a virtue of the clemency. Rollande de Vernois, thirty-five years old, was imprisoned in such a freezing dungeon that she promised to admit herself guilty of Magic if she might be allowed to go near a fire. As soon as she felt its warmth she fell into frightful convulsions, accompanied by fever and delirium. In this condition she was put to the torture, made every required statement, and was dragged in a dying condition to the stake. A storm broke out, extinguished the fire, and thereupon Boguet gloated over the sentence which he had pronounced, since she who in appearance was thus protected by heaven must really and incontestably be aided by the devil. This same judge burnt Pierre Gaudillon and Pierre le Gros for travelling by night, the one in the form of a hare and the other in that of a wolf.

But the prosecution which caused the greatest stir at the beginning of the seventeenth century was that of Messire Louis Gaufridi, curé of the parish of Accoules, at Marseilles. The scandal of this affair created a fatal precedent, which was only followed too faithfully. It was a case of priests. accusing a priest, of a minister dragged before a tribunal of his associates in the ministry. Constantine had said that if he found a priest dishonouring his calling by some shameful sin he would cover him with his own purple, which was a beautiful and royal saying, for the priesthood ought to be stainless, even as justice is infallible in the presence of public morality.²

In December 1610 a young woman of Marseilles went on a pilgrimage to Sainte-Baume in Provence, and there fell into ecstasy and convulsions. She was named Magdelaine de la Palud. Louise Capeau, another devotee, was similarly seized some short time after.³ The Dominicans and Capuchins believed that it was possession by the devil and had recourse to exorcisms. The result was that Magdelaine de la Palud and her fellow victim presented that spectacle which was renewed so often a century later during the epidemic of convulsions. They screamed, writhed, begged to be beaten and trampled underfoot. One day six men walked successively over the breast of Magdelaine without the slightest suffering on her part. While in this state she made confession of the most extraordinary licentiousness, saying that she had given herself, body and soul, to the devil, to whom she

---

¹ The account is in Bodin and in the record of Henri Boguet. Her physical peculiarity is described as *un trou qu'elle avait au dessous de sa parti gorrière*. The work of Boguet is entitled *Discours Exécrables des Sorciers*, 1602. It is exceedingly rare.

² The prosecution and execution of secular priests and monks recur frequently throughout the annals of sorcery.

³ The names appear to have been Madeleine de Mandol, daughter of the Seigneur de la Palud, and Louise Capel.

had been affianced by a priest named Gaufridi.[1] So far from incarcerating the distracted girl, she obtained a hearing, and the exorcising monks despatched three Capuchins to Marseilles for the purpose of secretly acquainting the ecclesiastical superiors with the state of affairs at Sainte-Baume, the object, if possible, being to bring the curé Gaufridi thither and confront him with the supposed demons.[2]

Furthermore, the monks put on record the infernal inspirations of the two hysterics, which were discourses full of ignorant and fanatical devotion, presenting religion as this was understood by the exorcists themselves. In a word, the possessed women seemed to be relating the dreams of those who exorcised them: it was precisely the phenomena of table-rapping and mediums in our own days. The devils assumed names not less incongruous than those of the spirits in America; they declaimed against printing and books, delivering sermons worthy of the most fervent and illiterate Capuchins. In the presence of demons made in their own image and their own likeness, the fathers were confirmed in the fact of the possession and in the veracity of the infernal spirits. The phantoms of their diseased imaginations assumed bodily shape and living manifestation in the two women, whose obscene admissions at once stimulated their curiosity and their indignation, full of secret lust. Such were their dispositions when the unhappy Louis Gaufridi was at length brought before them.

Gaufridi was an all too worldly priest, of agreeable countenance, weak character and more than dubious morality.[3] He had been the confessor of Magdelaine de la Palud and had inspired her with an insatiable passion, which, being changed by jealousy into hatred, became a fatality and drew the unfortunate priest into its whirlpool of madness, by which he was carried ultimately to the stake. Whatsoever was said by the accused in his own defence was turned against him. He called on God and Christ Jesus, on the Blessed Mother of Christ and the precursor St. John Baptist; but they answered: "You are excellent at reciting the Litanies of the Sabbath. By God, you understand Lucifer; by Jesus Christ, Beelzebub; by the Holy Virgin, the apostate mother of Antichrist; by St. John Baptist, the false prophet and precursor of Gog and Magog."

Gaufridi was put to the torture and promised mercy if he would sign the declarations of Magdelaine de la Palud. Distracted, circumvented, broken, the poor priest signed whatever was required; it was sufficient for his burning, and this was the object in view.[4] This also was the frightful spectacle which the Provençal Capuchins gave to the people as a lesson in

---

[1] The actual charges were (a) that Madeleine was seduced by Gaufridi when she was nine years old, (b) that he had taken her to the Sabbath, (c) that he had sent her 666 devils. To Louise he had sent four only.
[2] See *L'Histoire Admirable de la Possession et de la Conversion d'une Pénitente séduite par un Magicien*, by the Inquisitor Michaëlis, 1612.
[3] He was a priest of Marseilles and curé of Accoules.
[4] The confession included: (1) Visions of Lucifer, (2) compact with him, (3) obtaining the love of women by breathing upon them, (4) visiting the Black Sabbath, (5) celebration of Black Masses, etc.

violating the privileges of the sanctuary. They shewed how priests are killed, and the people remembered later on. A rabbi who witnessed the prodigies which went before the destruction of Jerusalem by Titus exclaimed: "O Holy Temple, what is it that possesses thee, and why frighten thyself in this manner?" Neither Chair of Peter nor bishops protested against the murder of Gaufridi, but the eighteenth century was to come, bringing the Revolution in its wake.

One of the possessed women[1] who had destroyed the curé of Accoules testified that the demon was leaving her to prepare the murder of another priest, whom she named prophetically in advance and in the absence of all personal knowledge: this was Urbain Grandier. It was then the reign of that terrible Cardinal de Richelieu, for whom absolute authority alone could guarantee the salvation of states; unfortunately his tendencies were political and subtle rather than truly Christian. One limitation which characterised this great man was a certain narrowness of heart, which made him sensible to personal offence and also implacable in revenge. And further, that which he was least ready to pardon in talent was independence; while he preferred men of parts for auxiliaries rather than flatterers, he took a certain pleasure in destroying whatsoever desired to shine apart from him. His ambition was to dominate all; Father Joseph was his right hand and Laubardemont his left.

There was then in the provinces, at Loudun, an ecclesiastic of remarkable genius and exalted character, possessed also of learning and talent but lacking in circumspection. Made to please multitudes and attract the sympathies of the great, he might on occasion have become a dangerous partisan; protestantism was at that period bestirring in France, and the curé of St. Peter's at Loudun, predisposed to the new ideas by his dislike of ecclesiastical celibacy, might prove at the head of such a party a preacher more brilliant than Calvin and not less daring than Luther. He was named Urbain Grandier. Serious differences with his bishop had already given instances of his ability and his inflexible character, but by mischance it was maladroit ability, since from enemies who were powerful he had appealed to the King and not, unhappily, to the Cardinal. The King held that he was right, but it remained for the Cardinal to teach him how far he was wrong. Grandier meanwhile had gone back in triumph to Loudon, and had indulged in the unclerical display of entering the town bearing a branch of laurel. From that time he was lost.[2]

The Lady Superior of the Ursuline nuns at Loudun was named Mother Jeanne des Anges in religion, otherwise Jeanne de Belfiel, grand-daughter

---

[1] Louise is heard of no further in the history of the period. Madeleine was cast out by her family and lived on alms at Avignon, till in 1653 the Parliament of Aix condemned her to perpetual seclusion.

[2] The historical facts are that Grandier insisted on one occasion in taking precedence of Richelieu, then Bishop of Luçon and in disgrace at Coussay. It is not even quite clear that the priest appealed to the King, but he was involved in much litigation on charges of immorality. It is just, however, to add that, according to Garinet, Grandier went to Paris and pleaded his cause before the King.

of the Baron de Cose. She could not be termed fervent in piety, and her convent was not to be ranked among the strictest in the country; in particular, nocturnal scenes took place which were attributed to spirits.[1] Relatives withdrew boarders, and the house was on the point of being denuded of all resources. Grandier was responsible for certain intrigues and was a little careless regarding them, while he was much too public a character for the idleness of a small town not to make a noise over his shortcomings. The pupils of the Ursulines heard them discussed mysteriously by their parents; the nuns spoke of them, deploring the scandal and dwelling over much upon him through whom it arose; of that which they talked by day they dreamed by night; and so it came about that at night they saw him appear in their dormitories under circumstances which were conformable with his alleged morals; they uttered cries, believed themselves obsessed, and in this manner the devil was let loose among them.

The directors of the nuns, who were mortal enemies of Grandier, did not fail to perceive the advantage they could draw from the affair in the interests of their rancour and in those of the convent.[2] They began to perform exorcisms—at first privately and afterwards in public. The friends of Grandier felt that there was a plot hatching, and were anxious that he should exchange his benefice, in order to leave Loudun, believing that everything would quiet down when he was gone. But Grandier was brave and could not tolerate yielding to calumny; he remained therefore and was arrested one morning as he entered his church, clothed in sacerdotal vestments. He was treated forthwith as a State prisoner; his papers were seized, seals were placed on his effects, and he was conducted, under a strong guard, to the fortress at Angers. Meanwhile a dungeon was prepared for him at Loudun which seemed intended for a wild beast rather than a man. Richelieu, informed of everything, had despatched Laubardemont to make an end of Grandier and forbade the parliament to take cognisance of the affair.

If the conduct of the Curé of Saint-Pierre had been that of a worldling, the demeanour of Grandier, a prisoner on a charge of Magic, was that of a hero and a martyr: so does adversity reveal great souls, and it is much easier to withstand suffering than prosperity. He wrote to his mother: "I bear my affliction with patience and pity yours more than my own. I am very unwell, having no bed; try to have mine brought me; for if the body does not rest the mind gives way. Send me also my breviary, a Bible, and St. Thomas for my consolation. For the rest, do not grieve; I hope that God will vindicate my innocence."[3]

There is no question that God does sooner or later take the part of persecuted innocence, but He does not invariably deliver it from enemies on earth, save indeed by death. This lesson was about to be learned by

[1] The first victim of the phenomena appears to have been the Lady Superior.
[2] The director of the convent was named Mignon, and he called to his assistance not only certain Carmelites but a secular priest of the district, who was a great believer in diabolical interventions.
[3] This letter is quoted by Garinet, pp. 218, 219.

Grandier. On our own part, do not let us represent men worse than they are in fact; his enemies did not believe in his innocence; they pursued him with fury, but he whom they pursued was for them a great criminal.

The phenomena of hysteria were little understood at the time, and somnambulism was quite unknown; the convulsions of nuns, the bodily motions exceeding all normal human power, their astonishing evidences of second sight, were things of a nature to convince the least credulous. A well-known atheist of the day, being the Sieur de Kériolet, counsellor in the parliament of Brittany, came to witness the exorcisms and to deride them. The nuns, who had never seen him, addressed him by name and published sins which he supposed to be unknown to anyone. He was so overwhelmed that he passed from one extreme to another, like all hot-headed natures; he shed tears, made his confession and dedicated his remaining days to the strictest asceticism.

The sophistry of the exorcists of Loudun was that absurd unreason which M. de Mirville has the courage to sustain at the present day: the devil is the author of all phenomena which cannot be explained by known laws of Nature. To this illogical maxim they joined another which was, so to speak, an article of faith: the devil who has been duly exorcised is compelled to speak the truth and can therefore be admitted as a witness in the cause of justice.

The unfortunate Grandier was not therefore delivered into the hands of malefactors but rather of raving maniacs, who, strong in their rectitude of conscience, gave the fullest publicity to this incredible prosecution. Such a scandal had never afflicted the Church—howling, writhing nuns, making the most obscene gestures, blaspheming, striving to cast themselves on Grandier like the Bacchantes on Orpheus; the most sacred things of religion mixed up with this hideous spectacle and drawn in the filth thereof; amidst all Grandier alone calm, shrugging his shoulders and defending himself with dignity and mildness; in fine, pallid, distraught judges, sweating profusely, and Laubardemont in his red robe, hovering over the conflict, like a vulture awaiting a corpse: such was the prosecution of Urbain Grandier.

Let us say for the honour of humanity that one is compelled to assume good faith in exorcists and judges alike, for such a conspiracy as would be involved in the legal murder of the accused is happily impossible. Monsters are as uncommon as heroes; the mass is composed of mediocrities, equally incapable of great virtues and great crimes. The holiest persons of the day believed in the possession at Loudun; even St. Vincent de Paul was not unacquainted with its history and was asked to give his opinion about it. Richelieu himself, though he might in any case have found some way of getting rid of Grandier, ended by believing him guilty. His death was the crime arising from the ignorance and prejudice of the period; it was a catastrophe rather than a murder.

We spare our readers the details of his tortures: he remained firm, resigned, patient, although confessing nothing; he did not even affect to despise his judges, but prayed mildly for the exorcists to spare him. "And you, my fathers," he said to them, "abate the rigour of my torments, and reduce not my soul to despair." Through this moan of complaining nature one discerns all the meekness of the Christian who forgives. To hide their emotion, the exorcists replied with invectives, and the executioners wept.[1] Three nuns, in one of their lucid moments, cast themselves before the tribunal, crying that Grandier was innocent, but it was believed that the devil was speaking by their mouth,[2] and their declaration only hastened the end. Urbain Grandier was burnt alive on August 18, 1634. He was patient and resigned to the end. When he was taken from the cart, his legs being broken, he fell heavily face down on the earth without uttering a single cry or groan. A Franciscan, named Father Grillau, squeezed through the crowd and raised up the sufferer, whom he embraced weeping, "I bring you," said he, "the blessing of your mother: she and I pray God for you."—"Thank you, my father," answered Grandier; "you alone pity me; console my poor mother and be a son unto her." The provost's lieutenant, deeply affected, then said to him: "Sir, forgive me the part I am compelled to take in your anguish." And Grandier answered: "You have not offended me and are obliged to fulfil the duties committed to your charge." They had promised to strangle him before the burning, but when the executioner sought to tighten the rope it proved to be knotted, and the unfortunate Curé de St. Pierre fell alive into the flames.

The chief exorcists, Fathers Tranquille and Lactance, died soon after in the delirium of violent frenzy; Father Surin, who succeeded them, became imbecile; Manoury, the surgeon who assisted at the torturing of Grandier, died haunted by the phantom of his victim. Laubardemont lost his son in a tragical manner and fell into disgrace with his master; the nuns remained idiots. So is it true that the question was one of a terrible and contagious malady, the mental disease of false zeal and false devotion. Providence punishes people by their own faults and instructs them by the sad consequences of their errors.

Ten years after the death of Grandier the Loudun scandals were renewed in Normandy, where the nuns of Louviers accused two priests of having bewitched them. Of these priests, one was already dead, but they violated the sanctity of the tomb to disinter his corpse. The details of the possession were identical with those of Loudun and Sainte-Baume. The hysterical women translated into foul language the nightmares of their directors. Both priests were condemned to the flames, and—to increase the horror—a living man and a corpse were bound to the same stake. The punishment of Mezentius, that fiction of a pagan poet, came so to be

---

[1] Notwithstanding the application of what was called the ordinary and extraordinary torture, no confession of guilt in respect of the charges was ever extracted from Grandier, who indeed refused to reply. Éliphas Lévi's picture of his deportment is throughout accurate as well as admirably told.

[2] This took place as stated, and, moreover, the inhabitants of the town, after a meeting in the town hall, wrote to the King complaining of the pretence, absurdity and vexation of the process. See Garinet, *Pièces Justificatives*, No. XVI.

realised by Christians; a Christian people assisted coldly at the sacrilegious execution, and the ministers did not realise that in thus profaning at once the priestly office and the dead, they gave a frightful precedent to impiety. When the call came, the eighteenth century arrived to extinguish the fires with the blood of priests, and, as it happens almost invariably, the good paid for the wicked. At the beginning of that century the burning of human beings still proceeded; though faith was dead, hypocrisy abandoned the youthful Labarre to the most horrible tortures because he refused to uncover when a procession went by. Voltaire was then in evidence and conscious in his heart of a vocation like that of Attila. While human passions were profaning religion, God sent this new destroyer to remove religion from a world which was no longer worthy of it.

In 1731 a young woman of Toulon, named Catherine Cadière, accused her confessor, the Jesuit Girard, of seduction and Magic. She was a stigmatised ecstatic who had long passed as a saint. Her history is one of lascivious swoons, secret flagellations and lewd sensations. Where is the sink of infamy with mysteries comparable to those of celibate imagination disordered by dangerous mysticism? The woman was not believed on her mere word and Father Girard escaped condemnation; the scandal for this reason was not less great, but the noise which it made was echoed by a burst of laughter: we have said that Voltaire was among us.

Superstitious people till then had explained extraordinary phenomena by the intervention of the devil and of spirits; equally absurd on its own part, the school of Voltaire, in the face of all evidence, denied the phenomena themselves. It was said by the one side that whatsoever we cannot explain comes from the devil; the answer on the other side was that the things which we cannot explain do not exist. By reproducing under analogous circumstances the same series of eccentric and wonderful facts, Nature protested in the one case against presumptuous ignorance and in the other against deficient science.

Physical disturbances have, in all times, accompanied certain nervous maladies; fools, epileptics, cataleptics, victims of hysteria have exceptional faculties, are subject to infectious hallucinations and produce occasionally, in the atmosphere or in surrounding objects, certain commotions and derangements. He who is hallucinated exteriorises his dreams and is tormented by his own shadow; the body is surrounded with its own reflections, distorted by the sufferings of the brain; the subject beholds his own image in the Astral Light; the powerful currents of that light, acting like a magnet, displace and overturn furniture; noises are then heard and voices sound as in dreams. These phenomena, so often repeated at this day that they have become common, were attributed by our fathers to phantoms and demons. Voltairian philosophy found it more easy to deny them, treating the ocular witnesses of the most incontestable facts as so many imbeciles and idiots.

What, for example, is better accredited than the extraordinary convulsions at the grave of Paris the deacon, or at the meetings of Saint-

Médard ecstatics? What is the explanation of the strange buffetings demanded by the convulsionaries? Blows rained by thousands on the head, compressions which would have crushed a hippopotamus, torsions of breasts with iron pincers, even crucifixion with nails driven into hands and feet? And then the superhuman contortions and levitations? The followers of Voltaire refused to see anything but sport and frolic therein; the Jansenists cried miracle; the true catholics sighed; science which should have intervened, and that only, to explain the fantastic disease, held aloof. It is to her nevertheless that there now belong the Ursulines of Loudun, the nuns of Louviers, the convulsionaries and the American mediums. The phenomena of magnetism have placed science on the path of new discoveries, and the coming chemical synthesis will lead our physicians to a knowledge of the Astral Light. When this universal force is once known, what will prevent them from determining the strength, number and direction of its magnets? A revolution will follow in science and there will be return to the Transcendental Magic of Chaldea.

Much has been talked about the presbytery of Cideville; De Mirville, Gougenot Desmousseaux and other uncritical believers have seen in the strange occurrences which took place therein a contemporary revelation of the devil; but the same things happened at Saint-Maur in 1706, and thither all Paris flocked. There were great rappings on walls, beds rocked without being touched, other furniture was displaced. The manifestations finished in a climax during which the master of the house, a young man of twenty-four or twenty-five years old, and a person of weak constitution, fell into a deep swoon and believed that he heard spirits speaking to him at great length, though he could never repeat subsequently a single word that they said.

One history of an apparition at the beginning of the eighteenth century may here follow; the simplicity of the account proves its authenticity; there are certain characteristics of truth which cannot be simulated by inventors.

A pious priest of Valognes, named Bézuel, was invited to dinner on January 7, 1708, by a lady related tò the Abbé de Saint-Pierre, the Abbé being also of the company, and the priest recounted, at their request, the appearance of one of his deceased comrades in open day, some twelve years previously. In 1695 he told them that he was a young scholar, about fifteen years old, and that he was acquainted with two lads, sons of Abaquène, a solicitor, who were scholars like himself. "The elder was my own age and the other, who was some eighteen months younger, was named Desfontaines; we walked together and shared our amusements; and whether or not Desfontaines had greater friendship for me, or was more lively, more affable, more intelligent than his brother, I know that I cared for him more. We were wandering in the cloister of the Capucins, in 1696, when he told me that he had been reading a story of two friends who had promised one another that whichever of them died first should bring news of his condition to him who survived; that one of them who did pass away redeemed his pledge and told the survivor astonishing things. Desfontaines then said that he had a favour to ask me, which was to make a similar promise, he doing likewise on his own part. I was, however, unwilling and indeed declined the proposal; several months passed away, during which he recurred frequently to the idea, I always resisting. About August 1696, when he was on the point of leaving to continue his studies at Caen, he pressed me so much, and with tears in his eyes, that at length I consented. He produced thereupon two little slips of paper on which he had written beforehand, one signed with his blood and in which he promised me, in the event of his death, to give me news of his state, the other in which I entered into a similar bond. I pricked my finger, and with the blood which issued therefrom I signed my own name. He was delighted to receive the promise and embraced me with a thousand thanks. Some time after he left, accompanied by his brother; the separation was grievous to both of us; we wrote from time to time, and then there was a silence for the space of six weeks, after which the event happened that I am about to relate. On July 31, 1697, being a Thursday and a day which I shall always remember, the late M. de Sortoville, with whom I lodged and who was always exceedingly good to me, begged me to go into a meadow adjoining the Franciscan monastery and help his people in haymaking. I had not been there for more than a quarter of an hour when, about half past two, I suddenly felt giddy and overcome with weakness. It was to no purpose that I tried to lean on my hay-fork; I felt obliged to lie down on the hay, and so remained for about half an hour, trying to recover my strength. The feeling passed away but, having never had such an experience previously, it caused me some surprise, and I feared that it was the beginning of an illness. I have no special recollection regarding the remainder of the day, but on the following night I slept less than usual.

"At the same hour next day, as I was walking in the meadow with M. de Saint-Simon, grandson of M. de Sortoville, then about ten years old, I was overcome in exactly the same way and sat down in the shade on a stone. It passed again and we continued our walk; nothing further occurred on that day and the next night I slept scarcely at all. Finally, on the morrow, being the second day of August, I was in the loft where they stacked the hay at precisely the same hour, when I was again seized with a similar giddiness and weakness, but more serious than before. I swooned and lost all consciousness. One of the servants saw me and asked what was the matter, to which it is said that I replied, stating that I had seen what I should have never believed. I do not, however, recollect either the question or answer. The memory which does remain with me is that I had seen someone in a state of nakedness to the waist, but it was not anyone whom I recognised. I was helped down the ladder; I held tight to the rungs; but when I saw Desfontaines, my comrade, at the foot of the ladder, the weakness returned, my head fell between two of the rungs and again I lost consciousness. I was laid upon a wide beam which served for a bench on the Grande Place des Capucins; I saw nothing of M. de Sortoville nor of his servants, though they were present, but I observed Desfontaines, still by the foot of the ladder, signalling for me to come to him, and I drew back on my seat as if to make room for him. Those who were by me, and whom I did not see, though my eyes were open, observed this movement. He did not respond and I rose to go towards him; he then came forward, and taking my left arm in his own right arm, he led me some paces forward into a quiet street, with arms still interlocked. The servants, thinking that my giddiness had passed and that I was going about some business of my own, went back to their work, with the exception of one youth, who told M. de Sortoville that I was talking to myself. He came up to me and heard me questioning and answering, as he has since told me. I was there for nearly three quarters of an hour, talking to Desfontaines, who said: 'I promised that if I died before you I would come and tell you. I was drowned the day before yesterday in the river at Caen. It was just about this time, and I was walking with some friends; it was exceedingly warm; we decided to bathe; a weakness came over me and I sank to the bottom. My companion, the Abbé de Menil-Jean, dived to bring me up. I caught hold of his leg, and as I clung very tight he may have thought that it was a salmon or he may have had to come up quickly, but he struck out so roughly with his leg that I received a blow upon the chest, throwing me again to the bottom, where the depth is considerable at that point!

"Desfontaines subsequently told me all that had happened in their walk and the subjects discussed between them. I was anxious to learn whether he was saved, whether he was damned, whether he was in purgatory, whether I was myself in a state of grace and whether I should follow him speedily; but he continued speaking as if he had not heard or refused to listen. I tried to embrace him several times, but I seemed to embrace nothing; yet I felt him still holding me tight by the arm, and when I attempted to turn away my head, so as not to see him because of the grief which it caused me, he tightened his grasp as if to compel me to look as well as to listen. He seemed taller than when I had last seen him and taller even than he was at the time of death, though he had grown a good deal during the eighteen months since we met. I saw him as far as his waist only and he was naked, his head bare and a white paper twisted in his beautiful fair hair over the forehead; the paper had writing on it, but I could read only the word: IN, etc. His voice was the same voice; he seemed neither gay nor sad, but in a calm and tranquil state. He begged me on his brother's return to give him certain messages for his father and mother; he begged me also to say the seven penitential psalms, which had been imposed on him as a penance the previous Sunday and which he had not yet recited. Finally, he again advised me to speak to his brother and then bade me farewell, saying as he went, 'Till I see you again,' which was our usual formula when we parted at the end of a walk. He told me also that at the time he was drowned his brother, who was making a translation, regretted having let him go apart from him, in case of an accident. He described so well where he was drowned, and the tree in the Avenue de Louvigny on which he had cut some words, that two years afterwards, when in the company of the late Chevalier de Gotot, one who was with him at the time, I pointed out the very spot, and counting the trees on one side, as Desfontaines had specified, I went straight to the tree, there to find the inscription. I learned also that it was true about the seven psalms which had been given him as a penance at confession. His brother also told me that he was writing his translation and reproached himself for not being with him.

"As a month went by before I was able to do as Desfontaines asked me in regard to his brother, he appeared to me on two other occasions before dinner in a country house a few miles away, to which I had been invited. Feeling unwell, I made an excuse of being tired, saying that it was nothing and that I should return. I went into a corner of the garden and Desfontaines reproached me for not having spoken to his brother; he talked to me for a quarter of an hour, but would not answer questions on my own part. The second appearance was in the morning, as I was going to Notre Dame de la Victoire, but the apparition was for a shorter time; be impressed on me about speaking to his brother and left me, repeating, 'Till I see you again'—still without answering my questions. One remarkable fact is that I always had a pain in the arm where he had taken a hold of me the first time, and it remained till I had spoken to his brother. For three days I had no sleep owing to the astonishment in which I was. After the first conversation I told M. de Varonville, my schoolfellow and neighbour, that Desfontaines had been drowned, that he had appeared to me and told me so. He hurried to his relations, asking whether this was true; they had just had news on the subject, but, owing to a misunderstanding, believed that it was the elder boy. He assured me that he had seen the letter of Desfontaines and he thought that this was correct; I maintained that it must be wrong, for Desfontaines himself had appeared to me. He went again to his relatives and returned in tears saying: 'It is only too true.'

"Nothing has happened to me since, and such was my experience simply. It has been told in many ways, but I have never related it otherwise than as I do now. The late Chevalier de Gotot stated that Desfontaines also appeared to M. de Menil-Jean, but I do not know him. He is fifty miles from here, near Argentan, and I can tell you no more."

We should notice the characteristics of dream which prevail throughout in this vision of a man who is awake, but in a state of semi-asphyxiation produced by the emanations of the hay. The astral intoxication following congestion of the brain will be recognised. The somnambulistic condition which followed showed M. Bézuel the last living reflection left by his friend in the Astral Light. He was naked and was visible down to the waist only, because the rest of his body was immersed in the water of the river. The supposed paper in his hair was probably a handkerchief used to confine his hair when bathing. Bézuel had further a somnambulistic intuition of all that took place, and it seemed to him that he was learning it from the lips of his friend. The friend appeared neither sad nor gay, an indication of the impression made upon him by an image which was lifeless and consisting only of reminiscence and reflection. On the occasion of the first vision, M. Bézuel, intoxicated by the scent of the hay, fell off the ladder and injured his arm; it seemed, with the logic of dreams, that his friend was grasping the arm, and when he came to himself he still felt the pain, which is explained quite naturally by the hurt that he had received. For the rest, the conversation of the deceased person was simply retrospective; there was nothing about death or the other life, proving once more how impossible is the barrier which separates this world from the next.

In the prophecy of Ezekiel life is represented by wheels which turn within one another; the elementary forms are symbolised by four beasts, which ascend and descend with the wheel and pursue one another without ever overtaking, like the signs of the Zodiac. The wheels of perpetual movement never return on themselves; forms never go back to the stations which they have quitted; to return whence one has come, the entire circle must have been traversed in a progress always the same and yet always new. The conclusion is that whatsoever manifests to us in this life is a phenomenon which belongs to this life and it is not given here below to our thought, to our imagination, or even to our hallucinations and our dreams, to overstep even for an instant the formidable barriers of death.

CHAPTER VII

THE MAGICAL ORIGIN OF FREEMASONRY

THAT great Kabalistical association known in Europe under the name of Masonry appeared suddenly in the world when revolt against the Church had just succeeded in dismembering Christian unity. The historians of the Order are one and all in a difficulty when seeking to explain its origin. According to some, it derived from a certain guild of Masons who were incorporated for the construction of the cathedral of Strasburg. Others refer its foundation to Cromwell, without pausing to consider whether the Rites of English Masonry in the days of the Protector were not more probably developed as a counterblast to this leader of Puritanical anarchy. In fine, some are so ignorant that they attribute to the Jesuits the maintenance and direction, if not indeed the invention, of a society long preserved in secret and always wrapped in mystery.[1] Setting aside this last view, which refutes itself, we can reconcile the others by admitting that the Masonic Brethren borrowed their name and some emblems of their art from the builders of Strasburg cathedral, and that their first public manifestation took place in England, owing to radical institutions and in spite of Cromwell's despotism. It may be added that the Templars were their models, the Rosicrucians their immediate progenitors,[2] and the Johannite sectarians their more remote ancestors. Their doctrine is that of Zoroaster and of Hermes, their law is progressive initiation, their principle is equality—regulated by the hierarchy and universal fraternity. They are successors of the school of Alexandria, as of all antique initiations, custodians of the secrets of the *Apocalypse* and the *Zohar*. Truth is the object of their worship, and they represent truth as light; they tolerate all forms of faith, profess one philosophy, seek truth only, teach reality, and their plan is to lead all human intelligence by gradual steps into the domain of reason. The allegorical end of Freemasonry is the rebuilding of Solomon's Temple; the real end is the restoration of social unity by an alliance between reason and faith and by reverting to the principle of the hierarchy,[3] based on science and virtue, the path of initiation and its ordeals serving as steps of ascent. Nothing, it will be seen, is more beautiful, nothing greater than are such ideas and dedications; unhappily the doctrines of unity and submission to the hierarchy have not been maintained in universal Masonry. In addition to that which was orthodox there

---

[1] This remark, in which I concur unreservedly, may be noted by students of Masonic history as an offset against the pretentious nonsense which has been talked on the subject by French makers of fable and especially by J. M. Ragon, the dullest and most imbecile of all.

[2] This opinion is showing signs of recrudescence at the present day, and it is well to say that there is no evidence to support it.

[3] It may be mentioned that Masonry, wheresoever established, is elective and not hierarchical.

arose a dissident Masonry, and all that is worst in the calamities of the French Revolution were the result of this schism.

Now, the Freemasons have their sacred legend, which is that of Hiram, completed by another concerning Cyrus and Zerubbabel. The legend of Hiram is as follows. When Solomon projected his Temple, he entrusted the plans to an architect called Hiram. This master builder, to ensure order in the work, divided the craftsmen according to their degrees of skill. They were a great multitude, and in order to recognise craftsmen, so that they might be classified according to merit or remunerated in proportion to their work, he provided Pass-Words and particular Signs for each of three categories, or otherwise for the Apprentices, the Companions and the Masters. It came about that three Companions coveted the rank of Master without having earned it by their ability. They set an ambush at the three chief gates of the Temple, and when Hiram was issuing from one of them, the first of these Companions demanded the Master-Word, threatening the architect with his rule. Hiram answered: "It is not thus that I received it." Thereupon the Companion in his fury struck him with the iron tool and gave him the first wound. The builder fled to the second gate, where he met with the second Companion, who made the same demand and received the same answer. On this occasion Hiram was struck with a square òr, as others say, with a lever. At the third gate there stood the third assassin, who completed the work with a mallet. The three companions concealed the corpse under a heap of rubbish, planted on the improvised grave a branch of acacia, and then took flight like Cain after the murder of Abel. Solomon, however, finding that his architect did not return, sent nine Masters to seek him, when the branch of acacia revealed the corpse. They drew it from beneath the rubbish, and as it had laid long therein, they uttered in so doing a word signifying that the flesh was falling from the bones. The last offices were rendered duly to Hiram, and twenty-seven Masters were despatched subsequently by Solomon in search of the murderers. The first of these was taken by surprise in a cavern; a lamp was burning near him, a stream flowed at his feet and a dagger lay for his defence beside him. The Master who had been first to enter recognised the assassin, seized the weapon and stabbed him with the exclamation *Nekam*—a word signifying vengeance. The head was carried to Solomon, who shuddered at the sight and said to the avenger: "Unhappy being, did you not know that I reserved to myself the right of punishment?" Then all the Masters fell on their knees before the king and entreated pardon for him whose zeal had carried him away. The second murderer was betrayed by one with whom he had found an asylum. He was concealed in a rock near to a burning bush; a rainbow shone above the rock, and a dog lay near him. Eluding the vigilance of the dog, the Masters seized the criminal, bound and carried him to Jerusalem, where he perished in the utmost tortures. The third assassin was slain by a lion, and the beast had to be overcome before the body could be secured. Other versions say that he defended himself with a hatchet when the Masters fell upon him, but they succeeded in disarming him and he was led to Solomon, who caused him to expiate his crime.[1]

Such is the first legend and its explanation now follows. Solomon personifies supreme science and wisdom. The Temple is the realisation and emblem of the hierarchic reign of truth and reason on earth. Hiram is the man who, by science and wisdom, has attained empire. He governs by justice and order, rendering to each according to his works. Each Degree is in correspondence with a word, which expresses the sense thereof. For Hiram the word is one, but it is expressed after three manners. One is for the Apprentices and can be uttered by them; it signifies Nature and is explained by Work. Another is for the Companions; in their case it signifies thought and is explained by Study. The third is for Masters; in their mouth it signifies truth and is explained by Wisdom. As to the word itself, it is used to designate God, Whose true name is indicible and incommunicable. Thus there are three degrees in the hierarchy and three entrances of the Temple; there are three modes of light and there are three forces in Nature, which forces are symbolised by the Rule that measures, the Lever which lifts and the Mallet which consolidates. The rebellion of brutal instincts against the hierarchic aristocracy of wisdom arms itself successfully with these three forces and turns them from their proper uses. There are three typical rebels—the rebel against Nature, the rebel against Science and the rebel against Truth. They were represented in the classical Hades by the three heads of Cerberus; in the Bible by Koran, Dathan and Abiram; while in the Masonic legend they are distinguished by names which vary in the different Rites. The first, who is usually called Abiram, or the murderer of Hiram, is he who strikes the Grand Master with the rule; this is the story of the just man immolated by human passion under the pretence of law. The second, named Mephibosheth, after a ridiculous and feeble pretender to the throne of David, attacks Hiram with the lever or the square. So does the popular square or lever of insensate equality become an instrument of tyranny in the hands of the multitude, and assails, still more grievously than the rule, the royalty of wisdom and virtue. The third in fine despatches Hiram with a mallet: so act the brutal instincts when they seek to establish order, in the name of violence and of fear, by crushing intelligence.[2]

The branch of acacia over the tomb of Hiram is like the cross on our altars; it is a sign of knowledge which outlives knowledge itself; it is the green sprig which presages another spring. When men have disturbed in this manner the order of Nature, Providence intervenes to restore it, as Solomon to avenge the death of the Master Builder. He who has struck with the rule shall perish by the poignard. He who has attacked with the lever or square shall make expiation under the axe of the law: it is the

[1] The Legend of Hiram has been told after several manners. English Masons will see that the present version is utterly incorrect, and it may be added further that it incorporates reveries borrowed from old High Grades.

[2] The names ascribed to the three assassins are High Grade inventions, and so also is all that follows concerning them.

eternal judgment on regicides. He who has slain with the mallet shall be the victim of that power which he misused. He who would slay with the rule is betrayed by the very lamp which lights him and by the stream from which he drinks: it is the law of retaliation. He who would destroy with the lever is surprised when his watchfulness fails like a sleeping dog, and he is given up by his own accomplices, for anarchy is the mother of treason. He who struck with the mallet is devoured by the lion, which is a variant of the sphinx of Œdipus, while he who can conquer the lion shall deserve to succeed Hiram. The decaying body of the Builder indicates that forms may change but the spirit remains. The spring of water in the vicinity of the first murderer recalls that deluge which punished crimes against Nature. The burning bush and rainbow which betray the second assassin typify life and light denouncing outrage on thought. Finally, the vanquished lion represents the triumph of mind over matter and the definite subjection of force to intelligence. From the dawn of the intellectual travail by which the Temple of unity is erected, Hiram has been slain often, but ever he has risen from the dead. He is Adonis destroyed by the wild boar, Osiris put to death by Typhon, Pythagoras in his proscription, Orpheus torn to pieces by Bacchantes, Moses abandoned in the caverns of Mount Nebo, Jesus crucified by Judas, Caiaphas and Pilate. Now those are true Masons who seek persistently to rebuild the Temple in accorance with the plan of Hiram.

Such is the great and the chief legend of Masonry; there are others that are no less beautiful and no less profound; but we do not feel justified in divulging their mysteries. Albeit we have received initiation only from God and our researches,[1] we shall keep the secrets of transcendental Freemasonry as we keep our own secrets. Having attained by our efforts to a grade of knowledge which imposes silence, we regard ourselves as pledged by our convictions even more than by an oath. Science is a *noblesse qui oblige*, and we shall in no wise fail to deserve the princely crown of the Rosy Cross. We also believe in the resurrection of Hiram.

The Rites of Masonry are designed to transmit a memorial of the legends of initiation and to preserve them among the Brethren. Now, if Masonry is thus holy and thus sublime, we may be asked how it came to be proscribed and condemned so often by the Church; but we have already replied to this question when its divisions and profanations were mentioned. Masonry is the Gnosis and the false Gnostics caused the condemnation of the true. The latter were driven into concealment, not through fear of the light, for the light is that which they desire, that which they seek and adore; but they stood in dread of the sacrilegious—that is to say, of false interpreters, calumniators, the derision of the sceptic, the enemies of all belief and all morality. Moreover, at the present day, there are many who think that they are Masons and yet do not know the meaning of their

[1] It is understood that Éliphas Lévi entered Masonry in the ordinary way, but it is quite true that vital integration therein and real understanding thereof are consequences of personal work.

Rites, having lost the Key of the Mysteries. They misconstrue even their symbolical pictures and those hieroglyphic signs which are emblazoned on the carpets of their Lodges. These pictures and signs are the pages of a book of absolute and universal science. They can be read by means of the Kabalistic keys and hold nothing in concealment for the initiate who already possesses those of Solomon.

Masonry has not merely been profaned but has served as the veil and pretext of anarchic conspiracies depending from the secret influence of the vindicators of Jacques de Molay, and of those who continued the schismatic work of the Temple. In place of avenging the death of Hiram they have avenged that of his assassins. The anarchists have resumed the rule, square and mallet, writing upon them the words Liberty, Equality, Fraternity—Liberty, that is to say, for all the lusts, Equality in degradation and Fraternity in the work of destruction. Such are the men whom the Church has condemned justly and will condemn for ever.

BOOK VI

MAGIC AND THE REVOLUTION

VAU

CHAPTER I

REMARKABLE AUTHORS OF THE EIGHTEENTH CENTURY

CHINA was practically unknown to the outside world until the end of the seventeenth century, when its vast empire, explored in part by our missionaries, began to be revealed by them and appeared like a necropolis of all sciences in the past. The Chinese may be compared to a race of mummies; nothing progresses with them, for they live in the immobility of their traditions, from which the spirit and the life have long since withdrawn. They know nothing any longer, but they have a vague recollection of everything. The genius of China is the dragon of the Hesperides—which defends the golden apples in the garden of science. Their human type of divinity, instead of conquering the dragon, like Cadmus, cowers fascinated and magnetised by the monster who flashes before it a changing mirage of its scales. Mystery alone is alive in China, science is in a state of lethargy, or at least is in a deep sleep and speaks only in dream. We have said that the Chinese Tarot is based on the same Kabalistic and absolute data as the Hebrew *Sepher Yetzirah*; but China has also a hieroglyphical book consisting exclusively of combinations of two figures; this is the *Y-Kim*,[1] attributed to the emperor Fo-Hi, and M. de Maison, in his *Letters on China*, states that it is utterly indecipherable. Its difficulties, however, are not greater than those of the *Zohar*, of which it appears to be a curious complement and is indeed a valuable appendix thereto. The *Zohar* explains the work of the Balance, or of universal equilibrium, and the *Y-Kim* is the hieroglyphic and ciphered demonstration thereof. The key of the work is a pantacle known as the Trigrams of Fo-Hi. According to a legend related in the *Vay-Ky*, a collection of great authority in China, composed by Leon-Tao-Yuen, under the dynasty of the Soms, some seven or eight hundred years ago, the emperor Fo-Hi was meditating one day on the bank of a river about the great secrets of Nature, when he saw a sphinx come out of the water, meaning an allegorical animal, having the composite form of a horse and a dragon. Its head was elongated like that of a horse, it

[1] It has been called the most ancient of all the Chinese books, being ascribed to the year 3468 B.C. It consists of 10 chapters.

had four feet and ended in the tail of a serpent; the back was covered with scales, on each of which there shone the symbol of the mysterious Trigrams; they were smaller towards the extremities than those on the breast and back, but were in perfect harmony throughout. The dragon was reflected in the water but with all its characteristics inverted. This serpentine horse, the inspirer or rather the bearer of inspirations, like the Pegasus of Greek mythology, that symbol of universal light, or like the serpent of Kronos, initiated Fo-Hi into universal science. The Trigrams served as the introduction; he numbered the scales and combined the Trigrams in such a manner that he conceived a synthesis of the sciences compared and united with one another by the pre-existent and necessary harmonies of Nature. The tables of the *Y-Kim* were the result of this marvellous combination. The numbers of Fo-Hi are the same as those of the Kabalah, while his pantacle is analogous to that of Solomon, as explained already in our *Doctrine and Ritual of Transcendental Magic*.[1] His tables correspond to the thirty-two Paths and the fifty Gates of Light; consequently the *Y-Kim* cannot be obscure for those who have the key of the *Sepher Yetsirah* and *Zohar*.[2]

The science of absolute philosophy has therefore existed in China; the Kims are commentaries on this Absolute which is hidden from the profane, and their relation to the *Y-Kim* is like that of the Pentateuch of Moses to the Revelations in the *Sepher Dzenioutha*, which is the *Book of Mysteries* and the key of the Hebrew *Zohar*.[3] Kong-fu-tzee, or Confucius, was the revealer or veiler of this Kabalah, the existence of which he might have denied, to turn the researches of the profane into a wrong path, just as that learned Talmudist Maimonides denied the realities of the Key of Solomon. After Confucius came the materialistic Fo, who substituted the traditions of Indian sorcery for the remnants of Egyptian Transcendental Magic. The cultus of Fo paralysed the progress of the sciences in China, and the abortive civilisation of this great people collapsed into routine and stupor.

A philosopher of sagacity and admirable profundity, the learned Leibnitz, who deserved most assuredly initiation into the supreme truths of absolute science, thought that he could discern in the *Y-Kim* his own discovery of the differential calculus, while in the straight and divided line he recognised the characters 1 0, employed in his own calculations. He was on the threshold of the truth, but, seeing it in only one of its details, he could not grasp it as a whole.

The most important discoveries on religious antiquities in China have

---

[1] See my translation of this work: *Transcendental Magic: Its Doctrine and Ritual*, 1896.

[2] It will be observed and appreciated at its proper value that Éliphas Lévi does not attempt to elucidate the Chinese puzzle of which he claims to possess the key, and the explanation is that if he had known his subject critically he would not have attempted to create Zoharic analogies which in the nature of things are non-existent.

[3] The *Book of Concealed Mystery* is not a key to the *Zohar*; it is one of the tracts inserted therein and its influence on the text at large is almost *nil*.

been the result of theological disputes.[1] This came about through the question whether the Jesuits were justified in permitting the worship of heaven and ancestral worship among the Chinese who were converted to Christianity—in other words, whether the educated Chinese regarded their heaven as God or simply as space and Nature. It was reasonable to have recourse to the educated themselves and to public good sense, but these do not constitute theological authorities. There was therefore much debate, much writing and more intriguing; the Jesuits were fundamentally right but were wrong in their mode of procedure, with the result that fresh difficulties were created which have not been yet overcome and which still continue in China to cost the blood of our indefatigable martyrs.

Whilst the conquests of religion in Asia were thus disputed, a great spirit of unrest was agitating Europe; the Christian faith seemed on the point of being extinguished, though on every side there was a rumour of new revelations and miracles. A man who had a definite position in science and in the world otherwise, namely, Emmanuel Swedenborg, was astonishing Sweden by his visions, and Germany was swarming with new *illuminati*. Dissident mysticism conspired to replace the mysteries of hierarchic religion by mysteries of anarchy; a catastrophe was in preparation and was imminent. Swedenborg, the most sincere and the mildest among the prophets of false illuminism, was not for this less dangerous than the others. As a fact, the pretence that all men are called to communicate immediately with heaven[2] replaces regular religious instruction and progressive initiation by every divagation of enthusiasm, by all excesses of imagination and of dream. The intelligent *illuminati* felt that religion was a great need of humanity and hence must never be destroyed; not only religion itself but the fanaticism which it carries along with it as a fatal consequence of enthusiasm inspired by ignorance, were, however, to be used as arms for the overthrow of hierarchic Church authority, they recognising that from the war of fanaticism there would issue a new hierarchy, of which they hoped to be founders and chiefs. "You shall be as gods, knowing all without having the trouble of learning anything; you shall be as kings, possessing everything without the trouble of acquiring anything." Such, in a summary form, are the promises of the revolutionary spirit to envious multitudes. The revolutionary spirit is the spirit of death; it is the old serpent of Genesis, which notwithstanding it is the father of movement and of progress, seeing that generations are renewed only by death. It is for this reason that the Indians worship Siva, the pitiless destroyer, whose symbolical form was that of physical love and material generation.

The system of Swedenborg is no other than the Kabalah, *minus* the

[1] It will be noticed that this remark is not borne out by the instance which is supposed to illustrate it and that the lucubration on China is a curious preamble to a study of remarkable authors of the eighteenth century, who had nothing to do with China.
[2] Emmanuel Swedenborg never gave expression to this view, and in respect of the criticism as a whole, it must be remarked that the communications which came to him came unawares, his psychic states not being self-induced.

The Great Hermetic Arcanum

principle of hierarchy;[1] it is the temple without the key-stone and without base; it is a vast edifice, fortunately all airy and fantastic, for had anyone attempted to realise it on this earth it would collapse upon the head of the first child who sought, not indeed to overthrow it, but merely to lean against one of its chief pillars. To organise anarchy is the problem which the revolutionaries have undertaken to solve, and it is with them for ever; it is the rock of Sisyphus which will invariably fall back upon them. To exist for a single moment they are and will ever be compelled fatally to improvise a despotism having no other justification than necessity, and it is one which is blind and violent like anarchy. Emancipation from the harmonious monarchy of reason is attained only by passing under the disorderly dictatorship of folly.

The means proposed indirectly by Swedenborg for communication with the supernatural world constitute an intermediate state allied to dream, ecstasy and catalepsy. The illuminated Swede affirmed the possibility of such a state, without furnishing any intimation as to the practices necessary for its attainment.[2] Perhaps his disciples, in order to supply the omission, might have had recourse to Indian Ceremonial Magic, when a genius came forward to complete the prophetic and Kabalistic intuitions of Swedenborg by a natural thaumaturgy. This man was a German physician named Mesmer. It was he who had the glory of rediscovering, apart from initiation and apart from occult knowledge, the universal agent of light and its prodigies. His *Aphorisms*, which scholars of his time regarded as a bundle of paradoxes, will ultimately form a basis for the physical synthesis.[3]

Mesmer postulated two modes in natural being; these are substance and life, producing that fixity and movement which constitute the equilibrium of things. He recognised further the existence of a first matter, which is fluidic, universal, capable of fixity and motion; its fixation determines the constitution of substances, while its continual motion modifies and renews forms. This fluidic matter is active and passive; as passive it indraws and as active it projects itself. In virtue of this matter the world and those who dwell therein attract and repel; it passes through all by a circulation comparable to that of the blood. It maintains and renews the life of all beings, is the agent of their force and may become the instrument of their will. Prodigies are results of exceptional wills or energies. The phenomena of cohesion and elasticity, of density or subtlety in bodies,

---

[1] The Kabalah has no principles of the hierarchy; its one counsel is the study of the Doctrine, and that study continually brought forward new developments of the deep meanings which lay behind (*a*) the Law, (*b*) the prophets and (*c*) the historical books of the Old Testament. The *Zohar* presupposes throughout a widely diffused knowledge of its Secret Doctrine, as already intimated.

[2] He was the recipient of a revelation and was not concerned with assisting those whom he addressed to attain the interior states into which he entered himself. He was bent only on delivering the message which he had received.

[3] Éliphas Lévi refers to a work entitled *Mesmer—Mémoires et Aphorismes Suivis des Procédés d'Eslon*, 1846. The Aphorisms of Anton Mesmer have been frequently reprinted.

are produced by various combinations of these two properties in the universal fluid or first matter. Disease, like all physical disorders, is owing to a derangement in the normal equilibrium of the first matter in this or that organised body. Organised bodies are sympathetic or antipathetic to one another, by reason of their particular equilibrium. Sympathetic bodies may cure each other, restoring their equilibrium mutually. This capacity of bodies to equilibrate one another by the attraction or projection of the first matter was called magnetism by Mesmer, and as it varies according to the forms in which it acts, he termed it animal magnetism when he studied its phenomena in living beings.

Mesmer proved his theory by his experiments, which were crowned with complete success. Having observed the analogy between the phenomena of animal magnetism and those of electricity, he made use of metallic conductors, connecting with a common reservoir containing earth and water, so as to absorb and project the two forces. The complicated apparatus of tubs has now been abandoned, as it can be replaced by a living chain of hands superposed upon a circular non-conducting body like a wooden table, or on silk or wool. He subsequently applied to living organised beings the processes of metallic magnetisation and attained certitude as to the reality and similitude of the phenomena which followed. One step only was left for him to take, and it was to affirm that the effects attributed in physics to the four imponderable fluids are diverse manifestations of one and the same force differentiated by its usages, and that this force—inseparable from the first and universal matter which it sets in motion—now resplendent, now igneous, now electric, now magnetic, has but one name, indicated by Moses in Genesis, when he describes its manifestation by the *fiat* of the Almighty before all substances and all forms: that word is THE LIGHT—יהי אור•

Let us now have the courage to affirm one truth which will be acknowledged hereafter. The great thing of the eighteenth century is not the *Encyclopædia*, not the sneering and derisive philosophy of Voltaire, not the negative metaphysics of Diderot and D'Alembert, not the malignant philanthropy of Rousseau: it is the sympathetic and miraculous physics of Mesmer. Mesmer is grand as Prometheus; he has given men that fire from heaven which Franklin could only direct. There was wanting to the genius of Mesmer neither the sanction of hatred nor the consecration of persecution and insult; he was hunted out of Germany, ridiculed in France, which, however, provided him with a fortune, for his cures were evident, and the patients who went to him paid him, though they may have stated afterwards that their restoration was a matter of chance, so that they might not draw down upon themselves the hostility of the learned. The authorised bodies did not even so far honour the thaumaturge as to examine his discovery, and the great man resigned himself perforce to pass for a skilful impostor. It was only the really instructed who were not hostile to mesmerism; sincerely religious persons were alarmed by the dangers of the new discovery, while the superstitious cried out at the scandal and the Magic. The wise foresaw abuses; the imbecile would not so much as tolerate the exercise of this marvellous power. Some thought that the miracles of the Saviour and His saints would be denied in the name of magnetism; others wondered how it would fare with the power of the devil. True religion, notwithstanding, has nothing to fear from the discovery of truth; and, further, in putting a limit to human power, does not magnetism give a new sanction to divine miracles instead of destroying them? It follows that the fools will ascribe fewer prodigies to the devil, which will leave them the less opportunity to exercise their hatred and their rage; but persons of real piety will not find this a ground of complaint. The devil must lose ground when light manifests and ignorance recedes; but the conquests of science and of light extend, strengthen and increase more and more our love of the empire and the glory of God.

CHAPTER II

THAUMATURGIC PERSONALITIES OF THE EIGHTEENTH CENTURY

THE eighteenth century was credulous about nothing but Magic, and the explanation is that vague beliefs are the religion of souls devoid of true faith. The miracles of Jesus Christ were denied, while resurrections were ascribed to the Comte de Saint-Germain. This exceptional personality was a mysterious theosophist who was credited with possessing the secrets of the Great Work, and the manufacture of diamonds and of precious stones. For the rest, he was a man of the world, agreeable in conversation and highly distinguished in manners. Madame de Genlis, who saw him almost daily during his early years, says that even his representations of gems in pictures had a natural fire and gleam, the secret of which could not be divined by any chemist or painter. None of his pictures are in evidence, and it can only be speculated whether he had contrived to fix light on canvas or whether he employed a preparation of mother-of-pearl, or some metallic coating.

The Comte de Saint-Germain professed the Catholic Religion and conformed to its practices with great fidelity. This notwithstanding, there were reports of suspicious evocations and strange apparitions; he claimed also to have the secret of eternal youth. Was this mysticism or was it madness? His family connections were unknown and to hear him talk of past events suggested that he had lived for many centuries. Of all that was in kinship with occult science he said but little, and when the benefit of initiation was demanded at his hands he pretended to know nothing on the subject. He chose his own disciples, required passive obedience on their part and then talked of a royalty to which they were called, being that of Melchisedek and Solomon, a royalty of initiation, which is a priesthood at the same time. "Be the torch of the world," he said. "If your light is that only of a planet, you will be as nothing in the sight of God. I reserve for you a splendour, of which the solar glory is a shadow. You shall guide the course of stars and those who rule empires shall be governed by you."

These promises, the proper meaning of which is quite intelligible to true adepts, are recorded substantially, if not in the words here given, by the anonymous author of a *History of Secret Societies in Germany*,[1] and they are evidence as to the school of initiation with which the Comte de Saint-Germain was connected. The following details have been so far unknown concerning him.

---
[1] The reference is probably to a French work, which in the absence of date and fuller description cannot be identified with certainty.

The Comte de Saint-Germain was born at Lentmeritz in Bohemia at the end of the seventeenth century. He was either the natural or an adopted son of a Rosicrucian who called himself *Comes Cabalicus*—the Companion Kabalist—ridiculed under the name of Comte de Gabalis by the unfortunate Abbé de Villars.[1] Saint-Germain never spoke of his father, but he mentions that he led a life of proscription and errantry in a world of forest, having his mother as companion. This was at the age of seven years, which, however, is to be understood symbolically and is that of the initiate when he is advanced to the Grade of Master. His mother was the science of the adepts, while the forest, in the same kind of language, signifies empires devoid of the true civilisation and light. The principles of Saint-Germain were those of the Rosy Cross, and in his own country he established a society from which he separated subsequently when anarchic doctrines became prevalent in fellowships which incorporated new partisans of the Gnosis. Hence he was disowned by his brethren, was charged even with treason, and some memorials on illuminism seem to hint that he was immured in the dungeons of the Castle of Ruel. On the other hand, Madame de Genlis tells us that he died in the Duchy of Holstein, a prey to his own conscience and terrors of the life beyond.[2] It is certain in any case that he vanished suddenly from Paris, no one exactly knowing where, and that his companions in illumination permitted the veil of silence and oblivion to fall as far as possible upon his memory. The association which he had formed under the title of Saint-Jakin—which has been turned into Saint Joachim—continued till the Revolution, when it dissolved or was transformed, like so many others. A story is told concerning it in a pamphlet against illuminism; it is derived from a correspondence in Vienna, and, though it is worth reproducing, there is nothing that can be termed certain or authentic therein.

"Owing to your introduction, I had a cordial welcome from M. N. Z., who had been informed already of my arrival. Of the harmonica he approved highly. He spoke first of all about certain trials, but of this I understood nothing; it is of late only that I have been able to grasp the meaning. Yesterday, towards evening, I accompanied him to his country

[1] The writer in question certifies (a) that the Comte de Gabalis was a German, (b) that he was a great nobleman and a great Kabalist, (c) that his lands were on the frontiers of Poland, (d) that he was a man of good presence who spoke French with a foreign accent. Saint-Germain testified on his own part to Prince Karl of Hesse that he was the son of Prince Ragoczy of Transylvania. Perhaps the latter place will be regarded as sufficiently in proximity to Poland to make the story of Éliphas Lévi a little less unlikely than it appears on the surface. But the prince in question was Franz-Leopold Ragoczy, who spent his life in conspiracies against the Austrian Empire, "with the object of regaining his independent power" and the freedom of his principality. No more unlikely person can be thought of as the original of the ridiculous Comte de Gabalis, and the Comte de Saint-Germain never intimated that he belonged to a line of Kabalists, least of all such a Kabalist and occultist as is depicted by the Abbé de Villars. See Mrs. Cooper Oakley's *Monograph on the Comte de St. Germain*, Milan, 1912.
[2] See Madame la Comtesse de Genlis: *Mémoires Inédites pour servir à l'Histoire des XVIIIme et XIXme Siècles*.

house, the grounds of which are very beautiful. Temples, grottos, cascades, labyrinths, caves form a long vista of enchantments; but an exceedingly high wall which encompasses the whole pleasaunce was extremely displeasing to me, for beyond this there is also a wonderful prospect. . . . I had brought the harmonica with me, at the instance of M. N. Z., with the idea of playing on it for a few minutes in a place indicated, and on receiving an agreed signal.[1] The visit to the garden over, he took me to a room in the front of the house and there left me, somewhat quickly and under a trivial pretext. It was now very late; he did not return; weariness and the wish to sleep began to come over me, when I was interrupted by the arrival of several coaches. I opened the window, but, being night, I could see nothing, and I was much puzzled by the low and mysterious whispering of those who seemed entering the house. Sleep now overcame me, and an hour must have passed away, when I was awakened by a servant who was sent to conduct me and also carry the instrument. He walked very quickly and far in advance of myself, I following mechanically, when I heard the sound of horns, which seemed to issue from the depths of a cave. At this moment I lost sight of my guide and, proceeding in the direction from which the noise seemed to be coming, I half descended a staircase leading to a vault, from which, to my utter surprise, a funeral chant arose, and I saw distinctly a corpse in an open coffin.

"On one side stood a man, clothed in white covered with blood; it appeared to me that a vein had been opened in his right arm. With the exception of those who were helping him, all present were shrouded in long black mantles and were armed with drawn swords. So far as I could judge in my state of terror, the entrance to the vault was strewn with human bones, heaped one upon another. The only light which illuminated the mournful spectacle was that of a flame, such as is produced by spirits of wine.

"Uncertain whether I should be able to overtake my guide, I retreated hurriedly and found him in search of myself a few paces away; there was a haggard look in his eyes, and taking my hand in rather an uneasy manner, he led me into a singular garden, where I began to think that I must have been transported by magic. The brilliance produced by a vast number of lamps, the murmur of falling waters, the singing of mechanical nightingales and the perfume which seemed to exhale everywhere exalted my imagination at the outset. I was hidden behind a green arbour, the interior of which was richly decorated, and thither they brought immediately a person in a fainting state, apparently the one who had occupied the coffin in the vault. It was at this point that I received the agreed signal to play my instrument. Disturbed very much by the whole scene, there

---

[1] See the *Essai sur la Secte des Illuminés*, which appeared anonymously in 1789, the author being the Marquis de Luchet. The story here reproduced is given in Note XV to the essay in question. It affirms that the Order of Initiated Knights and Brethren of Asia became the Order of St. Joachim about 1786. There is no mention of Saint-Germain in this Note.

is no doubt that a good deal escaped me,[1] but I could see that the swooning person came to himself as soon as I touched the harmonica; he also began to ask questions with an accent of astonishment, saying: 'Where am I? What is this voice?' Shouts of joy, accompanied by trumpets and timbrels, were the only answer. Everyone ran to arms and plunging into the depths of the garden were quickly out of sight. I am still in agitation as I write these lines; and if I had not taken the precaution to make my notes on the spot, I should regard it today as a dream."

The most inexplicable part of this scene is the presence of the uninitiated person who tells the story. How the association could thus risk the betrayal of its mysteries is a question that cannot be answered, but the mysteries themselves can be explained easily.[2] The successors of the old Rosicrucians, modifying little by little the austere and hierarchic methods of their precursors in initiation, had become a mystic sect and had embraced zealously the Templar magical doctrines, as a result of which they regarded themselves as the sole depositaries of the secrets intimated by the Gospel according to St. John. They regarded the narratives of that Gospel as an allegorical sequence of rites designed to complete initiation, and they believed that the history of Christ must be realised in the person of each one of the adepts. Furthermore, they recounted a Gnostic legend, according to which the Saviour, instead of being buried in the new tomb of Joseph of Arimathea, having been swathed and perfumed, was brought back to life in the house of St. John. This was the pretended mystery which they celebrated to the sound of horns and harmonica.[3] The Candidate was invited to offer up his life and was actually subjected to bleeding which caused him to swoon. This swoon was called death, and when he returned to himself his resurrection was celebrated amidst outbursts of joy and gladness. The varied emotions produced, the scenes, by turns mournful and brilliant, must have permanently impressed the candidate's imagination, and rendered him either fanatical or lucid. Many believed that a real resurrection took place in themselves and felt convinced that

---

[1] Éliphas Lévi explains in a note that the neophyte whose experience is related, and who was mistaken for a corpse, was in a state of somnambulism induced by magnetism. In respect of the green arbour, and the effects produced by the harmonica, he refers to Deleuze: *Histoire Critique du Magnétisme Animal*, 2nd edition, 1829. It contains curious accounts of the magnetic chain and trough, magnetised trees, music, the voice of the mesmerist and the instruments employed by him. Lévi adds that the author was a partisan of mesmerism, which does not leave his opinions open to suspicion. I do not know what this is intended to convey, but the work of Deleuze was of authority in its own day and is still worth reading.

[2] It will be observed that Éliphas Lévi is taking the story more seriously than he proposed to do at the beginning. If therefore I may on my own part take the Marquis de Luchet for a moment in the same manner and assume that he was right in saying that the Order of Saint Joachim was a transformation of the Knights and Brethren of Asia, it seems certain that the latter did not owe their origin to Saint-Germain and that their connection with Rosicrucianism was of the Masonic kind only, members of the fifth degree being called True Brothers Rose Croix, otherwise Masters of the Sages, Royal Priests, and Brothers of the Grade of Melchisedek.

[3] Compare the ribaldries of the Marquis de Luchet respecting the Harmonica and his supplementary account of its use in the evocations of Lavâter.

MAGIC AND THE REVOLUTION

they were no longer subject to death. The heads of the society thus had at the service of their concealed projects the most formidable of all instruments, namely madness, and secured on the part of their adepts that blind and tireless devotion which unreason produces more often and more surely than goodwill.

The sect of Saint-Jakin was therefore an order of Gnostics steeped in the illusions of the Magic of Fascination; it drew from Rosicrucians and Templars; and its particular name was one of the two names—*Jachin* and *Boaz*—engraven on the chief pillars of Solomon's Temple. In Hebrew the initial letter of *Jachin* is *Yod*, a sacred letter of the Hebrew alphabet, and also the initial of Jehovah, which Divine Name was indeed veiled from the profane under that of *Jachin*, whence the designation Saint-Jakin. The members of this order were theosophists, unwisely addicted to theurgic processes.[1]

All that is told of the mysterious Comte de Saint-Germain supports the idea that he was a skilful physician and a distinguished chemist. He is said to have known how to fuse diamonds so that there was no trace of the operation; he could also purify precious stones, thus making the most common and imperfect of high value. That imbecile and anonymous author[2] whom we have already cited places the latter claim to his credit but denies that he ever made gold, as if one did not make gold in the making of precious stones. Saint-Germain also invented, according to the same authority, and bequeathed to the industrial sciences, the art of imparting greater brilliance and ductility to copper—another invention sufficient to prove the fortune of him who devised it. Performances of this kind make us forgive the Comte de Saint-Germain for having been acquainted with Queen Cleopatra and for chatting familiarly with the Queen of Sheba. He was otherwise good-natured and gallant; he was one who loved children and amused himself by providing them with delicious sweetmeats and marvellous toys; he was dark and of small stature, dressed richly but with great taste and cultivating all the refinements of luxury. He is said to have been received familiarly by Louis XV, and was engrossed with him over questions of diamonds and other precious stones. It is probable that this monarch, entirely governed by courtesans and given up to pleasure, was rather yielding to some caprice of feminine curiosity than to any serious concern for science when he invited Saint-

---

[1] *Jachin* is connected in Kabalism with the *Sephira Netzach*, because it is the right-hand pillar, and, on account of *Netzach*, *Jachin* is in correspondence with צבאות ירוד and צבאות י׳. The Divine Name *Tetragrammaton* cannot be said on Kabalistical authority to be veiled in *Netzach*. It was really veiled in Adonai because of *Shekinah*, and the cohabiting glory between the cherubim was the manifestation, vestment and concealment of Jehovah.

[2] There is no secret as to the authorship of the tract on Illuminism, and Lévi could have been enlightened on the subject by his friend, J. M. Ragon. So far from being imbecile, the monograph of the Marquis de Luchet is entertaining if it is not brilliant. As to the transmutations of Saint-Germain, it is meant that there is no evidence of gold being produced by his methods, but it is otherwise in respect of precious stones. For the exoneration of De Luchet it does not signify that the evidence is bad.

Germain to certain private audiences. The Comte was the fashion for a moment, and as he was an amiable and youthful Methuselah, who knew how to combine the tattle of a roué with the ecstasies of a theosophist, he was the rage in certain circles, though speedily replaced by other phantasiasts. So goes the world.

It is said that Saint-Germain was no other than that mysterious Althotas who was the Master in Magic of another adept with whom we are about to be occupied and who took the Kabalistic name of Acharat. The supposition has no foundation, as will be seen in due course.

Whilst the Comte de Saint-Germain was thus in request at Paris, another mysterious adept was on his way through the world, recruiting apostles for the philosophy of Hermes. He was an alchemist who called himself Lascaris and gave out that he was an Eastern archimandrite, charged with collecting alms for a Greek convent. The distinction was this, that instead of demanding money, Lascaris seemed occupied, so to speak, in sowing his path with gold and leaving the trail of it behind him wherever he went. His appearances were momentary only and his guises many; here he was old and in the next place still a young man. He did not make gold in public on his own part, but caused it to be made by his disciples, with whom he left at parting a little of the powder of projection. Nothing is better established than the transmutations operated by these emissaries of Lascaris. M. Louis Figuier, in his learned work on the alchemists, does not question either their reality or their importance. Now, in physics above all, there is nothing more inexorable than facts, and it must be therefore concluded from these that the Philosophical Stone is not a matter of reverie, if the vast tradition of occultism, the ancient mythologies and the serious researches of great men in all ages are not otherwise sufficient to establish its real existence.[1] A modern chemist, who had not failed to publish his secret, has arrived at the extraction of gold from silver by a ruinous process, for the silver sacrificed by him does not produce in gold more than the tenth of its value, or thereabouts. Agrippa, who never attained the universal dissolvent, was, notwithstanding, more fortunate than our chemist, for he did obtain gold which was equivalent in value to the silver employed in his process and did not therefore lose his labour absolutely, if to employ it in research after the grand secrets of Nature can be called loss.

To set men upon researches which might lead them to the absolute philosophy by the attraction of gold, such would appear to have been the end of the propaganda connected with the name of Lascaris; reflection on Hermetic books would of necessity lead those who studied to a knowledge of the Kabalah. As a fact, the initiates of the eighteenth

---

[1] See *L'Alchimie et les Alchimistes*, by Louis Figuier, pp. 320 *et seq*. I have intimated that it is very difficult to trust this writer in matters of historical fact, but he represents Lascaris as appearing in Germany at the end of the seventeenth century, being then about fifty years old, and in any case it is a mistake to say that he was in evidence when the Comte de Saint-Germain was making a sensation in Paris. Lascaris had long since vanished from the theatre of Hermetic events.

century thought that their time had come—some for the foundation of a new hierarchy, others for the subversion of an authority and for setting on the summits of the social order the level of equality. The Secret Societies sent their scouts throughout the world to sound opinion, and at need awaken it. After Saint-Germain and Lascaris came Mesmer, and Mesmer was succeeded by Cagliostro. But they were not all of the same school: Saint-Germain was the ambassador of illuminated theosophists, while Lascaris represented the naturalists attached to the tradition of Hermes. Cagliostro was the agent of the Templars, and this is how he came to announce, in a circular addressed to all Masons in London, that the time had come to build the Temple of the Eternal. Like the Templars, Cagliostro was addicted to the practices of Black Magic and to the fatal science of evocations. He divined past and present, predicted things to come, wrought marvellous cures and pretended to make gold. He introduced a new Rite under the name of Egyptian Masonry and sought to restore the mysterious worship of Isis. Wearing a *nemys* like that of the Theban sphinx, he presided in person over nocturnal assemblies, in chambers emblazoned with hieroglyphics and lighted by torches. His priestesses were young girls, whom he called doves, and he placed them in a condition of ecstasy by means of hydromancy in order to obtain oracles, water being an excellent conductor, a powerful reflector, and highly refracting medium for the Astral Light, as proved by sea and cloud mirages.

It is obvious that Cagliostro was a successor of Mesmer and had the key of mediumistic phenomena; he was himself a medium, meaning that he was a man whose nervous organisation was exceptionally impressionable, and to this he joined a fund of ingenuity and assurance, public exaggeration and the imagination—especially of women—supplying the rest. Cagliostro had an extravagant success; his bust was to be seen everywhere—inscribed "The Divine Cagliostro". A reaction equivalent to the enthusiasm was of course to be foreseen; after having been a god, he became an intriguer and impostor, the debaucher of his wife, a scoundrel in fine, to whom the Roman Inquisition shewed grace by merely condemning him to perpetual imprisonment. The fact that his wife sold him lends colour to the idea that previously he had sold his wife.[1] He was taken in a snare, his prosecution followed and his accusers published as much of the process as they pleased. The revolution came in the meantime, and everyone forgot Cagliostro.

This adept is, however, by no means without importance in the history of Magic; his Seal is as significant as that of Solomon and attests his initiation into the highest secrets of science. As explained by the Kabalistic letters of the names Acharat and Althotas, it expresses the chief characteristics of the Great Arcanum and the Great Work. It is a

---

[1] It was in the presence of the rack that the testimony of his wife was extracted, and I suppose that there is no one at this day who will count it as infidelity on her part.

serpent pierced by an arrow, thus representing the letter *Aleph*, an image of the union between active and passive, spirit and life, will and light. The arrow is that of the antique Apollo, while the serpent is the python of fable, the green dragon of Hermetic philosophy. The letter *Aleph* represents equilibrated unity. This pantacle is reproduced under various forms in the talismans of old Magic, but occasionally the serpent is replaced by the peacock of Juno, the peacock with the royal head and the tail of many colours. This is an emblem of analysed light, that bird of the *Magnum Opus*, the plumage of which is all sparkling with gold. At other times, instead of the emblazoned peacock, there is a white lamb, the young solar ram bearing the cross, as still seen in the armorial bearings of the city of Rouen. The peacock, the ram and the serpent have the same hieroglyphical meaning—that of the passive principle and the sceptre of Juno. The cross and arrow signify the active principle, will, magical action, the coagulation of the dissolvant, the fixation of the volatile by projection and the penetration of earth by fire. The union of the two is the universal balance, the Great Arcanum, the Great Work, the equilibrium of *Jachin* and *Boaz*. The initials L.P.D., which accompany this figure, signify Liberty, Power, Duty, and also Light, Proportion, Density; Law, Principle, and Right. The Freemasons have changed the order of these initials, and in the form of L∴D∴P∴[1] they render them as *Liberté de Penser*, Liberty of Thought, inscribing these on a symbolical bridge, but for those who are not initiated they substitute *Liberté de Passer*, Liberty of Passage. In the records of the prosecution of Cagliostro it is said that his examination elicited another meaning as follows: *Lilia destrue pedibus*: Trample the lilies underfoot; and in support of this version may be cited a Masonic medal of the sixteenth or seventeenth century, depicting a branch of lilies severed by a sword, having these words on the exergue: *Talem dabit ultio messem*—Revenge shall give this harvest.

The name Acharat, assumed by Cagliostro, is written Kabalistically thus: אש, אור, את, and expresses the triple unity: אש, the unity of principle and beginning; אור, the unity of life and perpetuity of regenerating movement; and את, the unity of end in an absolute synthesis.

The name Althotas, or that of Cagliostro's master, is composed of the word *Thot*, with the syllables *Al* and *As*, which, if read Kabalistically, are *Sala*, meaning messenger or envoy. The name as a whole therefore signifies: *Thot*, the messenger of the Egyptians, and such in effect was he whom Cagliostro recognised as his master above all others.[2]

Another title adopted by Cagliostro was that of the Grand Copht, and his doctrine had the twofold object of moral and physical regeneration. The precepts of moral regeneration according to the Grand Copht

[1] This device is inscribed on the symbolic bridge which is mentioned in the Grade of Knight of the East, or of-the Sword.

[2] According to the account of himself which Cagliostro gave at the famous trial arising out of the Diamond Necklace affair, Acharat was the name which he bore in the years of childhood which he spent at Medina. His "governor" was Althotas, who has been sometimes identified with Kölmer, the instructor of Weishaupt in Magic.

were as follows: "You shall go up Mount Sinai with Moses; you shall ascend Calvary; with Phaleg you shall climb Thabor, and shall stand on Carmel with Elias. You shall build your tabernacle on the summit of the mountain; it shall consist of three wings or divisions, but these shall be joined together and that in the centre shall have three storeys. The refectory shall be on the ground floor. Above it there shall be a circular chamber with twelve beds round the walls and one bed in the centre: this shall be the place of sleep and dreams. The uppermost room shall be square, having four windows in each of the four quarters; and this shall be the room of light. There, and alone, you shall pray for forty days and sleep for forty nights in the dormitory of the Twelve Masters. Then shall you receive the signatures of the seven genii and the pentagram traced on a sheet of virgin parchment. It is the sign which no man knoweth, save he who receiveth it. It is the secret character inscribed on the white stone mentioned in the prophecy of the youngest of the Twelve Masters. Your spirit shall be illuminated by divine fire and your body shall become as pure as that of a child. Your penetration shall be without limits and great shall be also your power; you shall enter into that perfect repose which is the beginning of immortality; it shall be possible for you to say truly and apart from all pride: I am he who is."

This enigma signifies that in order to attain moral regeneration, the transcendent Kabalah must be studied, understood and realised. The three chambers are the alliance of physical life, religious aspirations and philosophical light; the Twelve Masters are the great revealer, whose symbols must be understood; the signatures of the seven spirits mean the knowledge of the Great Arcanum. The whole is therefore allegorical, and it is no more a question of building a house of three storeys than a temple at Jerusalem in Masonry.

Let us now turn to the secret of physical regeneration, to attain which—according to the occult prescription of the Grand Copht—a retreat of forty days, after the manner of a jubilee, must be made once in every fifty years, beginning during the full moon of May, in the company of one faithful person only. It must be also a fast of forty days, drinking May-dew—collected from sprouting corn with a cloth of pure white linen —and eating new and tender herbs. The repast should begin with a large glass of dew and end with a biscuit or crust of bread. There should be slight bleeding on the seventeenth day. Balm of Azoth[1] should then be taken morning and evening, beginning with a dose of six drops and increasing by two drops daily till the end of the thirty-second day. At the dawn which follows thereafter renew the slight bleeding; then take to your bed and remain in it till the end of the fortieth day.

On the first awakening after the bleeding, take the first grain of

[1] In his *Lexicon Alchimiae*, 1612, Martinus Rulandus explains that, according to the system of Paracelsus, Azoth was the Universal Medicine, though for others it is one of the names ascribed to the Philosophical Stone. It was evidently neither in the process of Cagliostro, but—if questioned—he might have identified it with Philosophical Mercury, a substance which can be extracted from any metallic body.

Universal Medicine. A swoon of three hours will be followed by convulsions, sweats and much purging, necessitating a change both of bed and linen. At this stage a broth of lean beef must be taken, seasoned with rice, sage, valerian, vervain and balm. On the day following take the second grain of Universal Medicine, which is Astral Mercury combined with Sulphur of Gold. On the next day have a warm bath. On the thirty-sixth day drink a glass of Egyptian wine, and on the thirty-seventh take the third and last grain of Universal Medicine. A profound sleep will follow, during which the hair, teeth, nails and skin will be renewed. The prescription for the thirty-eighth day is another warm bath, steeping aromatic herbs in the water, of the same kind as those specified for the broth. On the thirty-ninth day drink ten drops of Elixir of Acharat in two spoonfuls of red wine. The work will be finished on the fortieth day, and the aged man will be renewed in youth.[1]

By means of this jubilary regimen Cagliostro claimed to have lived for many centuries. It will be seen that it is a variation of the famous Bath of Immortality in use among the Menandrian Gnostics.[2] The question is whether Cagliostro believed in it seriously. However this may be, before his judges he shewed much firmness and presence of mind, professing that he was a catholic who honoured the pope as supreme chief of the religious hierarchy. On matters relating to the occult sciences he replied enigmatically and when accused of being absurd and incomprehensible he told his examiners that they had no ground of judgment, at which they were offended, and ordered him to enumerate the seven deadly sins, Having recited lust, avarice, envy, gluttony and sloth, they reminded him that he had omitted pride and anger. To this the accused retorted: "Pardon me; I had not forgotten them, but I did not include them out of respect for yourselves and for fear of offending you further."

He was condemned to death, which was afterwards commuted to perpetual imprisonment. In his dungeon Cagliostro asked to make his confession and himself designated the priest, who was a man of his own figure and stature.[3] The confessor visited him and was seen to take his departure at the end of a certain time. Some hours after the gaoler entered the cell and found the body of a strangled man clothed in the garments of Cagliostro, but the priest himself was never seen again. Lovers of the marvellous declare that the Grand Copht is at this day in America, being the supreme and invisible pontiff of the believers in spirit-rapping.

[1] It is interesting to note that Mr. W. R. H. Trowbridge, who has made the latest attempt to exonerate Cagliostro, has omitted all reference to the regeneration processes and the alleged attempt to renew thereby the youth of Cardinal de Rohan.
[2] As seen already, Menander was the successor of Simon Magus, and the baptism which he performed was claimed to confer immortality.
[3] This story has been altered from the original narrative to make it appear that Cagliostro escaped. He did nothing of the sort, for the monk proved the stronger of the two. Prince Bernard of Saxe-Weimar is the authority for the account, and he is said to have guaranteed its accuracy.

CHAPTER III

PROPHECIES OF CAZOTTE

THE school of unknown philosophers founded by Martines de Pasqually and continued by L. C. de Saint-Martin seems to have incorporated the last adepts of true initiation. Saint-Martin was acquainted with the ancient key of the Tarot—the mystery, that is to say, of sacred alphabets and hieratic hieroglyphics. He has left many very curious pantacles which have never been engraved and of which we possess copies. One of them is the traditional key of the Great Work and is called by Saint-Martin the key of hell, because it is that of riches.[1] The Martinists were the last Christians in the cohort of *illuminés*, and it was they who initiated the famous Cazotte.

We have said that during the eighteenth century a schism took place in illuminism: on the one hand, the wardens of the traditions concerning Nature and science wished to restore the hierarchy; there were others, on the contrary, who desired to level all things by disclosing the Great Arcanum, thus rendering the royalty and priesthood alike impossible in the world. Among the latter, some were ambitious and unscrupulous, seeking to erect a throne for themselves over the ruins of the world. Others were dupes and zanies. The true initiates beheld with dismay the launching of society towards the abyss, and they foresaw all the terrors of anarchy. That revolution which was destined at a later period to manifest before the dying genius of Vergniaud under the sombre figure of Saturn devouring his children had already shewn itself fully armed in the prophetic dreams of Cazotte. On a certain evening, when he was surrounded by blind instruments of the Jacobinism to come, he predicted the doom of all—for the strongest and weakest the scaffold, for the enthusiasts, suicide—and his prophecy, which at the moment was rather like a sombre jest, was destined to be realised amply.[2] As a fact, it was only the calculus of probabilities, and it proved strictly correct because it dealt with chances which had already become fatal consequences. La Harpe, who was impressed by the prediction, amplified the details, to make it appear more marvellous.[3] He mentioned, for example, the

---

[1] Saint-Martin did not continue the school of theurgic Masonry founded by Martines de Pasqually. He abandoned the school and all active connection with Rites and Lodges. The evidence for his acquaintance with the Tarot rests on the fact that his *Tableau Natural des Rapports qui existent entre Dieu, l'Homme et l'Univers* happens to be divided into 22 sections, and there are 22 Tarot Trumps Major. On the same evidence the same assertion is made in respect of the Apocalypse. That which seemed adequate for Éliphas Lévi continues to be found sufficient for the school of Martinism today and for its Grand Master, Papus.

[2] See Deleuze: *Mémoires sur la Faculté de la Prévision*, 1836.

[3] The reader who is in search of romances may also consult P. Christian: *Histoire de la Magie*, published about 1871. It pretends that Court de Gebelin left an account in MS. of the interrogation of Count Cagliostro in the presence of many Masonic

exact number of times that a certain guest of the moment would draw the razor across his throat. Poetic licence of this kind may be forgiven to the tellers of unusual stories; such adornments are of the substance of style and poetry rather than untruths.

The gift of absolute liberty to men who are unequal by Nature is an organisation of social war; when those who should restrain the headlong instincts of the crowd are so mad as to unloose them, it does not need a great magician to foresee that they will be the first to be devoured, since animal lusts are bound to prey upon one another until the appearance of a bold and skilful huntsman who will end them by shot and snare. Cazotte foresaw Marat, as Marat in his turn foresaw reaction and a dictator. Cazotte made his first appearance in public as the author of some literary trifles, and it is said that he owed his initiation to the romance of *Le Diable Amoureux*. There is no question that it is full of magical intuitions, and love, that supreme ordeal of life, is depicted in its pages under the true light of the doctrine of adeptship. Passion in a state of delirium and folly invincible for those who are slaves of imagination, physical love is but death in the guise of allurement, seeking to renew its harvest by means of birth. The physical Venus is death, painted and habited like a courtesan; Cupid also is a destroyer, like his mother, for whom he recruits victims. When the courtesan is satiated, death unmasks and calls in turn for its prey. This is why the Church—which safeguards birth by sanctifying marriage—lays bare in their true colours the debaucheries which are mortal, by condemning without pity all the disorders of love. If she who is beloved is not indeed an angel, earning immortality by sacrifice to duty in the arms of him whom she loves, she is a *stryge* who expends, exhausts and slays him, finally exposing herself before him in all the hideousness of her animal egoism. Woe to the victims of the *Le Diable Amoureux*, thrice woe to those who are beguiled by the lascivious endearments of Biondetta. Speedily the gracious countenance of the girl will change into that camel's head which appears so tragically at the end of the romance of Cazotte.

According to the Kabalists there are two queens of the *stryges* in *Sheol* —one is Lilith, the mother of abortions, and the other is Nehamah, fatal and murderous in her beauty. When a man is false to the spouse set apart for him by heaven, when he is abandoned to the disorders of a sterile passion, God withdraws his legitimate bride and delivers him to the embraces of Nehamah, who assumes at need all charms of maidenhood and of love; she turns the hearts of fathers, and at her instigation they abandon all the duties owing to their children; she brings married men to widowhood; while those who are consecrated to God she coerces into sacrilegious marriage. When she assumes the rôle of a wife she is, however

dignitaries, including Cazotte, at the Masonic Convention of Paris. The date was May 10, 1785. Cagliostro on that occasion predicted the chief events of the French Revolution, and, at the suggestion of Cazotte, gave the name, then unknown, of the Corsican, Napoleon Bonaparte.

unmasked easily, for on her marriage day she appears in a state of baldness, that hair which is the veil of modesty for womanhood being forbidden her on this occasion. Later on she assumes airs of despair and disgust with existence; she preaches suicide, deserts him who cohabits with her, having first sealed him between the eyes with an infernal star. The Kabalists say further that Nehamah may become a mother but she never rears her children, as she gives them to her fatal sister to devour.

These Kabalistic allegories, which are found in the Hebrew book concerning the Revolution of Souls, included by Rosenroth in the collection of the *Kabbala Denudata*[1] and otherwise met with in Talmudic commentaries on the *Sota*, must have been either known or divined by the author of *Le Diable Amoureux*. Hence we are told that after the publication of his novel, Cazotte had a visit from an unknown person who was wrapped in a mantle, after the traditional manner of emissaries of the Secret Tribunal. The visitor made signs to Cazotte which he failed to understand and then asked whether indeed he had not been initiated. On receiving a reply in the negative, the stranger assumed a less sombre expression and then said: "I perceive that you are not an unfaithful recipient of our secrets but rather a vessel of election prepared for knowledge. Do you wish to rule in reality over human passions and over impure spirits?" Cazotte displayed his curiosity; a long talk followed; it was the preface to other meetings; and the author of *Le Diable Amoureux* was called to initiation at the end. He became a devout supporter of order and authority as a consequence and also a redoubtable enemy of anarchists.

We have seen that, according to the symbolism of Cagliostro, there is a mountain into which those must go up who are on the quest of regeneration; this mountain is white with light, like Tabor, or red with fire and blood, like Sinai and Calvary. The *Zohar* says that there are two chromatic syntheses; one of them is white and is that of peace and moral light; the other, which is red, is that of war and material life. The Jacobins had plotted to unroll the standard of blood, and their altar was erected on the red mountain. Cazotte was enrolled under the banner of light, and his mystical tabernacle was established on the white mountain. That which was stained with blood triumphed for a moment, and Cazotte was proscribed. The heroic girl who was his daughter saved him from the slaughter at the Abbey; it so happened that the prefix denoting nobility was not attached to her name and she was spared therefore that horrible toast of fraternity which immortalised the filial piety of Mlle de Sombreuil, who, to be vindicated from the charge of aristocracy, drank the health of her father in the blood-stained glass of cut-throats.

Cazotte was in a position to foretell his own death, because conscience

[1] The *Tractatus de Revolutionibus Animarum* was the work of R. Isaac de Loria, a German Kabalist. It is contained in the second volume of *Kabbala Denudata*. It is not allegorical and it has no Talmudic or Zoharic authority. As it was translated into French in 1905, most people can judge for themselves on the subject.

compelled him to fight against anarchy even to the last. He obeyed it, was arrested for the second time and brought before the revolutionary tribunal as one <u>condemned</u> already. The President who pronounced his sentence added an allocution full of esteem and regret, pledging his victim to be worthy of himself unto the end and to die nobly as he had lived. Even in episodes of the tribunal, the revolution was a civil war and the brethren exchanged salutations as they condemned one another to death. The explanation is that there was the sincerity of conviction on both sides and both were entitled to respect. Whosoever dies for that which he thinks to be true is a hero in even his deception, and the anarchists of the ensanguined mountain were not only intrepid when despatching others to the scaffold, but ascended it themselves without blanching. Let God and posterity be their judges.

CHAPTER IV

THE FRENCH REVOLUTION

ONCE there was a man in the world who was soured on discovering that his disposition was cowardly and vicious, and he visited his consequent disgust on society at large. He was an ill-starred lover of Nature, and Nature in her wrath armed him with eloquence as with a scourge. He dared to plead the cause of ignorance in the face of science, of savagery in the face of civilisation, of all low-life deeps in the face of all social heights. Instinctively the populace pelted this maniac, yet he was welcomed by the great and lionised by women. His success was so signal that, by revulsion, his hatred of humanity increased, and he ended in suicide as the final issue of his rage and disgust. After his death the world was shaken in its attempts to realise the dreams of Jean Jacques Rousseau, and that silent conspiracy which ever since the murder of Jacques de Molay had sworn destruction to the social edifice, inaugurated in Rue Platrière, and in the very house where Rousseau had once lived, a Masonic Lodge, with the fanatic of Geneva as its patron saint. This Lodge became the centre of the revolutionary propaganda, and thither came a prince of the blood royal, vowing destruction to the successors of Philip the Fair over the tomb of the Templar.

It was the nobility of the eighteenth century which corrupted the people; the aristocracy of that period were seized with a mania for equality, which took its rise in the orgies of the Regency; low company was kept for the pleasure of it and the court obtained diversion in talking the language of the slums. The archives of the Order of the Temple[1] testify that the Regent was its Grand Master, that he had as his successors the Duc de Maine, the princes of Bourbon-Condé and Bourbon-Conti, and the Duc de Cossé-Brissac. Cagliostro drew auxiliaries from the middle class to swell the membership of his Egyptian Rite; everyone was eager to obey the secret and irresistible impulse which drove decadent civilisation to its destruction. Events did not tarry, but as if impelled by hands unseen, they were heaped one upon another, after the manner foreseen by Cazotte. The unfortunate Louis XVI was led by his worst enemies, who at once prearranged and stultified the paltry project of evasion which brought about the catastrophe of Varennes, just as they had done with the orgy at Versailles and the massacre of August 10. On every side they compromised the king; at every turn they saved him from the fury of the people, to foment that fury and ensure the dire event which had

---

[1] The reference is here to the latest development of Templary under the ægis of Fabré-Palaprat. It came into public knowledge about 1805, and its invention is not much earlier. Its documents were fictitious, like its claims

been in preparation for centuries. A scaffold was essential to complete the revenge of the Templars.

Amidst the pressure of civil war, the National Assembly suspended the powers of the king and assigned him the Luxembourg as his residence; but another and more secret assembly had ruled otherwise. A prison was to be the residence of the fallen monarch, and that prison was none other than the old palace of the Templars, which had survived, with keep and turrets, to await the royal victim doomed by inexorable memories. There he was duly interned, while the flower of French ecclesiasticism was either in exile or at the Abbey. Artillery thundered on the Pont Neuf, menacing posters proclaimed that the country was in danger, unknown personages organised successive slaughters, while a hideous and gigantic being, covered with a long beard, was to be seen wheresoever there were priests to murder. "Behold," he cried with a savage sneer, "this is for the Albigenses and the Vaudois; this is for the Templars, this for St. Bartholomew and this for the exiles of the Cevennes." As one who was beside himself, he smote unceasingly, now with the sabre and now with axe or club. Arms broke and were replaced in his hands; from head to foot he was clothed in blood, swearing with frightful blasphemies that in blood only would he wash. It was this man who proposed the toast of the nation to the angelical Mlle de Sombreuil. Meanwhile another angel prayed and wept in the tower of the Temple, offering to God her own sufferings and those of two children to obtain pardon for the royalty of France. All the agonies and all the tears of that virgin martyr, the saintly Mme Elizabeth, were necessary for the expiation of the imbecile joys which characterised courtesans like Mme de Pompadour and Mme du Barry.

Jacobinism had received its distinctive name before the old Church of the Jacobins was chosen as the headquarters of conspiracy; it was derived from the name Jacques—an ominous symbol and one which spelt revolution. French iconoclasts have always been called Jacques; that philosopher whose fatal celebrity prepared new Jacqueries and was a peg on which to hang the sanguinary projects of Johannite schemers bore the name of Jean Jacques, while those who were prime movers in the French Revolution had sworn in secret the destruction of throne and altar over the tomb of Jacques de Molay. At the very moment when Louis XVI suffered under the axe of revolution, the man with a long beard—that wandering Jew, significant of vengeance and murder—ascended the scaffold and, confronting the appalled spectators, took the royal blood in both hands, casting it over the heads of the people, and crying with his terrible voice: "People of France, I baptise you in the name of Jacques and of liberty."[1] So ended half of the work, and it was henceforth against the Pope that the army of the Temple directed all

---

[1] Éliphas Lévi mentions in a note that he quotes these words as they were given to him by an old man who heard them. They are cited differently in the *Journal* of Prudhomme.

its efforts. Spoliation of churches, profanation of sacred things, mock processions, inauguration of the cultus of reason in the metropolis of Paris—these were the signals in chief of the war in its new phase. The Pope was burnt in effigy at the Palais Royal, and presently the armies of the Republic prepared to march on Rome. Jacques de Molay and his companions were martyrs possibly, but their avengers dishonoured their memory. Royalty was regenerated on the scaffold of Louis XVI; the Church triumphed in the captivity of Pius VI, when he was taken a prisoner to Valence, perishing of fatigue and suffering. But the unworthy sucessors of that old chivalry of the Temple perished in their turn, overwhelmed by disastrous victory.

Signal abuses had characterised the ecclesiastical state and grave scandals were entailed by the misfortune of great riches; but when the riches melted away, the pre-eminent virtues returned. Such transitory disasters and such a spiritual triumph were predicted in the Apocalypse of St. Methodius, to which reference has been made already. We have a black letter copy of the work mentioned, printed in 1527 and embellished with amazing designs. Unworthy priests are shewn in the act of casting the sacred elements to swine; the populace in a state of rebellion are seen assassinating the priests and breaking their sacramental vessels on their heads; the Pope appears as a prisoner in the hands of soldiers; a crowned knight raises with one hand the standard of France, and with the other draws his sword against Italy. Finally, two eagles are depicted on either side of a cock, bearing a crown on his head and a double *fleur de lys* on his breast. One of the eagles combines with griffins and unicorns to drive the vulture from his eyrie; and there is a host of other marvels. This singular book may be compared with an illustrated edition of the prophecies attributed to Abbé Joachim, the Calabrian, wherein are exhibited portraits of all the popes to come, with the allegorical signs of their respective pontificates, down to the coming of Anti-Christ. These are strange chronicles of futurity, pictured as things of the past; they seem to intimate a succession of worlds wherein events are repeated, so that the prevision of things to come is the evocation of shadows already lost in the past.

CHAPTER V

PHENOMENA OF MEDIOMANIA

IN the year 1772 a certain parishioner of Saint-Mandé, named Loiseaut, being at church, believed that he saw an extraordinary person kneeling close by him; this was a very swarthy man, whose only garment was a pair of coarse worsted drawers. His beard was long, his hair woolly, and about his neck there was a ruddy circular scar. He carried a book, having the following inscription emblazoned in golden letters: *Ecce Agnus Dei.*

Loiseaut observed with astonishment that no one but himself seemed aware of this strange presence, but he finished his devotions and returned home, where the same personage was awaiting him. He drew nearer to ask who he was and what might his business be, when the fantastic visitor vanished. Loiseaut retired to bed in a fever and unable to sleep. The same night he found his room illuminated suddenly by a ruddy glow; he sprang up in bed, believing that the place was on fire; and then on a table in the very centre of the room he saw a gold plate, wherein the head of his visitor was swimming in blood, encompassed by a red nimbus. The eyes rolled terribly, the mouth opened, a strange and hissing voice said: "I await the heads of kings, the heads of the courtesans of kings; I await Herod and Herodias." The nimbus faded and the sick man saw no more.[1]

Some days after he had recovered sufficiently to resume his usual occupations, as he was crossing the Place Louis XV, a beggar accosted him, and Loiseaut, without looking, threw a coin into his hat. "Thank you," said the recipient, "it is a king's head; but here," and he pointed towards the middle place of the thoroughfare, "there will fall another, and it is that for which I am waiting." Loiseaut looked with astonishment towards the speaker and uttered a cry when he recognised the strange figure of his vision. "Be silent," said the mendicant; "they will take you for a fool, as no one but yourself can see me. You have recognised me, I know, and to you I confess that I am John Baptist, the Precursor. I am here to predict the punishment which will befall the successors of Herod and the heirs of Caiaphas; you may repeat all that I tell you."

From this time forward Loiseaut believed that St. John was present visibly at his side, almost from day to day. The vision spoke to him long and frequently on the woes which would befall France and the Church. Loiseaut related his vision to several persons, who were not only impressed but became seers on their own part. They formed among themselves a mystical society which met in great secrecy. It was their custom to sit in a

---

[1] I have failed to trace this story to its source, but Éliphas Lévi was curiously instructed in the byways of French occult history, and though he could seldom resist the decoration and improvement of his narratives, they had always a basis in fact.

circle, holding hands and awaiting communications in silence. This might continue for hours, and then the figure of the Baptist would appear in the midst of them. They fell, concurrently or successively, into the magnetic sleep, and saw passing before their eyes the future scenes of the Revolution, with the restoration which would come thereafter.

The spiritual director of this sect or circle was a monk named Dom Gerle, who became also their leader on the death of Loiseaut in 1788.[1] At the epoch of the Revolution, however, having been won over by republican enthusiasm, Dom Gerle was expelled by the other members, acting on the inspirations of their chief somnambulist, who was known as Sister Françoise André. He had a somnambulist of his own, and in a Parisian garret he followed what was then the new craft of a mesmerist. The séeress in question was an old and nearly blind woman, named Catherine Théot; she prophesied, and her predictions were realised; she cured many who were sick; and as her forecasts had a political cast invariably, the police of the *Comité de salut public* were not slow in taking up the matter.

One evening Catherine Théot was in an ecstasy, surrounded by her adepts. "Hearken," she exclaimed, "I hear the sound of his footsteps; he is the mysterious chosen one of Providence, the angel of revolution, at once its saviour and victim, king of ruins and regeneration. Do you see him? He draws nigh. He also has been encircled by the ruddy nimbus of the Precursor; it is he who shall bear all crimes of those who are about to immolate him. Great are thy destinies, O thou who shalt close the abyss by casting thyself therein. Do you not behold him, adorned as if for a festival, carrying flowers in his hands—garlands which are crowns of his martyrdom." Then sobbing and melting into tears: "How cruel is thine ordeal, my son; and how many ingrates shall curse thy memory through the ages. Rise up, and kneel down: he comes; the king comes—he is the king of bloody sacrifices."

At this moment the door opened quickly; a man entered enveloped in a cloak and having his hat drawn over his eyes. Those who were present rose up; Catherine Théot stretched forth her arms towards the newcomer and said as her hands trembled: "I knew that you must come, and I have awaited your coming. He who is at my right side, but unseen by you, shewed you to me yesterday, when an accusation was lodged against us. We are accused of conspiring for the king, and of a king I have indeed spoken; it is he whom the Precursor reveals to me at this present moment, having a crown steeped in blood, and I know over whose head it is placed —your own, Maximilian."

---

[1] Christian Antoine Gerle was born in 1740 and died in 1805. He was a Carthusian, who came into some prominence under the Constituent Assembly. On April 10, 1790, Dom Gerle proposed a decree that "the Catholic, Apostolic and Roman Church was and should remain always the religion of the nation, and that its worship should be alone authorised". See Albert Sorel: *L'Europe et la Révolution Française*, vol. ii, p. 121. He was imprisoned at the Conciergerie but was liberated, and during the reign of Napoleon he was appointed to an office in the Home Department.

At this name the unknown started, as if a red-hot steel had entered his breast. He cast a swift and anxious glance about him, after which his expression became again impassible.

"What would you say? I fail to understand," he murmured in a short and abrupt manner.

"I would say," replied Catherine Théot, "that the sun will beam brightly on that day when a man clothed in blue and bearing a sceptre of flowers shall be for one moment the king and saviour of the world. I would say that you shall be great as Moses and as Orpehus, when, trampling on the head of that monster which is ready to devour you, you shall testify to headsmen and to victims that God is. Cease from this masking, Robespierre; shew us rather without paling that valiant head which God is about to cast in the empty scale of his balance. The head of Louis XVI is heavy and yours can only be its counterpoise."

"Do you threaten?" asked Robespierre coldly, letting his cloak fall. "Do you think by this juggling to startle my patriotism and influence my conscience? Do you hope by fanatical measures and old wives' fables to surprise my resolves as you have played the spy on my proceedings? You have looked for me, it would seem, and woe to you because you have looked. Since you compel the curiosity-seeker, the anonymous visitor and observer, to be Maximilian Robespierre, representative of the people, as such I denounce you to the committee of public weal, and I shall proceed to have you arrested."

Having said these words, Robespierre cast his cloak round his powdered head and walked stiffly to the door. No one dared to detain and none to address him. Catherine Théot clasped her hands and said: "Respect his will, for he is king and pontiff of the new age. If he strike us, it is that God wills to strike us; lay bare the throat before the knife of Providence."

The initiates of Catherine Théot waited expecting their arrest through the whole night, but no one appeared. They separated on the following day. Two or three further days and nights elapsed, during which the members of the sect made no attempt at concealment. On the fifth day Catherine Théot and those who were called her accomplices were denounced to the Jacobins by a secret enemy of Robespierre who insinuated skilfully to his hearers certain doubts against the tribune—a dictatorship had been mentioned, the very name of king was pronounced. Robespierre knew, and how came he to tolerate it? Robespierre shrugged his shoulders, but on the morrow Catherine Théot, Dom Gerle and some others were arrested and consigned to those prisons which, once entered, opened only to furnish his daily task to the headsman.

The story of Robespierre's interview with Catherine Théot had transpired one knows not how.[1] Already the counter-police of the

---

[1] She is said to have been imprisoned in the Bastille, but this seems to be an error, for it is certain that she died in the Conciergerie at the age of 70. She called herself the mother of God, prophesied the speedy advent of a Messiah and promised that eternal life would then begin for the elect.

MAGIC AND THE REVOLUTION

Thermidorians were watching the presumed dictator, whom they accused of mysticism because he believed in God. Robespierre, notwithstanding, was neither the friend nor enemy of the sect of New Johannites. He went to Catherine Théot that he might take account of phenomena, and dissatisfied at having been recognised he departed with threats which he did not attempt to fulfil; those who converted the conventicle of the old monk and ecstatic into a sect of conspiracy hoped to derive from the proceeding a doubt or an opportunity for ridicule attaching to the reputation of the incorruptible Maximilian. The prophecy of Catherine Théot was fulfilled by the inauguration of the worship of the Surpeme Being and the swift reaction of Thermidor.

During this time the sect which had gathered about Sister André, whose revelations were recorded by a Sieur Ducy, continued their visions and miracles. The fixed notion which they cherished was to preserve the legitimacy by the future reign of Louis XVII.[1] Times out of number they saved in dream the poor little orphan of the Temple and believed also that they had saved him literally. Old prophecies promised the throne of the lilies to a young man who had been once a captive. So Bridget, St. Hildegarde, Bernard Tollard, Lichtemberger—all foretold a miraculous restoration after great disasters.[2] The Neo-Johannites were the interpreters and multipliers of these forecasts; a Louis XVII never failed them; they had seven or eight in succession, all perfectly authentic and not less perfectly preserved. It is to the influence of this sect that we owe at a later period the revelations of the peasant Martin de Gallardon and the prodigies of Vintras.

In this magnetic circle, as in the assemblies of Quakers or Shakers of Great Britain, enthusiasm proved contagious, and was propagated from one to another. After the death of Sister André, second sight and the gift of prophecy devolved upon a certain Legros, who was at Charenton when Martin was incarcerated provisionally therein. He recognised a brother in the Beauceron peasant whom he had never seen. All these partisans, by force of willing Louis XVII, created him in a certain sense; that is to say, they worked such efficacious hallucinations that mediums were made in the image and likeness of the magnetic type, and believing themselves to be literally the royal child escaped from the Temple, they attracted all the reflections of this gentle and frail victim, so that they even remembered circumstances known only to the family of Louis XVI. This phenomenon, however incredible it may appear, is neither impossible nor unheard of. Paracelsus states that if, by an extraordinary effort of

---

[1] See my *Studies in Mysticism*, pp. 99-111, for a summary account of the Saviours of Louis XVII.

[2] St. Hildegarde died in 1179 at the age of 81. She wrote three books of Revelations, which were approved by the Council of Trèves, and Latin authorities have termed her one of the most illustrious mystics of Germany. In the fifteenth century the Council of Basle approved the Revelations of St. Bridget, who was born about 1307 and she died on July 23, 1373. A translation in full of her memorial was published at Avignon in four small volumes, dated 1850.

will, one can picture oneself as another person, one would know thereby and forthwith the inmost thought of that person, and would attract his most secret memories. Often after a conversation which has placed us in thought-affinity with a companion in conversation, we dream reminiscences of his private life. Among the simulators of Louis XVII we must therefore recognise some who were not impostors, but hallucinated beings, and among these last is the Swiss who is named Naündorff, a visionary like Swedenborg, one indeed so contagious in his conviction that old servants of the royal family have recognised him and cast themselves weeping at his feet. He bore the particular signs and scars of Louis XVII; he recounted his infancy with a startling appearance of truth and entered into minute details, which are decisive for private remembrances. His very features would have been those of the orphan of Louis XVI, had he really lived. One thing only in fine was wanting for the pretender to have been Louis XVII truly, and that is not to have been Naündorff.[1]

Such was the contagious magnetic power of this deluded person that even his death did not undeceive any of the believers in his reign to come. We have seen one of the most convinced, to whom we timidly objected —when he spoke of the approaching restoration of what he called the true legitimacy—that his Louis XVII was dead. "Is it then more difficult for God to raise him from death than it was for those who preceded us to save him from the Temple?" Such was the answer given us—and this with a smile so triumphant that almost it seemed disdainful. We had nothing to rejoin on our own part, but were rather compelled to bow in the presence of such a conviction.

---

[1] Out of a great body of claimants, computed by one writer to have been forty and by another two hundred in number, there are four who may rank as competitors at least one with another for recognition as the escaped Dauphin: they are the Baron de Richemont, Augustus Mèves, Eleazar Williams and Naündorff

CHAPTER VI

THE GERMAN ILLUMINATI

GERMANY is the land of metaphysical mysticism and phantoms. A phantom itself of the old Roman Empire, it seems always to invoke the mighty shade of Hermann, consecrating in his honour the simulacrum of the captive eagles of Varus. The patriotism of young Germany is invariably that of the Germans in elder days. They have no thought of invading the laughing land of Italy; they accept the situation, as it stands, simply as a matter of revenge; but they would die a thousand times in the defence of their hearths and homes. They love their old castles, their old legends of the banks of the Rhine; they read with the uttermost patience the darksome treatises of their philosophy; they behold in the fogs of their sky and in the smoke of their pipes a thousand things inexpressible, by which they are initiated into the marvels of the other world. Long before there was any question of mediums and their evocations in America and France, Prussia had its *illuminati* and seers, who had habitual communications with the dead. At Berlin, a great noble built a house destined for evocations; King Frederick William was very curious about all such mysteries and was often immured in this house with an adept named Steinert. His experiences were so signal that a state of exhaustion supervened and he had to be restored with drops of some magical elixir analogous to that of Cagliostro. There is a secret correspondence belonging to the reign in question which is cited by the Marquis de Luchet in his work against the *illuminati*, and it contains a description of the dark chamber in which the evocations were performed. It was a square apartment, divided by a transparent veil; the magical furnace or altar of perfumes was erected in front of the veil and behind was a pedestal on which the spirit manifested. In his German work upon Magic, Eckartshausen describes the whole of the fantastic apparatus, being a system of machines and operations by which imagination was helped to create the phantoms desired, those who consulted the oracle being in a kind of waking somnambulism, comparable to the nervous excitement produced by opium or hasheesh. Those who are contented with the explanations given by the author just mentioned will regard the apparitions as magic-lantern effects, but there is more in it assuredly than this, while the magic lantern was only an accessory instrument in the business and one in no sense necessary for the production of the phenomenon. The images of persons once known on earth and now called up by thought do not appear as reflections of coloured glass; the pictures painted by a lantern do not speak, nor do they give answers to questions on matters of conscience. The King of Prussia, to whom the house belonged, was well acquainted with all the apparatus and was not therefore duped by jugglery, as the author of the secret correspondence pretends. The natural means paved the way for the prodigy but did not perform the latter; and the things which occurred were of a kind to surprise and disturb the most inveterate sceptic.[1] Schroepfer, moreover, made use of no magic lantern and no veil, but those who came to him drank a kind of punch which he prepared; the forms which then appeared by his mediation were like those of the American Home—that is to say, partially materialised—and they caused a curious sensation in persons who sought to touch them. The experience was analogous to an electric disturbance, making the flesh creep, and there would have been no such sensation if people had moistened their hands before touching the apparition. Schroepfer acted in good faith, as does also the American Home; he believed in the reality of the spirits evoked by him, and he killed himself when he began to doubt it.[2]

Lavater, who also died violently, was utterly given over to evocations; he had two spirits at his command and belonged to a circle which cultivated catalepsy by the help of a harmonica. A magical chain was formed; a species of imbecile served as the spirit's interpreter and wrote under his control.[3] This spirit gave out that he was a Jewish Kabalist who died before the birth of Jesus Christ, and the things which the medium recorded under this influence were worthy of Cahagnet's somnambulists.[4] There was, for example, a revelation on sufferings in the life beyond, the communicating spirit stating that the soul of the Emperor Francis was compelled to calculate the number and exact condition of all the snail-shells which may exist and have existed in the whole universe. He made known also that the true names of the three Magi were not, as tradition tells us, Gaspar, Melchior and Balthazar, but on the contrary Vrasapharmion, Melchisedek and Baleathrasaron; it is like reading the names written by our modern process of table-turning. The spirit also testified that he was himself doing penance for having threatened his father with the magical sword and that he felt disposed to make his friends a present

[1] The work of De Luchet is quite worthless from the evidential standpoint, but the so-called correspondence is cited in a Note on pp. 182–186 of the essay. It appears that the House Magical had been sold to King Frederick William, but the person who assisted at the evocations is called *un grand Seigneur*, which may or may not veil the royal identity. Moreover, Steinert was the adept who compounded the "magical elixir", and was pensioned on this account; but it is not stated that he was the magus of the ceremonial proceedings. I have been unable to check the recital of Eckartshausen, which is very difficult to meet with in England.

[2] In the *Secret Tradition in Freemasonry* I have indicated that Schroepfer is, on the whole, rather likely to have possessed some psychic powers, which, notwithstanding his story, ran the usual course of imposture. As he practised evocation perpetually, his suicide can be accounted for owing to the conditions which supervened on this account. There seems no real reason to suppose that he killed himself because he doubted his powers; however, the question does not signify.

[3] It is just to say that another side of Lavater is shewn in his *Secret Journal of a Self-Observer*, which is a very curious memorial—or human document, as it would be termed in our modern language of inexactitude. It contains no suggestion of evocations and dealings with Jewish Kabalists, in or out of the flesh.

[4] Cahagnet is the author of the following works: *Arcanes de la Vie Future*, 3 vols., 1848–1854; *Lumière des Morts*, 1851; *Magie Magnétique*, 2nd Edition, 1858; *Sanctuaire du Spiritualisme*, 1850; *Révélations d'outre Tombe*, 1856.

of his portrait. Paper, paints and brushes were placed at his request behind a screen; he was then seen to design on the screen the outline of a small hand; a slight friction was audible on the paper; when it ceased everyone pressed forward and found rudely painted the likeness of an old Rabbi vested in black, with a white ruffle over the shoulders and a black skullcap, a costume altogether eccentric for a personage who was anterior to Jesus Christ. The painting, for the rest, was smudged and ill-drawn, resembling the work of a child amusing himself by daubing with eyes shut.[1] The written instructions of the medium under the inspiration of Gablidone vie in their obscurity with the characteristics of German metaphysicians. "The attribute of majesty must not be conferred lightly," says this authority, "for majesty is a derivation from Mage, seeing that the Magi were pontiffs and kings; they were therefore the primeval majesties. It is against the majesty of God that we offend when we sin mortally; we wound Him as Father, casting death into the sources of life. The fountain of the Father is light and life; that of the Son is blood and water; while the splendour of the Holy Spirit is fire and gold. We sin against the Father by falsehood, against the Son by hatred and against the Holy Spirit by debauchery, which is the work of death and destruction." The good Lavater received these communications like oracles, and when he asked for some further illuminations Gablidone proceeded as follows: "The great revealer of mysteries shall come, and he will be born in the next century. The religion of the patriarchs will then be known on earth; it will explain to mankind the triad of *Agion, Helion, Tetragrammaton*; and the Saviour whose body is girt with a triangle shall be shewn on the fourth step of the altar; the apex of the triangle will be red and the device of mystery thereon will be: *Venite ad patres osphal*. One of the auditors demanded the meaning of the last word, and the medium wrote as follows without other explanations: *Alphos, M: Aphon, Eliphismatis*. Certain interpreters have concluded that the magus whose advent was announced in the course of the nineteenth century would be named Maphon and would be the son of Eliphisma, but this reading may be somewhat speculative.

There is nothing more dangerous than mysticism, for the mania which it begets baffles every combination of human wisdom. It is ever the fools who upset the world, and that which great statesmen never foresee is the desperate work of a maniac. The architect of the temple of Diana at Ephesus promised himself eternal glory, but he counted without Erostratus. The Girondins did not foresee Marat. What is needed to alter the equilibrium of the world? asked Pascal, on the subject of Cromwell. The answer is, a speck of gravel formed by chance in the entrails of a man. So do the great events come about through causes which in themselves are

[1] This account is taken from Note XV, appended to the *Essai sur la Secte des Illuminés*, but the Marquis de Luchet depended on another writer, the latter drawing from Lavater's *Spiritus Familiaris Gablidone*, published at Frankfort and Leipsic in 1787.

nothing. When any temple of civilisation crashes down, it is always the work of a blind man, like Samson, who shakes the pillars thereof. Some wretched preacher, belonging to the dregs of the people, is suffering from insomnia and believes himself elected to deliver the world from antichrist. Accordingly he stabs Henry IV and reveals to France in its consternation the name of Ravaillac. The German thaumaturgists regarded Napoleon as the Apollyon mentioned in the Apocalypse and one of their neophytes, named Stabs, came forward to kill the military Atlas, who at the given moment was carrying on his shoulders a world snatched from the chaos of anarchy. But that magnetic influence which the Emperor called this star was more potent than the fanatical impulse of the German occult circles. Stabs could not or dared not strike; Napoleon himself questioned him; he admired his resolution and courage; but, as he understood his own greatness, he would not detract from the new Scevola by forgiving him; he shewed his estimation indeed by taking him seriously and allowing him to be shot.

Carl Sand, who killed Kotzebue, was also an unfortunate derelict child of mysticism, misled by the secret societies, in which vengeance was sworn upon daggers. Kotzebue may have deserved cudgelling, but the weapon of Sand reinstated and made him a martyr. It is indeed grand to perish as the enemy and victim of those who wreak vengeance by means of ambuscades and assassinations. The secret societies of Germany practised rites which were less or more comparable to those of Magic. In the brotherhood of Mopses, for example, the mysteries of the Sabbath and the secret reception of Templars were renewed in mitigated and almost humorous forms. The Baphometic Goat was replaced by a dog, as if Hermanubis were substituted for Pan, or science for Nature—the latter being an equivalent change, since Nature is known solely by the intermediation of science. The two sexes were admitted by the Mopses, as was the case at the Sabbath; the reception was accompanied by barkings and grimaces, and, as among the Templars, the Neophyte was invited to take his choice between kissing the back parts of the devil, the Grand Master or the Mopse, which was a small image of cardboard, covered with silk, and representing a dog, called *Mops* in German. The salutation in question was the condition of reception and recalls that which was offered to the Goat of Mendes in the initiations of the Sabbath. The Mopses took no pledges other than on their word of honour, which is the most sacred of all oaths for self-respecting people. Their meetings were occasions for dancing and festivity—again like those of the Sabbath—except that the ladies were clothed, and did not hang live cats from their girdles or eat little children: it was altogether a civilised Sabbath.[1]

Magic had its epic in Germany and the Sabbath its great poet; the

[1] It is suggested by Clavel that when Charles VI suppressed Masonry in Austria, owing to a Bull of Pope Clement XII, the brethren of certain Lodges instituted the Order of Mopses to fill the gap. See *Histoire Pittoresque de la Francmaçonnerie*, 3rd edition, 1844, p. 154. Ragon reproduces the opinion in his *Manuel de l'Inité*, 1861, p. 88.

CHAPTER VII

EMPIRE AND RESTORATION

NAPOLEON filled the world with wonders, and in that world was himself the greatest wonder of all. The Empress Josephine, his wife, curious and credulous as a creole, passed from enchantments to enchantments. A glory of this kind had, as we are told, been promised her by an old gipsy woman, and the folk of the countryside still believe that she was herself the Emperor's good genius. As a fact, she was a sweet and modest counsellor who would have saved him from many perils, had he always listened to her warnings, but he was impelled forward by fatality, or rather by providence, and that which was to befall him had been decreed beforehand. In a prophecy attributed to St. Césaire but signed Jean de Vatiguerro, and found in the *Liber Mirabilis*, a collection of predictions printed in 1524,[1] there are the following astonishing sentences:

"The churches shall be defiled and profaned, and the public worship suspended. The eagle shall take flight over the world and overcome many nations. The greatest prince and most august soveriegn in all the West shall be put to rout after a supernatural defeat. A most noble prince shall be sent into captivity by his enemies and shall mourn in thinking of those who were devoted to him. Before peace is restored to France, the same events shall be repeated again and again. The eagle shall be crowned with a triple diadem, shall return victorious to his eyrie and shall leave it only to ascend into heaven."

After predicting the spoliation of churches and the murder of priests, Nostradamus foretells the birth of an emperor in the vicinity of Italy and says that his reign will cost France a great outpouring of blood, while those who belong to him will betray him and charge him with the spilling of blood.

"An Emperor shall be born near Italy,
Who shall cost dear to the Empire:
They shall say, With what people he keepeth company!
He shall be found less a prince than a butcher.

From a simple soldier he shall come to have the supreme command,
From a short gown he shall come to the long one;
Valiant in arms, no worse man in the Church,
He shall vex the priests, as water doth a sponge."[2]

---

[1] *Liber Mirabilis: qui Prophetias: Revelationesque: nec non res mirandas: preteritas: presentes: et futuras aperte demonstrat*, 1522. The work is in two parts, of which the first is in Latin and the second in French.

[2] I have used the seventeenth-century English translation. The original says: *En l'Eglise au plus pire, traiter les prêtres comme l'eau fait l'éponge.* I do not quite see how Lévi's explanation follows, but the point is not worth discussing.

epic was the colossal drama of *Faust*—that completed Babel of human genius. Goethe was initiated into all mysteries of magical philosophy; in his youth he had even practised the ceremonial part. The result of his daring experiments was to produce in him, for the time being, a profound disgust with life and a strong inclination towards death. As a fact, he accomplished his suicide not by a literal act but in a book; he composed the romance of *Werther*, the fatal work which preaches death and has had so many proselytes; then, victorious over discouragement and disgust, and having entered the serene realms of peace and truth, he wrote *Faust*. It is a magnificent commentary on one of the most beautiful episodes in the Gospel—the parable of the prodigal son. It is initiation into sin by rebellious science, into suffering by sin, into expiation and harmonious science by suffering. Human genius, represented by Faust, employs as its lackey the spirit of evil, who aspires to become master; it exhausts quickly all the delight that is attributed by imagination to unlawful love; it goes through orgies of folly; then, drawn by the charm of sovereign beauty, it rises from the abyss of disillusion to the heights of abstraction and imperishable beauty. There Mephistopheles is at his ease no longer; the implacable laughter turns sad; Voltaire gives place to Chateaubriand. In proportion, as the light manifests the angel of Darkness writhes and tosses; he is bound by celestial angels; he admires them against his will; he loves, weeps and is conquered.

In the first part of the drama, we see Faust separated by violence from Marguérite; the heavenly voices cry that she is saved, even as she is being led to execution. But can that Faust be lost who is always loved by Marguérite? Is not his heart already espoused to heaven? The great work of redemption in virtue of solidarity moves on to its fulfilment. How should the victim ever be consoled for her sufferings, did she not convert her executioner? Is not forgiveness the revenge of the children of heaven? The love which has first reached the empyrean draws science after it by sympathy; Christianity uprises in its admirable synthesis. The new Eve has washed the mark from the forehead of Cain with the blood of Abel, and she weeps with joy over her two children, who hold her in their joint embrace. To make room for the extension of heaven, hell—which has become useless—ceases. The problem of evil has found its definitive solution, and good—alone necessary and alone triumphant—shall reign henceforth eternally.

Hereof is the glorious dream of the greatest of all poets, but the philosopher, by misfortune, forgets the laws of equilibrium; he would swallow up light in a shadowless splendour and motion in an absolute repose, which would signify cessation of life. So long as there is visible light there will be shadow in proportion therewith. Repose will never be happiness unless equilibrated by an analogous and contrary movement. So long as there shall be free benediction, blasphemy will remain possible; so long as heaven remains, a hell there will also be. It is the unchangeable law of Nature and the eternal will of that justice whose other name is God.

This is to say that at the moment when the Church experiences the greatest calamities, he will overwhelm the priests with benefits. In a collection of prophecies published in 1820, and of which we possess a copy, the following phrase occurs after a prediction concerning Napoleon I: "And the nephew will accomplish that which the uncle failed to do." The celebrated Mlle Lenormand had in her library a volume in boards with a parchment back, containing the *Treatise of Olivarius on Prophecies*, followed by ten manuscript pages, in which the reign of Napoleon and his downfall were announced formally. The seeress imparted the contents of this work to the Empress Josephine. Having mentioned Mlle Lenormand, a few further words may be added about this singular woman: she was stout and extremely plain, emphatic in talk, ludicrous in style, but a waking somnambulist of conspicious lucidity. She was the fashionable seeress under the First Empire and the Restoration. There is nothing more wearisome than are her writings, but as a teller of fortunes by cards she was most successful.

Cartomancy, as restored in France by Etteilla, is literally the questioning of fate by signs agreed on beforehand. These in combination with numbers suggest oracles to the medium, who is biologised by staring at them. The signs are drawn by chance, after having shuffled them slowly; they are arranged according to Kabalistic numbers, and they respond invariably to the thoughts of those who question them, seriously and in good faith, for all of us carry a world of presentiments within us which any pretext will formulate. Susceptible and sensitive natures receive from us a magnetic shock which conveys to them the impression of our nervous state. The medium can then read our fears and hopes in ripples of water, forms of clouds, counters cast haphazard on the ground, in the marks made on a plate by the grouts of coffee, in the lottery of a card-game, or in the Tarot symbols.

As an erudite Kabalistic book, all combinations of which reveal the harmonies pre-existing between signs, letters and numbers, the practical value of the Tarot is truly and above all marvellous. But we cannot with impunity, by such means, extort from ourselves the secrets of our intimate communication with the universal light. The questioning of cards and Tarots is a literal evocation, which cannot be performed apart from danger and crime. By evocations we compel our astral body to appear before us; in divination we force it to speak. We provide a body for our chimeras by so doing, and we make a proximate reality of that future which will actually become ours when it is called up by power of the word and is embraced by faith. To acquire the habit of divination and of magnetic consultations is to make a compact with vertigo, and we have established already that vertigo is hell.

Mlle Lenormand was infatuated with herself and with her art; she thought that the world could not go on without her and that she was necessary to the equilibrium of Europe. At the Congress of Aix-la-Chapelle, the seeress made her appearance with all her properties, did business at all the customs, and pestered all the authorities, so that they were compelled in a sense to concern themselves with her; she was truly the fly on the wheel, and what a fly! On her return she published her impressions with a frontispiece representing herself surrounded by all the powers who consulted her and trembled in her presence.[1]

The great events which had just come to pass in the world turned all minds towards mysticism; a religious reaction began and the royalties constituting the Holy Alliance felt the need of attaching their united sceptres to the cross. The Emperor Alexander in particular believed that the hour was come for Holy Russia to convert the world to universal orthodoxy. The intriguing and turbulent sect of the Saviours of Louis XVII sought to profit by this tendency for the foundation of a new priesthood, and it succeeded in introducing one of its seeresses to the notice of the Russian Emperor. Madame Bouche was the name of this new Catherine Théot, but she was called Sister Salome by the sect.[2] She spent eighteen months at the Imperial Court and had many secret conferences with Alexander, but he had more of pious imagination than true enthusiasm; he delighted in the marvellous and pretended that it amused him. It came about that his confidants in this class of interests presented him with another prophetess, and Sister Salome was forgotten. Her successor was Madame de Krudener, an amiable coquette full of piety and virtue, who created but was not herself Valérie.[3] It was, however, her ambition to pass as the heroine of her own book, and when one of her intimate friends pressed her to identify the hero, she mentioned an eminent personality of that period. "Ah, then," said her friend, "the catastrophe of your book is not in conformity with the facts, for the gentleman in question is not dead." But Madame de Krudener replied, "Oh, my dear, he is little better than dead," and the retort was her fortune. The influence of Madame de Krudener on the somewhat weak mind of Alexander was strong enough to concern his advisers; he was often shut up with her in prayer, but in the end she was lost by excess of zeal. One day the Emperor was taking leave of her when she threw herself before him, conjuring him not to go out and explaining how God had made known to her that he was in great danger, that there was a plot against his life, and that an assassin was concealed in the palace. The Emperor was alarmed and summoned the guards; a search followed, and some poor wretch was ultimately discovered with a dagger. In confusion he finished

---

[1] *Les Dernières Prophéties de Mlle Lenormand* appeared in 1843 and are joyful reading. She was born at Alençon in 1772 and died on June 25, 1843.

[2] I have failed to verify the statement that this person had access to the Emperor Alexander.

[3] It should be understood that *Valérie* appeared at Paris in 1803, when the writer was thirty-nine years old. Her acquaintance with the Russian Emperor was eleven years later, and it was during the intervening period that her spiritual development took place. She was no longer an amiable coquette, though the description may once have applied to her. There is no question that the portrait of *Valérie* was, and was intended to be, her own portrait. As to the identity of her hero, he was her husband's secretary and there was no intimacy between them in the evil sense of the term, though she was not of unblemished reputation in other respects.

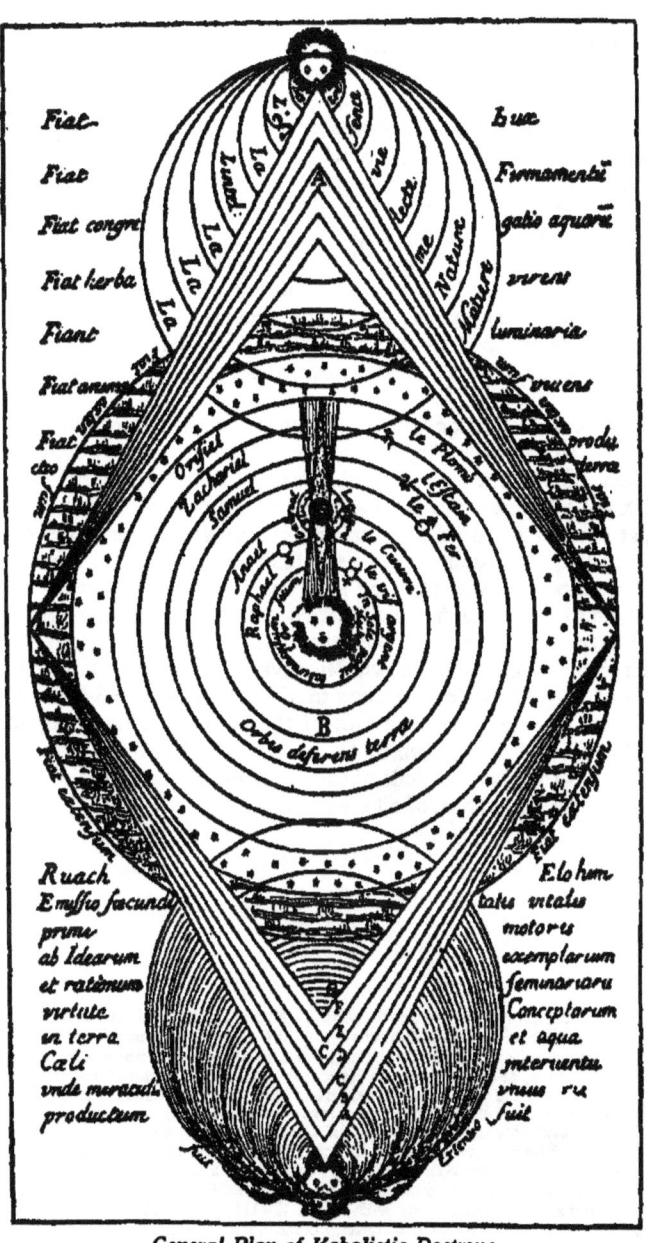

General Plan of Kabalistic Doctrine

by confessing that he had been introduced by Madame de Krudener herself.[1] Was it true, and had the lady played the part of Latude, in the vicinity of Madame de Pompadour? Was it false, and, secreted by the Emperor's enemies, was the man's mission—in the event of the murder failing—to destroy Madame de Krudener? Either way, the poor prophetess was lost, for the Emperor, in his shame at being regarded as a dupe, sent her about her business without hearing her, and she had reason to think herself fortunate in escaping so easily.

The little church of Louis XVII did not conclude that it was beaten by the disgrace of Madame Bouche, while in that of Madame de Krudener it beheld a Divine punishment. The prophecies continued and were reinforced, as required, by miracles. In the reign of Louis XVIII they put forward a peasant of La Beauce, named Martin,[2] who declared that he had seen an angel.

From the description which he gave the angel in question was in the guise of a lackey belonging to some good family; he had a long surtout, cut very close at the waist and of a yellow colour; he was pale and thin, with a hat which was probably adorned with gold lace. The strange thing is that the seer managed to be taken seriously and obtained an interview with the king, furnishing one more instance of the resources in persistence and boldness. It is said that the king was astonished by revelations concerning his private life, in which there is nothing that is impossible or even of an extraordinary nature, now that the phenomena of magnetism are better authenticated and known. Moreover, Louis XVIII was sufficiently sceptical to be credulous. Doubt in the presence of existence and its harmonies, scepticism in the face of the eternal mathematics and immutable laws of life, by which Divinity is manifested everywhere—this assuredly is the most imbecile of superstitions and the least excusable, as it is the most dangerous, of all credulities.

---

[1] It was the Empress Elizabeth, wife of Alexander, who first brought Madame de Krudener to the notice of her husband. She shewed him some of her letters to draw him under religious influence. The King and mystic met, under singular circumstances, on June 4, 1815. Madame de Krudener was 13 years older than the Emperor, with pale, emaciated and drawn features. The story repeated by Éliphas Lévi, whencesoever it may come, is an execrable calumny. The acquaintance began at Würtemberg and continued during the Emperor's residence in Paris, or till September 28, 1815. Those were the days which ended in the proclamation of the Holy Alliance, and Madame de Krudener's part in that work is a matter of history.

[2] Thomas Ignatius Martin is said to have foretold the revolution of 1830, but the fact is dubious. In his interview with Louis XVIII he is said also to have told the French King that he was not the rightful occupant of the French throne, but this is more than dubious. The particular legitimacy which he supported was that of Naündorff.

BOOK VII

MAGIC IN THE NINETEENTH CENTURY

I ZAIN

CHAPTER 1

MAGNETIC MYSTICS AND MATERIALISTS

THE denial of the fundamental doctrine of catholic religion, formulated so magnificently in the poem of *Faust*, had borne its fruits in the world. Morality, deprived of its eternal sanction, became doubtful and unsettled. A materialistic mystic turned about the system of Swedenborg to create on earth a paradise of attractions in proportion to destinies. By the word "attractions" Fourier understood the sensuous passions, and to these he promised an integral and absolute expansion. God, who is the Supreme Reason, marks such condemned doctrines with a terrible seal; the disciples of Fourier began by absurdity and ended in madness.[1]

They believed seriously that the ocean would be presently transformed into an immeasurable bowl of lemonade; they believed also in the future creation of anti-lions and anti-serpents, in epistolary correspondence to be established between the planets. We forbear speaking of the famous tail, thirty-two feet in length, with which it is reported that the human species was to be adorned, because it would appear that they had the generosity to set this notion aside as, according to their master, a purely hypothetical question. To such absurdities does the denial of equilibrium lead. And at the bottom of all these follies there is more logic than would be thought. The same reason which necessitates suffering in humanity renders indispensable the bitterness of sea-water; grant the integral expansion of instincts, and you can no longer admit the existence of wild beasts; endow man with the capacity of satisfying his appetites as the sum of all morality, and he will still have something to envy in orang-outangs and monkeys. To deny hell is also to deny heaven, seeing that, according to the most exalted interpretation of the Great Hermetic Dogma, hell is the equilibrating reason of heaven, for harmony results from the analogy of contraries. *Quod superius, sicut quod inferius.* Superiority presupposes inferiority; the depth determines the height, and to fill up the valleys is to efface mountains; so also to take away shadows would be to destroy light, as this is only visible by the graduated contrast of darkness and day; an universal obscurity would be produced by all-

---

[1] See *La France Mystique*, by Alexandre Erdan, vol. ii, pp. 135 *et seq.* for notices of four chief disciples of Fourier, the maddest being Victor Hennequin.

dazzling brilliance. The very existence of colours in light is due to the presence of shadow; it is the triple alliance of day and night, the luminous image of dogma, the light made shadow, as the Saviour is the Word made man. All this rests on the same law, which is the first law of creation, the one absolute law of Nature, being that of the distinction and harmonious balancing of opposing forces in universal equilibrium.

That which has revolted public conscience is not the dogma of hell but its rash interpretation. Those barbarous dreams of the middle ages, those atrocious and obscene tortures, sculptured on the porticos of churches, that infamous cauldron for the cooking of human flesh which lives for ever, so that it may for ever suffer, while the elect are rejoiced by the smoke—all this is absurd and impious; but none of it belongs to the sacred doctrine of the Church. The cruelty attributed to God constitutes the most frightful of blasphemies, and it is precisely for this reason that evil is for ever irremediable while the will of man rejects the divine goodness. God inflicts the tortures of reprobation on those who are damned only as He causes the death of the suicide. "Work in order to possess, and you will be happy"—so speaks the Supreme Justice to man.—"I would possess and enjoy without labour."—"You will then be a robber and will suffer."—"I will rebel."—"You will be broken and will suffer further."—"I will rebel for ever."—"Then shall you suffer eternally." Such is the decree of the Absolute Reason and the Sovereign Justice: what can be answered hereto by human pride and folly?

Religion has no greater enemy than unbridled mysticism, which mistakes its feverish visions for divine revelations. It is not the theologians who have created the devil's empire, but the false devotees and sorcerers. To believe a vision of the brain rather than the authority of public reason or piety has been ever the beginning of heresy in religion and of folly in the order of human philosophy; a fool would not be a fool if he believed in the reason of others. Visions have never been wanting to piety in revolt, nor chimeras to reason which excommunicates and banishes itself. From this point of view, magnetism has its dangers assuredly, for the state which it induces leads to hallucination as easily as to lucid intuition. We are dealing in this chapter, on the one hand, with mystic magnetisers, with materialistic magnetisers on the other hand, and we would warn them in the name of science concerning the risks which they run. Divinations, magnetic experiences and evocations belong to one and the same order of phenomena, being those which cannot be misemployed without danger to reason and life.

Some thirty or forty years ago a choirmaster of Notre Dame, who, for the rest, was an exceedingly pious and estimable man, became infatuated with mesmerism and gave himself up to its experiences; he also devoted more time than was reasonable to the study of the mystics, and above all the vertiginous Swedenborg. Mental exhaustion followed, and as it was accompanied by sleeplessness, he used to rise and continue his studies; if this failed to quiet the restlessness of his brain, he took the key of the church, entered it by the *Porte Rouge*, repaired to the choir, which was lighted only by the feeble lamp of the High Altar, took refuge in his stall and there remained till morning, immersed in prayers and profound meditation.

There came a night when eternal damnation formed the subject of his reflections, in connection with the menacing doctrine of the small number of the elect. He was unable to reconcile such rigorous exclusion of the majority with the infinite goodness of that God Who, according to Holy Scripture, wills the salvation of all and their attainment of truth. He thought also of those fiery torments which the most cruel of earthly tyrants would not, were it possible, inflict for one day only on his worst enemy. Doubt entered his heart by all its avenues, and he had recourse to the conciliating explanations of theology. The Church does not define the fire of hell; according to the Gospel it is eternal, but it is nowhere written that the greater number of men are destined to suffer eternally. Many of the condemned may undergo only the privation of God; above all the Church forbids absolutely the assumption of individual damnation. Pagans can be saved by the baptism of desire, scandalous sinners by sudden and perfect contrition, and in fine we must hope for all, as we must pray also for all, save one only, being he of whom the Saviour said that it would have been better for him had that man never been born.

The last thought brought the choirmaster to a pause, and it came upon him suddenly that a single man was thus carrying officially the burden of condemnation for centuries; that Judas Iscariot, who is the subject of reference in the passage of Scripture quoted, after so far repenting his crime that he died because of it, had become the scapegoat of humanity, the Atlas of hell, the Prometheus of damnation. Yet he it was whom the Saviour on the threshold of death had termed his friend. The choirmaster's eyes filled with tears, redemption seemed ineffectual if it failed to save Judas. "For him and for him only," he exclaimed in his exaltation, "would I have died a second time, had I been the Saviour. Yet is not Jesus Christ a thousand times better than I am, and what must He then be doing in heaven, if I am weeping on earth for His hapless apostle? . . . What He is doing," added the priest, his exaltation increasing, "is to pity me and console me; I feel it. He is telling my heart that the pariah of the Gospel is saved and that he will become, by the long malediction which still weighs upon his memory, the redeemer of all pariahs. . . . Now, if it be so, a new gospel must be proclaimed to the world, and it will be one of infinite, universal mercy—in the name of the regenerated Judas. . . . But I am astray, I am a heretic, a reprobate . . . and yet, no—for I am sincere." Then, clasping his hands fervently, the choirmaster added: "My God, vouchsafe me that which Thou didst not refuse unto faith of old and which Thou dost not refuse now—a miracle to convince and reassure me, a miracle as the testimony of a new mission."

The enthusiast then rose, and in that silence of the night which is so formidable at the foot of altars, in the vastness of the mute and darksome church, he pronounced the following evocation in loud tones, but slowly and solemnly: "Thou who hast been cursed for eighteen centuries, thou for whom I weep, for thou dost seem to have taken hell solely unto thyself, so that heaven may be left for us; thou, unfortunate Judas, if it be true that the blood of thy Master has purified thee, so that thou art saved indeed, come and lay thy hands upon me, for the priesthood of mercy and love."

While the echo of these words was still murmuring through the affrighted arches, the choirmaster rose up, crossed the choir and knelt under the lamp before the High Altar. He tells us—for the account is related by himself—that he felt positively and really two warm and living hands placed upon his head, as bishops impose them on the day of ordination. He was not sleeping or swooning and he felt them; it was a real contact which lasted for several minutes. He became certain that God had heard him, that a miracle had been performed, new duties had been imposed, and that a new life was for him begun; from tomorrow he must be a new man. But on the morrow the unhappy choirmaster was mad.

The dream of a heaven without hell, the dream of Faust, has made other victims innumerable in this hapless century of doubt and egoism, which has only succeeded on its own part in the realisation of a hell without a heaven. God Himself has become of no effect in a system where all is permissible, where all things count for good. Men who have reached the point where they fear no longer a Supreme Judge find it easy to dispense with that God of simple folk, Who is less of a God in reality than the simple folk themselves. The fools, who vaunt themselves as conquerors of the devil, end by making themselves gods. Our age is above all that of these pseudo-divine mummers, and we have known all grades of them. The god Ganneau, a good and too poetic nature, who would have given his shirt to the poor, who reinstated thieves, who admired Lacenaire, and who would not have hurt a fly; the god Cheneau, a dealer in buttons in the rue Croix des Petits-Champs, a visionary like Swedenborg, and recording his inspirations in the style of Jeannot;[1] the god Tourreil, an excellent personage who deified woman and decided that Adam had been extracted from Eve; the god Auguste Comte, who preserved the catholic religion intact with only two exceptions, being the existence of God and the immortality of the soul; the god Wronski, he being a true scholar, who had the glory and the happiness to rediscover the first theorems of the Kabalah, and who, having sold their communication for 150,000 francs to a wealthy imbecile named Arson, has borne witness in one of his most serious works that the said Arson, having refused to pay him in full, has become actually and literally the beast of the Apocalypse. With a view to enforcing payment, Wronski published a pamphlet entitled *Yes or No— that is to say, have you or have you not, yes or no, purchased from me for 150,000 francs my discovery of the absolute?*

Lest we should be accused of injustice towards one whose works have

[1] He was the prophet of a third and final alliance between God and man.

proved useful to ourselves, and whose eulogium has been pronounced in our former publications, we will give verbatim the passage in Wronski's *Reform of Philosophy*, p. 512, which calls the attention of an indifferent universe to the pamphlet above mentioned. It will also offer a curious specimen of the style adopted by this merchant in the Absolute.

"This fact of the discovery of the Absolute, against which people have appeared to rebel so strongly, has already been established undeniably by means of a great scandal, that of the famous *Yes or No*, not less decisive by the brilliant victory of truth which followed therefrom than remarkable by the sudden manifestation of the symbolic being foreshadowed in the Apocalypse, the monster of creation who bears the name Mystery on his forehead, and who on this occasion, fearing to be mortally wounded, can no longer hide his hideous contortions in darkness, but comes through the medium of newspapers and by other modes of publicity to expose in the open day his infernal rage and the height of his imposture, etc."

It is good to know that this unfortunate Arson, here accused, had already expended on the hierophant some forty or fifty thousand francs. We have attained after Wronski that Absolute which he sold so dearly, and we have given it without price to our readers, for truth is due to the world, and none has the right to appropriate or turn it into trade and merchandise. May this one act of justice atone for the error of a man who perished in a condition approaching want after having worked so hard, though not indeed for science, but to enrich himself by means of knowledge that he may have been unworthy to understand or to possess.[1]

---

[1] It is said that after the rupture of his relations with Wronski, M. Arson instituted a kind of humanitarian religion on his own account, and combined it with some aspect of metempsychosis speculations.

CHAPTER II

HALLUCINATIONS

A ROOT of ambition or cupidity is found invariably beneath the fanaticism of all the sects. Christ Jesus Himself reprimanded often and severely those of His disciples who cleaved to Him, during the days of His privations and exile in His own land, with the hope that they would come into a kingdom wherein they would occupy the seats of the mighty. The more egregious the expectations are, the more they inveigle some imaginations; and people are then prepared to pay for the felicity of hope with their whole purse and indeed their whole personality. It is thus that the god Wronski ruined those imbeciles to whom he promised the Absolute; it is thus that the god Auguste Comte drew an annuity of 6000 francs at the expense of his worshippers, among whom he had distributed fantastic dignities in advance, to become realisable when his doctrine should have conquered the world. It is thus that certain mediums draw money from innumerable dupes by promising them treasures which the spirits always make away with. Some of these impostors really believe in their promises, and it is these precisely who are the most unwearying and the boldest in their intrigues. Money, miracles, prophecies, none of these fail them, because theirs is that absolute of will and action which really works wonders, so that they are magicians without knowing it.

From this point of view, that sect which may be termed the Saviours of Louis XVII belongs to the history of Magic. The mania of these people is so contagious that it draws within the circle of their belief even those who have come forward to combat them. They procure the most important and rare documents, collect the most exceptional testimonies, evoke forgotten memories, command the army of dreams, ensure the apparition of angels to Martin, of blood to Rose Tamissier, of an angel in tatters to Eugène Vintras. The last history is curious on account of its extraordinary consequences, and we shall therefore recite it.

In 1839, the Saviours of Louis XVII, who had filled the almanacs with prophecies for 1840, seemed to have assumed that if the whole world could be made to expect a revolution, that revolution would not fail to be accomplished; but having no longer their prophet Martin, they set about to secure another. Some of their most zealous agents were then in Normandy, of which the pretended Louis XVII claimed to be Duke. They cast their eyes on a devout labourer, with an excitable but weak brain, and they planned the following device. They framed a letter addressed to the prince, meaning the pretender, filled it with emphatic promises concerning the reign to come, in combination with mystical expressions calculated to influence a person of feeble mentality, and then arranged that it should come into the hands of the peasant in question, who was named Eugène Vintras, under circumstances as to which he may be left to speak for himself.

"*August* 6, 1839.

"Towards nine o'clock I was occupied in writing, when there was a knock at the door of the room in which I sat, and supposing that it was a workman who came on business, I said rather brusquely: 'Come in.' Much to my atsonishment, in place of the expected workman, I saw an old man in rags. I asked merely what he wanted. He answered with much tranquillity, 'Don't disturb yourself, Pierre Michel.' Now, these names are never used in addressing me, for I am known everywhere as Eugène, and even in signing documents I do not make use of my first names. I was conscious of a certain emotion at the old man's answer, and this increased when he said: 'I am utterly tired, and wherever I appear they treat me with disdain, or as a thief.' The words alarmed me considerably, though they were spoken in a saddened and even a woeful tone. I arose and placed a ten-sous piece in his hand, saying, 'I do not take you for that, my good man,' and while speaking, I made him understand that I wished to see him out. He received it in silence but turned his back with a pained air. No sooner had he set foot on the last step than I shut the door and locked it. I did not hear him go down, so I called a workman and told him to come up to my room. Under some business pretext I was wishing him to search with me all the possible places which might conceal my old man, whom I had not seen go out. The workman came accordingly. I left the room in his company, again locking my door. I hunted through all the nooks and corners, but saw nothing.

"I was about to enter the factory when I heard on a sudden the bell ringing for mass and felt glad that, notwithstanding the disturbance, I could assist at the sacred ceremony. I ran back to my room to obtain a prayer book and, on the table where I had been writing, I found a letter addressed to Mme de Generès in London; it was written and signed by M. Paul de Montfleury of Caen, and embodied a refutation of heresy, together with a profession of orthodox faith. The address notwithstanding, this letter was intended to place before the Duke of Normandy the most important truths of our holy Catholic, Apostolic and Roman religion. On the document was laid the ten-sous piece which I had given to the old man."

In another communication Pierre Michel admits that the face of his visitor was not unknown to him, but that he was struck with strange fear by his sudden appearance, that he barred and barricaded the door when he went out and listened a long time, hoping to hear him go down. As Vintras heard nothing, there is no doubt that the mendicant took off his shoes so that he might descend, making no noise. Vintras ran to the window but did not see him depart, the explanation being that he had done so some time previously. Our witness, in the end, is upset, calls for help, looks everywhere, finally coming across the letter which he was meant to read, but it is for him evidently a letter fallen from heaven. Behold Vintras, devoted henceforth to Louis XVII, behold him also a visionary for the rest of his days, as the apparition of the old mendicant never quits him henceforward. Then seeing that he addressed Vintras as Pierre Michel, the latter regards him as the archangel Michael, by an association of ideas which is analogous to that of dreams.[1] The deluded supporters of Louis XVII had divined, with the second sight of maniacs, the right moment for impressing the feeble wits of Vintras so as to make him by a single experience at once an *illuminé* and a prophet.

The sect of Louis XVII consists more especially of persons belonging to the service of the legitimate royalty, and when Vintras became their medium he was the faithful mirror of their imagination filled with romanesque memories and obsolete mysticism. In the visions of the new prophet there were everywhere lilies steeped in blood,[2] angels habited like knights, saints disguised as troubadours. Thereafter came hosts affixed on blue silk. Vintras had bloody sweats, his blood appeared on hosts, where it pictured hearts with inscriptions in the handwriting and spelling of Vintras; empty chalices were filled suddenly with wine, and where the wine fell the stains were like those of blood. The initiates believed that they heard delightful music and breathed unknown perfumes; priests, invited to witness the prodigies, were carried away in the current of enthusiasm. One of them, from the diocese of Tours, an old and venerable ecclesiastic, left his cure to follow the prophet.[3] We have personally seen this priest; he has narrated the marvels of Vintras with the most perfect accent of conviction; he has shewn us hosts intincted with blood in a most inexplicable manner; he has communicated to us copies of official proceedings signed by more than fifty witnesses, all honourable persons, occupying positions in the world—artists, physicians, lawyers, a Chevalier de Razac and a Duchesse d'Armaillé. Doctors have analysed the crimson fluid which flowed from the hosts and have certified that it was human blood; the very enemies of Vintras—and he has cruel enemies —do not dispute the miracles, but refer them to the devil. "Now," said the Abbé Chavoz, the priest of Touraine whom we have mentioned, "can you tolerate the notion of the demon falsifying the blood of Christ Jesus on hosts which have been regularly consecrated?" Abbé Chavoz is a real priest, and the signs in question appeared in hosts which had been hallowed by him. This notwithstanding, the sect of Vintras is anarchic and absurd, and God would not therefore perform miracles in its favour. There remains the natural explanation of such phenomena, and in the course of the

[1] The discourses of St. Michael with Vintras are said to have concerned (*a*) the destinies of France, (*b*) the future of religion, (*c*) the reform of the clergy. The Blessed Virgin, St. Joseph and Christ Himself also visited the seer, according to his own testimony.
[2] *L'Œuvre de la Miséricorde prit une teinte fleur-de-lys très prononcée.*—Alexandre Erdan.
[3] See my *Mysteries of Magic: a Digest of the Writings of Éliphas Lévi*

present work it has been indicated sufficiently to make further development needless.

Vintras, whom his partisans represent as a new Christ, has also had his Iscariots; two members of the sect, a certain Gozzoli and another named Alexandre Geoffroi, published the most scandalous revelations against him.[1] According to them, the devotees of Tilly-sur-Seules—which was the place of their residence—were given over to the most obscene practices; they celebrated in their private chapel, which they termed the upper chamber, sacrilegious masses, at which the elect assisted in a state of complete nudity. At a given moment all present fell into a paroxysm, and with tears and cries of "Love, Love," they cast themselves into each other's arms; the rest we may be permitted to suppress. It was like the orgies of the old Gnostics, but without even taking the precaution to extinguish the lights. Alexandre Geoffroi testifies that Vintras initiated him into a kind of prayer which consisted in the monstrous act of Onan, committed at the foot of the altar, but here the accuser is too odious to be believed on his own word. Abbé Chavoz, to whom we mentioned these infamous impeachments, explained that they must be attributed to the hatred of two men who had been expelled from the association for having been guilty on their own part of the acts which they attributed to Vintras. However it may be, moral disorders engender naturally those of a physical kind, and abnormal excitements of the nervous system produce almost invariably eccentric irregularities in morals: if therefore Vintras is innocent, he might have been and may yet be guilty. His sect was condemned formally by Gregory XVI in his brief, dated November 8, 1843.

We append a specimen of the style which this *illuminé* adopted; he is a man without education and his bombastic writings swarm with grammatical errors.

"Sleep, sleep, ye indolent mortals; rest, and still rest on your soft couches; smile at your dreams of festivals and grandeurs. The angel of the covenant has come down on your mountains; he has written his name even in the cups of your flowers; the rings on his feet have touched the rivers which are your pride and hope; the oaks of your forests have borrowed the tincture of a new morning from the radiance of his brow; the sea has made answer to his glance with a yearning leap. She has gone before him; prostrate yourselves upon the earth and be not alarmed at the continuous sound heard in the graves beneath. Sleep, and still sleep. He is engraving his name on the high hills; he is calling on time to speed his ship, and I have seen the oldest of the old smile at him. Sleep therefore and sleep; Elias, in the West, sets a cross at the gate of the temple; he seals it with fire and with the steel of a dagger."

Still the temple, and still fire and dagger. It is strange assuredly how the fools reflect one another; all fanaticisms interweave their inspirations

---

[1] The charges are contained in a pamphlet entitled *Le Prophète Vintras*, published by Gozzoli in 1851. I do not think that Geoffroi wrote anything.

and the prophet of Louis XVII is here an echo of the vengeance-cry of the Templars.

It is true that Vintras does not hold himself responsible for what he writes; this is how he speaks on the subject. "If my mind counted for anything in these condemned works, I should bow my head and fear would possess my soul. But the work is not my work, and I have had no concurrence therein, either by research or desire. Calm is within me; my couch knows no vigils; watches have not wearied my eyes; my sleep is pure, as when God first gave it; I can say to my God with a free heart: *Custodi animam meum et erue me: non erubescam, quoniam speravi in te.*"

Another reputed reformer, he who posed as the Messiah of prisons and the scaffold, namely Lacenaire, with whom we do not assuredly seek to compare Vintras, wrote thus in his prison: "As a chaste and pure virgin, I wake and I sleep, ever in dreams of love. Who shall teach me the meaning of remorse?" The argument of Vintras, in order to legalise his inspiration, is not therefore conclusive, for it has also served Lacenaire, to excuse and even legitimise not only reveries but crimes

Condemned by the Pope, the sect of Tilly-sur-Seules condemned the Pope in their turn, and Vintras, on his private warrant, constituted himself sovereign pontiff. The shape of his priestly vestments was revealed to him; he wears a golden diadem, having an Indian lingam over the forehead; he is vested in a purple robe and carries a magical sceptre terminated by a hand, the fingers of which are closed except the thumb and little finger, being those consecrated to Venus and Mercury, emblematic of the antique hermaphrodite, the emblem of the old ceremonial orgies and the obscene pageants of the Sabbath. So do the memories and reflections of Black Magic, transmitted by the Astral Light, connect the mysteries of India and the profane worship of Baphomet with the ecstasies of this contagious being whose infirmary is at London, and who continues there to make proselytes and victims.[1]

The exaltation of the unfortunate prophet is by no means exempt from terrors and remorse, whatever he may have alleged to the contrary, and mournful confessions escape him from time to time. An example occurs in a letter written to one of his most intimate friends. "I am always expecting new torments. Tomorrow the Verger family will come, and I shall behold in their faces the purity of their soul manifested in their joy of spirit. It will recall my past happiness; names will be mentioned which I pronounced lovingly myself in days not far away. That which will be a delight for others will bring me new tortures. I shall sit at the table, and whilst my heart is pierced with a sword I shall have to smile. O, if perchance those terrible words which I have heard were not eternal, I might still embrace my cruel torment. Pardon, most dear, I cannot live without loving God. Listen, if your human charity permits you, as minister of the living God;

---

[1] Vintras was arrested at Tilly-sur-Seules in 1842 on a charge of roguery; he was tried at Caen and condemned to five years' imprisonment. After his release in 1848 he found an asylum in England.

I do not protest; he whom your Master has spewed out of his mouth must be anathematised by you: On the night of Monday, being May 17 or 18, a frightful dream struck a mortal blow at soul and body alike. I was at Sainte-Paix, and there was no one in the house, though the doors were open. I had ascended hurriedly to the holy chapel and was about to open the door when I saw emblazoned thereon in characters of fire: 'Dare not to enter this place, thou whom I have spewed from my mouth.' ... I could not retreat; I fell down overcome on the first step; and you can judge of my terror when I saw on every side a vast and deep abyss, with hideous monsters therein who hailed me as their brother. The thought came to me at that moment that the holy archangel also once called me his brother. What a difference! His salutation caused my soul to leap with the most intense joy; and at theirs I writhed in convulsions similar to those which they had experienced through the power with which God endowed my cross of grace at their apparition on April 28 last.

"I tried to cling to something, so that I might not fall into the bottomless gulf. I turned to the Mother of God, the divine Mary, and called on her to help me. She was deaf to my voice. During all this time I continued writhing, leaving strips of my skin on the rugged points which bordered this terrible abyss. Suddenly whirlpools of flame rose towards me from that depth wherein I was about to fall. I heard yells of ferocious joy and could pray no longer, when a voice more terrific than long echoes of thunder in a violent tempest filled my ears, uttering these words: 'You think to overcome me but it is you who are conquered. I have taught you to be humble after my manner. Come, taste of my sweetness; be numbered among my elect, and learn also to know the tyrant of heaven; join with us in uttering blasphemies and imprecations against him; all else is useless, so far as you are concerned.' Then after a scream of laughter the voice added: 'Behold Mary, her whom you called your shield against us; behold her gracious smile and listen to her gentle voice.'

"Dear friend, I saw her above the abyss; her eyes of celestial blue were filled with fire, her red lips were violet, her mild and divine voice had become hard and terrible, and like a thunderbolt she hurled these words at me: 'Writhe, proud one, in those fiery regions inhabited by demons.'

"All my blood flowed back to my heart; it seemed that the hour had struck wherein an earthly hell was to replace the hell that is eternal; I could still utter a few words of the *Ave Maria*. How the time passed I knew not, but on returning the servant was asleep and said that it was late. O, if only I revealed to the enemies of the Work of Mercy that which passes within me, would they not cry victory? They would say that here indeed was evidence of monomania. Would God that it were so, for I should have less to lament. And yet fear nothing; if God will not hear my voice when it pleads my own cause, I will pray Him to double my sufferings, on condition that He hides them from my enemies."

Here triumphant hallucination reaches the point of the sublime; Vintras consents to be damned, provided he is not classed as a fool. It is the last instinct of reason's inestimable value, surviving reason itself. The drunken man is afraid only of being regarded as drunk; the monomaniac chooses death rather than admit his delirium. The explanation is that, according to the beautiful sentence of Cebes, already quoted, there is only one good desirable for man; it is that wisdom which is the practice of reason: there is also one only true and supreme misfortune to dread, which is madness.

CHAPTER III

MESMERISTS AND SOMNAMBULISTS

THE Church in its great wisdom forbids us to consult oracles and to violate by indiscreet curiosity the secrets of futurity. In our day the voice of the Church is no longer heeded; the people go back to diviners and pythonesses; the somnambulists have become prophets for those who believe no longer in the Gospel precepts. It is not realised that preoccupation over a predicted event suppresses our freedom in a sense and paralyses our means of defence; by consulting Magic, to foresee future events, we give earnests to fatality. The somnambulists are the sibyls of our epoch, as the sibyls were somnambulists of antiquity; happy are those querents who do not place their credulity at the service of immoral or senseless magnetists, for by the very fact of their friendly consultations they place themselves in communion with the immorality or folly of those who inspire the oracle; the business of the mesmerist is easy and his dupes are manifold. Among those who are devoted to magnetism it is therefore important to know who are in earnest.

Among these, M. le Baron Du Potet must be placed in the front rank, and his conscientious work has already done much to advance the science of Mesmer. He has opened at Paris a practical school of magnetism, to which the public is admitted for instruction in the processes and verification of the phenomena obtained.

Baron Du Potet is of an exceptional and highly intuitive nature. Like all our contemporaries, including the most instructed, he knows nothing of the Kabalah and its mysteries, but magnetism has notwithstanding revealed to him the science of Magic, and as it is still dread in his eyes, he has concealed that which he has found, even while feeling it necessary to reveal it. The book which he has written on the subject is sold only to his adepts, and then under the seal absolute of secrecy.[1] We have entered into no bond with M. Du Potet, but we shall reserve his secret out of respect for the convictions of a hierophant. It is sufficient to say that his work is the most remarkable of all products of pure intuition. We do not regard it as dangerous, because the writer indicates forces without being precise as to their use. He is aware that we can do good or evil, can destroy or save, by means of magnetic processes, but the nature of these is not clearly and practically put forward, on which we offer him our felicitations, for the right of life and death presupposes a divine sovereignty, and we should regard its possessor as unworthy if he consented to sell it—in what manner soever.

[1] See *La France Mystique*, vol. i, pp. 36 *et seq.*, for a contemporary account of Du Potet and of the periodical magnetic *séances* which took place *au dessus du restaurant des Frères Provençaux, au Perron du Palais-Royal*.

M. Du Potet establishes triumphantly the existence of that universal light wherein lucids perceive all images and all reflections of thought. He assists the vital projection of this light by means of an absorbent apparatus which he calls the Magic Mirror; it is simply a circle or square covered with powdered charcoal, finely sifted. In this negative space the combined light projected by the magnetic subject and the operator soon tinges and realises the forms corresponding to their nervous impressions. The somnambulist sees manifested therein all dreams of opium and hasheesh, and if he were not distracted from the spectacle convulsions would follow.

The phenomena are analogous to those of hydromancy as practised by Cagliostro; the process of staring at water dazzles and troubles the sight; the fatigue of the eye, in its turn, favours hallucinations of the brain. Cagliostro sought to secure for his experiments virgin subjects in a state of perfect innocence, so as to set aside interference due to nervous divagations occasioned by erotic reminiscences. Du Potet's Magic Mirror is perhaps more fatiguing for the nervous system as a whole, but the dazzlements of hydromancy would have a more dangerous effect upon the brain.[1]

M. Du Potet is one of those deeply convinced men who suffer bravely the disdain of science and the pre-judgment of opinion, repeating beneath his breath the profession of secret faith cherished by Galileo: *E pur si muove*. It has been discovered quite recently that the tables turn, as the earth itself turns, and that human magnetisation imparts to portable articles, made subject to the influence of mediums, a specific movement of rotation. Objects of extraordinary weight can be lifted and transported through space by this force, for weight exists only by reason of equilibrium between the two forces of the Astral Light. Augment the action of one of them and the other will give way immediately. Now, if the nervous apparatus indraws and expels this light, rendering it positive or negative according to the personal super-excitation of the subject, all inert bodies submitted to its action and impregnated with its life will become lighter or heavier, following the flux and reflux of the light, which—in the new equilibrium of its movement—draws porous bodies and non-conductors about a living centre, as planets in space are drawn, balanced and gravitate about their sun.

This excentric power of attraction or projection supposes invariably a diseased condition in the person who is the subject thereof; the mediums are all excentric and badly equilibrated beings; mediomania supposes or occasions a sequence of other nervous manias, fixed notions deordinated appetites, disorderly erotomania, tendencies to murder or suicide. Among persons so effected moral responsibility seems to exist no more; they do evil with good as their motive; they shed tears of emotion in a church and may be surprised at bacchanalian orgies. They have a way of explaining

[1] According to another account, the Magic Mirror was an ordinary circle of evocation drawn with charcoal. Wandering spirits were supposed to be conjured therein.

everything—by the devil or the spirits which obsess and carry them away. What would you have of them? They live no more in themselves; some mysterious creature animates them and acts in their place; this being is named "Legion".

The reiterated efforts of a healthy person to develop mediumistic faculties cause fatigue, disease and may even derange reason. It is this which happened to Victor Hennequin, formerly an editor of *La Démocratie Pacifique* and, after 1848, a member of the National Assembly. He was a young barrister, with a plentiful flow of eloquence, wanting neither education nor talent, but he was infatuated with the reveries of Fourier. Being banished as an after-consequence of December 2, he took up table-turning during his enforced inactivity; he fell a victim all too soon to mediomania and believed himself an instrument for the revelations of the soul of the earth. He published a book entitled *Save the Human Race*; it was a medley of socialistic and Christian reminiscences; a last gleam of reason flickered therein; but the experiences continued and folly triumphed. In a final work of which only one volume was issued, Victor Hennequin represents God in the guise of an immense polypus located at the centre of the earth, having antennae and horns turned inwards like tendrils all over his brain, as also over that of his wife Octavia. Soon afterwards it was reported that Victor Hennequin had died from the consquences of a maniacal paroxysm in a madhouse.[1]

We have also heard of a lady belonging to the aristocracy who gave herself up to communications with pretended spirits in tables and who, scandalised beyond measure at the unsuitable replies of her particular piece of furniture, undertook a journey to Rome to submit the heretical article to the chair of St. Peter. She carried it with her and had an *auto-da-fé* in the capital of the Christian world. Better to burn her furniture than to court madness, and to say the truth it was an imminent danger for the lady here in question. Let us not laugh at the episode—for we are children of an age of reason in which men who pass as serious, like the Comte de Mirville, ascribe to the devil unexplained phenomena of Nature.

In a drama which is well known on the boulevards there is much to be heard of a magician who, requiring a formidable auxiliary, created an automaton, being a monster with the paws of a lion, a bull's horns and the scales of leviathan. To this hybrid sphinx he imparted life, but took flight incontinently, being terrified at the work of his hands. The monster followed in pursuit, appeared between him and his betrothed, set fire to his house, burnt his father, carried off his son, and continuing the chase to the sea, followed him on board a ship which he caused to be engulfed; but finally made an end of himself amidst thunder. This awful spectacle, rendered visible by fear, has been realised in the history of humanity;

---

[1] His madness is said otherwise to have been partial, or characterised by many lucid intervals. His second work was *Religion*, and it preached the doctrine of reincarnation, with periodical changes of sex. It described the Deity as an infinite substance in which circulated myriads of soul-entities.

poetry has personified the phantom of evil and has endowed it with all forces of Nature. It has sought to enlist the chimera as an aid to morality, and has then gone in fear of the ugliness begotten by its own dreams. From this time forward the monster has pursued us through the ages; it makes grimaces between us and the objects of our love; an impure nightmare, it strangles our children in their sleep; it carries through creation, that father's house of humanity, the inextinguishable torch of hell; it burns and tortures our parents everlastingly; it spreads black wings to hide heaven from our eyes; it shrieks to us: "Hope no more." It mounts the crupper and gallops behind us like remorse; it plunges into the ocean of despair the last rock of our hopes; it is the old Persian Ahriman, the Egyptian Typhon, the darksome god confessed by the heretics of Manes, the Comte de Mirville and the Black Magic of the devil; it is the world's horror and the idol of bad Christians. Men have tried to laugh at it and have been afraid; they have caricatured it and trembled, for the cartoons have seemed to take life and to mock at those who made them. All this notwithstanding, its reign is over, though it will not perish overwhelmed by a bolt from heaven; science has conquered the lightning and converted it into torches; the monster will dissolve before the brightness of science and truth; the genius of ignorance and darkness can only be blasted by the light.

CHAPTER IV

THE FANTASTIC SIDE OF MAGICAL LITERATURE

It is now twenty years since Alphonse Esquiros,[1] one of the friends of our childhood, issued a work of high fantasy, entitled the *Magician*. All that the romanticism of that period conceived to be most bizarre was embodied in the story; the author provided his magus with a seraglio of dead ladies, embalmed according to a process which has since been discovered by Gannal. The characters included an automaton of bronze who preached chastity, a hermaphrodite who was in love with the moon and conducted a regular correspondence with that satellite: there were other wonderful things which one has forgotten at this day. Alphonse Esquiros may be said to have founded a school of Fantasiasts in Magic by the publication of this romance, its most distinguished present representative being the young and interesting Henri Delaage, who is a productive writer, an unrecognised thaumaturgist and a gifted charmer. His style is not less astonishing than were the notions of Alphonse Esquiros, his initiator and master. Thus, in his book dealing with those who have risen from the dead, he remarks as follows concerning some objection against Christianity: "I take this objection by the throat and, when I loose my grasp, the earth shall resound sullenly under the weight of its strangled corpse." It is true that his reply to the objection comes to very little; but what would you, when an objection has been strangled and when the earth has resounded sullenly under the weight of its body?

We have said that Henri Delaage is an unrecognised thaumaturgist. As a fact he has informed a person of our acquaintance that during a winter when influenza was prevalent, it was sufficient for him to enter a room and every one who happened to be therein was cured immediately. Unhappily he became himself a victim of the miracle, for he contracted a slight hoarseness which has never left him. Many of our friends declare that he has the gift of ubiquity; he is left at the office of *La Patrie* and is found again with his publisher Dantu; one retires in dismay and goes home, there to find—Delaage awaiting one's arrival. He is a skilful charmer. A society lady who had been reading one of his books testified that she knew nothing better written or more beautiful, but it is not to his works alone that Delaage imparts beauty. We had been reading an article signed "Fiorentino" which said that the physical attractions of the young magician equalled or even surpassed those of angels. We encountered Delaage and

---

[1] His other works include the *Gospel of the People*, 1840, to which Éliphas Lévi refers subsequently. For this he was imprisoned. In 1847 he published a *Histoire des Montagnards*. At the end of 1851 he was compelled to leave France, and seems to have lived in England. Henri Alphonse Esquiros was born in 1814.

questioned him with curiosity on this singular revelation. Delaage then put his hand in his waistcoat, turned three parts round and looked smilingly to heaven; it happened fortunately that we were carrying the *Enchiridion* of Leo III, which is known to preserve from enchantments, so that the charmer's angelical beauty was hidden from our eyes. Let us offer on our part a more serious eulogium to Henri Delaage than do those who admire his good looks; he is sincere when he says that he is a catholic and when he proclaims loudly his love and respect for religion. Now religion can make you a saint, and this title is more estimable and glorious than that of a sorcerer.[1]

It is owing to his rank as a publicist that we have placed this young man in the first place among the Fantasiasts of Magic, but in all other respects it belongs to the Comte D'Ourches, a man of venerable age who has devoted his life and fortune to mesmeric experiments. Ladies in a state of somnambulism, and any furniture at his house, give themselves up to frenzied dances; the furniture becomes worn out and is broken, but it is said that the ladies are all the better for their gyrations.

For a long time the Comte D'Ourches has been dominated by a fixed idea, which is the fear of being buried alive, and he has written a number of memorials on the need for verifying decease in a more certain way than obtains usually. He has some justification for such a fear on his own part because his temperament is plethoric, while his extreme nervous susceptibility, continually superexcited by experiments with fair somnambulists, may expose him to attacks of apoplexy. In magnetism he is the pupil of Abbé Faria and in necromancy he belongs to the school of Baron de Guldenstubbé. The latter has published a work entitled *Practical Experimental Pneumatology, or the Reality of Spirits and the Marvellous Phenomenon of their Direct Writing*. He gives an account of his discovery as follows: "It was in the course of the year 1850, or about three years prior to the epidemic of table-rapping, that the author sought to introduce into France the circles of American spiritualism, the mysterious Rochester knockings and the purely automatic writing of mediums. Unfortunately he met with many obstacles raised by other mesmerists. Those who were committed to the hypothesis of a magnetic fluid, and even those who styled themselves Spiritual Mesmerists, but who were really inferior inducers of somnambulism, treated the mysterious knockings of American Spiritualism as visionary follies. It was therefore only after more than six months that the author was able to form his first circle on the American plan, and then thanks to the zealous concurrence of M. Roustan, a former member of the *Société des Magnétiseurs Spiritualistes*, a simple man who was full of enthusiasm for the holy cause of spiritualism. We were joined

---

[1] Henri Delaage seems to have taken the question of physical beauty rather seriously to heart. In 1850, under the title of *Perfectionnement physique de la Race Humaine*, he made a collection of processes and methods for acquiring beauty, drawn —as he claimed—from Chaldean Magi and Hermetic Philosophers.

by a number of other persons, amongst whom was the Abbé Châtel,[1] founder of the Église Française, who, despite his rationalistic tendencies, ended by admitting the reality of objective and supernatural revelation, as an indispensable condition of spiritualism and all practical religions. Setting aside the moral conditions which are equally requisite, it is known that American circles are based on the distinction of positive and electric or negative magnetic currents.

"The circles consist of twelve persons, representing in equal proportions the positive and negative or sensitive elements. This distinction does not follow the sex of the members, though generally women are negative and sensitive, while men are positive and magnetic. The mental and physical constitution of each individual must be studied before forming the circles, for some delicate women have masculine qualities, while some strong men are, morally speaking, women. A table is placed in a clear and ventilated spot; the medium is seated at one end and entirely isolated; by his calm and contemplative quietude he serves as a conductor for the electricity, and it may be noted that a good somnambulist is usually an excellent medium. The six electrical or negative dispositions, which are generally recognised by their emotional qualities and their sensibility, are placed at the right of the medium, the most sensitive of all being next him. The same rule is followed with the positive personalities, who are at the left of the medium, with the most positive among them next to him. In order to form a chain, the twelve persons each place their right hand on the table and their left hand on that of their neighbour, thus making a circle round the table. Observe that the medium or mediums, if there be more than one, are entirely isolated from those who form the chain.

"After a number of séances, certain remarkable phenomena have been obtained, such as simultaneous shocks, felt by all present at the moment of mental evocation on the part of the most intelligent persons. It is the same with mysterious knockings and other strange sounds; many people, including those least sensitive, have had simultaneous visions, though remaining in the ordinary waking state. Sensitive persons have acquired that most wonderful gift of mediumship, namely automatic writing, as the result of an invisible attraction which uses the non-intelligent instrument of a human arm to express its ideas. For the rest, non-sensitive persons experience the mysterious influence of an external wind, but the effect is not strong enough to put their limbs in motion. All these phenomena, obtained according to the mode of American spiritualism, have the defect of being more or less indirect, because it is impossible in these experiences to dispense with the mediation of a human being or medium.

---

[1] The Église Française was forcibly closed about 1840, but in 1848 an attempt was made to reopen it in a small room. A particular kind of Mass was celebrated in the French language, and it appears that the church had fixed festivals of its own. In doctrinal matters Abbé Châtel regarded the relation between God and the universe as comparable to that between the soul and body, "but in an infinitely more excellent manner". Paradise, Purgatory and Hell were alike abolished, and in their place two states were substituted, one of glory and felicity, the other of reparation.

It is the same with the table-turning which invaded Europe in the middle of the year 1853.

"The author has had many table experiences with his honourable friend, the Comte d'Ourches, one of the most instructed persons in Magic and the Occult Sciences. We attained by degrees the point when tables moved apart from any contact whatever, while the Comte d'Ourches has caused them to rise, also without contact. The author has made tables rush across a room with great rapidity, and not only without contact but without the magnetic aid of a circle of sitters. The vibration of piano-chords under similar circumstances took place on January 20, 1856, in the presence of the Comte de Szapary and Comte d'Ourches. Now all such phenomena are proof positive of certain occult forces, but they do not demonstrate adequately the real and substantial existence of unseen intelligences, independent of our will and imagination, though the limits of these have been vastly extended in respect of their possibilities. Hence the reproach made against American spiritualists, because their communications with the world of spirits are so insignificant in character, being confined to mysterious knockings and other sound vibrations. As a fact, there is no direct phenomenon at once intelligent and material, independent of our will and imagination, to compare with the direct writing of spirits, who have neither been invoked nor evoked, and it is this only which offers irrefutable proof as to the reality of the supernatural world.

"The author, being always in search of such proof, at once intelligent and palpable, concerning the substantial reality of the supernatural world in order to demonstrate by certain facts the immortality of the soul, has never wearied of addressing fervent prayers to the Eternal, that He might vouchsafe to indicate an infallible means for strengthening that faith in immortality which is the eternal basis of religion. The Eternal, Whose mercy is infinite, has abundantly answered this feeble prayer. On August 1, 1856, the idea came to the author of trying whether spirits could write directly—that is, apart from the presence of a medium. Remembering the marvellous direct writing of the Decalogue, communicated to Moses, and that other writing, equally direct and mysterious, at the feast of Belshazzar, recorded by Daniel; having further heard about those modern mysteries of Stratford in America, where certain strange and illegible characters were found upon slips of paper, apparently apart from mediumship, the author sought to establish the actuality of such important phenomena, if indeed within the limits of possibility.

"He therefore placed a sheet of blank letter paper and a sharply pointed pencil in a box, which he then locked and carried the key about him, imparting his design to no one. Twelve days he waited in vain, but what was his astonishment on August 13, 1856, when he found certain mysterious characters traced on the paper. He repeated the experiment ten times on that day, placing a new sheet of paper each time in the box, with the same result invariably. On the following day he made twenty experiments but left the box open, without losing sight of it. He witnessed the formation of characters and words in the Esthonian language with no motion of the pencil. The latter being obviously useless, he decided to dispense with it and placed blank paper sometimes on a table of his own, sometimes on the pedestals of old statues, on sarcophagi, on urns, etc., in the Louvre, at St. Denis, at the church of St. Étienne du Mont, etc. Similar experiments were made in different cemeteries of Paris, but the author has no liking for cemeteries, while most spirits prefer the localities where they have lived on earth to those in which their mortal remains are laid to rest."

We are far from disputing the singular phenomena observed by Baron de Guldenstubbé, but would point out to him that the discovery had been made previously by Lavater and that the water-colour portrait[1] painted by the Kabalist Gablidone is of far greater importance than the few lines of writing obtained on his part. Speaking next in the name of science, we would tell him, not indeed for his benefit, seeing that he will not believe us, but for serious observers of these strange phenomena, that the writings obtained by him do not come from the other world but have been made unconsciously by himself. We would say to him that your experiments, so unduly multiplied, and the excessive tension of your will, have destroyed the equilibrium of your fluidic and astral body; you have compelled it to realise your dreams and it has traced, in characters borrowed from your own remembrance, the reflections of your imagination and of your thoughts. Had you been placed in a perfectly lucid state of magnetic sleep, you would have seen a luminous counterpart of your hand, lengthened out like a shadow in the setting sun; you would have seen it trace on the paper prepared by yourself or your friends those characters which have so much surprised you. That corporeal light which emanates from the earth and from you is contained by a fluidic envelope of extreme elasticity, and that envelope is formed from the quintessence of your vital spirits and your blood. This quintessence derives from the light a colour determined by your secret will; it is made in the likeness of your dream, and the characters are impressed on the paper as signs on the bodies of unborn children are imprinted by the imagination of their mothers. That which seems to you ink is your blackened and transfigured blood. You are expending yourself in proportion as such writings multiply. If you continue your experiments your brain will be weakened gradually and your memory will suffer. You will experience unspeakable pains in the joints of the limbs and fingers, and you will finally die, either struck down suddenly or after a prolonged agony, characterised by hallucinations and madness. So much for Baron de Guldenstubbé.

To the Comte d'Ourches we would say: You will not be buried alive, but you run the risk of dying by the very precautions which you are taking against such a possibility. The awakening of those who are so buried can

[1] See the appendix to *Essai sur le Secte des Illuminés*, by the Marquis de Luchet, already quoted.

only be rapid and brief, but they may live long underground, conserved by the Astral Light in a complete state of lucid somnambulism. Their souls are then bound to the sleeping body by an invisible chain, and if those souls are greedy and criminal they can draw on the quintessence of the blood in persons who are naturally asleep; they can transmit this sap to their interred bodies for their longer preservation, in the vague hope that they may be restored ultimately to life. It is this frightful phenomenon which is called vampirism, and its reality has been established by many cases as well attested as the most serious things in history. If you question the possibility of this magnetic life of the human body under earth, read the following account of an English officer, named Osborne, the good faith of which was attested to Baron Du Potet by General Ventura.

"On June 6, 1838," says Mr. Osborne, "the monotony of our camp-life was happily interrupted by the arrival of an individual who was famous throughout the Punjab. He was the subject of great veneration among the Sikhs because of his power to remain buried underground for so long a time as he pleased. Such extraordinary stories are told of this man, and their authenticity has been guaranteed by so many reputable persons, that we were most anxious to see him. He told us on his own part that he had followed this business of interment for a number of years in various parts of India. Among serious and creditable people who have borne witness in his favour I may mention Captain Wade, the political agent at Lodhran. This officer has told me most seriously that he himself assisted at the resurrection of the said fakir after a burial which took place several months previously, in the presence of General Ventura, the Maharajah and the principal Sikh chiefs. The details concerning the interment as given to Captain Wade, and those which he added on his own authority respecting the exhumation, are as follows.

"After certain precautions which lasted for several days and the details of which are distasteful, the fakir announced that he was ready to undergo the trial. The Maharajah, Sikh chiefs and General Ventura assembled round a grave of stonework constructed for the express purpose. In their presence the fakir sealed up with wax every opening of his body by which air could enter, with the exception of the mouth; he then cast off his garments, was enveloped in a linen bag and, by his own wish, his tongue was turned back so that it obstructed the gullet. He fell after this into a kind of lethargy. The bag which contained him was closed up, and a seal was placed thereon by the Maharajah. It was then put into a sealed and padlocked chest, which was lowered into the grave. A large quantity of earth was thrown on it; it was trodden down and barley was sown therein. Finally sentinels were stationed round the spot, with orders to watch day and night.

"These precautions notwithstanding, the Maharajah still had doubts; thrice during the period of ten months, during which the fakir was to remain interred, he visited the grave and had it opened in his presence, but the body was in the sack, just as it had been placed therein, cold and inanimate to all appearance. When the ten months had expired the fakir was exhumed finally. General Ventura and Captain Wade undid the padlocks, broke the seals and raised the chest from the grave. The fakir was taken out, but there was no indication of life either at heart or pulse. As a first means to reanimate him, one of the spectators inserted his finger very gently in the mouth and restored the tongue to its natural position. The top of the head was the sole seat of any sensible heat. By pouring warm water slowly over the body, some signs of life were obtained by degrees. After two hours of attention, the fakir rose up and began to move about smiling.

"The extraordinary being declared that he had delicious dreams during his entombment, but that the time of awaking was always exceedingly painful and that he was in a state of vertigo before his return to consciousness; his age is about thirty years, his countenance is ill-favoured and his expression somewhat crafty. We had long conversations with him, and he offered to be buried in our presence. We took him at his word and appointed a meeting at Lahore, where we promised that he would remain underground throughout our stay in that city."

Such was the story of Osborne. The question was whether the fakir would really allow himself to be interred once more. The new experiment might well be decisive. But that which happened was as follows.

"Fifteen days after the fakir's visit to their camp, the English officers arrived at Lahore. They chose a spot which seemed favourable for the coming operations, had a mural tomb constructed, as well as a very solid chest, and then awaited the fakir. He came on the day following, expressing an ardent desire to prove that he was no impostor. He stated further that he had made the necessary preparations for an experiment, but his demeanour evidenced a certain disquiet and despondency. He began to stipulate concerning his compensation, which was fixed at fifteen hundred rupees down and two thousand rupees annually, which the officers undertook to obtain from the king. Satisfied on this point, he wished to be informed as to the precautions that they were proposing to take. The officers shewed him the chest, the keys belonging thereto, and warned him that sentinels chosen among the English soldiers would watch round the place for a week. The fakir cried out and gave vent to much abuse of the *Firinghees* and sceptics, who sought to rob him of his reputation. He expressed also a fear that some attempt would be made on his life and refusing to trust himself entirely to the surveillance of Europeans, he demanded that duplicate keys should be comitted to one of his co-religionists, further insisting—and this indeed above all—that the sentries should not be enemies of his faith. The officers declined to entertain these conditions; several interviews followed, leading to no result; and finally the fakir intimated, through one of the Sikh chiefs, that the Maharajah having menaced him with his anger if he did not fulfil his engagement with the English, it was his wish to undertake the trial, though he rested assured that the sole object of the officers was to deprive him of life, and that he would never come forth from his tomb. The officers admitted that, as to the last point, they all shared his conviction, adding that as they did not wish to have his death as a reproach against them, they relieved him of his promise.

"Are such hesitations and fears proof positive against the fakir? Does it follow that all who have testified previously how they had beheld with their own eyes and occurrences to which he owes his celebrity have been guilty of deception themselves or were the victims of skilful trickery? We confess that, having regard to the extent and quality of the evidence, we cannot doubt that the fakir was frequently and literally interred; and even admitting that after his burial he has on each occasion continued to communicate with the world above ground, it would still be inexplicable how he could be deprived of respiration during the time which intervened between his burial and that moment when his accomplices came to his aid. Mr. Osborne adds in a note a quotation from the *Medical Topography of Lodhiana*, by Dr. MacGregor, an English physician, who assisted at one of the exhumations, was a witness of the fakir's lethargy, of his gradual return to life, and who tries seriously to explain it. Mr. Boileau, another English officer, in a work published some years ago, recounts how he witnessed another experience which reproduced all the facts in precisely the same manner. Those who are anxious to satisfy their curiosity more fully, those who discern in the narrative an indication of a curious physiological fact, may refer with confidence to the sources which are here indicated."

A number of official records of the exhumation of vampires are still extant. In each case the flesh was in a remarkable state of preservation, but blood oozed from the body, the hair had grown in an abnormal manner and protruded in tufts through the chinks of the coffin. There was no sign of life in the respiratory apparatus, save in the heart only, and this seemed to have become a vegetable rather than an animal organ. To kill the vampire a stake had to be driven through the breast, and then a frightful cry shewed that the somnambulist of the grave had awakened with a start into a veritable death. To render such death definitive, swords were driven point upwards into the vampire's grave, for the phantoms of Astral Light are disintegrated by the action of metallic points, which attract that light towards the common reservoir and dissipate its coagulated clusters. To reassure nervous people, it may be added that cases of vampirism are fortunately exceedingly rare, and that no one who is healthy in mind and body can be personally victimised, unless he or she has been abandoned, body and soul, to the creature in its lifetime by some criminal complicity or irregular passion.

The following history of a vampire is related by Tournefort in his *Voyage to the Levant*.[1]

"In the island of Mycona we witnessed a very singular scene, being the

---

[1] Joseph Pitton de Tournefort: *Relation d'un Voyage du Levant*, 1717, 2 vols. It was translated into English and published in 3 vols., 1741.

alleged return of a deceased person after interment. In northern Europe those who come back in this manner are called vampires, while the Greeks designated them under the name of *Broucolaques*. The case in question was that of a peasant of Mycona who was naturally gloomy and quarrelsome. It is a circumstance worthy of note, on account of parallel instances. He was killed in the countryside, no one knew why or by whom. Two days after his burial in a church of the city, a report went abroad that he was seen nightly wandering about at a great pace. He also visited houses, turned over the furniture, put out the lights, embraced people from behind and performed innumerable other tricks. At first it was a laughing matter, but it took a serious turn when reliable people began to complain. The priests themselves certified to the fact, and no doubt they had their reasons. Recourse was had to masses, said for the purpose, but the peasant continued the same course with no sign of amendment. After several meetings of the chief persons, priests and monks of the town it was concluded to wait for the expiration of nine days after the interment, following I know not what ancient procedure. On the tenth day a mass was said in the church wherein the body had been buried, for the purpose of expelling the demon who was thought to have entered into it. The mass over, the corpse was disinterred and the heart removed. It was necessary to burn incense owing to the evil smell, but the combination made bad worse and almost stifled those present. It was testified that a thick smoke exhaled from the corpse, and we who were present at the operations did not venture to suggest that it was really the smoke of the incense. There were also those who affirmed that the blood of the unfortunate person was abnormally scarlet, while yet others declared that the flesh was still warm, whence it was concluded that the deceased person was seriously wrong in not being properly dead, or rather in allowing himself to be brought to life by the devil. This is precisely the idea which obtains concerning the vampire, and that word began to be repeated persistently. A crowd assembled, loudly protesting that the body was obviously not rigid when it was carried to the church for burial and that it was therefore a veritable vampire.

"Appeal being made to us, we expressed the opinion that the person was undoubtedly dead, and as for the supposed scarlet blood, it was easy to see that it was only bad-smelling slime. For the rest, we attempted to cure or at least not provoke further their excited imaginations by explaining the fumes and warmth attributed to the corpse. Such arguments notwithstanding, it was determined to burn the heart of the deceased person, but after this had been done he was not more amenable than formerly and indeed created greater stir. He was accused of beating people at night, of breaking down doors and windows, tearing garments and emptying pitchers and bottles. Altogether, the deceased made himself highly objectionable. There is reason to believe that he spared no house save that of the consul, in which we happened to be lodging. Every imagination was overwrought, people of good sense being affected as much as others. A disease of the brain seemed abroad, as dangerous as that of madness; entire families abandoned their houses and carried their pallets to the outskirts, there to pass the night. Even then they complained of fresh insults, and the most sober retired into the country. Citizens who were imbued with a sense of public zeal decided that one essential detail had been missed, so far, in the observance; from their point of view, the mass should have been celebrated after, and not before, removing the heart from the body. With this precaution it was pretended that the devil would have been taken by surprise and would not have attempted to return; but unfortunately they began with the mass, which gave him time to depart, and he was able to come back at his ease. These considerations left matters in their original state of difficulty. There were meetings and still meetings, both evening and morning; there were processions for three days and three nights; fasts were imposed on the priests; houses were visited by them, *aspergillus* in hand; there was sprinkling with holy water and doors were purified. Even the mouth of the miserable vampire was filled with holy water.

"In the midst of such prepossessions our course was to say nothing; we should have been regarded as jesters and infidels. What, however, was to be done to help the inhabitants? Every morning brought a fresh scene in the comedy by the recital of new pranks of this nightbird, who was even accused of committing the most abominable crimes. We did, however, represent more than once to the governor of the town that in our own country, under such circumstances, a watch would not fail to be set, to take note of what passed. The precaution was ultimately taken, and led to the arrest of some vagabonds who were undoubtedly at the bottom of the disorder. It was, of course, relaxed too soon, and two days subsequently, to atone for the fast which the said wastrels had undergone in prison, they betook themselves to emptying the wine jars in some of the abandoned houses. After driving in numberless drawn swords over the grave of the body, people now returned to their prayers, combined with disinterring the corpse as caprice led them, when an Albanian, who happened to be there, pointed out in an authoritative tone that it was highly ridiculous, in a case of the kind, to make use of the swords of Christians; these being cross-handled effectually prevented the devil from leaving the body, and his recommendation was therefore to substitute Turkish sabres. The advice of this expert came to nothing; the vampire was not more tractable, and they knew not what saint to invoke, when all with one voice, as if a word of command had been given, cried out through the whole town that the vampire must be burned completely, after which they might defy the devil, and that certainly it was better to have recourse to this extremity rather than that the island should be deserted. As a fact, certain families were preparing already for their departure.

"The vampire was therefore carried, by order of the governors, to the extremity of the isle of St. George, where a great pyre had been prepared with tar, lest even dry wood should not kindle quickly enough. What remained of the miserable body was cast therein and speedily consumed.

This was on the first day of January, 1701. Henceforth there were no complaints against the vampire; it was agreed that the devil had that time been overreached and songs were made to deride him."

It is to be observed in this account of Tournefort that he admits the reality of the visions which paralysed the whole people. He does not deny the flexibility or warmth of the corpse but seeks to explain these with the praiseworthy object of reassuring those who were concerned. He does not mention the decomposition of the body but only its evil smell, which is not less characteristic of vampire corpses than of venomous toadstools. Finally he allows that once the body was burned, the wonders and visions ceased. But we have wandered far from the subject of Fantasiasts in Magic; let us return to them and, forgetting the problem of vampires, a word shall be said on the cartomancist, Edmond. He is the pet sorcerer of ladies in the Quartier de Notre Dame de Lorette and he occupies, in the Rue Fontaine St. Georges, No. 30, a dainty little room, where the vestibule is always full of clients, including those occasionally of the male sex. Edmond is a man of tall stature, somewhat stout, of pale complexion, open countenance and sympathetic voice. He appears to believe in his own art and carries on conscientiously the methods of people like Etteilla and Mlle Lenormand. We have questioned him as to his processes, and he has answered frankly and civilly that he has been passionately devoted to the occult sciences from childhood; that he began divination early; that he is unacquainted with the philosophical secrets of transcendental knowledge; and that the keys of the Kabalah of Solomon are not in his possession. He states, however, that he is highly sensitive and that the mere proximity of his clients impresses him so keenly that in a way he feels their destiny. "I seem to hear singular noises and clankings of chains about those who are doomed to the scaffold, cries and moans round those who will die violently. Supernatural odours assail and almost stifle me. One day in the presence of a veiled lady, clothed in black, I began to tremble at an odour of straw and blood. 'Madam,' I cried, 'pray leave here, for you are surrounded by an atmosphere of murder and prison.'—'You say truly,' she answered, unveiling her pale face, 'I have been accused of infanticide and have just come out of prison. Since you have seen the past, tell me also the future.'"

One of our friends and disciples in Kabalism, utterly unknown to Edmond, went on a day to consult him, and having paid in advance he awaited the oracles, when Edmond, rising respectfully, begged him to take back his money. "I have nothing to tell you," he explained; "your destiny is closed against me by the key of occultism; whatsoever I might say you would know already as well as myself." He showed him out with many bows.

Edmond is also occupied with judicial astrology; he erects horoscopes and judges nativities at very moderate prices. In a word, he deals with everything belonging to his business, which is otherwise a wearisome and disenchanting thing. With how many disordered brains and diseased hearts must he be continually in relation, and the imbecile requirements of some, the unjust reproaches of others, the tiring confidences, the demand for philtres and spells, the obsessions of fools, all combine in making him gain his income hardly. To sum up, Edmond is a somnambulist like Alexis; he is self-magnetised by his cards and by the diabolical figures which adorn them; he wears black and gives his consultations in a black cabinet; in a word, he is the prophet of mystery.

CHAPTER V

SOME PRIVATE RECOLLECTIONS OF THE WRITER

ON a certain morning in 1839 the author of this book had a visit from Alphonse Esquiros, who said: "Let us pay our respects to the Mapah."[1] The natural question arose: "But in any case, who or what is the Mapah?" ... "He is a god," was the answer.... "Many thanks," said the author, "but I pay my devotions only to gods unseen." ... "Come notwithstanding; he is the most eloquent, most radiant and magnificent fool in the visible order of things".... "My friend, I am in terror of fools: their complaint is contagious." ... "Granted, *dilectissime*, and yet I am calling on you." ... "Admitted, and things being so, we will pay our respects to the Mapah."

In an appalling garret there was a bearded man of majestic demeanour, who invariably wore over his clothes the tattered cloak of a woman, and had in consequence rather the air of a destitute dervish. He was surrounded by several men, bearded and ecstatic like himself, and in addition to these there was a woman with motionless features, who seemed like an entranced somnambulist. The prophet's manner was abrupt and yet sympathetic; he had hallucinated eyes and an infectious quality of eloquence. He spoke with emphasis, warmed to his subject quickly, chafed and fumed till a white froth gathered on his lips. Abbé Lamennais was once termed "old ninety-three fulfilling its Easter duties". The catch phrase is more suited to the Mapah and his mysticism, as will be shewn by a fragment from one of his lyrical enthusiasms.

"Transgression was inevitable for man: it was decreed by his destiny, that he might be the instrument of his own reconstruction, that the greatness and majesty of God might be manifested in the majesty and greatness of human toil, passing through its successive phases of light and darkness. But primitive unity was destroyed by the Fall; suffering entered the world in the guise of the serpent, and the Tree of Life became the Tree of Death. Things being at this pass, God said to the woman: 'In sorrow thou shalt bring forth children,' yet added afterwards: 'Thou shalt crush the serpent's head.' And the first slave was a woman; she accepted her divine mission, and the pains of travail began. From the first hour of the Fall, the task of humanity has been, for this reason, a great and terrible task of initiation.

---

[1] I wish that it were possible to quote the moving panegyric on Ganneau in a letter addressed by Éliphas Lévi to Alexandre Erdan and printed by him in *La France Mystique*, vol. ii, pp. 184–188. He is described as one of the *élite* of intelligence, an artist, a poet of original and inexhaustible eloquence. He was sometimes bizarre but never absurd or wearisome. He was, finally, one of those hearts under the inspiration of which the zealous will crucify themselves with joy for the ungrateful. Erdan once saw Ganneau addressing a crowd in the Place de la Concorde, "uplifting his great arms and raising to heaven his beautiful Christ-like head".

For this also the terms of that initiation are all equally sacred in the eyes of God. Their *Alpha* is our common mother Eve, while the *Omega* is Liberty, who is our common mother also.

"I beheld a vast ship, having a gigantic mast with its crow's nest at the top; one of the ship's extremities looked to the West, the other to the East. On the western side it was poised upon the cloudy summits of three mountains, their bases lost in a raging sea. On the flank of each mountain was inscribed its ominous name. The first was Golgotha, the second Mont St. Jean, but the third was St. Helena. In the middle way of the mast, on the western side, there was erected a five-armed cross,[1] on which a woman was expiring. The inscription above her head was: FRANCE: JUNE 18, 1815: GOOD FRIDAY. The five arms of the cross represented the five divisions of the globe: the woman's head rested on Europe and was encircled by a cloud. But at the end of the ship to the East there was no darkness; and the keel paused at the threshold of the city of God, by the summit of a triumphal arch in the full rays of the sun. Here the woman reappeared, but this time transfigured and glorious. She rolled away the stone from the sepulchre, and on that stone was written: RESTORATION, days of the tomb: July 29, 1830: EASTER."

It will be seen that the Mapah was a successor of Catherine Théot and Dom Gerle; and yet—such is the strange sympathy between follies—he told us one day confidentially that he was Louis XVII returned to earth for a work of regeneration, while the woman who shared his life was Marie Antoinette of France. He explained further that his revolutionary theories were the last word of the violent pretensions of Cain, destined as such to ensure, by a fatal reaction, the victory of the just Abel. Now Esquiros and I visited the Mapah to enjoy his extravagances, but our imaginations were overcome by his eloquence. We were two college friends, like Louis Lambert and Balzac, and we had nourished dreams in common concerning impossible renunciations and unheard-of heroisms. After visiting Ganneau—for this was the name of the Mapah—we took it into our heads that it would be a great thing to communicate the last word of revolution to the world and to seal the abyss of anarchy, like Curtius, by casting ourselves therein. Our students' extravagance gave birth to the *Gospel of the People* and the *Bible of Liberty*, follies for which Esquiros and his ill-starred friend paid but too dearly. Hereof is the danger of enthusiastic manias; they are catching; one does not approach with impunity the edge of the precipice of madness.

The incident which now follows is a different and more terrible fatality. A nervous and delicate young man named Sobrier was numbered among the Mapah's disciples; he lost his head completely and believed himself predestined to save the world by provoking the supreme crisis of a universal revolution. The days of 1848 drew towards the threshold. A commotion had led to some change in the ministry, but the episode seemed closed. Paris had an air of contentment and the boulevards were illu-

[1] I suppose that this would be a St. Andrew's cross with the addition of a vertical branch, on which would rest the head of the crucified person.

minated. Suddenly a young man appeared in the populous streets of the Quartier Saint-Martin. He was preceded by two street arabs, one bearing a torch and the other beating to arms. A large crowd gathered; the young man got upon a post and harangued the people. His words were incoherent and incendiary, but the gist was to proceed to the Boulevard des Capucines and acquaint the ministry with the will of the people. The demoniac repeated the same harangue at every corner of the streets and presently he was marching at the head of a great concourse, a pistol in each hand, still heralded by torch and tambour. The frequenters of the boulevards joined out of mere curiosity, and subsequently it was a crowd no longer but the massed populace surging through the Boulevard des Italiens. In the midst of this the young man and his street Arabs disappeared, but before the Hotel des Capucines a pistol-shot was fired upon the people. This shot started the revolution, and it was fired by a fool.

Throughout that night two carts loaded with corpses perambulated the streets by torchlight; on the morrow all Paris was barricaded, and Sobrier was reported at home in a state of unconsciousness. It was he who, without knowing what he did, had for a moment shaken the world. Ganneau and Sobrier are dead and no harm is done them by reciting this terrible instance of the magnetism of enthusiasts and the fatalities which may be entailed by the nervous diseases of certain persons. The story is drawn from a reliable source and its revelations may sooth the conscience of that Belisarius of poetry who is the author of the *History of the Girondins*.

The magnetic phenomena produced by Ganneau continued even after his death. His widow, a woman of no education and little intelligence, the daughter of an honest peasant of Auvergne, remained in the static somnambulism in which she had been placed by her husband.[1] Like the child which assumes the form of its mother's imagination, she has become a living image of Marie Antoinette, when a prisoner at the Conciergerie. Her manners are those of a queen who is widowed and desolate for ever; a complaint sometimes escapes her, as though she were weary of her dream, but she is sovereignly indignant with any who seek to awake her. For the rest, she has no symptom of mental alienation; her outward conduct is reasonable, her life perfectly honourable and regular. Nothing is more pathetic, to our thinking, than this persistent obsession of a being fondly loved who lives again in a conjugal hallucination. Had Artemis existed literally it would be permissible to believe that Mausol was also a powerful mesmerist, and that he had gained and fixed for ever the affections of an extremely sensitive woman, outside all limits of free will and reason.

---

[1] There was a son of this marriage, and in 1855 M. Alexandre Erdan was inquiring what had become of him.

CHAPTER VI

THE OCCULT SCIENCES

THE secret of the occult sciences is that of Nature herself; it is the secret of the generation of angels and worlds; it is that of God's own omnipotence. "Ye shall be as the Elohim, knowing good and evil." So testified the serpent of Genesis, and so did the Tree of Knowledge become the Tree of Death. For six thousand years the martyrs of science have toiled and perished at the foot of this Tree, so that it may become once more the Tree of Life.

That Absolute which is sought by the foolish and found only by the wise is the truth, the reality and the reason of universal equilibrium. Such equilibrium is the harmony which proceeds from the analogy of opposites. Humanity has sought so far to balance itself as if on one leg—now on one and now again on the other. Civilisations have sprung up and have fallen, through the anarchic alienation of despotism, or alternatively through the despotic anarchy of revolt. Here superstitious enthusiasms and there the pitiful schemes of materialistic instinct have misguided the nations; but at last it is God Himself Who impels the world towards believing reason and reasonable beliefs. We have had enough and to spare of the prophets apart from philosophy and the philosophers destitute of religion. Blind believers and sceptics are on a par with each other, and both are equally remote from eternal salvation.

In the chaos of universal doubt, and amidst the conflict of science and faith, the great men and the seers figure as sickly artists, seeking the ideal beauty at the risk of their reason and their life. Look at them now even— these sublime children. They are whimsical and nervous like women; a shadow maims them; reason injures; they are unjust even to each other; and though assuredly on the quest of crowns, in their fantastic excesses they are the first to be guilty of that which Pythagoras forbids in one of his admirable symbols; they are the first to revile crowns and to trample them under their feet. They are fanatics of glory; but the good God has bound them by the chains of opinion, so that they may not be openly dangerous.

Genius is judged by the tribunal of mediocrity, and this judgment is without appeal, because, being the light of the world, genius is accounted as a thing that is null and dead whenever it ceases to enlighten. The ecstasy of the poet is controlled by the indifference of the prosaic multitude, and every enthusiast who is rejected by general good sense is a fool and not a genius. Do not count the great artists as bondsmen of the ignorant crowd, for it is the crowd which imparts to their talent the balance of reason.

Light is the equilibrium between shadow and brightness. Motion is the

Apocalyptic Key

equilibrium between inertia and activity. Authority is the equilibrium between liberty and power. Wisdom is equilibrium in thought; virtue is equilibrium in the affections; beauty is equilibrium in form. Outlines that are lovely are true outlines, and the magnificence of Nature is an algebra of graces and splendours. Whatsoever is true is beautiful; all that is beautiful should be true. Heaven and hell are the equilibrium of moral life; good and evil are the equilibrium of liberty.

The Great Work is the attainment of that middle point in which equilibrating force abides. Furthermore, the reactions of equilibrated force do everywhere conserve universal life by the perpetual motion of birth and death. It is for this reason that the philosophers have compared their gold to the sun. For the same reason that same gold cures all diseases of the soul and communicates immortality. Those who have found this middle point are true and wonderworking adepts of science and reason. They are masters of the wealth of worlds, confidants and friends of the princes of heaven itself, and Nature obeys them because they will what is willed by the law which is the motive power of nature. It is this which the Saviour of the world spoke of as the Kingdom of Heaven; this also is the *Sanctum Regnum* of the Holy Kabalah. It is the Crown and Ring of Solomon; it is the Sceptre of Joseph which the stars obeyed in heaven and the harvests on earth.

We have discovered this secret of omnipotence; it is not for sale in the market; but if God had commanded us to set a price thereon, we question whether the whole fortune of the buyers would seem its equivalent. Not for ourselves but for them, we should demand in addition their undivided soul and their entire life.

CHAPTER VII

SUMMARY AND CONCLUSION

IT remains for us to summarise and conclude. To summarise the history of a science is to summarise the science itself, and we are therefore to recapitulate the great principles of initiation, as preserved and transmitted through all the ages. Magical science is the absolute science of equilibrium. It is essentially religious; it presided at the formation of dogmas in the antique world and has been thus the nursing mother of all civilisations. O chaste and mysterious mother who, in giving milk of poetry and inspiration to the dawning generations, didst cover thy face and breast. Before all things she directs us to believe in God and to adore without seeking to define Him, since a God in definition is to some extent a finite God. And after Deity she points to eternal mathematics and equilibrated forces as to the sovereign principles of things. It is said in the Bible that God has ordered all things according to weight, number and measure. *Omnia in pondere et numero et mensura disposuit Deus*. Weight is equilibrium, number is quantity, measure is proportion—these three, and these are the eternal or divine basis of the science of Nature. Here now is the formula of equilibrium: Harmony results from the analogy of contraries. Number is the scale of analogies, the proportion of which is measure. The entire occult philosophy of the *Zohar* might be termed the science of equilibrium.[1] The key of numbers is found in the *Sepher Yetzirah;* their generation is analogous to the affiliation of ideas and the production of forms. On this account the illuminated hierophants of the Kabalah combined the hieroglyphic signs of numbers, ideas and forms in their sacred alphabet. The combinations of this alphabet give equations of ideas, and comprise by way of indication all possible combinations in natural forms. According to Genesis, God made man in His image, but as man is the living synthesis of creation, it follows that creation itself is made in the likeness of God. There are three things in the universe—the Spirit, the plastic mediator and matter. The ancients assigned to spirit, as its immediate instrument, that igneous fluid to which they gave the generic name of Sulphur; to the plastic mediator they assigned the name of Mercury, because of the symbolism represented by the Caduceus; to matter they gave the name of Salt, because of the fixed salt which remains after combustion, resisting the further action of fire. Sulphur was compared with the Father on account of the generative action of fire; Mercury with the Mother, because of its power of attraction and reproduction; and Salt, in

---

[1] To suggest that the *Zohar* exists to propound and interpret a thesis of equilibrium is like saying that the vast text is written about the legend of the Edomite Kings or that it is a violent attack on Christianity, because there is a reference to each of these subjects. The symbolism of the Balance is practically confined to a single tract imbedded in the *Zohar*.

fine, was the Child, or that substance which is subjected to education by Nature. For them also the creative substance was one, and the name which they gave it was Light. Positive or igneous light was volatile Sulphur; light in the negative state, or made visible by the vibrations of fire, was the fluidic or ethereal Mercury; and light neutralised, or shadow, the coagulated or fixed composite under the form of earth, was termed Salt.

After such manner did Hermes Trismegistus formulate his symbol, which is called the Emerald Tablet: "That which is above is like that which is below, and that which is below is like that which is above for the operations of the wonders of the one thing."[1] This means that the universal movement is produced by the analogies of fixed and volatile, the volatile tending to be fixed and the fixed to become volatile, thus producing a continual exchange between the modes of the one substance, and from the fact of the exchange the combinations of universal form in everlasting renewal.

The fire is Osiris, or the sun; the light is Isis, or the moon; they are the father and mother of that grand Telesma which is the universal substance —not that they are its creators, but rather its generating powers, the combined effort of which produces the fixed or earth, whence Hermes says that this force has reached its plenary manifestation when earth has been formed therefrom. Osiris is not therefore God, even for the great hierophants of the Egyptian sanctuary; he is the igneous or luminous shadow of the intellectual principle of life, and hence in the supreme moment of initiation a flying voice whispered in the ear of the adept that dubious revelation: "Osiris is a black god." Woe to the recipient whose understanding had not been raised by faith above the purely physical symbols of Egyptian revelation. Such words would become for him a formula of atheism, and his mind would be struck with blindness. But for the believer, more exalted in intelligence, those same words sounded like an earnest of the most sublime hopes. It was as if the initiator said to him: "My child, you mistake a lamp for the sun, but that lamp is only a star of night. Still, the true sun exists; leave therefore the night and seek the day."

That which the ancients understood by the four elements in no wise signified simple bodies, but rather the four elementary manifestations of the one substance. These modes were represented by the sphinx, its wings corresponding to air, the woman's breasts to water, the body of the bull to earth, and the lion's claws to fire. The one substance, thrice threefold in essential mode and tetradic in the form of manifestation—such is the secret of the three pyramids, triangular in respect of their elevation, square at the base and guarded by the sphinx. In raising these monuments Egypt attempted to erect the Herculean pillars of universal science. Sands have accumulated, centuries have passed, but the pyramids in their eternal

---

[1] "God stretched forth His right hand and created the world above, and He stretched forth His left hand and created the world below.... God created the world below on the model of the world above, for the image is found beneath of all that abides on high."—*Zohar*, Part II, fol. 20a.

greatness still propound to the nations that enigma of which the solution is lost. As to the sphinx, it seems to have sunk in the dust of ages. The great empires of Daniel have reigned by turn upon the earth and have gone down into the tomb, overwhelmed by their own weight. Conquests on the field of battle, monuments of labours, results of human passions—all are engulfed with the symbolic body of the sphinx; now only the human head rises over the desert sands as if looking for the universal empire of thought.

Divine or die—such was the terrible dilemma proposed by the sphinx to the Candidates for Theban royalty. The reason is that the secrets of science are actually those of life; the alternatives are to reign or to serve, to be or not to be. The natural forces will break us if we do not put them to use for the conquest of the world. There is no mean between the height of kinghood and the abyss of the victim state, unless we are content to be counted among those who are nothing because they ask not why or what they are.

The composite form of the sphinx also represents by hieroglyphical analogy the four properties of the universal agent—that is to say, the Astral Light—dissolving, coagulating, heating and cooling. These four properties, directed by the will of man, can modify all phases of Nature, producing life or death, health or disease, love or hatred, wealth even or poverty, in accordance with the given impulsion. They can place all the reflections of the light at the service of imagination; they are the paradoxical solution of the wildest questions which can be set for Transcendental Magic. Specimens of these paradoxical questions shall here follow, together with the answers thereto: (1) Is it possible to escape death? (2) Is there such a thing as the Philosophical Stone, and what must be done to find it? (3) Is it possible to be served by spirits? (4) What is meant by the Key, Ring and Seal of Solomon? (5) Is it possible to predict the future by reliable calculations? (6) Can good or evil be worked at will by means of magical power? (7) What must be done to become a true magician? (8) What are the precise forces put in operation by Black Magic?

We term these questions paradoxical because they are outside all that is understood as science, while at the same time they seem negatived by faith. If propounded by an uninitiated person they are merely foolhardy, while their complete solution, if given by an adept, would seem like a sacrilege. God and Nature alike have closed the Sanctuary of Transcendent Science, and this in such a manner that, beyond a certain limit, he who knows would speak to no purpose, because he would not be understood. The revelation of the Great Magical Secret is therefore happily impossible. The replies which we are about to give will be the last possible expression of the word in Magic, and they will be put in all clearness, but we do not guarantee to make them comprehensible to our readers.

In respect of the first and second, it is possible to escape death after two manners—in time and in eternity. We escape it in time by the cure of diseases and by avoiding the infirmities of old age; we escape it in respect of eternity by perpetuating in memory personal identity amidst the transformations of existence. Let it be certified (1) that the life resulting from motion can only be maintained by the succession and the perfecting of forms; (2) that the science of perpetual motion is the science of life; (3) that the purpose of this science is the correct apprehension of equilibrated influences; (4) that all renewal operates by destruction, each generation therefore involving a death and each death a generation. Let us now further certify, with the ancient sages, that the universal principle of life is a substantial movement or a substance which is eternally and essentially moved and mover, invisible and impalpable, in a volatile state and manifesting materially when it becomes fixed by the phenomena of polarisation. This substance is indefectible, incorruptible and consequently immortal; but its manifestations in the world of form are subject to eternal mutation by the perpetuity of movement. Thus all dies because all lives, and if it were possible to make any form eternal, then motion would be arrested and the only real death would be thus created. To imprison a soul for ever in a mummified human body, such would be the terrible solution of that magical paradox concerning pretended immortality in the same body and on the same earth. All is regenerated by the universal dissolvent of the first substance. The force of this dissolvent is concentrated in the quintessence—that is to say, at the equilibrating centre of a dual polarity. The four elements of the ancients are the four forces of the universal magnet, represented by the figure of a cross, which cross revolves indefinitely about its own centre and so propounds the enigma respecting the quadrature of the circle. The Creative Word speaks from the middle of the cross and cries: "It is finished." It is in the exact proportion of the four elementary forms that we must seek the Universal Medicine of bodies, even as the Medicine of the Soul is offered by religion in Him Who gives Himself eternally on the cross for the salvation of the world. The magnetic state and polarisation of the heavenly bodies results from their equilibrated gravitation about suns, which are the common reservoirs of their electro-magnetism. The vibration of the quintessence about common reservoirs manifests by light, and the polarisation of light is revealed by colours. White is the colour of the quintessence; this colour condenses towards its negative pole as blue and becomes fixed as black; while it condenses towards its positive pole as yellow and becomes fixed as red. Thus centrifugal life proceeds always from black to red, passing by white, and centripetal life returns from red to black, following the same path. The four intermediates or mixed hues produce with the three primary colours what are called the seven colours of the prism and the solar spectrum. These seven colours form seven atmospheres or seven luminous zones round each sun, and the planet which is dominant in each zone is magnetised in a manner analogous to the colour of its atmosphere. In the depths of the earth, metals are formed like planets in the sky, by the particular influences of a latent light which decomposes when traversing certain regions. To take possession of a subject in which the metallic light is latent, before it becomes specialised, and drive it to the extreme positive pole—that is to say, to the live red—by the help of a fire derived from the light itself—such is the secret in full of the Great Work. It will be understood that this positive light at its extreme degree of condensation is life itself in a fixed state, serving as a universal dissolvent and as a medicine for all Kingdoms of Nature. But to extract from marcassite, stibium and philosophical arsenic the living and bisexual metallic sperm, we must have a prime dissolvent which is a mineral saline menstruum, and there must be, moreover, the concurrence of magnetism and electricity. The rest proceeds of itself in a single vessel, being the athanor, and by the graduated fire of one lamp. The adepts say that it is a work of women and children.

The heat, light, electricity and magnetism of modern chemists and physicists were for the ancients elementary phenomenal manifestations of one substance, called *Aour*, *Od* and *Ob*—that is to say, אור, אוּר, אוּב. *Od* is the active, *Ob* the passive, and *Aour* is the name of the bisexual and equilibrated composite which is signified when the Hermetic philosophers speak of gold. Vulgar gold is metalised. *Aour* and philosophical gold is the same *Aour* in the state of a soluble gem. Theoretically, according to the transcendental science of antiquity, the Philosophical Stone which heals all diseases and accomplishes the transmutation of metals exists therefore incontestably. Does it, however, or can it, exist in fact? If we answer this in the affirmative, no one will believe, and the simple statement shall stand as a paradoxical solution of the paradoxes expressed by the two first questions, without dealing with the problem as to what must be done in order to find the Philosophical Stone. M. de la Palisse would reply in our place that in order to find one must of necessity seek, unless indeed discovery is a matter of chance. Enough has been said to direct and facilitate research.

The third and fourth questions concern the ministry of spirits and the Key, Seal and Ring of Solomon. When the Saviour of the world, at His temptation in the desert, overcame the three lusts which keep the soul in bondage—that is to say, the lust of the appetites, lust of ambition and lust of greed—it is written that the angels came down to serve Him. The explanation is that spirits are subject to the sovereign spirit, and he is the sovereign spirit who binds the rebellious turbulence and unlawful propensities of the flesh. It should be noted at the same time that to reverse the natural order of communication subsisting between things which are is opposed to the law of Providence. We do not find that the Saviour of the world and His apostles evoked the souls of the dead. The immortality of the soul, being one of the most consoling dogmas of religion, is reserved for the aspirations of faith and will never be proved by facts accessible to the criticism of science. Loss of reason, or its distraction at the very least, is hence and will be always the penalty for those who dare to pry into the other life with the eyes of this world only. Hence also magical traditions always represent the spirits of the dead as responding to evocations with sad and angry countenances. They complain of being troubled in their repose and they proffer only reproaches and menaces. The Keys of Solomon are religious and rational forces expressed by signs, and their use is not so much in the evocation of spirits as to shield us from aberration in experiences relative to the occult sciences. The Seal is the synthesis of the Keys and the Ring indicates its use. The Ring of Solomon is at once round and square and it represents the mystery of the quadrature of the circle. It is composed of seven squares so arranged that they form a circle. Their bezels are round and square, one being of gold and the other of silver. The Ring should be a filagree of the seven metals. In the silver setting a white stone is placed and in the gold one there is a red stone. The white stone bears the sign of the Macrocosm, while the Microcosm is on the red stone. When the Ring is worn upon the finger, one of the stones should be turned inwards and the other outward, accordingly as it is desired to command spirits of light or darkness. The plenary powers of this Ring can be accounted for in a few words. The will is omnipotent when armed with the living forces of Nature. Thought is idle and dead until it manifests by word or sign; it can therefore neither spur nor direct will. The sign, being the indispensable form of thought, is the necessary instrument of will. The more perfect the sign the more powerfully is the thought formulated, and the will is consequently directed with more force. Blind faith moves mountains, and what therefore would be possible to faith if enlightened by complete and indubitable science? If the soul could concentrate its plenary understanding and energy in the utterance of a single word, would not that word be all-powerful? The Ring of Solomon, with its double seal, typifies all science and faith of the Magi expressed by one sign. It symbolises the powers of heaven and earth and the sacred laws which rule them, whether in the celestial Macrocosm or in the Microcosm of man. It is the talisman of talismans and the pantacle which is above pantacles. As a sign of life it is omnipotent, but it is without efficacy as a dead sign: intelligence and faith, the intelligence of Nature and faith in its eternally Active Cause—of such is the life of signs.

The profound study of natural mysteries may alienate the casual observer from God because mental fatigue paralyses the aspirations of the heart. It is in this sense that the occult sciences may be dangerous and even fatal for certain personalities. Mathematical exactitude, the absolute rigour of natural laws, their harmony and simplicity, suggest to many an inevitable, eternal, inexorable mechanism, and for such as these Providence recedes behind the iron wheels of a clock in perpetual motion. They fail to reflect on the indubitable fact of freedom and autocracy in thinking beings. A man disposes at his will of creatures organised like himself; he can snare birds in the air, fish in the water and wild beasts in the forest; he can cut down or burn entire forests; he can mine and blast rocks, or even mountains; he can modify all forms about him; and yet, notwithstanding the supreme analogies of Nature, he refuses to believe that other intelligent beings might at their will disintegrate and consume worlds, extinguish suns by a breath or reduce them to starry dust—beings so great that they are too much for our faculty of sight, even as we, in our turn, are probably inappreciable to the eye of the mite or worm. And if such beings exist without the universe being destroyed a thousand times over, must we not admit that they are under obedience to a supreme will, a wise and omnipotent force, which forbids them to annihilate worlds, even as it forbids us to destroy the swallow's nest and the chrysalis of the butterfly? For the Magus who is conscious of this power in the deep places of his nature, and who discerns in universal law the instruments of eternal justice, the Seal of Solomon, his Keys and his Ring are tokens of supreme royalty.

The next questions concern the prediction of things to come by means of reliable calculations and the working of good or evil by magical influence. The answers are in this wise. Two chess players of equal skill being seated at a table and having opened the game, which of them will win? Assuredly the more watchful of the two. If I knew the preoccupations of both, I could foresee certainly the result of their match. To foresee is to win at chess, and it is the same in the game of life. In life nothing comes by chance; chance is the unforeseen, but that which the ignorant fail to perceive in advance has been accounted for already by the sage. All events, like all forms, result either from a conflict or from a balancing of forces, which forces can be represented by numbers. The future may thus be determined in advance by calculation. Every extreme action is counterpoised by an equivalent reaction. So laughter presages tears, and for this reason our Saviour said: "Blessed are those who mourn." He said also, and again for the same reason: "He that exalteth himself shall be abased, and he that humbleth himself shall be exalted." Today Nebuchadnezzar is a god; tomorrow he will be changed into a beast. Today Alexander makes his triumphal entry into Babylon and has incense offered to him on all the altars; but tomorrow he will die in a state of degraded drunkenness. The future is in the past, and the past is also in the future. When genius foresees, it remembers. Effects are linked together so inevitably and so exactly to their causes, and become on their own part the causes for further effects in such conformity with the first as regards their manner of production, that a single fact may reveal to a seer an entire succession of mysteries. The coming of Christ makes that of Anti-Christ a certainty; but the advent of Anti-Christ will precede the triumph of the Holy Spirit. The money-seeking epoch in which we now live is the precursor of more lavish charities and of greater good works than the world has yet known.

But it must be understood that the will of man modifies blind causes and that a single impetus started by him may change the equilibrium of an entire world. If such is man's power in the world under his dominion, what must be that of the intelligences which rule the suns? The least of the *Egregores*, with a breath, and by dilating suddenly the latent caloric of our earth, might shatter and reduce it into a cloud of dust. Man also can dissipate by a breath all the happiness of one of his kind. Human beings are magnetised like worlds; like suns, they irradiate their particular light; some are more absorbent, some give forth more freely. No one is isolated in this world; each is a fatality or a providence. Augustus and Cinna encounter; both are proud and implacable; and hereof is fatality. That fatality makes Cinna seek to slay Augustus, who is impelled as fatally to punish him; but he elects to forgive. Here fatality is changed into providence, and the epoch of Augustus, inaugurated by this sublime beneficence, was worthy to witness the birth of Him Who said: "Forgive your enemies." By extending his mercy to Cinna, Augustus atoned for all the revenge of Octavius. So long as man is subject to the dictates of fatality, he is profane—that is to say, a man who must be excluded from the sanctuary of knowledge, because in his hands knowledge would become a terrible instrument of destruction. On the contrary, the man who is free, who governs by understanding the blind instincts of life, is essentially a preserver and repairer, for Nature is the domain of his power and the temple of his immortality. When the uninitiated seeks to do good the result is evil. On the other hand, the true initate can never will to do evil; if he strikes it is to chastise and to cure. The breath of the uninitiated is deadly, that of the initiate is lifegiving. He who is profane suffers that others may suffer also, but the initiate endures in order that others may be spared. He who is profane steeps his arrows in his own blood and poisons them; he who is initiated cures the most cruel wounds by a single drop of his blood.

The last questions are what must be done to become a true magician and in what precisely do the powers of Black Magic consist? Now, he who disposes of the secret forces of Nature and yet does not risk being crushed by them—he is a true magician. He is known by his works and by his end which is always a great sacrifice. Zoroaster created the primitive doctrine and civilisations of the East, after which he vanished in a tempest like Œdipus. Orpheus gave poetry to Greece and with that poetry the beauty of all high things; he then perished in an orgy in which he refused to join. All his virtues notwithstanding, Julian was only an initiate of Black Magic; his death was that of a victim and not of a martyr; it was an annihilation and a defeat: he failed to understand his epoch. Though acquainted with the Doctrine of Transcendental Magic, he misapplied the Ritual. Apollonius of Tyana and Synesius were simply wonderful philosophers; they cultivated the true science but did nothing for posterity. At their period the Magi of the Gospel reigned in the three parts of the known world, and the oracles were silenced by the cries of the babe of Bethlehem. The King of Kings, the Magus of all Magi, had come into the world and the ritualworships, the laws, the empires, all were changed. There is a void in the world of marvels between Jesus Christ and Napoleon. That incarnate word of battle, that armed Messiah who was the bearer of the last name, came blindly and unconsciously to complete the Christian message. This revelation had so far taught us how to die, but the Napoleonic civilisation has shown us how to conquer. The two messages—sacrifice and victory, how to suffer, to die, to strive and to overcome—contrary as they are in appearance—comprise in their union the great secret of honour. Cross of the

Saviour and cross of valour, you are incomplete when apart from one another, for only he knows how to conquer who has learned self-devotion, even to death, and how can this be attained except by belief in eternal life? Though he died in appearance, Napoleon is destined to return in the person of one who will realise his spirit. Solomon and Charlemagne will return also in the person of a single monarch; and then St. John the Evangelist, who according to tradition shall be reborn at the end of time, will appear as sovereign pontiff, the apostle of understanding and of love. The combination of these two rulers, announced by all the prophets, will bring about the wonder of the world's regeneration. The science of the true magician will be then at its zenith, for so far our workers of miracles have been for the most part sorcerers and bondsmen—that is to say, the blind instruments of chance. Now, the masters whom fatality casts upon the world are soon overthrown thereby, and those who conquer in the name of their passions shall fall the prey of those passions. When Prometheus in his jealousy of Jupiter stole the thunderbolts of the gods, he sought to create an immortal eagle, but what he made and immortalised was a vulture. We hear in another fable of that impious king Ixion, who would have ravished the queen of heaven, but that which he received in his arms was a faithless cloud, and he was bound by fiery serpents to the inexorable wheel of destiny. These profound allegories are a warning to false adepts, profaners of Magic Science and partisans of Black Magic. The power of Black Magic is a contagion of vertigo and an epidemic of unreason. The fatality of passion is like a fiery serpent which twists and writhes about the world devouring the souls therein. But intelligence—peaceable, smiling and full of love—represented by the Mother of God, sets her foot upon its head. Fatality consumes itself and is that old serpent of Kronos eternally devouring its tail. Rather there are two hostile serpents striving one with another, until such time as harmony intervenes to enchant them and make them interlace peaceably around the caduceus of Hermes.

Conclusion

The most intemperate and absurd of all faiths is to believe that there is no universal and absolute intelligent principle. It is a faith, since it involves the negation of the indefinite and indefinable; it is intemperate, for it is isolating and desolating; it is absurd, because it supposes complete nothing in place of most complete perfection. In Nature all is preserved by equilibrium and renewed by activity. Equilibrium in order and activity signifies progress. The science of equilibrium and movement is the absolute science of Nature. Man by its aid can produce and direct natural phenomena as he rises ever towards intelligence that is higher and more perfect than his own. Moral equilibrium is the concurrence of science and faith, distinct in their forces but joined in their action to endow the spirit and heart of man with that rule which is reason. The science which denies faith is not less unreasonable than the faith which denies science.

The object of faith cannot be defined and still less denied by science; science, on the contrary, is itself called to substantiate the rational basis of the hypotheses of faith. An isolated belief does not constitute faith, because it lacks authority and hence moral guarantee; it tends to fanaticism and superstition. Faith is the confidence which is imparted by religion—that is to say, by the communion of belief. True religion is constituted by universal suffrage. It is therefore ever and essentially catholic—that is to say, universal. It is an ideal dictatorship proclaimed generally in the revolutionary domain of the unknown. When the law of equilibrium is understood more adequately it will put an end to all the wars and revolutions of the old world. There has been conflict between powers as between moral forces. The papacy is blamed because it clings to temporal power, but what is forgotten is the protestant tendency towards usurpation of spiritual power. So long as the royalties put forward a pretension to be popes, so long will the popes be driven, by the same law of equilibrium, to the pretension of being kings. The whole world continues to dream of unity in political power, but it does not understand the power resident in equilibrated dualism. Confronted by the royal usurpers of spiritual power, if the Pope were king no longer, he would be no longer anything. In the temporal order he is subject, like others, to the prejudgments of his time; he dare not therefore abdicate his temporal power, if such abdication would be a scandal for a considerable part of the world. When the sovereign opinion of the universe shall have proclaimed publicly that a temporal prince cannot be Pope; when the Czar of all the Russias and the King of Great Britain shall have renounced their derisive priesthood, the Pope will know that which remains to be done on his own part. Till then he must struggle, and if needs be must die, to maintain the integrity of St. Peter's patrimony.

The science of moral equilibrium will put an end to religious disputes and philosophical blasphemies. Men of understanding will be also men of religion when it comes to be recognised that religion does not impeach the freedom of conscience, and when those who are truly religious shall respect that science which recognises on its own part the existence and necessity of a universal religion. Such science will flood the philosophy of history with new light, and will furnish a synthetic plan of all the natural sciences. The law of equilibrated forces and of organic compensations will reveal a new chemistry and a new physics. So from discovery to discovery we shall work back to Hermetic philosophy, and shall be astonished at those prodigies of simplicity and brilliance which have been for so long and long forgotten.

Philosophy in that day will be exact like mathematics, for true ideas—being those which are identical with the living orders and so constituting the science of reality—shall combine with reason and justice to furnish exact proportions and equations as rigorous as numbers. Error thenceforth will be possible to ignorance alone, and true knowledge will be free from self-deception. Aestheticism will be subordinated no longer to caprices of taste which change as fashions change. If the beautiful is the splendour of the true, we shall be able to calculate without error the radiation of a light of which the source shall be certainly known and determined with exact precision. Poetry will abound no longer with foolish and subversive tendencies, nor will poets be those dangerous enchanters whom Plato crowned with flowers and banished from his republic; they will be rather magicians of reason and gracious mathematicians of harmony. Does this mean that the earth will become an Eldorado? No, for so long as humanity exists, there will be children, meaning those who are weak, small, ignorant and poor. But society will be governed by its true masters, and there will be no irremediable evil in human life. It will be understood that the divine miracles are those of eternal order, and the phantoms of imagination will be worshipped no longer on the faith of unexplained wonders. The abnormal character of certain phenomena is only a proof of our ignorance in the presence of the laws of Nature. When God designs to communicate the knowledge of Himself He enlightens our reason and does not seek to confound or surprise it. In that day we shall know the utmost limit of the power of man who is created in the image of God; we shall realise that he also is a creator in his own sphere and that his goodness, directed by Eternal Reason, is a lower providence for beings which are placed by Nature under his influence and domination. Religion will then and for evermore have nothing to fear from progress, and will follow in the course thereof. The Blessed Vincent de Lerins, a doctor justly venerated in the golden chain of catholicism, expresses admirably this accord between progress and conservative authority. According to him, true faith is worthy of our confidence only on account of that invariable authority which safeguards its dogmas from the caprices of human ignorance. "This notwithstanding," adds Vincent de Lerins, "such immobility is not death; on the contrary, it preserves a germ of life for the future. That which we believe today without understanding will be understood by the future, which will rejoice in the knowledge thereof. *Posteritas intellectum gratuletur, quod ante vestustas non intellectum venerabutur.* If therefore we are asked whether all progress is excluded from the religion of Christ Jesus, the answer is no, assuredly, for great is the progress expected. Who indeed would be so jealous of humanity and at such enmity with God as to wish to hinder progress? But the condition is that it should be progress in reality, and not change of belief. Progress is the growth and development of each thing according to its class and its nature. Disorder is confusion and the medley of things and their nature. There must be undoubtedly a difference in the degrees of intelligence, science and wisdom, as much for men in general as for each man in particular, according to the natural succession of epochs in the Church, but only so that all be conserved and that dogma shall ever cherish the same spirit and maintain the same definition. Religion should develop souls successively, as life develops bodies which remain the same through all the stages of their growth. How great is the difference between the infantile flower of early years and the maturity of age! The old, notwithstanding, are the same in respect of personality as they were in boyhood; it is the exterior and the appearances which have changed. The limbs of an infant in the cradle are exceedingly frail, yet are they the same organs, having the same root principles, as those of the man; and this must be so, for otherwise there is deformity or death.

"The analogy obtains in the religion of Jesus Christ, for progress therein is fulfilled according to the same conditions and following similar laws. It grows with the years, with the years it increases in strength, but nothing is added to the sum total of its being. It was born complete and perfect in respect of proportions, and it grows and extends without changing. Our fathers sowed the wheat, and our nephews ought not to reap tares. The intermediate crops change nothing in the nature of the grain; we leave it perforce as we take it. Catholicism planted roses, and is it for us to substitute brambles? No, unquestionably; otherwise, woe to us. The balm and cinnamon of this spiritual paradise must not change in our hands to aconite and poison. All whatsoever which in the Church, that lovely land of God, has been sown by the fathers must be cultivated and nourished by the sons. This only must grow, and this alone blossom; but it may increase, and it should develop. As a fact, God permits that the dogmas of this heavenly philosophy shall be studied, developed, polished in a certain sense; but that which is forbidden is to change them, and that which is a crime is to prune them or to mutilate. May new light come down on them and the wise distinctions multiply, but let them ever preserve their fulness, their integrity and their native quality."

Let us therefore take it for granted that all conquests of science in the past have been achieved for the profit of the universal Church, and, with Vincent de Lerins, let us allocate thereto the undivided heritage of all progress to come. Unto her be the great aspirations of Zoroaster and all discoveries of Hermes; hers be the Key of the Holy Arch and the Ring of Solomon, for she represents the holy and immutable hierarchy. She is stronger by reason of her struggles and is grounded by her apparent falls in still greater stability. She suffers in order that she may reign; she is cast down that she may be exalted in her rising; and she dies that she may rise again. "We must be prepared," says Comte Joseph de Maistre, "for a great event in the divine order; we are moving towards it at an accelerated pace, which must be manifest to all observers, while striking oracles announce that the hour is at hand. Many prophecies in the *Apocalypse* have reference to these modern times. One writer has gone so far as to say that the event is already inaugurated and that the French nation is destined to become the great instrument of the most mighty of all revolutions. There is perhaps no truly religious man in all Europe—I speak of the educated classes—who is not in expectation of something extraordinary at this present moment. Does a general presentiment of the kind count for nothing? Go back through past ages, even to the birth of our Saviour. At that period a high and mysterious voice, beginning in the Eastern realms, proclaimed that the East was about to triumph, that a conqueror would come out of Judea, that a divine infant was given us, that He would descend from highest heaven and restore the golden age upon the earth. Such ideas were spread abroad everywhere, and as they lent themselves to poetry, above all things, they were taken over by the greatest of Latin poets and emblazoned with brilliant hues in his *Pollio*. To-day, as in the time of Virgil, the universe is in expectation, and how on our part shall we despise such strong persuasion, or by what right condemn those who are devoted to sacred researches on the indications of divine signs? If you seek proof of what is in store, look at the sciences themselves; consider the progress of chemistry, of astronomy also, and you will see where they are leading. Would you think, for example, that Newton takes us back to Pythagoras and that it will be proved presently that the heavenly bodies are set in motion, like human bodies, by intelligences joined thereto? We know not how, but this is what is on the point of being verified beyond all dispute. Such doctrine may seem paradoxical and even ridiculous, because current opinion imposes this view; but let us wait till the natural affinity of religion and science marry both in the mind of a single man of genius. His advent cannot be far off, and then the opinions which now seem bizarre or irrational will become axioms which no one will question, while people will talk of our present stupidity as they now speak of mediæval superstition."[1]

According to St. Thomas, and it is a beautiful utterance: "All that God wills is just, but that which is just should not be so designated only because God wills it"—*Non ex hoc dicitur justum quod Deus illud vult*. The moral doctrine of the future is contained herein, and from its fruitful principle one deduction follows immediately: not only is it good from the standpoint of faith to do what is ordained by God, but even from the standpoint of reason it is excellent and rational to obey Him. Man can therefore say: I do good not only because God wills it but because I also will. The will of humanity may be thus at once free and in conformity, tor reason—demonstrating in an irrecusable fashion the wisdom of the prescriptions of faith—will act on its proper impulse by following the divine law, of which reason thus becomes, as it were, the human sanction. From that time forward superstition and impiety will be no longer possible, while from these considerations it follows that in religion and in practical—that is to say, in moral—philosophy, there will be an absolute authority, and moral dogmas will alone be revealed and established. Till then we shall have the pain and consternation of seeing daily the most simple and universal questions of right and duty challenged; while if blasphemies are reduced to silence, it is one thing to impose such silence but another to persuade and convert.

So long as Transcendental Magic was profaned by the wickedness of

[1] Joseph de Maistre: *Soirées de St. Pétersbourg*, 1821. p. 308

men, the Church of necessity proscribed it. False Gnostics have discredited that name of Gnosticism which was once so pure; sorcerers have outraged the children of the Magi; but religion, that friend of tradition and guardian of the treasures of antiquity, can no longer reject a doctrine anterior to the Bible and in perfect accord with traditional respect for the past, as well as with our most vital hopes for progress in the future. The common people are initiated by toil and by faith into the right of property and knowledge. There will always be such a people, as there will be children always; but when the aristocracy, endowed with wisdom, shall become a mother to the people, the path of personal, successive, gradual emancipation will be open to all, and he that is called will thereby be enabled through his own efforts to attain the rank of the elect. This is that mystery of the future which antique initiation concealed in its dark recesses. The miracles of Nature made subject to the will of man are reserved for the elect to come. The crook of the priesthood shall become the rod of miracles; it was so in the time of Moses and of Hermes; it will be so again. The sceptre of the Magus will be that of the world's king or emperor; and that person will by right be first among men who shall have shewn himself greatest of all in knowledge and in virtue. Magic, at that time, will be no longer an occult science except for the ignorant; it will be one that is incontestable for all. Then shall universal revelation resolder one to another all links of its golden chain; the human epic will close and even the efforts of Titans will have served only to restore the altar of the true God. All forms which have clothed the divine thought successively will be reborn immortal and perfect. All those features sketched by the successive art of nations will be united to form the perfect image of God. Having been purified and brought out of chaos, dogma will give birth naturally to an infallible ethic, and the social order will be constituted on this basis. Systems which are now in warfare are dreams of the twilight; let them pass. The sun shines and the earth follows its course; distracted is he who doubts that the day is coming. Distracted also are those who say that catholicism is only a dead trunk and that we must put the axe thereto. They do not see that beneath its dry bark the living tree is renewed unceasingly. Truth has no past and no future; it is eternal; it is not that which ends; it is our dream only. Hammer and hatchet, which destroy in the sight of man, are in God's hand as the knife of a pruner, and the dead branches—being superstitions and heresies in religion, science and politics—can alone be lopped from the tree of everlasting convictions and beliefs.

It has been the purpose of this History of Magic to demonstrate that, at the beginning, the symbols of religion were those also of science, which was then in concealment. May religion and science, reunited in the future, give help and shew love to one another, like two sisters, for theirs has been one cradle.

APPENDIX

AUTHOR'S PREFACE PREFIXED TO THE FIRST EDITION

THE works of Éliphas Lévi on the science of the ancient Magi are intended to form a complete course, divided into three parts. The first part contains the Doctrine and Ritual of Transcendental Magic; the second is The History of Magic; and the third will be published later under the title of The Key to the Great Mysteries. Taken separately, each of these parts gives a complete instruction and seems to contain the whole science; but in order to a full understanding of one it is indispensable to study the two others carefully.

The triadic division of our undertaking has been imposed by the science itself, because our discovery of its great mysteries rests entirely upon the significance which the old hierophants attached to numbers. THREE was for them the generating number, and in the exposition of every doctrine they had regard to (*a*) the theory on which it was based, (*b*) its realisation and (*c*) its application to all possible uses. Whether philosophical or religious, thus were dogmas formed; and thus the dogmatic synthesis of that Christianity which was heir of the magi imposes on our faith the recognition of Three Persons in one God and three mysteries in universal religion.

We have followed in the arrangement of the two works already published, and shall follow in the third work, the plan indicated by the Kabalah—that is to say, by the purest tradition of occultism. Our Doctrine and Ritual are each divided into twenty-two chapters distinguished by the twenty-two letters of the Hebrew alphabet. We have set at the head of each chapter the letter thereto belonging and the Latin words which, according to the best writers, represent its hieroglyphical meaning. For example, at the head of the first chapter will be found:

1 א A
THE RECIPIENT
Disciplina
Ensoph
Kether

The explanation is that the letter *Aleph*—equivalent to A in Latin, and having the number 1 as its numerical value—signifies the Recipient, the man who is called to initiation, the qualified personality, corresponding to the Bachelor of the Tarot. It signifies also *disciplina*, or dogmatic syllepsis; *Ensoph*, or being in its general and primary conception; and finally, *Kether*, or the Crown, which, in Kabalistic theology, is the first and obscure idea of Divinity. The chapter in question is the development of the title and the title contains hieroglyphically the whole chapter.

The History of Magic, which follows, narrates and explains, according to the general theory of the science furnished in the Doctrine and Ritual, the realisation of that science through the ages. As the Introduction explains, it

[1] For the sake of completeness I have included this preface, though from some points of view it might have been reasonably omitted altogether.

APPENDIX

i, constituted in harmony with the number seven—the septenary being the number of the creative week and of Divine Realisation.

The Key to the Great Mysteries will be established on the number four—which is that of the enigmatic forms of the sphinx and of elementary manifestations. It is also the number of the square and of force. In the book referred, to, certitude will be established on irremovable bases. The enigma of the sphinx will have its complete solution and our readers will be provided with that Key of things kept secret from the foundation of the world which the learned Postel only dared to depict enigmatically in one of his most obscure books, giving no satisfactory explanation.

The History of Magic explains the affirmations found in the Doctrine and Ritual; the Key of the Great Mysteries will complete and explain the History of Magic. In this manner, for the attentive reader at least, we trust that nothing will be found wanting in our revelation of the secrets of Jewish Kabalism and of Supreme Magic—whether that of Zoroaster or of Hermes.

The writer of these books gives lessons willingly to serious and interested persons in search of these; but once and for all he desires to forewarn his readers that he tells no fortunes, does not teach divination, makes no predictions, composes no philtres and lends himself to no sorcery and no evocation. He is a man of science, not a man of deception. He condemns energetically whatsoever is condemned by religion, and hence he must not be confounded with persons who can be approached without hesitation on a question of applying their knowledge to a dangerous or illicit use. For the rest, he welcomes honest criticism, but he fails to understand certain hostilities. Serious study and conscientious labour are superior to all attacks; and the first blessings which they procure, for those who can appreciate them, are profound peace and universal benevolence.

ÉLIPHAS LÉVI.

INDEX

ABEL, 43, 108
Abiram, 285
Abraham, 30, 60, 72, 98, 103, 129, 152, 178
Abraham the Jew, 250, 264, 265
Absolute, 29, 331, 358
Acharat, 301, 302, 304
Achilles, 121, 132
Adam, 36, 55, 56, 59, 105, 159, 193, 204, 230, 330
Adam, Book of the Penitence of, 56
Adam Kadmon, 64
Adhi-Nari, 72
Adolphus of Schleswig, 199
Adonai, 99, 183, 196
Aeschylus, 88
Agamemnon, 132
Agde, Council of, 192
Agesilaus, 112
Agla, 99, 101, 196
Agrippa, H. Cornelius, 91, 252
Ahih, 99, 230
Ahriman, 35, 39, 45
Al, 230
Albertus Magnus, 90, 203, 205
Albigenses, 118, 310
Alchemy, 87, 127, 163, 164, 204, 205, 206, 217, 247, 250, 251, 266, 267, 302, 365
Alcides, 88
Alcmene, 112
Aleph, 51, 302
Alexandria, School of, 80, 99, 101, 152, 173
Alfarabius, 206
Alphabet, Hebrew, 82, 99, 101, 152, 173
Alphons XI, 240
Alihotas, 301, 302
Amasis, King, 92
Ammonius, 142, 176
Amphion, 86
Analogy, 44, 150, 372
André, Françoise, 313, 315
Antichrist, 65
Apis, 84
Apocalypse, 58, 61, 98, 148, 283, 372
Apocrypha, 149
Apollonius of Tyana, 162–165, 368
Apuleius, 168–170
Ararita, 230
Arcanum, Great. *See* Great Secret

Archedemus, 123
Aristeus, 206
Aristotle, 65, 113, 205, 246
Arius, 174
Ark of the Covenant, 57
Aroux, Eugène, 260, 263
Art, Royal, 29, 81, 110
Art, Sacerdotal, 110, 112
Artephius, 206
Asclepios, 107
Astarte, 70
Astrology, 89
Athanor, 164
Augury, 140
Augustine, St., 34, 170
Aupetit, Pierre, 270

BABEL, 108, 109
Bacchantes, 115, 131, 140
Bacchus, 131, 134
Baldwin II, 209
Ballanche, 89
Balmes, James, 151
Balneum Mariæ, 164
Baphomet, 211
Bartolocci, 203
Beausoleil, Baron de, 267
Bel, 183
Belphegor, 109
Belshazzar, 137
Belus, 69, 70
Benjamin, Tribe of, 139
Bermechobus, 58
Bernard of Sienna, St., 240
Bernard of Saxe-Weimar, Prince, 304
Berthe, 186
Berthelot, 79
Beth, 5
Binah, 107
Blaquerne, Hermit, 248
Boaz, 43, 57, 152, 302
Bodinus, 262, 270, 271
Boguet, Henri, 271
Bohani, 72
Böhme, Jacob, 124, 267
Boismont, Brierre de, 120, 160, 192
Bonaventura, St., 63
Boniface, Bishop of Mayence, 192

INDEX

Book of Ceremonial Magic, 119, 175, 197, 229, 230
Bossuet, 33, 49
Bouche, Madame, 324
Brahma, 60
Brahmans, 165
Brennus, 183
Bryant, Jacob, 65, 122
Buddha, 74

CADMUS, 86, 131
Caduceus, 131, 369
Cagliostro, Count, 301–304, 305, 340
Cahagnet, 318
Cain, 43, 58, 59, 60, 72, 78, 88, 108, 124
Calchas, 132
Calf, Golden, 84
Calvin, John, 118
Camul, 183
Canaan, 59, 109
Cardan, Jerome, 177
Cartomancy, 133, 323. *See* Tarot
Cazotte, Jacques, 308
Cebes, Table of, 127, 269, 338
Cedron, 57
Certon, Salomon, 141
Chamos, 109
Charistia, 138
Charity, 151, 152
Charlemagne, 194, 195, 196, 198, 199, 200, 369
Charles Martel, 192
Charles the Bald, 202
Charles VI, 240
Charles VI of Austria, 320
Charles VII, 212
Charles IX, 262
Charvoz, Abbé, 334
Chastity, 135
Chateaubriand, 166, 186
Chilperic, 188, 189
Chokmah, 33, 107
Christ, 29, 36, 43, 48, 57, 58, 129, 137, 147, 148, 149, 207, 209, 210, 211, 212, 328, 364, 368
Christian, P., 305
Church, Catholic, 37, 41, 52, 107, 129, 147, 222, 328, 329
Circe, 91
Clairvoyance, 40, 68, 77
Clavel, 320
Clement, St., 171
Clement V, Pope, 207
Cleopatra, 206
Clothilde, St., 187–188

Clovis, 188–189
Cocytus, 126
Cœlum Sephiroticum, 123
Comte, Auguste, 330, 332
Confucius, 30, 289
Constance of Provence, 202
Cooper-Oakley, Isabel, 296
Corinth, Bride of, 180 *et seq.*
Cornuphis, 112
Cosmopolite, *i.e.* Alexander Seton, 267
Cremer, John, 247
Crollius, Oswald, 267
Cross of Eden, 171
Cuvier, 183
Cyprian, Prayer of St., 168

DAATH, 107
Dacier, 123, 150
Daleth, 51
Damis, 163, 164
Daniel, 92
Dante, 51, 127, 260, 262, 263
Darboy, Monsignor, 177
Davies, 123
Dea, Bona, 135
De Cauzons, P., 202
De Cossé-Brissac, Duc, 309
De Gabalis, Comte, 194
De Genlis, Madame, 296
Dejanira, 121
Delaage, Henri, 343, 344
Delancre, 270
De Lerins, Blessed Vincent, 371
Deleuze, 298, 305
De Luchet, Marquis, 297, 298, 318, 347
Delrio, 270
Deluge, 56, 59, 108
De Maine, Duc, 309
De Maistre, Comte Joseph, 32, 48, 102, 150, 191, 373
De Medicis, Catherine, 262
De Mirville, Comte, 192, 221, 252, 341, 342
Democritus, 110
De Paul, St. Vincent, 151
Desbillons, 254, 255
Desmousseux, G., 278
D'Espagnet, 267
De Sombreuil, Mdlle, 307, 310
Deussen, 75
De Vatiguerro, Jean, 322
De Villanova, Arnaldus, 247
De Villars, Abbé, 104, 296
Devil, 36, 37, 38, 39, 158 *et seq.*, 219 *et seq.*

INDEX

Diana, 140
Dionysius, 177, 178
Dionysius the Younger, 123
Diseases, Astral, 139
Doctrine and Ritual of Transcendental Magic, 37, 48, 108, 147, 185, 289
Dodona, Oaks of, 87
Dominic, St., 205, 224
Donatists, 118
D'Ourches, Comte, 344, 346, 347
Dositheus, 153
Dreams, 141
Druids, 183-185, 186, 198
Du Fresnoy, Lenglet, 247
Duperron, Anquetil, 75
Du Potet, Baron, 68, 69, 77, 119, 339, 340, 348
Dupuis, 30
Dzenioutha Sepher, 289

ECKHARTSHAUSEN, Karl von, 317
Ecstasy, 77, 104, 120
Eden and Earthly Paradise, 56, 58, 107, 193
Edmond, 353, 354
Egeria, 134
Elementary Spirits, 105, 194
Eleusis, 122, 140, 260
Elizabeth, Mme, 310
Elohim, Elohim T'zabaoth, 122, 196, 220
Empusæ, 91
Enchiridion, 174, 195-197, 344
Enoch, 259
Enoch, Book of, 55, 57, 58, 59
Ensoph, 58, 123
Equilibrium, 131, 142, 358, 359, 361, 369-371
Erdan, A., 327, 355, 357
Eros and Anteros, 152
Esquiros, Alphonse, 343, 355, 356
Etteilla, 81, 240, 323
Eucharist, 151, 172
Eudoxus, 65
Euripides, 140
Eurydice, 89
Eve, 40, 108, 193, 230, 330
Evil, 37, 38
Ezekiel, 92, 207, 282

FABER, Rev. G. S., 122
Fabré-Palaprat, 309
Faith and Science, 35, 36, 47, 151, 369, 370
Figuier, Louis, 79, 247, 300

Fire, Secret, 164
Flamel, Nicholas, 250-252, 261, 264, 265
Fludd, Robert, 267
Fo-Hi, 288-289
Fontenelle, 136
Fourier, 108, 222, 327
Four Sons of Aymon, 195
Franck, Adolphe, 61
Fredegonde, 188, 189, 190
Frederick William, King, 317
Freemasonry, Freemasons, 32, 34, 43, 48, 67, 209, 283-287
French Revolution, 159

GAFFAREL, 217
Ganneau, 330, 355-357
Garden of Olives, 57
Garden of Pomegranates, 43
Garinet, Jules, 188, 193, 194, 199, 203, 276
Gaufridi, Louis, 271, 272
Geber, 206
Genebrard, 248
Geoffrey de St. Omer, 207
Geomancy, 133
Gerle, Dom, 313, 314, 356
Gilles de Laval, 213-218, 220, 270
Gimel, 51
Gipsies, 234-241
Girard, 277
Glauber, Richard, 267
Gnosis, Gnosticism, Gnostics, 32, 65, 72, 155, 165, 171, 172, 173, 174, 207, 211, 223, 260, 286, 299, 304, 374
Goethe and the *Faust*, 166, 233, 242, 321, 327, 330
Goetia, 72, 74, 90, 105, 134, 149
Golden Ass, 169-170
Golden Fleece, 86-88
Golden Legend, 166, 167
Graces, Three, 138
Grandier, Urbain, 273-276
Gregory, St., 138
Gregory of Tours, 189, 192
Gregory XVI, Pope, 335
Grimoires, Various, 119, 217, 224, 226-233
Gringonneur, Jacques, 82
Guldenstubbe, Baron de, 222, 344, 347
Gymnosophists, 74

HAGAR, 61
Ham, 61, 88, 108, 109, 116
He, 82

INDEX

Hecate, 140
Helena, 154
Helmont, J. B. van, 267
Hennequin, Victor, 341
Henry III, 262, 263
Heraclitus, 110
Hercules, 87, 110, 121
Hermanubis, 84
Hermes, 65, 79, 80, 121, 204
Hierarchy, Descending, 191
Hierophants, 160
Hiram, 284–287
Hod, 43
Home, 318
Homer, 87, 121
Honorius II, 228, 229
Honorius III, 224
Hugh de Payens, 207, 209, 210
Hussites, 118
Hypatia, 176
Hyphasis, 162, 163

I A O, 125
Iliad, 88
Illuminati, 32, 65, 130, 317
Immortality, 96
Irminsul, 183
Isaac de Loria, 307
Isaiah, 36
Isis, 46, 84, 124, 186, 362
Ixion, 126
lynx, 82

JACHIN, 43, 57, 152, 302
Jacob, 33, 34, 139
Jason, 87, 88
Jean d'Arras, 187
Jean de Meung, 261
Jean Hachette, 184
Jechiel, Rabbi, 190, 191, 202, 203
Jehovah, 85, 99, 101, 196, 230, 232
Joachim, Abbé, 311
Joan, Pope, 47
Joan of Arc, 184, 187, 212, 213
Johannite Doctrine, 149, 209, 210, 211, 260, 283, 310, 315
John, St., 48, 57, 58, 61, 98, 124, 171, 175, 207, 210, 248, 259, 298, 369
Jonah, 171
Joseph, 81
Josephine, Empress, 322, 323
Jude, St., 55
Julian the Apostate, 162, 165, 368
Juno, 87

Jupiter, 34, 88, 105, 134, 140; Jupiter and Semele, 41
Justina, Legend of, 166–167
Juvenal, 135

KABALAH, 30, 41, 43–48, 51, 52, 55–58, 60, 61, 64, 72, 74, 81, 98, 106, 123, 124, 127, 130, 147, 148, 149, 161, 171, 183, 184, 206, 207, 247, 248, 249, 250, 252, 265, 266, 288, 289, 290, 292, 299, 300, 302, 303, 306, 307. *See* Zohar
Kether, 33
Keturah, 72
Khnoubis, 125
Khunrath, Heinrich, 48, 206, 265–266
Kircher, Athanasius, 81, 136
Klodswinthe, 188
Kolmer, 302
Koran, 192
Kotzebue, 320
Koung-Tseu, 130
Krishna, 74
Krudener, Madame de, 324–325

LABARUM, 197
Lacenaire, 336
Lactantius, 126
La Harpe, 305
Lamech, 78
Lamennais, Abbé, 355
Lamia, 91
Land, Promised, 139
Larva, 105, 106, 118, 120
Lascaris, 300, 301
Lavater, 318, 347
Laysis, 93
Leibnitz, 289
Lemures, 126
Lenormand, 323, 324, 353
Leo III, Pope, 174, 175, 196
Leon-Tao-Yuan, 288
Lethe, 97, 126
L'Étoile, 263
Liber Mirabilis, 58
Light, Astral, 37, 39, 40, 68, 69, 70, 77, 79, 96, 101, 104, 105, 116, 119, 137, 142, 149, 153, 157, 159, 160, 163, 174, 217, 251, 258, 301, 336, 363
Lilith, 306
Little Albert, 139, 205
Loiseaut, 312
Lopukhin, 59
Louis, St., 190, 203
Louis the Pious, 194, 202

INDEX

Louis XVI, 309, 310, 311, 315
Louis XVII, 315, 316, 324, 325, 332, 334, 336, 356
Louis XVIII, 325
Lucifer, 36, 38, 158, 159, 161
Lucretia, 135
Lully, Raymund, 242-249
Luther, Martin, 48, 261-262

MACROCOSM, 366
Magi, 29, 66, 68, 70, 71, 75, 130, 139, 152, 157, 183, 368
Magi, the Three, 29, 74, 130
Magic: as the science of the ancient Magi, 29; as certitude in philosophy and religion, 29; its profanation, 32; as the science of the devil, 35; its Great Secret, 40; opens the Temple of Nature, 49; does not explain the mysteries of religion, 49; its chief attraction, 49; distinction between good and evil, 58; spurious Magic of India, 58; term of, 68; its perfect doctrine in Egypt, 79; its summary in the Emerald Tablet, 79; miracles of Moses not referable to Magic, 84; Magic of Light, 152; Magic of the old sanctuaries, 162; Magic of works, 206; why Magic is proscribed by the Church, 374; the future of Magic, 374
Magic, Black, 40, 72, 77, 90, 91, 109, 116, 118, 119, 124, 159, 171, 180, 200, 204, 213, 223, 263, 270, 336, 342, 363, 368
Magnetism, 41
Mahomet, 48, 192
Maia, 137
Maimonides, 289
Malkuth, 43
Manes, 65, 127
Manicheans, 39, 165
Mapah. *See* Ganneau
Marat, 60, 306, 319
Marcellinus, 165
Marcos, 172, 173
Mars, 87
Martin de Gallardon, 315, 332
Martinists, 39
Mary the Virgin, 35, 45, 89, 131, 136, 137, 149, 150, 201, 369
Matter, Jacques, 172, 211
Mead, G. R. S., 67, 68, 82
Medea, 87, 88, 91
Medicine, Universal, 121, 304, 364
Mediums, 142, 312 *et seq.*, 341, 344-347
Melchisedek, 152, 295

Melusine, 187
Memphis, 112, 122
Menander, 157, 304
Mercury, 79, 101, 163, 250, 251, 268, 361, 362; Hymn of, 141; Astral, 303
Mesmer, Anton, 68, 292-293
Methodius, St., 58, 311
Meves, Aug., 316
Microcosm, 206, 366
Minerva, 87, 132
Minos, 140
Mithraic Mysteries, 108
Molay, Jacques de, 212, 309, 310
Moloch, 109
Montanists, 172
Mopses, Order of, 320
Morien, 206
Moses, 34, 40, 57, 81, 84, 85, 98, 107, 122, 129, 220, 250, 374; Wand of, 34, 57, 81, 107
Muller, Philip, 267
Musæus, 88
Mustapha, Benjamin, 267
Mysteries, Ancient, 34
Mysteries, Greek, 122

NAPOLEON, 306, 322, 323
Naude, Gabriel, 225, 268, 316
Necromancy, 128
Nehamah, 307
Nero, 155, 157
Netzach, 33, 43
Nicæa, Council of, 174
Nicholas IV, Pope, 247
Nicodemus, Gospel of, 57
Nimrod, 69
Ninus, 70, 71
Noah, 56, 60
Norton, Samuel, 267
Nostradamus, Michael, 322
Numa, 66, 69, 92, 134, 136

OBERON, 195
Odyssey, 88
Œdipus, 88, 121, 368
Olivarius, 323
Om, 75
Omphale, 121
Oracles, 149
Orleans, Council of, 192
Orpheus, 30, 86, 88, 89, 90, 115, 121, 131, 134, 368
Ortelius, 267

INDEX

Osiris, 46, 84, 171, 362
Ostanes, 206
Oupnek'hat, 74–77

PAN, 149
Pantacle of Jupiter, 144
Pantacle of Mars, 144
Pantacle of Mercury, 144
Pantacle of Saturn, 144
Pantacle of the Moon, 144
Pantacle of the Sun, 144
Pantacle of Venus, 144
Pantarba, 164
Pantheism, 74
Pantheus, 129, 134
Paracelsus, 105, 185, 206, 257-259
Paradise, Earthly, 56, 107, 126
Paris the Deacon, 157
Parmenides, 136
Pascal, 63, 319
Pasqually, Martines de, 39, 90, 305
Paths, Thirty-Two, 82
Patricius, Franciscus, 66, 67, 68
Paul, St., 36
Penelope, 132
Pentegrams, 29
Pentheus, 131
Pepin the Short, 192
Pernety, A. J., 87
Peter, St., 154, 155, 157, 175
Peter Lombard, 205
Peter the Venerable, 205
Petronius, 155
Pharamond, 190
Pharaoh and his Magicians, 40, 84
Philalethes, 267
Philip, St., 153
Philip the Fair, 207, 212, 309
Philostratus, 162, 163
Photius, 207
Physiognomy, 95
Picus de Mirandula, 104
Pignorius, L., 81
Pillars, 125
Pison, Lucius, 66
Pistorius, 82
Planis Campe, David de, 268
Platina, 224, 226
Plato, 67, 88, 112, 113, 122, 123, 124, 127, 144, 176, 371
Pliny, 66
Plotinus, 142, 176
Polonus, Martinus, 224
Polycrates, 92
Porphyry, 139, 140, 142, 176

Postel, William, 58, 253–257
Pot of Manna, 57
Poterius, 267
Prometheus, 88, 105, 170, 205
Proserpine, 134, 140
Protestantism, 129, 152
Protoplastes, 105
Psyche, 169
Punishment, Eternal, 33
Puritans, 118
Pyramids, 148
Pyrrhos, 110
Pythagoras, 90, 92–97, 122, 125, 136, 373

RAGON, J. M., 77, 283
Regnum Sanctum, 29, 359
Reichstheater of Müller, 200
Reincarnation, 96–97
Reuchlin, John, 30
Richard Cœur de Lion, 211
Richemont, Baron de, 316
Robert the Pious, 202
Robespierre, 60, 314, 315
Roland, 195
Romance of the Rose, 107, 263
Romarius, 206
Rose-Nobles, 246
Rosenroth, Baron Knorr von, 61, 307
Rosicrucians, 32, 48, 107, 197, 261, 264, 265, 268, 283, 296, 298, 299
Rossetti, Gabriele, 260
Rousseau, 60, 115, 151, 309
Rulandus, Martinus, 79, 303

SAINT-FOIX, 184
Saint-Germain, Comte de, 295, 299–301
Saint-Martin, L. C. de, 39, 305
Saint-Medard, 277–278
Saint-Simon, 46
Saint-Victor, Adam de, 58
Salic Laws, 190–192
Salmanas, 206
Salt, 59, 104, 164, 362
Samaria, 153, 168
Sand, Carl, 320
Sardanapalus, 70, 71
Satan, 36–39, 124, 137, 161
Schroepfer, 318
Schuré, Edouard, 92
Second Birth, 121
Secret, Great, 29, 44, 127, 165, 302; Great Magical, 363
Secret Societies, 51

INDEX

Secret Tradition in Freemasonry, 209, 318
Semiramis, 69, 70
Sephiroth, 33, 43, 74, 99, 107, 123, 197
Sergius IV, Pope, 226
Seth, 56, 57, 58, 59, 60, 98
Shelley, P. B., 141
Sibyls, 132
Simon Magus, 152–157, 172, 304
Sisyphus, 126
Sixtus IV, 226
Sobrier, 357
Socrates, 72, 110
Solomon, 129, 283–287, 295, 369; Keys of, 101, 289, 363, 365, 367; Ring of, 359, 363, 365, 366, 367; Seal of, 363, 365, 366, 367; Star of, 80, 197; Pillars of, 43, 47; Temple of, 129, 130, 144, 152, 207, 284–286
Sphinx, 341, 363
Spirits, Return of, 102–103
Sprenger, 270
Star, Blazing, 29
Steinert, 317
Stone, Corner, 148; Stone of the Philosophers, 164; Philosophical Stone, 205, 266, 365
Stryges, 91, 128
Sulphur, 101, 163, 362
Superstition, 138
Swedenborg, Emmanuel, 64, 290–292, 316, 327, 328
Sword of the Cherubim, 108
Sylvester II, Pope, 224, 226
Synesius, 171, 176, 177, 368

TABLE of Bembo, 81; Table of Denderah, 30; Tables of the Law, 57
Tablet of Emerald, 79, 80
Tabor, 303
Talleyrand, 228
Talmud, 41, 147, 148, 191
Tantalus, 126
Taranis, 183
Tarchon, 92
Tarot, 68, 82, 84, 101, 133, 238–240, 305, 323; Chinese, 288–289
Tavernier, 258
Telesma, 79, 362
Templar, Knights, 34, 207–212, 223, 248, 299, 309, 310, 311, 336
Temple, Second, 209
Temporal Power, 369–370
Tenarus, 126

Teresa, St., 35
Tertullian, 36, 169, 173
Tetrad, 93, 94
Teutas, 183, 184
Thales, 125
Thebes, 30, 82
Theoclet, 210
Theosophy, 124
Théot, Catherine, 313–315, 324, 356
Thomas Aquinas, St., 33, 203, 205, 373
Thoth, 184; Book of, 58, 112. *See* Tarot
Tieck, Ludwig, 269
Tigellinus, 155
Tiresias, 131, 132
Tissot, Hilarion, 159, 220, 269
Toldoth Jeshu, Sepher, 147, 210
Torneburg, John, 267
Torreblanca, F., 91, 159, 270
Tournefort, 350, 353
Tree of Knowledge, 56, 107, 108, 244
Tree of Life, 56
Trent, Council of, 253, 255
Trevisan, Bernard, 252
Tribunal, Secret, 198–200
Trigonum, 288
Trimalcyon, 155
Trithemius, Abbot, 252, 264
Trois-Echelles, 125
Trophonius, 125
Tullus Hostilius, 66
Typhon, 46

VAILLANT, 237, 239, 240
Valentine, Basil, 172, 252
Vampires, 106, 128, 130, 350–354
Vau, 51
Vaudois, 118, 310
Vedas, 72
Velleda, 186
Venus, 70, 86, 137, 139
Vienna, Council of, 248
Vintras, Eugene, 173, 332–338
Virgil, 89
Vishnu, 72, 74
Voltaire, 30, 102, 108, 136, 277, 278

WESTCOTT, W Wynn, 82
William of Brunswick, 199
William of Loris, 261, 263
William of Malmesbury, 225
Williams, Eleazar, 316
Woman, 44, 46, 186–189

383

INDEX

Wonders, Seven, 144-146
Word, Sacred, etc., 30, 43, 81, 90, 114, 122; 123, 144, 147, 148, 174, 220, 222, 253, 328, 364
Work, Great, 87, 126, 163, 164, 204, 264, 266, 305, 359, 365
Wronski, Hoene, 330-332

YETZIRAH, Sepher, 41, 57, 58, 60, 61, 64, 81, 82, 148, 178, 250, 253, 266, 288, 361

Y-Kim, 288-289

ZAIN, 51
Zedekias, 193
Zerubbabel, 209, 284
Zohar, Sepher Ha, 41, 45, 47, 51, 56, 60, 61, 63, 64, 86, 96, 104, 108, 122, 123, 126, 130, 148, 152, 164, 170, 172, 173, 196, 204, 253, 266, 283, 289, 307, 361, 362
Zoroaster, 30, 65, 66, 67, 69, 70, 71, 74, 80, 87, 368, 372

www.ingramcontent.com/pod-product-compliance
Lightning Source LLC
Chambersburg PA
CBHW071312150426
43191CB00007B/597